Hacker's Guide by

Rating golf courses as a member of *Team Hacker* isn't all fun and games. It not just golf, golf and more golf. Being a course rater includes things that don't show up in a review. There is beer to drink, food to sample, balls to lose, tees to break and miles to drive. Here is a quick look at what our reviewers had to do to bring you these ratings:

2,229
How many golf balls lost?
(3.5 golf balls per person)

6,368
How many golf tees broken?
(10 tees per round)

955
How many bags of chips bought?
(1.5 per round)

1,274
How many hot dogs eaten?
(2 hot dogs per person)

1,592
How many beers drunk?
(2.5 per person, 12 ounces each)

354
How many hours writing reviews?
(1.25 hours per review)

25,470
How many practice balls hit?
(a bucket of 40 per person)

1019
How many hours driving?
(50 MPH per rater for each course)

50,940
How many miles driven?
(40 miles each way per course)

2215
How much gas was used?
(23 miles/gallon)

58,581
How many strokes taken?
(20-handicap, 72 par)

NOTE: These figures are based on an estimated 2.25 raters per course for 283 golf courses.

Why do you need this book?

This isn't a slick marketing brochure you're reading. We don't sugarcoat our opinions within these pages. These are insights and ratings of golf courses by regular hackers just like you.

Welcome to the *Hacker's Guide to Minnesota & Western Wisconsin Golf Courses*, a complete rating and review of every 18-hole public golf course across Minnesota and thirty-five courses in Wisconsin. Every public golf course from International Falls to Rochester, Willmar to Albert Lea, the Iron Range to the Arrowhead. Public, semi-private, resort and executive eighteens. They have all been personally reviewed and played by a member of *Team Hacker*—real golfers rating real golf courses.

In 2008, nothing like this existed in the market so we decided to do something about it and create a golf course guide that looks at the entire golf experience—hospitality, playability, usability, facility and value—not just the beauty of a golf course.

As you leaf through these pages you'll quickly turn to your favorite courses. How did they do? Surprised?

Ever get invited to play a course that you've never played before? Play a course that was too hard for you? Felt you didn't get your money's worth? Inside these pages you'll find the information you'll need to make better choices.

We hope you enjoy our new book and if you like this one, you're going to want to buy our future guides, too. Also, don't forget to visit *Hackers Central* at **www.hackerscentralonline.com.**

We'd love to hear what you think so send us an e-mail.

Bruce D. Stasch
Publisher
ultimatehacker@hackersguides.com
877-939-0458

Please Leave Page Blank

HACKER'S GUIDE™
Real Ratings by Real People! ®

To Minnesota & Western Wisconsin Golf Courses

The Complete Ratings Guide for Every 18-Hole Public Golf Course Across Minnesota & Western Wisconsin

(that's 283 you betcha!)

Publisher & Production Supervisor
Bruce D. Stasch, the Ultimate Hacker

Published and distributed by:
Apex Golf Enterprises
a division of Apex Mountain Holdings Corporation
4317 Washburn Avenue North
Minneapolis, MN 55412
877-939-0458
inquiries@hackersguides.com
www.hackersguides.com
www.hackerscentralonline.com

Dedication

Again, like the first time, I'd like to dedicate this book to my parents Marcia and Jesse Stasch. Although they are not here to see the publication of the *Hacker's Guide* series, they would say "way to go champ!"

Also, to my lovely and tolerant wife Eve. Although not a golfer herself, she knows that these books would not have happened unless she gave her support to all the time and energy it took to complete them.

Finally, to hackers everywhere. Without you there is no *Hacker's Guide.*

HACKER'S GUIDE™
Real Ratings by Real People! ®

To Minnesota & Western Wisconsin Golf Courses

The Complete Ratings Guide for Every 18-Hole Public Golf Course Across Minnesota & Western Wisconsin

The reviews published in this guide are based on the opinions of assigned raters, with numerical ratings reflecting the average scores given by all reviewers assigned to a particular course. The same scoring system has been used by all reviewers and the values and write-ups are solely the opinion of the reviewers. Course data including phone numbers, addresses, distances and other factual information were correct to the best of our knowledge when this guide was published. The publisher cannot accept responsibility for facts that have become outdated or for errors or omissions. For the most accurate information, please consult a course's website or our site at: www.hackerscentralonline.com.

Cover Design & Illustrations by Kevin Cannon and Zander Cannon

© 2008-2010 Apex Golf Enterprises
Real Ratings by Real People® is a registered trademark and Hacker's Guide™ is a trademark of Apex Golf Enterprises a division of Apex Mountain Holdings Corporation.

ISBN-13: 978-0-615-34180-4
ISBN-10: 0-615-34180-2
Printed in the United States of America

Acknowledgements

A guide like this cannot be completed by one person. It took *Team Hacker*, a group of enthusiastic and dedicated golfers that personally visited every course listed in this book to do it. For this guide, no fewer than 55 golfers just like you became part of the team. *Team Hacker* members that contributed to this guide included:

Adam Johnson *(St. Paul)*; Al Cooper *(Albertville)*; Al Lemke *(Ramsey)*; Andrew Jackola *(North St. Paul)*; Bill Cantwell *(Pine City)*; Brett Mueller *(St. Paul)*; Bruce Mohnkern *(Big Lake)*; Carlin Koffarnus *(Unity, WI)*; Cathy Erickson *(Two Harbors)*; Dan Westmoreland *(Minnetonka)*; Dave Buzza *(Minneapolis)*; Dave Prehal *(Eagan)*; Deborah Bohnhoff *(Nerstrand)*; Dennis Delmont *(Maplewood)*; Dick Pontinen *(Shoreview)*; Doug Naylor *(Warroad)*; Duncan Ryhorchuk *(Hanover)*; Ed Shukle *(Mound)*; Eric Hart *(Rochester)*; Erick Wienke *(Sioux Falls, SD)*; Galen Bronson *(Bemidji)*; Ginny Toughill *(Albertville)*; Glen Moe *(South Haven)*; Glen Roseen *(Wyoming)*; Jay Anderson *(Wisconsin Rapids, WI)*; Jay Rasmussen *(Minneapolis)*; Jeff Carlson *(Eagan)*; Jeff Meyer *(Moorhead)*; Jesse Zeien *(New Brighton)*; Jim Bykowski *(Falcon Heights)*; John Erickson *(St. James)*; Jordan Buri *(Farmington)*; Jordan Osterman *(New Hope)*; Justin Rice *(Minneapolis)*; Kenneth Willwert, Jr. *(St. Paul)*; Kevin Lay *(Lakeville)*; Kimberly Lundquist *(Culver)*; Kimberly Stasch *(Cold Spring)*; Larry Bohjanen *(Hibbing)*; Margaret Moe *(South Haven)*; Mark Alewine *(Rosemount)*; Mark Johnson *(Lake Elmo)*; Mark Wilson *(Rosseau)*; Mary Doody *(St. Paul)*; Matt Wenner *(St. Peter)*; Nathan Eidem *(Rochester)*; Pat Barrett *(Lake Elmo)*; Rex Schmidt *(Bloomington)*; Richard Camp *(Eden Prairie)*; Robin Collins *(Staples)*; Susan Holstrom-Johnson *(Alexandria)*; Tyler Wirth *(Alexandria)*; and Warren Wessel *(Maplewood)*.

Also, many others helped during the production of this book; from our attorney to our printer, distributor, designer and illustrator. Without these folks, the idea of rating every public golf course in Minnesota & western Wisconsin would have never happened. In addition, six sets of eyes are better than one so to my proofreaders, Heidi Hogg, Amanda Hall, and Eve Sotnak, thank you for correcting my mistakes.

Table of Contents

Please Leave Page Blank

Why do we call them Hacker's Guides?

National Golf Foundation (NGF) research shows that _only 22% of all golfers regularly score better than 90 for 18 holes_ on a regulation length course. For females, the percentage is just 7% and for males it is 25%. The average 18-hole score on a full-size course is 97 for men and 114 for women. It's an even 100 for all golfers. Only 6% of the men and 1% of the women say they break 80 regularly. When asked what they'd like to shoot, most golfers say they'd be satisfied if they could shoot 85 on an 18-hole regulation course on a regular basis. The average scores have changed very little over the years. With these statistics in mind, we are targeting the _78% of the golfing public that are hackers_. All of the golf magazines and golf guides on the market target the hard-core, highly active and economically well-off golfer, but that group only represents 22% of the market. The *Hacker's Guides* are real course ratings for real people.

How does our Hacker Rating System work?

The goal of the *Hacker Rating System* is to assess a course on its friendliness to an average golfer, not a pro. So a *Hacker's Guide* rating might be different than other guides and some favorite courses might have a rating that is different than what you'd expect. The rating system analyzes a golf course on forty different factors in five different categories. These categories each have a value that adds up to a maximum rating of 1000 points. The rating categories are broken out into five distinct areas: Hospitality (25%) = 250 points, Playability (30%) = 300

points, Usability (20%) = 200 points, Facility (15%) = 150 points and Value (10%) = 100 points. Each rating category is then broken into 8-10 areas that are assessments of specific factors. The formula that was used to come up with a final rating is proprietary.

The Hacker Rating System

The *Hacker Rating System* is a scoring system that looks at a golf course from the perspective of the "hacker" or modestly skilled player. It takes into account both on- and off-course factors when coming up with an overall rating. Each of the 40 factors that make up the scoring are weighted within each category (for example 8.25 out of 10) and each category makes up a certain percentage of the total score. A perfect score in all categories would be 1000 points.

Independent raters from *Team Hacker* visited each course during the summer/fall. They played each course, talked to the management, drove the cart, toured the facility, ate in the restaurant or bar, warmed up on the putting green and practiced hitting golf balls on the range. They did not ask for or receive any special treatment so that they could experience the golf course from the perspective of an average customer. Some of the factors that were considered:

Hospitality (25%) = 250 points

Professionalism. Friendliness of staff and guests. Does the beverage cart appear often? Check-in. Does the course reach out to women? Pace-of-play. How friendly were the natives? Quality of the food and food service.

Playability (30%) = 300 points

Is this course suitable for a 20+ handicap golfer? Course conditions - cart paths, fairways, tees & greens. Lots of hazards? Safe outs for average players. Hilly or can you walk?

Usability (20%) = 200 points

Signage easy to understand? Flow from hole to hole and from the course to the clubhouse. What about the website? Online tee times? Getting to the first tee?

Facility (15%) = 150 points

Overall conditions of the clubhouse, driving range, putting area and parking lot. The bar and restaurant. Walkable? Short distances between holes. What is missing?

Value (10%) = 100 points

Did you get your money's worth? Cart rental prices. Food. What about memberships? Deals and specials. Would you come back?

Who is Team Hacker?

Every one of the golf courses in the *Hacker's Guide* has been personally rated by a member of *Team Hacker*. *Team Hacker* members come from the ranks of teachers, seniors, salespeople, students; real golfers rating real courses. A member will typically have an average handicap of 80-110 for men and 95-125 for women.

This team has personally visited each golf course, met with course management, answered an extensive list of assessment questions and played the golf course just like any other golfer. They did not request any special VIP treatment from the course while they were there. In addition to the course rating, each course in this guide has also been given a 400-word review based on that team member's personal playing experience. No other golf course directory or rating guide exists that spends as much time assessing a course in this manner.

How can I join Team Hacker?

Team Hacker members are not paid to provide golf course ratings. They are just a group of men and women that enjoy golf and are willing to provide their opinions to the millions of fellow golfers out there. They don't do this for a living, don't work for a golf course that they rated, and feel that their opinions will help others decide what golf course to play.

Anyone is eligible to become a member of *Team Hacker*. All they need to do is visit our website **www.hackerscentralonline.com** and fill out the registration form. We will contact you when we add to our team.

What are the perks?

Although you can't make a living rating golf courses for *Team Hacker* (wouldn't that be nice?) there are a few perks. The biggest is being able to play golf courses for free or at a big discount. Also, you'll receive *Team Hacker* gear and chances to win free golf trips.

Why this guide is different

Existing rating books and systems only seem to look at the golf course's difficulty and fail to consider other factors that affect having an enjoyable golfing experience. Scores appear arbitrary and most books don't even know who is actually making the rating. For all we  know it could be the golf pro rating his own course. For 95% of men and 99% of women, breaking 80 is a rarity and shooting par will only be a dream. So playing the famous courses that the professionals do will only frustrate us. This guide is for the rest of us that are defined as hackers (you know who you are).

By creating this book, we wanted to dig deeper and look at a broader range of factors that make up the golfing experience and we wanted the same people who rated the courses to be the same people that would read our book. Hackers should know what hackers want from a golf course.

How to use this book

Keep it in your car or golf bag. Use it as your golf travel planner. Play the Top 25 in one of the rating categories. If you are a beginner, look for courses that provide the right amount of challenge for your game. If you play a lot of golf, look for a better golfing experience, not just a better golf course. Hey, if it is a nice sunny day and you just drove past a course you never heard of, pull out the book. When you're done, tell us about it at **www.hackerscentralonline.com**.

How to use Hacker's Central

Since a book is only as current as its last printing, we've also built an extensive online community called *Hacker's Central*. Here you'll find a site that has everything you'll find in this book as well as blogs, course maps, course photos, course news, podcast interviews, news feeds, on-line tee times and everything else golf you can do online. Also, as we rate new courses, they appear online first. Become part of the *Hacker's Central* community at **www.hackerscentralonline.com.**

How do I read a Hacker Review?

1

Course Details: Includes basic contact info, type of course (public, semi-private), par and website.

4

Region: For this guide, courses are from one of seven regions in Minnesota and western Wisconsin. They are: NorthWest, NorthEast, WestCentral, TwinCities, South-West, SouthEast and Wisconsin.

BOULDER POINTE

9575 Glenborough Drive
Elko, MN 55020
Clubhouse: 952-461-4900
Golf Shop: 952-461-4900
Type: Public   Par: 71

www.boulderpointegolf.com

Tees	Men's	Women's	Yards
Red	64.7/118	69.0/122	4794
Gold	67.6/123	72.5/129	5426
White	69.5/126		5833
Black	71.2/131		6224

Region: Twin Cities

Course Rating

HOSPITALITY	6.12
PLAYABILITY	7.50
USABIL	7.35
FACILI	7.01
VALUE	6.15

OVERALL SCORE
692

Greens Fee: $34.00 (weekend)
1/2 Cart Fee: $15.00 (weekend)

2

Scoring Details: Includes tee boxes for men and women, par rating, slope rating and yardages. Some tee box options for courses with more than 18 holes may have been excluded because of space.

3

Favorite Icon: If a course has ranked in the Top 25 in any category or in overall score, they have received a *Hacker's Favorite Award*.

5

Course Ratings: Weighted scores based on how 40 different questions were answered by a course rater. Each category score is based on a total of 10 points (e.g., 6.35 out of 10).

6

Overall Score: Courses score a maximum total of 1000 points. This score is based on the weighting of the five categories.

7

Fees: Obtained from each course's website weekend fees information and were current as of December 2009.

Minnesota's Golf Obsession

How many golfers are there in the U.S.?

There are 29.5 million golfers in the United States.[1] A golfer is defined as a person that has played at least one round in the last year. More importantly, there are 17.3 million "core" golfers (those that golf at least 8 times/year). The *National Golf Foundation* (NGF) estimates that there are 500 million rounds of golf played annually in the United States.

How many golf courses are there in the U.S.?

There are approximately 16,000 courses in the United States. The top five states for golf are Florida, South Carolina, North Carolina, California and Arizona (Minnesota ranks #11 in the total number of courses).

How many golfers are there in Minnesota?

The State of Minnesota has a population of 5.19 million people[2] and often ranks 1st or 2nd in the country with the highest level of participation by its residents. Minnesota has 733,000 golfers which represent 2.9% of the U.S. golf population.

How many "core" golfers are there in Minnesota?

Of the 733,000 Minnesota golfers, the core Minnesota golfers represent 11.8% of the total or 87,000 golfers. These golfers play an average of 20+ rounds annually.

How many golf courses are in Minnesota?

According to the Minnesota Golf Association[3], Minnesota has 508 golf courses in the state: 55 private, 351 public/daily fee, 83 municipal, and 19 resort, with nearly 90 percent of Minnesota golf courses open to the public (457 courses). Almost half of the public courses are 9-holes.

[1]National statistics are from 2007 and were provided by the *National Golf Foundation*.
[2]State population is based on 2007 *U.S. Census Bureau* estimate.
[3]State golf course data is based on 2008 *Minnesota Golf Association* statistics.

"The Swing of Things"
an introduction to golf in Minnesota

by Eric N. Hart, Associate Director of Golf

How do you properly introduce a visitor to the beautiful state of Minnesota? Well, for starters, you don't do it during the winter. The first snowfall is enchanting, and a white Christmas is nice, but… for most adults, the fascination fades faster than the snow ever melts. Suffice it to say, snow's best presentation is made in Colorado or in snow globes.

No. If you want to give someone a warm Minnesota welcome, you do it during "Golf Season." That's right, we're a two-season state… There's "Golf Season" (bookended by March and November) and "Waiting for Golf Season." That's not to say that some of us don't try to play golf year round… we do… even in the snow. The snow often provides the best opportunity we have all year to find our tee shots. We just try not to lick our clubs as much. You betcha, we Minnesotans live for golf, with more golfers per capita than any other state. In addition, more golf balls reside in our 10,000 lakes than in the collective water bodies of any other state, an achievement not yet acknowledged by Mr. Guinness, or his book. (But he credits us as the Lutefisk Capital of the nation. Gee, thanks.) Ya sure, Minnesota and golf were clearly made for each other.

Prior to Minnesota becoming a state in 1858, its future as a great golf destination was set. You may have heard the "larger than life" tales of the great Minnesotan, Paul Bunyan. And yet, until now, you were likely unaware of the true genius of the legendary lumberjack. In an interview granted exclusively to the *Hacker's Guide*, a relative of a man named Paul offered his perspective on the historical giant's contribution to the state and the game of golf.

"Contrary to popular opinion Mr. Bunyan and his Babe did not clear patches of trees as pick-up-stick contests to get through the winter… (He spent his winters in Arizona and California as any Minnesota snowbird would) … No, Mr. Bunyan was an avid golfer. Using a 17,400 lb. ball of twine, Paul scattered giant divots across forested fairways preparing the rugged northern terrain for 508 examples of greatness that over the next 150 years would be built."

Wow. Really? Uff da. That's hard to believe! (This Paul guy is a fisherman too.) But it's true… Minnesota does indeed have 508 golf courses, of which nearly 90% are accessible to the public, and… you can still see that Bunyanesque "golf" ball of twine in Darwin, Minnesota.

Yes, here in Minnesota we're known for doing big and bigger, especially when it comes to golf. We have America's largest green, named the Jolly Green Giant… the nation's only golf-ball-looking building, called the Metrodome… (The other domes look like ping pong balls.) … the nation's biggest sports related paradox in a miniature golf course under the roof of a 10 million square foot shopping center… at the Mall of America… and we invented Spam. We are proud of our state and its many historical accomplishments, including being the only state whose courses have hosted every USGA tournament. We invented the "breakfast of champions" (Wheaties) and we bask in the glow of championships (see Minnesota Twins). We are resilient and hopeful in the face of failure (see Minnesota Vikings). We are enthusiastic and downright giddy about our golf, a reality on full display at 2009's most attended professional event, the PGA Championship at Hazeltine National in Chaska. (Host of the 2016 Ryder Cup as well.) Yes, Minnesota is a great golf state and we definitely have our act together. (We invented the stapler.)

We are the "who's who" of the golf world… as in no one's ever heard of you or me, but we don't care. And why should we? Our public golf courses are heralded among the "elite" by media giants across the country… From "The Classic" and "Deacon's Lodge" of the Brainerd Golf Trail… To a veritable trilogy that rivals Bandon's in Oregon, with "The Legend," "The Quarry,"

(near a town named Biwabik) and "The Wilderness" in the "Iron Range" of Northern Minnesota. Adding to the greatness of our courses… For less than the cost of a round at Pebble Beach, you can play all five of these! What's more, for every "big name" course here, there are a dozen or so equally great lesser knowns, no less worthy of your time and attention. We won't lie, of course it would be nice to be a member at Hazeltine or Somerby, and to play them whenever we want… but we'll play "The Refuge" or "Rush Creek" any day and still feel just as fortunate.

In fact, ask any Minnesota golfer to name their favorite course and you're likely to get a different response from each one. Yes, there are that many great courses here. And when you have that many great

courses in one state it raises the expectations of course conditions and service exponentially. While it's worth pointing out that many of us are more aware of the conditions of the rough and hazards than we are of the fairways, we expect supremacy from our courses, and we're spoiled in that we actually get it. You may not be impressed to hear that (Minneapolis-based) Caribou Coffee founder John Puckett considers Minnesota a golf "mocha"… But perhaps Arnold Palmer's praising of Minnesota as a golf "mecca" will sway you. He even scoffed at the notion of a "short" golf season in Minnesota, wondering where else in the country you can play 7 months of golf more comfortably. (Note: Nintendo Wii in your basement doesn't count.)

I bet you'd laugh if I told you that Minnesota has more shoreline miles than Florida, Hawaii and California combined. Don't believe me? Look it up. (Seriously. Stop laughing.) So what if they're lake shorelines? We may not have a desert, an ocean, or the Rockies, but we can go toe to toe with the beauty of any other landscape in America. Big or small, we've got it all. From "The Jewel" of the mighty Mississippi, to a 9-hole gem by a pine lined creek in La Crescent, where there's a "Willingers" there's a way… to play great golf. Pun intended.

We're a non-discriminating golf state, with something for literally everyone. So pack up your clubs, your kids and your spouse and join the legions of Minnesota hackers crisscrossing our State.

2010 Hacker's Favorite Course Award

Since the *Hacker's Guide* is so particular in what it determines is a good golfing experience, we wanted to acknowledge golf courses that, according to our *Team Hacker* raters, represent the best the area has to offer. The *Hacker's Favorite Course Award* is awarded to those courses that scored in the Top 25 for any of the five rating categories (Hospitality, Playability, Usability, Facility & Value) as well as the Top 25 courses in Overall Score. Some courses may find themselves award winners in more than one category or categories. Each course will have received a certificate suitable for framing and hopefully are displaying that award in a prominent place in their golf shop.

On the next few pages you will see who finished in the Top 25 in each category and on each course review is listed what category(s) the course was awarded a *2010 Hacker's Favorite Course Award*.

H — Hospitality   **F** — Facility

P — Playability   **V** — Value

U — Usability

Congratulations to all the winners!

NOTE: *Eighty-five different courses received a Hacker's Favorite Course Award in 2010. Some more than once.*

2010 Hacker's Favorite Winners

TOP TWENTY FIVE
TOTAL SCORE (out of 1000 points)

Rank	Course	City	Score	Page
1(t)	Coffee Mill	Wabasha	867	81
1(t)	Eagle's Landing	Fort Ripley	867	105
1(t)	Little Crow	Spicer	867	169
4	The Jewel	Lake City	866	260
5	Ruttger's - The Lakes	Deerwood	864	238
6	The Refuge	Oak Grove	862	266
7	Crosswoods	Crosslake	861	88
8(t)	Breezy Point - White Birch	Breezy Point	859	69
8(t)	Falls Country Club	Int'l Falls	859	116
10	Cragun's - Dutch's Legacy	Brainerd	858	86
11	Wapicada	Sauk Rapids	857	286
12	Territory	St. Cloud	856	257
13(t)	Cragun's - Bobby's Legacy	Brainerd	855	85
13(t)	Greystone	Sauk Center	855	136
15	River Oaks	Cottage Grove	852	231
16	Deer Run	Victoria	851	96
17	Purple Hawk	Cambridge	849	222
18(t)	Braemar	Edina	847	67
18(t)	Grand View - The Preserve	Pequot Lakes	847	133
18(t)	Rose Lake	Fairmont	847	234
18(t)	Village Green	Moorhead	847	283
22	The Wilderness	Tower	846	269
23(t)	Eagle Creek	Willmar	845	100
23(t)	Giant's Ridge - The Quarry	Biwabik	845	126
25	Blackberry Ridge	Sartell	844	63

2010 Hacker's Favorite Winners

TOP TWENTY FIVE

HOSPITALITY (out of 10 points)

Rank	Course	City	Score	Page
1	The Jewel	Lake City	9.20	260
2	Valley High	Houston	9.14	278
3(t)	Mount Frontenac	Frontenac	9.08	193
3(t)	Island Pine	Atwater	9.08	151
5(t)	The Wilderness	Tower	9.07	269
5(t)	Blackberry Ridge	Sartell	9.07	63
5(t)	Mesaba	Hibbing	9.07	185
5(t)	Bemidji T & C	Bemidji	9.07	61
9	New Prague	New Prague	9.05	194
10	Ruttger's - The Lakes	Deerwood	9.02	238
11	Detroit Country Club	Detroit Lakes	9.01	97
12(t)	Coffee Mill	Wabasha	8.98	81
12(t)	Cragun's - Dutch's Legacy	Brainerd	8.98	86
12(t)	Rich Spring	Cold Spring	8.98	225
15(t)	Virginia	Virginia	8.97	285
15(t)	Lynx National	Sauk Center	8.97	174
17	Geneva	Alexandria	8.92	124
18	Princeton	Princeton	8.91	221
19	Wapicada	Sauk Rapids	8.90	286
20(t)	Little Crow	Spicer	8.89	169
20(t)	Soldiers Memorial	Rochester	8.89	244
21(t)	Greystone	Sauk Center	8.88	136
21(t)	Green Lea	Albert Lea	8.88	134
21(t)	Eagle Ridge	Coleraine	8.88	101
25	Cragun's - Bobby's Legacy	Brainerd	8.87	85

2010 Hacker's Favorite Winners

TOP TWENTY FIVE

PLAYABILITY (out of 10 points)

Rank	Course	City	Score	Page
1	Cragun's - Bobby's Legacy	Brainerd	9.09	85
2(t)	Cragun's - Dutch's Legacy	Brainerd	9.05	86
2(t)	Dacotah Ridge	Morton	9.05	92
4	The Refuge	Oak Grove	9.00	266
5	Territory	St. Cloud	8.97	257
6(t)	Giant's Ridge - The Quarry	Biwabik	8.96	126
6(t)	Grand View - The Preserve	Pequot Lakes	8.96	133
8(t)	Giant's Ridge - The Legend	Biwabik	8.91	125
8(t)	River Oaks	Cottage Grove	8.91	231
10	The Wilderness	Tower	8.90	269
11(t)	The Jewel	Lake City	8.87	260
11(t)	Mississippi Dunes	Cottage Grove	8.87	188
13	Wapicada	Sauk Rapids	8.86	286
14	Blueberry Pines	Menahga	8.85	64
15(t)	Coffee Mill	Wabasha	8.84	81
15(t)	Falls Country Club	Int'l Falls	8.84	116
17	Majestic Oaks - Signature	Ham Lake	8.83	179
18	Chaska Town	Chaska	8.81	78
19(t)	Izaty's - Blackbrook	Onamia	8.80	153
19(t)	Prestwick	Woodbury	8.80	220
21	Golden Eagle	Fifty Lakes	8.79	128
22(t)	New Prague	New Prague	8.76	194
22(t)	The Bridges	Winona	8.76	258
24	Le Sueur	Le Sueur	8.74	163
25	Bunker Hills	Coon Rapids	8.73	73

2010 Hacker's Favorite Winners

TOP TWENTY FIVE

USABILITY (out of 10 points)

Rank	Course	City	Score	Page
1(t)	Breezy Point - White Birch	Breezy Point	9.31	69
1(t)	Applewood Hills	Stillwater	9.31	56
1(t)	Breezy Point - Traditional	Breezy Point	9.31	68
4	Chaska Town	Chaska	9.22	78
5(t)	Crosswoods	Crosslake	9.16	88
5(t)	Elk River	Elk River	9.16	108
7	The Refuge	Oak Grove	9.15	266
8	Wild Marsh	Buffalo	9.07	294
9(t)	River Oaks	Cottage Grove	9.06	231
9(t)	Hidden Haven	Cedar	9.06	145
11(t)	Territory	St. Cloud	9.00	257
11(t)	Cedar Creek	Albertville	9.00	75
13	Emerald Green - Silv/Plat	Hastings	8.99	111
14	The Links at Northfork	Ramsey	8.98	261
15(t)	Little Crow	Spicer	8.93	169
15(t)	Eagle's Landing	Fort Ripley	8.93	105
15(t)	Purple Hawk	Cambridge	8.93	222
15(t)	Green Lea	Albert Lea	8.93	134
15(t)	Balmoral	Battle Lake	8.93	59
20	Stonebrooke	Shakopee	8.92	250
21	Stones Throw	Milaca	8.91	252
22	Madden's - Pine Beach West	Brainerd	8.90	176
23(t)	Oakcrest	Rosseau	8.85	204
23(t)	Virginia	Virginia	8.85	285
25	Wapicada	Sauk Rapids	8.84	286

2010 Hacker's Favorite Winners

TOP TWENTY FIVE
FACILITY (out of 10 points)

Rank	Course	City	Score	Page
1	Golden Eagle	Fifty Lakes	9.19	128
2	The Refuge	Chaska	9.16	266
3	Mississippi Dunes	Cottage Grove	9.15	188
4	Madden's - The Classic	Brainerd	9.13	177
5	The Jewel	Lake City	9.11	260
6	Blackberry Ridge	Sartell	9.10	63
7	Grand View - The Pines	Nisswa	9.08	132
8	Cragun's - Dutch's Legacy	Brainerd	9.05	86
9	Cragun's - Bobby's Legacy	Brainerd	9.03	85
10	Grand View - The Preserve	Pequot Lakes	9.02	133
11	Crystal Lake	Lakeville	9.01	90
12	Braemar	Edina	8.99	67
13	Wapicada	Sauk Rapids	8.98	286
14	Deer Run	Victoria	8.97	96
15	Le Sueur	Le Sueur	8.89	163
16	Coffee Mill	Wabasha	8.83	81
17	Fiddlestix	Isle	8.75	118
18(t)	Chaska Town	Chaska	8.71	78
18(t)	Minnesota National	McGregor	8.71	186
20	Legends	Prior Lake	8.69	165
21(t)	Stonebrooke	Shakopee	8.68	250
21(t)	Wendigo	Grand Rapids	8.68	290
23(t)	Little Falls	Little Falls	8.67	170
23(t)	The Wilderness	Tower	8.67	269
25	Rose Lake	Fairmont	8.64	234

2010 Hacker's Favorite Winners

TOP TWENTY FIVE

VALUE (out of 10 points)

Rank	Course	City	Score	Page
1	Pine Island	Pine Island	8.33	214
2	Eagle's Landing	Fort Ripley	8.15	105
3	Mount Frontenac	Frontenac	8.00	193
4	Coffee Mill	Wabasha	7.98	81
5	Meadow Greens	Austin	7.97	182
6(t)	Perham Lakeside	Perham	7.96	210
6(t)	Hiawatha	Minneapolis	7.96	142
6(t)	Eastwood	Rochester	7.96	106
9	Hayden Hills	Dayton	7.93	139
10	Little Crow	Spicer	7.92	169
11	Village Green	Moorhead	7.87	283
12(t)	Eagle Creek	Willmar	7.85	100
12(t)	Greystone	Sauk Center	7.85	136
14	Rich Spring	Cold Spring	7.82	225
15	Koronis Hills	Paynesville	7.80	156
16	Valley High	Houston	7.78	278
17	Thief River	Thief River Falls	7.77	272
18	Crow River	Hutchinson	7.75	89
19(t)	Elk River	Elk River	7.71	108
19(t)	Oak Summit	Rochester	7.71	203
19(t)	Cedar Creek	Albertville	7.71	75
22	Izaty's - Blackbrook	Onamia	7.70	153
23(t)	Ruttger's - The Lakes	Deerwood	7.69	238
23(t)	Tanners Brook	Forest Lake	7.69	256
25	St. James	St. James	7.68	249

Courses by Region

FACT:
Minnesota has over 10,000 lakes and 508 golf courses.

SouthEast Region

SouthWest Region

NorthEast Region

NorthWest Region

WestCentral Region

Twin Cities Region (page 1)

Twin Cities Region (page 2)

Minnesota Courses by Name

Course	City	Region	Page
Afton Alps	Hastings	TC	53
Albany	Albany	WC	54
Albion Ridges	Annandale	WC	55
Applewood Hills	Stillwater	TC	56
Atikwa	Alexandria	NE	57
Baker National	Medina	TC	58
Balmoral	Battle Lake	WC	59
Bellwood Oaks	Hastings	TC	60
Bemidji Town & Country	Bemidji	NW	61
Black Bear	Backus	NW	62
Blackberry Ridge	Sartell	WC	63
Blueberry Pines	Menahga	NW	64
Bluff Creek	Chanhassen	TC	65
Boulder Pointe	Elko	TC	66
Braemar	Edina	TC	67
Breezy Point - Traditional	Breezy Point	NW	68
Breezy Point - White Birch	Breezy Point	NW	69
Brooktree	Owatonna	SE	70
Brookview	Golden Valley	TC	71
Bulrush	Rush City	NE	72
Bunker Hills	Coon Rapids	TC	73
Cannon	Cannon Falls	SE	74
Cedar Creek	Albertville	TC	75
Cedar River	Adams	SE	76
Cedar Valley	Winona	SE	77
Chaska Town	Chaska	TC	78
Chisago Lakes	Lindstrom	NE	79
Chomonix	Lino Lakes	TC	80
Coffee Mill	Wabasha	SE	81
Columbia	Minneapolis	TC	82
Como	St. Paul	TC	83
Country Air	Lake Elmo	TC	84

Minnesota Courses by Name

Course	City	Region	Page
Cragun's - Bobby's Legacy	Brainerd	NW	85
Cragun's - Dutch's Legacy	Brainerd	NW	86
Creeksbend	New Prague	SE	87
Crosswoods	Crosslake	NE	88
Crow River	Hutchinson	WC	89
Crystal Lake	Lakeville	TC	90
Cuyuna	Deerwood	NE	91
Dacotah Ridge	Morton	SW	92
Dahlgreen	Chaska	TC	93
Daytona	Dayton	TC	94
Deacon's Lodge	Breezy Point	NW	95
Deer Run	Victoria	TC	96
Detroit Country Club	Detroit Lakes	NW	97
Dodge	Dodge Center	SE	98
Dwan	Bloomington	TC	99
Eagle Creek	Willmar	WC	100
Eagle Ridge	Coleraine	NE	101
Eagle Trace	Clearwater	WC	102
Eagle Valley	Woodbury	TC	103
Eagle View	Park Rapids	NW	104
Eagle's Landing	Ft. Ripley	WC	105
Eastwood	Rochester	SE	106
Edinburgh USA	Brooklyn Park	TC	107
Elk River	Elk River	TC	108
Elm Creek	Plymouth	TC	109
Emerald Greens - Brnz/Gold	Hastings	TC	110
Emerald Greens - Silv/Plat	Hastings	TC	111
Emily Greens	Emily	NE	112
Enger Park	Duluth	NE	113
Fair Haven	Menahga	NE	114
Falcon Ridge	Stacy	NE	115
Falls Country Club	Inter. Falls	NW	116
Faribault	Faribault	SE	117

Minnesota Courses by Name

Course	City	Region	Page
Fiddlestix	Isle	NE	118
Forest Hills	Detroit Lakes	NW	119
Fountain Valley	Farmington	TC	120
Fox Hollow	St. Michael	TC	121
Francis A. Gross	Minneapolis	TC	122
Gem Lake Hills	White Bear Lake	TC	123
Geneva	Alexandria	WC	124
Giant's Ridge - The Legend	Biwabik	NE	125
Giant's Ridge - The Quarry	Biwabik	NE	126
Glencoe	Glencoe	SW	127
Golden Eagle	Fifty Lakes	NE	128
Goodrich	Maplewood	TC	129
Gopher Hills	Cannon Falls	SE	130
Grand National	Hinkley	NE	131
Grand View - The Pines	Nisswa	NW	132
Grand View - The Preserve	Pequot Lakes	NW	133
Green Lea	Albert Lea	SE	134
Greenhaven	Anoka	TC	135
Greystone	Sauk Center	WC	136
Hardwoods	Milaca	NE	137
Hawley	Hawley	NW	138
Hayden Hills	Dayton	TC	139
Headwaters	Park Rapids	NW	140
Heritage Links	Lakeville	TC	141
Hiawatha	Minneapolis	TC	142
Hidden Creek	Owatonna	SE	143
Hidden Greens	Hastings	TC	144
Hidden Haven	Cedar	TC	145
Highland National	St. Paul	TC	146
Hollydale	Plymouth	TC	147
Hyland Greens	Bloomington	TC	148
Inver Wood	Inv. Grove Hghts.	TC	149
Irish Hills	Pine River	NE	150

Minnesota Courses by Name

Course	City	Region	Page
Island Pine	Atwater	WC	151
Island View	Waconia	WC	152
Izaty's Blackbrook	Onamia	NE	153
Keller	St. Paul	TC	154
Kimball	Kimball	WC	155
Koronis Hills	Paynesville	WC	156
Lake City	Lake City	SE	157
Lake Miltona	Miltona	WC	158
Lake Pepin	Lake City	SE	159
Lakeview	Detroit Lakes	NW	160
Lakeview	Mound	TC	162
Lakeview National	Two Harbors	NW	161
Le Sueur	Le Sueur	SW	163
Legacy	Faribault	SE	164
Legends	Prior Lake	TC	165
Les Bolstad	St. Paul	TC	166
Lester Park	Duluth	NE	167
Litchfield	Litchfield	WC	168
Little Crow	Spicer	WC	169
Little Falls	Little Falls	WC	170
Logger's Trail	Stillwater	TC	171
Long Prairie	Long Prairie	WC	172
Long Bow	Walker	NW	173
Lynx National	Sauk Center	WC	174
Madden's - The Classic	Brainerd	NW	175
Madden's - Pine Beach West	Brainerd	NW	176
Madden's - Pine Beach East	Brainerd	NW	177
Majestic Oaks - Crossroads	Ham Lake	TC	178
Majestic Oaks - Signature	Ham Lake	TC	179
Manitou Ridge	White Bear Lake	TC	180
Marshall	Marshall	SW	181
Meadow Greens	Austin	SE	182
Meadow Lakes	Rochester	SE	183

Minnesota Courses by Name

Course	City	Region	Page
Meadowbrook	Hopkins	TC	184
Mesaba	Hibbing	NE	185
Minnesota National	McGregor	NE	186
Minnewaska	Glenwood	WC	187
Mississippi Dunes	Cottage Grove	TC	188
Mississippi Nat'l - Highlands	Red Wing	SE	189
Mississippi Nat'l - Lowlands	Red Wing	SE	190
Montgomery	Montgomery	SE	191
Monticello	Monticello	TC	192
Mount Frontenac	Frontenac	SE	193
New Prague	New Prague	WC	194
New Ulm	New Ulm	SW	195
North Links	North Mankato	SW	196
Northern Hills	Rochester	SE	197
Northfield	Northfield	SE	198
Oak Glen	Stillwater	TC	199
Oak Harbor	Baudette	NW	200
Oak Hill	Rice	NW	201
Oak Marsh	Oakdale	TC	202
Oak Summit	Rochester	SE	203
Oakcrest	Rosseau	NW	204
Oakdale	Buffalo Lake	SW	205
Oneka Ridge	White Bear Lake	TC	206
Ortonville	Ortonville	WC	207
Parkview	Eagan	TC	208
Pebble Creek	Becker	TC	209
Perham Lakeside	Perham	NW	210
Pezhekee National	Glenwood	NW	211
Phalen Park	St. Paul	TC	212
Pheasant Acres	Rogers	TC	213
Pine Island	Pine Island	SE	214
Pine Ridge	Motley	WC	215
Pioneer Creek	Maple Plain	TC	216

Minnesota Courses by Name

Course	City	Region	Page
Pokegama	Grand Rapids	NW	217
Pomme De Terre	Morris	WC	218
Prairie View	Worthington	SW	219
Prestwick	Woodbury	TC	220
Princeton	Princeton	NE	221
Purple Hawk	Cambridge	NE	222
Red Wing	Red Wing	SE	223
Redwood Falls	Redwood Falls	SW	224
Rich Springs	Cold Spring	WC	225
Rich Valley	Rosemount	TC	226
Ridges at Sand Creek	Jordan	TC	227
Ridgewood	Longville	NE	228
River Oaks	Cottage Grove	TC	229
River Oaks	Austin	SE	230
River Oaks	Cold Spring	WC	231
Rivers' Bend	Preston	SE	232
Riverwood National	Otsego	TC	233
Rose Lake	Fairmont	SW	234
Rum River Hills	Ramsey	TC	235
Rush Creek	Maple Grove	TC	236
Ruttger's - Sugarbrooke	Cohasset	NE	237
Ruttger's - The Lakes	Deerwood	NE	238
Sanbrook	Isanti	NE	239
Sawmill	Stillwater	TC	240
Shadowbrooke	Lester Prairie	WC	241
Shamrock	Corcoran	TC	242
Shoreland	St. Peter	SW	243
Soldiers Memorial	Rochester	SE	244
Southbrook	Annandale	WC	245
Southern Hills	Farmington	TC	246
Spring Brook	Mora	NE	247
St. Charles	St. Charles	SE	248
St. James	St. James	SW	249

Minnesota Courses by Name

Course	City	Region	Page
Stonebrooke	Shakopee	TC	250
Stoneridge	Stillwater	TC	251
Stones Throw	Milaca	NE	252
Straight River	Owatonna	SE	253
Sundance	Dayton	TC	254
Superior National	Lutsen	NE	255
Tanners Brook	Forest Lake	TC	256
Territory	St. Cloud	WC	257
The Bridges	Winona	SE	258
The Crossings	Montevideo	WC	259
The Jewel	Lake City	SE	260
The Links at Northfork	Ramsey	TC	261
The Meadows	Moorhead	NW	262
The Meadows	Prior Lake	TC	263
The Oaks	Hayfield	SE	264
The Ponds	St. Francis	TC	265
The Refuge	Oak Grove	TC	266
The Summit	Cannon Falls	SE	267
The Vintage	Staples	NW	268
The Wilderness	Tower	NE	269
The Wilds	Prior Lake	TC	270
Theodore Wirth	Minneapolis	TC	271
Thief River	Thief River Falls	NW	272
Thumper Pond	Ottertail	WC	273
Tianna	Walker	NW	274
Timber Creek	Watertown	TC	275
Tipsinah Mounds	Elbow Lake	WC	276
Tyler Community	Tyler	SW	277
Valley High	Houston	SE	278
Valley View	Belle Plaine	TC	279
Valleywood	Apple Valley	TC	280
Victory Links	Blaine	TC	281
Viking Meadows	Cedar	TC	282

Minnesota Courses by Name

Course	City	Region	Page
Village Green	Moorhead	NW	283
Vintage	Otsego	TC	284
Virginia	Virginia	NE	285
Wapicada	Sauk Rapids	WC	286
Warroad Estates	Warroad	NW	287
Waseca Lakeside	Waseca	SE	288
Wedgewood Cove	Albert Lea	SE	289
Wendigo	Grand Rapids	NE	290
Whispering Pines	Annandale	WC	291
Whitefish	Pequot Lakes	NE	292
Whitetail Run	Wadena	NW	293
Wild Marsh	Buffalo	TC	294
Wildflower	Detroit Lakes	NW	295
Willingers	Northfield	SE	296
Willow Creek	Rochester	SE	297
Worthington	Worthington	SW	298
Zumbrota	Zumbrota	SE	299

Wisconsin Courses by Name

Course	City	Region	Page
Amery	Amery	WISC	301
Badlands	Roberts	WISC	302
Big Fish	Hayward	WISC	303
Bristol Ridge	Somerset	WISC	304
Clifton Highlands	Prescott	WISC	305
Clifton Hollow	River Falls	WISC	306
Coldwater Canyon	Wisconsin Dells	WISC	307
Cumberland	Cumberland	WISC	308
Frederic	Frederic	WISC	309
Hayward Golf & Tennis	Hayward	WISC	310
Hayward National	Hayward	WISC	311

Wisconsin Courses by Name

Course	City	Region	Page
Hiawatha	Tomah	WISC	312
Hudson	Hudson	WISC	313
Kilkarney Hills	River Falls	WISC	314
Krooked Kreek	Osceola	WISC	315
Lake Wissota	Chippewa Falls	WISC	316
Lakewoods - Forest Ridges	Cable	WISC	317
Luck	Luck	WISC	318
Nemadji	Superior	WISC	319
New Richmond	New Richmond	WISC	320
Pheasant Hills	Hammond	WISC	321
River Falls	River Falls	WISC	322
River Run	Sparta	WISC	323
Rolling Oaks	Barron	WISC	324
Siren National	Siren	WISC	325
Skyline	Black River Falls	WISC	326
Spring Valley	Spring Valley	WISC	327
St. Croix National	Somerset	WISC	328
Teal Wing	Hayward	WISC	329
Trempeleau Mountain	Trempeleau	WISC	330
Troy Burne	Hudson	WISC	331
Turtleback	Rice Lake	WISC	332
Viroqua Hills	Viroqua	WISC	333
White Eagle	Hudson	WISC	334
Whitetail	Colfax	WISC	335

Minnesota Courses by City

City	Course	Region	Page
Adams	Cedar River	SE	76
Albany	Albany	WC	54
Albert Lea	Green Lea	SE	134
Albert Lea	Wedgewood Cove	SE	289
Albertville	Cedar Creek	TC	75
Alexandria	Atikwa	NE	57
Alexandria	Geneva	WC	124
Annandale	Albion Ridges	WC	55
Annandale	Southbrook	WC	245
Annandale	Whispering Pines	WC	291
Anoka	Greenhaven	TC	135
Apple Valley	Valleywood	TC	280
Atwater	Island Pine	WC	151
Austin	Meadow Greens	SE	182
Austin	River Oaks	SE	230
Backus	Black Bear	NW	62
Battle Lake	Balmoral	WC	59
Baudette	Oak Harbor	NW	200
Becker	Pebble Creek	TC	209
Belle Plaine	Valley View	TC	279
Bemidji	Bemidji Town & Country	NW	61
Biwabik	Giant's Ridge - The Legend	NE	125
Biwabik	Giant's Ridge - The Quarry	NE	126
Blaine	Victory Links	TC	281
Bloomington	Dwan	TC	99
Bloomington	Hyland Greens	TC	148
Brainerd	Cragun's - Bobby's Legacy	NW	85
Brainerd	Cragun's - Dutch's Legacy	NW	86
Brainerd	Madden's - The Classic	NW	175
Brainerd	Madden's - Pine Beach West	NW	176
Brainerd	Madden's - Pine Beach East	NW	177
Breezy Point	Breezy Point - Traditional	NW	68
Breezy Point	Breezy Point - White Birch	NW	69

Minnesota Courses by City

City	Course	Region	Page
Breezy Point	Breezy Point - Deacon's Lodge	NE	95
Brooklyn Park	Edinburgh USA	TC	107
Buffalo	Wild Marsh	TC	205
Buffalo Lake	Oakdale	SW	294
Cambridge	Purple Hawk	NE	222
Cannon Falls	Cannon	SE	74
Cannon Falls	Gopher Hills	SE	130
Cannon Falls	The Summit	SE	267
Cedar	Hidden Haven	TC	145
Cedar	Viking Meadows	TC	282
Chanhassen	Bluff Creek	TC	65
Chaska	Chaska Town	TC	78
Chaska	Dahlgreen	TC	93
Clearwater	Eagle Trace	WC	102
Cohasset	Ruttger's - Sugarbrooke	NE	237
Cold Spring	Rich Springs	WC	225
Cold Spring	River Oaks	WC	231
Coleraine	Eagle Ridge	NE	101
Coon Rapids	Bunker Hills	TC	73
Corcoran	Shamrock	TC	242
Cottage Grove	Mississippi Dunes	TC	188
Cottage Grove	River Oaks	TC	229
Crosslake	Crosswoods	NE	88
Dayton	Daytona	TC	94
Dayton	Hayden Hills	TC	139
Dayton	Sundance	TC	254
Deerwood	Cuyuna	NE	91
Deerwood	Ruttger's - The Lakes	NE	238
Detroit Lakes	Detroit Country Club	NW	97
Detroit Lakes	Forest Hills	NW	119
Detroit Lakes	Lakeview	NW	160
Detroit Lakes	Wildflower	NW	295
Dodge Center	Dodge	SE	98

Minnesota Courses by City

City	Course	Region	Page
Duluth	Enger Park	NE	113
Duluth	Lester Park	NE	167
Eagan	Parkview	TC	208
Edina	Braemar	TC	67
Elbow Lake	Tipsinah Mounds	WC	276
Elk River	Elk River	TC	66
Elko	Boulder Pointe	TC	108
Emily	Emily Greens	NE	112
Fairmont	Rose Lake	SW	234
Faribault	Faribault	SE	117
Faribault	Legacy	SE	164
Farmington	Fountain Valley	TC	120
Farmington	Southern Hills	TC	246
Fifty Lakes	Golden Eagle	NE	128
Fort Ripley	Eagle's Landing	WC	256
Forest Lake	Tanners Brook	TC	105
Frontenac	Mount Frontenac	SE	193
Glencoe	Glencoe	SW	127
Glenwood	Minnewaska	WC	187
Glenwood	Pezhekee National	NW	211
Golden Valley	Brookview	TC	71
Grand Rapids	Pokegama	NW	217
Grand Rapids	Wendigo	NE	290
Ham Lake	Majestic Oaks - Crossroads	TC	178
Ham Lake	Majestic Oaks - Signature	TC	179
Hastings	Afton Alps	TC	53
Hastings	Bellwood Oaks	TC	60
Hastings	Emerald Greens - Brnz/Gold	TC	110
Hastings	Emerald Greens - Silv/Plat	TC	111
Hastings	Hidden Greens	NW	144
Hawley	Hawley	SE	138
Hayfield	The Oaks	NE	264
Hibbing	Mesaba	NE	185

Minnesota Courses by City

City	Course	Region	Page
Hinkley	Grand National	NE	131
Hopkins	Meadowbrook	TC	184
Houston	Valley High	SE	278
Hutchinson	Crow River	WC	89
Internation'l Falls	Falls Country Club	NW	116
Inv. Grove Hghts.	Inver Wood	TC	149
Isanti	Sanbrook	NE	239
Isle	Fiddlestix	NE	118
Jordan	Ridges at Sand Creek	TC	227
Kimball	Kimball	WC	155
Lake City	Lake City	SE	157
Lake City	Lake Pepin	SE	159
Lake City	The Jewel	SE	260
Lake Elmo	Country Air	TC	84
Lakeville	Crystal Lake	TC	90
Lakeville	Heritage Links	TC	141
Le Sueur	Le Sueur	SW	163
Lester Prairie	Shadowbrooke	WC	241
Lindstrom	Chisago Lakes	NE	79
Lino Lakes	Chomonix	TC	80
Litchfield	Litchfield	WC	168
Little Falls	Little Falls	WC	170
Long Prairie	Long Prairie	WC	172
Longville	Ridgewood	NE	228
Lutsen	Superior National	NE	255
Maple Grove	Rush Creek	TC	236
Maple Plain	Pioneer Creek	TC	216
Maplewood	Goodrich	TC	129
Marshall	Marshall	SW	181
McGregor	Minnesota National	NE	186
Medina	Baker National	TC	58
Menahga	Blueberry Pines	NW	64

Minnesota Courses by City

City	Course	Region	Page
Menahga	Fair Haven	NE	114
Milaca	Hardwoods	NE	137
Milaca	Stones Throw	NE	252
Miltona	Lake Miltona	WC	158
Minneapolis	Columbia	TC	82
Minneapolis	Francis A. Gross	TC	122
Minneapolis	Hiawatha	TC	142
Minneapolis	Theodore Wirth	TC	271
Montevideo	The Crossings	WC	259
Montgomery	Montgomery	SE	191
Monticello	Monticello	TC	192
Moorhead	The Meadows	NW	262
Moorhead	Village Green	NW	283
Mora	Spring Brook	NE	247
Morris	Pomme De Terre	WC	218
Morton	Dacotah Ridge	SW	92
Motley	Pine Ridge	WC	215
Mound	Lakeview	TC	161
New Prague	Creeksbend	SE	87
New Prague	New Prague	WC	194
New Ulm	New Ulm	SW	195
Nisswa	Grand View - The Pines	NW	132
North Mankato	North Links	SW	196
Northfield	Northfield	SE	198
Northfield	Willingers	SE	296
Oak Grove	The Refuge	TC	266
Oakdale	Oak Marsh	TC	202
Onamia	Izaty's Blackbrook	NE	153
Ortonville	Ortonville	WC	207
Otsego	Riverwood National	TC	233
Otsego	Vintage	TC	284
Ottertail	Thumper Pond	WC	273
Owatonna	Brooktree	SE	70

Minnesota Courses by City

City	Course	Region	Page
Owatonna	Hidden Creek	SE	143
Owatonna	Straight River	SE	253
Park Rapids	Eagle View	NW	104
Park Rapids	Headwaters	NW	140
Paynesville	Koronis Hills	WC	156
Pequot Lakes	Grand View - The Preserve	NW	133
Pequot Lakes	Whitefish	NE	292
Perham	Perham Lakeside	NW	210
Pine Island	Pine Island	SE	214
Pine River	Irish Hills	NE	150
Plymouth	Elm Creek	TC	109
Plymouth	Hollydale	TC	147
Preston	Rivers' Bend	SE	232
Princeton	Princeton	NE	221
Prior Lake	Legends	TC	165
Prior Lake	The Meadows	TC	263
Prior Lake	The Wilds	TC	270
Ramsey	Rum River Hills	TC	235
Ramsey	The Links at Northfork	TC	261
Red Wing	Mississippi Nat'l - Highlands	SE	189
Red Wing	Mississippi Nat'l - Lowlands	SE	190
Red Wing	Red Wing	SE	223
Redwood Falls	Redwood Falls	SW	224
Rice	Oak Hill	NW	201
Rochester	Eastwood	SE	106
Rochester	Meadow Lakes	SE	183
Rochester	Northern Hills	SE	197
Rochester	Oak Summit	SE	203
Rochester	Soldiers Memorial	SE	244
Rochester	Willow Creek	SE	297
Rogers	Pheasant Acres	TC	213
Rosemount	Rich Valley	TC	226
Rosseau	Oakcrest	NW	204

Minnesota Courses by City

City	Course	Region	Page
Rush City	Bulrush	NE	72
Sartell	Blackberry Ridge	WC	63
Sauk Center	Greystone	WC	136
Sauk Center	Lynx National	WC	174
Sauk Rapids	Wapicada	WC	286
Shakopee	Stonebrooke	TC	250
Spicer	Little Crow	WC	169
St. Charles	St. Charles	SE	248
St. Cloud	Territory	WC	257
St. Francis	The Ponds	TC	265
St. James	St. James	SW	249
St. Michael	Fox Hollow	TC	121
St. Paul	Como	TC	83
St. Paul	Highland National	TC	146
St. Paul	Keller	TC	154
St. Paul	Les Bolstad	TC	166
St. Paul	Phalen Park	TC	212
St. Peter	Shoreland	SW	243
Stacy	Falcon Ridge	NE	115
Staples	The Vintage	NW	268
Stillwater	Applewood Hills	TC	56
Stillwater	Logger's Trail	TC	171
Stillwater	Oak Glen	TC	199
Stillwater	Sawmill	TC	240
Stillwater	Stoneridge	TC	251
Thief River Falls	Thief River	NW	272
Tower	The Wilderness	NE	269
Two Harbors	Lakeview National	NW	162
Tyler	Tyler Community	SW	277
Victoria	Deer Run	TC	96
Virginia	Virginia	NE	285
Wabasha	Coffee Mill	SE	81
Waconia	Island View	WC	152

Minnesota Courses by City

City	Course	Region	Page
Wadena	Whitetail Run	NW	293
Walker	Long Bow	NW	173
Walker	Tianna	NW	274
Warroad	Warroad Estates	NW	287
Waseca	Waseca Lakeside	SE	288
Watertown	Timber Creek	TC	275
White Bear Lake	Gem Lake Hills	TC	123
White Bear Lake	Manitou Ridge	TC	180
White Bear Lake	Oneka Ridge	TC	206
Willmar	Eagle Creek	WC	100
Winona	Cedar Valley	SE	77
Winona	The Bridges	SE	258
Woodbury	Eagle Valley	TC	103
Woodbury	Prestwick	TC	220
Worthington	Prairie View	SW	219
Worthington	Worthington	SW	298
Zumbrota	Zumbrota	SE	299

Wisconsin Courses by City

City	Course	Region	Page
Amery	Amery	WISC	301
Barron	Rolling Oaks	WISC	324
Black River Falls	Skyline	WISC	326
Cable	Lakewoods - Forest Ridges	WISC	317
Chippewa Falls	Lake Wissota	WISC	316
Colfax	Whitetail	WISC	335
Cumberland	Cumberland	WISC	308
Frederic	Frederic	WISC	309
Hammond	Pheasant Hills	WISC	321
Hayward	Big Fish	WISC	303

Wisconsin Courses by City

City	Course	Region	Page
Hayward	Hayward Golf & Tennis	WISC	310
Hayward	Hayward National	WISC	311
Hayward	Teal Wing	WISC	329
Hudson	Hudson	WISC	313
Hudson	Troy Burne	WISC	331
Hudson	White Eagle	WISC	334
Lake Wissota	Chippewa Falls	WISC	316
Luck	Luck	WISC	318
New Richmond	New Richmond	WISC	320
Osceola	Krooked Kreek	WISC	315
Prescott	Clifton Highlands	WISC	305
Rice Lake	Turtleback	WISC	332
River Falls	Clifton Hollow	WISC	306
River Falls	Kilkarney Hills	WISC	314
River Falls	River Falls	WISC	322
Roberts	Badlands	WISC	302
Siren	Siren National	WISC	325
Somerset	Bristol Ridge	WISC	304
Somerset	St. Croix National	WISC	328
Sparta	River Run	WISC	323
Spring Valley	Spring Valley	WISC	327
Superior	Nemadji	WISC	319
Tomah	Hiawatha	WISC	312
Trempeleau	Trempeleau Mountain	WISC	330
Viroqua	Viroqua Hills	WISC	333
Wisconsin Dells	Coldwater Canyon	WISC	307

AFTON ALPS

6600 Peller Avenue South
Hastings, MN 55033
Clubhouse: 651-436-1320
Golf Shop: 651-436-1320
Type: Public   Par: 72

www.aftonalps.com

Tees	Men's	Women's	Yards
Red		68.6/117	4789
White	67.7/114	72.8/127	5556
Blue	68.9/116	74.3/130	5823

Region: Twin Cities

Course Rating

HOSPITALITY	7.33
PLAYABILITY	6.49
USABILITY	6.45
FACILITY	5.69
VALUE	5.48

OVERALL SCORE
647

Greens Fee: $26.00 (weekend)
1/2 Cart Fee: $12.00 (weekend)

Afton Alps Golf Course in Hastings, Minnesota, is part of the year-round Afton Alps recreational area, and located adjacent to Afton State Park, but technically has a Hastings, Minnesota address. It is open to the public and a nicely distanced course at 5823 yards from the blue tees. Golf carts are available, and necessary.

There are two practice greens and one is set up for chipping. The course does not offer a driving range. In the clubhouse there is lots of seating, a grill, and they do have full bar service. There is also a limited amount of golf items for purchase. The staff was very friendly and after our round came out to meet us and ask if we wanted them to keep the grill opened for us, as they were getting ready to close, but would be happy to stay if we wanted.

Afton Alps really is two different golf courses in one. The front nine plays very nicely and is well laid out. Greens are reachable in regulation, and we found the course to be very wide open and hazards placed in the appropriate locations. We did enjoy the front nine, but found the back nine to be far different. The back nine is laid out almost entirely within the Afton Alps ski slopes, making for a very hilly and sometimes odd layout. You are literally playing golf on the same slopes that you can ski on in the winter. It really seemed to be an afterthought to have holes here, tee boxes poorly placed, blind shots around corners, ski lifts surrounding holes and snowmaking machines and piping around the course. On the plus side, there are some very scenic vantage points on the back nine, with some nice views of the St. Croix River Valley. We even spotted three deer and a raccoon on the course.

We found this course just okay. Guess it would be fair to say we felt kind of "duped." We came for 18 holes of golf and we got 9. The second nine was more of a tour of the ski resort without the snow. Would we return? Maybe, but there are many more comparable choices that would be more enjoyable. Most likely, the next time we'd return, it would be with our skis, to experience the more appropriate use of this particular parcel of real estate.

ID: 5503308MN

ALBANY

500 Church Ave
Albany, MN 56307
Clubhouse: 320-845-2505
Golf Shop: 320-845-2505
Type: Public   Par: 72

www.albanygc.com

Tees	Men's	Women's	Yards
Red		65.8/106	4534
Gold	64.1/109		5070
White	68.4/117		6027
Blue	70.7/122		6531

Region: WestCentral

Course Rating

HOSPITALITY	7.73
PLAYABILITY	7.15
USABILITY	7.85
FACILITY	6.95
VALUE	7.32

OVERALL SCORE
742

Green Fee: $30 (weekend)
1/2 Cart Fee: $13 (weekend)

The large freeway sign for Albany Golf Club in Albany, Minnesota, (located 20 miles west of St. Cloud) makes the course easy to find. Parking is across the street from the course, but driving a golf cart to your car to load up your clubs makes the parking situation convenient.

The clubhouse, which feels like a private or semi-private club, is very clean and is large enough for banquets or parties. Oversized restrooms include lockers and showers. The pro shop doesn't have a huge selection of merchandise—especially for women—and prices are comparable to other courses.

We played this course on a weekday, which could explain why food service was minimal. Premade sandwiches and micro pizzas were available, but there wasn't a menu or grill service. The beer prices were reasonable and bar service was good. Also perhaps because of our weekday round, there wasn't water or a beverage cart on the course. However, there is a pop machine—and nice restrooms—on the front nine.

The course is well maintained with beautiful flowers and gardens. Large stone markers on the tees have nice diagrams, showing the layout and yardages for each hole. Pin placements are marked with red, white and blue flags. The fairways are large and somewhat forgiving, and the rough is short enough to hit out of without much problem. Even so, the trees came into play more often than we expected. The greens are in nice condition and are very fast. The freeway traffic can be heard constantly, but it is not distracting.

The many bunkers are easy to avoid; however, the sand is hard and gravelly. The few water hazards are mostly visible from the tees or markers. Only one hole has water completely across the fairway. On the day *Team Hacker* was there, most of the water hazards had algae and were murky, so it was difficult to see or retrieve a ball.

ID: 5630709MN

ALBION RIDGES

Region: WestCentral

7771 20th Street Northwest
Annandale, MN 55302
Clubhouse: 320-963-5500
Golf Shop: 320-963-5500
Type: Public   Par: 36/36/36

www.albionridges.com

Tees	Men's	Women's	Yards
Rock/Granite - white	67.3/124	72.5/125	5708
Rock/Granite - black	71.1/132		6555
Granite/Boulder - white	66.5/125	66.1/111	5525
Granite/Boulder - black	71.5/136		6630
Boulder/Rock - white	66.9/123	65.6/110	5637
Boulder/Rock - black	71.1/131		6549

Course Rating

HOSPITALITY	7.94
PLAYABILITY	8.01
USABILITY	8.52
FACILITY	8.05
VALUE	7.53

OVERALL SCORE
805

Green Fee: $32 (weekend)
1/2 Cart Fee: $11 (weekend)

About forty-five minutes from Minneapolis or St. Cloud and located amongst the hills and farms is a surprise called Albion Ridges in Annandale, Minnesota. The 27-hole golf course has something for all abilities. Granite plays 2,798 yards from the whites while Rock and Boulder play 2,910 and 2,727 respectively.

First glance at the Granite nine appears pretty straight forward, but you soon realize shot placement will be rewarded. Even though there is ample room off most tee boxes you don't want to find yourself in the rough too often or hacker status will be secure. We really enjoyed the par 3 #3 and par 4 #9 holes. Both are nicely laid out and a challenge at any level. #7 was another favorite on the Granite 9 luckily the wind was not a problem the sunny fall day we played. Our second 9 was Boulder. First hole is a dog leg left around Fred's silo. From the looks of the side of the silo more than few errant hacker shots have found it tough to cut the corner. There are aiming boulders on each hole and we suggest using them. There are several opportunities to cut distance off on this nine whether over water or shortening corners, but the prudent play may be straight forward as the hole lies. Boulder is different and a very fun 9 that has great variety.

Weekend green fees at Albion Ridges are $32 plus cart. Their website has great information ranging from directions to the interesting history of the course. The scorecard page has pictures of each hole that gives you an idea of what it is really like. Tee times are available by phone or online. The clubhouse is large and has plenty of room for larger groups before and after rounds. However, it is lightly merchandised and offers only minimal choices for refreshments. The staff was very accommodating and eager to help in anyway they could. Power carts are available and located conveniently right outside. Driving range and putting green are available to get you ready for your round.

ID: 5530209MN

APPLEWOOD HILLS Exec. 18

Region: Twin Cities

11840 60th Street North
Stillwater, MN 55082
Clubhouse: 651-439-7276
Golf Shop: 651-439-7276
Type: Public   Par: 62

www.applewoodhillsgolf.com

U

Course Rating

HOSPITALITY	8.59
PLAYABILITY	8.16
USABILITY	9.31
FACILITY	7.97
VALUE	6.61

Tees	Men's	Women's	Yards
Red		59.1/95	3392
White	60.0/98	61.8/102	3891
Blue	60.6/100		4110

OVERALL SCORE
831

Greens Fee: $26.50 (weekend)
1/2 Cart Fee: $15.00 (weekend)

Jobs, kids, yard work, softball, picnics…there are a host of summertime reasons why we may not always have time for a full round of golf. The solution: Applewood Hills Golf Course in Stillwater, Minnesota, an 18 hole, par-62 executive course that is like almost no other in the Twin Cities. Located just off of Highway 36 at Manning Avenue, Applewood Hills provides a serene, rural setting for a leisurely round of golf on a short but challenging course.

For most golfers, the phrase "executive course" evokes a yawning, defeated response usually accompanied by one of the aforementioned reasons why a full round is untenable. Not so with Applewood Hills. This course is a destination, not a last resort. A beautiful rolling course, lined with blooming apple trees on nearly every fairway, Applewood Hills provides a distinctive golf experience for the beginner and the seasoned golfer alike.

Although Applewood Hills is an executive course, do not leave your driver at home. You will almost certainly need it for the handful of fairways that measure 350 yards or longer. The course layout is relatively imaginative with fairways of varied lengths and shapes, which allows most golfers to play every club in their bag. Even the par-3 holes, which vary in length from 90 to 220 yards, challenge the golfer and provide a demanding "tune-up" for the irons. The greens are likewise varied, from the frustrating "postage-stamp" greens to those that sprawl with entertaining contours. The course is well managed with lush green fairways and ankle-length rough. The only meaningful complaint about this course is a few dead spots on the greens around the curtain. However, even these few dead spots paled in comparison to the overall golf experience.

Applewood Hills is a very walkable course and, at just over $20 per round, very affordable as well. The course also offers league play for men, women, seniors and juniors and twilight rates and enticing internet offers for free or discounted golf. Whether you are short on time, interested in focusing on your short game, or just looking for a break from the menu of your standard courses, Applewood Hills is a great destination.

56

ID: 5508208MN

ATIKWA

2100 Arrowwood Lane NW
Alexandria, MN 56308
Clubhouse: 320-762-8337
Golf Shop: 320-762-8337
Type: Public   Par: 72

www.arrowwoodresort.com

Tees	Men's	Women's	Yards
Red		69.7/114	5017
Gold	65.6/114		5148
White	68.4/119	73.9/123	5770
Blue	69.9/124		6167

Course Rating

HOSPITALITY   7.33
PLAYABILITY   7.15
USABILITY   7.00
FACILITY   7.33
VALUE   5.50

VERALL SCORE
703

Green Fee: $42 (weekend)
1/2 Cart Fee: $13 (weekend)

Right off the shores of Lake Darling in Alexandria, Minnesota, you can find Arrowwood Resort and Conference Center and its championship golf course, Atikwa Golf Club. We were not disappointed when we played the course.

Walking into the clubhouse, there's nothing too extraordinary or fancy about the place. The smaller clubhouse feels like a comfortable living room, and it has the basic necessities. The check-in and start was smooth, and they got us on the course as soon as possible.

We were impressed with the course before the round even started when our four beers turned into six, due to the course's buy four, get two free policy. Also, while out on the course, the beverage cart impressively appeared whenever we needed it, so we were never thirsty even on a very warm afternoon.

Atikwa delivers a very playable layout with a variety of different demands. Both the front and back nine start out with relatively straightforward par 5s, so a golfer should have a good chance at starting out either side with a decent score under his or her belt.

The course alternates between a more wide-open play in the opening and closing holes on each nine, and closer to target golf in the middle half of each nine, particularly the front side. These different styles give all levels of golfers a chance to hit shorter, straighter shots or longer, more forgiving shots.

The course is cut out of a very natural scene, so there are plenty of challenges that a hacker faces while at Atikwa. However, outside of the demanding par-3 #15, there isn't anything about the course that is so challenging it might scare a hacker away. The course is designed to give a player a fair chance to score while at the same time not rolling over and letting the hacker spray it just anywhere without finding trouble. For a fair price and a high quality of play, Atikwa is a great stop in northern Minnesota for any level of golfer.

57

ID: 5630809MN

BAKER NATIONAL

2935 Parkview Drive
Medina, MN 55340
Clubhouse: 763-694-7670
Golf Shop: 763-694-7670
Type: Public   Par: 72

www.bakernational.com

Tees	Men's	Women's	Yards
Yellow		72.0/131	5313
White	71.8/131	77.5/142	6294
Black	73.9/135		6762

Region: Twin Cities

Course Rating

HOSPITALITY   7.88
PLAYABILITY   8.50
USABILITY   7.84
FACILITY   8.17
VALUE   7.47

OVERALL SCORE
806

Greens Fee: $36.00 (weekend)
1/2 Cart Fee: $15.00 (weekend)

Baker National Golf Course in Medina, Minnesota, is located within the Three Rivers Park District and is the hacker's dream setting. With an expansive practice area, a championship 18-hole course, an executive 9-hole course and a well-stocked clubhouse, you can spend your chosen amount of time leisurely perfecting your golf game.

The course entrance and clubhouse (pro shop) were easy to find even though it is set back off of any highway, but that does mean no car noises to distract you. The pro shop is well stocked, and the staff were very pleasant and helpful. They eagerly checked our foursome in and directed us to the practice ranges and putting greens. Yes, practice ranges and putting greens.

When warmed up we hopped into the electric carts and drove them to the first tee. Although the course can be walked, the rolling fairways will test your stamina and on the back nine some "next tees" are a good walk away from the last hole's green. The nice lady starter checked our time and wished us good luck.

The championship course was very lush and the setting could not be more picturesque. The fairways were a tad narrow but the rough was not very punishing. Plus on the front nine, we found out first hand, you can spray your drive and still find your ball in a playable lie. The back nine holes are tighter and you do need to play some position golf rather than just "grip it and rip it" all the time. What was nice to see was that every sprinkler head did have a yardage marker on it and the 150-yard marker was very visible. All of the greens challenged our putting skills as the greens all seemed to have two or three tiers. The greens are large in size; hence it built up our self-esteem when we landed on from outside 150 yards. The pace of play for a Sunday was average, just over 4½ hours for the round but we did see the beverage cart every three holes.

Overall, Baker National Golf Course is a hacker's dream setting and we would definitely make a return trip each summer.

58

BALMORAL

28294 State Highway 78
Battle Lake, MN 56515
Clubhouse: 218-864-5414
Golf Shop: 218-367-2055
Type: Semi-Private   Par: 72

www.golfbalmoral.com

Course Rating

HOSPITALITY	8.65
PLAYABILITY	7.90
USABILITY	8.93
FACILITY	7.33
VALUE	7.19

U

OVERALL SCORE
814

Green Fee: $32 (weekend)
1/2 Cart Fee: $14 (weekend)

Tees	Men's	Women's	Yards
Red		70.1/117	5287
Gold	67.3/115		5640
White	69.1/119		6025
Blue	70.1/120		6255

When we visited Balmoral Golf Course in Battle Lake, Minnesota, it was a fine day for golfing—had we been in Scotland (perhaps on the Balmoral Estate with the Queen). But here in Minnesota, the blustery day kept the temperatures around the mid 50s, and there was a continuous light mist. Other than that, Balmoral proved to be a great course.

Balmoral Golf Course is located south of Ottertail on Highway 78, on the southeast corner of Ottertail Lake. It is a quaint, old course that is well kept, has lots of mature trees, has enough challenge to keep things interesting and yet is a course you can score on. What we liked best about Balmoral is that it is an easily walkable course: about 6100 yards from the white tees, with short walks from the green to the next tee. The course is also very scenic; along with the trees, there are rolling hills and a few ponds. Don't fear those ponds, however—there are no forced carries, but the ponds will make you think twice about cutting a corner.

This course's playability is great. Fairways are wide, most with at least a little dogleg. Rolling hills don't have too much side slope. Greens are large and generally well sloped, but they putted very true. The fairways were in good condition and the rough was not too deep. While there are quite a few trees, rarely did an errant shot put us in jail; there's almost always a clear shot back to the fairway.

The staff is friendly and efficient. The clubhouse has a small grill as well as sandwiches and chips; the bar offers pop as well as beer and some mixed drinks. Prices were very reasonable for food and beverage. Tee times are available by phone or online, and we'd guess that you could even do a walk-on in the middle of the week, unless a league is in process. At times we had to wait for golfers ahead of us, but not so much as to be truly annoying. In truth, Balmoral Golf Course is a great course that you should play whenever you're in the Ottertail area.

ID: 5651509MN

BELLWOOD OAKS

13239 210th Street East
Hastings, MN 55033
Clubhouse: 651-437-4141
Golf Shop: 651-437-4141
Type: Public   Par: 73

www.bellwoodoaksgolf.com

Course Rating

HOSPITALITY	6.80
PLAYABILITY	7.30
USABILITY	8.06
FACILITY	7.57
VALUE	5.31

Tees	Men's	Women's	Yards
Red		70.0/120	5124
Gold	69.5/121	74.4/129	5916
White	72.1/126	77.6/135	6487
Blue	73.5/129		6791

OVERALL SCORE

717

Greens Fee: $29.00 (weekend)
1/2 Cart Fee: $15.00 (weekend)

Bellwood Oaks Golf Club is located about five minutes south of Hastings, Minnesota, just off Highway 61. We golfed on a Monday morning and there were 10 to 12 golfers at the first tee. We were on time and had no wait at the first hole. There is a practice green and an 8-station driving range on site. Check-in is in a small building close to the first tee.

If you are hungry, or think you are going to be, better make sure you get something before you get here. There is a very limited amount of snacks and microwave sandwiches available. A few tables in the check-in building is the extent of the clubhouse amenities.

We really liked this course. It was a "no frills" experience other than the golf, but the round itself was very enjoyable. We found the course to be exceedingly well kept, and very hacker friendly. There is not an abundance of flora and fauna, but the holes are nevertheless very nice and give you a peaceful feeling. The rough was a bit on the long side, but not overly so. Greens were large, and flat for the most part; some gradual slopes here and there make them challenging on only a few holes. The greens were in excellent condition and the flags on this particular day were very fairly placed. The thing we liked most about this course was the fact that all holes were very reachable in regulation. If you drive an average distance and keep the ball in the fairway, you will have an excellent chance to reach the green and score well. If you do have the cursed slice or hook on your drives, don't worry, the course is open enough that you still have a chance to recover and score. There are 34 groomed bunkers on the course, and 3 holes have water, but all were fairly placed and the water was flagged with a striped pole to let you know it was there. Out-of-bounds markers come into play on only a few holes, and you really are out-of-bounds when you cross them.

Again, the best part of the day was the golf, just like it should be. Great course, in great condition, and very hacker friendly. This is a course we will surely visit again.

ID: 5503308MN

BEMIDJI

2425 Birchmont Beach Road
Bemidji, MN 56601
Clubhouse: 218-751-4535
Golf Shop: 218-751-9215
Type: Semi-Private   Par: 72
www.bemidjigolf.com

H

Course Rating

HOSPITALITY	9.07
PLAYABILITY	8.42
USABILITY	8.06
FACILITY	6.98
VALUE	6.97

OVERALL SCORE
815

Tees	Men's	Women's	Yards
Red		69.2/117	5027
Gold	66.4/116	71.3/122	5401
White	70.1/123	75.8/131	6210
Blue	71.6/126		6535

Green Fee: $47 (weekend)
1/2 Cart Fee: $16 (weekend)

Located on the north shore of Lake Bemidji, Bemidji Town & Country Club is the jewel of northwestern Minnesota. The view from the #9 green looks over the clubhouse and down on Lake Bemidji. This has to be one of the most beautiful vistas on any course in Minnesota.

The course is easy to get to—it's just north of the city of Bemidji, across the road from Lake Bemidji and Lake Bemidji State Park. If the course has a negative, it would be the hill one must climb to get from the parking lot to the clubhouse. However, golfers who rent a cart can check in and drive the cart down to get their clubs.

There is a driving range and two practice greens, one for chipping and the other for putting. Range balls are $5 per bag. Lessons with the golf pro are $45 for a 45-minute lesson. Prices for rounds seemed about average for this area: weekdays $47, weekends $50 and twilight $30, with carts at $16 per person.

The clubhouse has a bar and restaurant with a full menu and is very popular for weddings and meetings. The staff is very professional. The food is second to none, and the restaurant also has that magnificent view of the lake. Out on the course water comes into play on four holes, but as hackers we did not find those holes to be too threatening. There are 37 well-maintained sand traps on the course, but if you are accustomed to the white sand on some courses, you would be disappointed here. The main hazards are the many trees that line the fairways. The rough has been cut low under the trees, however, so you can still get out even though you may have to punch out and lose a stroke. The greens are in very good condition and seem quite fast, especially if you are used to playing a course not maintained as well. The fairways are also in top condition and very easy to hit from. We thoroughly enjoyed playing at Bemidji Town & Country Club; one of the best in northern Minnesota!

BLACK BEAR

2677 16th Street SW
Backus, MN 56435
Clubhouse: 218-587-8800
Golf Shop: 218-587-8800
Type: Public   Par: 72

www.blackbeargolfcomplex.com

Tees	Men's	Women's	Yards
Forward		69.3/111	4817
Middle	69.3/118	75.0/123	5840
Back	71.1/122		6231

NOTE: website was not working at presstime (Jan-2010).

Region: NorthWest

Course Rating

HOSPITALITY	8.03
PLAYABILITY	5.66
USABILITY	5.69
FACILITY	6.32
VALUE	7.47

OVERALL SCORE
654

Green Fee: $27.50 (weekend)
1/2 Cart Fee: included in fee

The Black Bear Golf Complex in Backus, Minnesota, is located north and east of Pine River, not far from the White Fish Chain of Lakes. Because the course is off the beaten path, we feel they could use more signage for better directions.

The clubhouse is pretty basic: They don't offer clothing or equipment for sale, and there is a limited menu of grill items. The green fee is inexpensive at $27.50 for 18 with a cart, and range balls are a reasonable $1.50 for a small bucket or $3 for a large one. The golf carts are older gas-powered carts—which is odd since the course itself is only 10 years old—but they are in good shape.

The back nine and the driving range are across the road from the front nine and the clubhouse, but neither the signs nor the scorecard indicated where to go for the back nine or how to get from green to tee, so we had to ask for directions a couple times.

The course is mostly wide open. For a northern course, there aren't that many trees, but there is a good amount of elevation change. A few tee boxes are relatively small; many of them are narrow and don't offer a lot of variety for different skill levels. There are three sets of tees, and the length goes from the forward tees at 4685 yards to the back tees at 6064 yards. Some of the holes seem to play much too short. You have par 5s at 382 and 396 yards from the middle tees, and there is a par 4 that is 220 yards.

This is not an easily walkable course—some of the green-to-tee distances seem close to a mile. The fairways are in okay condition—not great, but not terrible. The most notable part of the course is the greens. Some of them have a severe slope, so you could hit a ball that would almost go in but then turn around and roll off the green. For a resort course the greens are cut awfully short. This, combined with the slope and size of the greens, makes Black Bear a not very hacker-friendly course.

62

BLACKBERRY RIDGE

Region: WestCentral

3125 Club House Road
Sartell, MN 56377
Clubhouse: 320-257-4653
Golf Shop: 320-257-4653
Type: Public   Par: 72

www.blackberryridgegolf.com

H
F

Course Rating

HOSPITALITY	9.07
PLAYABILITY	8.72
USABILITY	8.05
FACILITY	9.10
VALUE	5.78

OVERALL SCORE
844

Green Fee: $33 (weekend)
1/2 Cart Fee: $14.25 (weekend)

Tees	Men's	Women's	Yards
Red		70.6/120	5112
Gold	68.3/132	74.0/127	5698
White	70.8/137		6238
Blue	72.5/141		6625
Black	74.2/144		6992

Blackberry Ridge Golf Club is located in Sartell, Minnesota, just minutes north of St. Cloud. The clubhouse has a full restaurant and bar, and the pro shop has a wide range of golf equipment and accessories. Getting on the course was not a problem even though we had no reservations.

We got our electric cart—complete with GPS—and drove a few feet to the 1st tee box, which actually has five separate tee boxes to accommodate golfers of every ability. Everything on the course is first class. This championship course, designed by Joel Goldstrand, is very scenic and challenging. There are mature trees lining the fairways, rolling hills and wetlands.

The well-mowed fairways have bent grass and are in great shape. The rough was mowed and, except for the wetlands, we lost only a few balls. The greens are fast, smooth and pristine. Cart paths are smooth, and they easily led from the green to the next tee box. Water comes into play on about half of the holes, but sand traps with fine, soft sand are present on almost every hole.

The 1st hole is a dogleg left around trees and over a water hazard to a small green. Three of the four par-3 holes require drives over wetlands. In fact, wetlands come into play on 14 holes! The par-5 hole #5 has three doglegs with wetlands along most of the left side of the fairway and wetlands on the right side for the last 100 yards. Number 13 has an S-shaped dogleg with wetlands on both sides and the final shot over the wetlands. These are some examples of the tricky variations in the course. It requires some thinking to do well.

It is interesting that there is about a half-mile difference between the lengths of the red and black tees (about a hundred yards per hole average), but everyone would walk the same distance. The course is long and the GPS is useful, so a cart is a plus, but the course is definitely walkable. In short, Blackberry Ridge is a difficult but enjoyable course, and with five different lengths, all level of golfers can do well here.

63

ID: 5637709MN

BLUEBERRY PINES

39161 US Highway 71
Menahga, MN 56464
Clubhouse: 218-564-4653
Golf Shop: 218-564-4653
Type: Public   Par: 72

www.blueberrypinesgolf.com

P

Course Rating

HOSPITALITY	8.08
PLAYABILITY	8.85
USABILITY	8.50
FACILITY	8.61
VALUE	6.83

OVERALL SCORE
835

Green Fee: $40 (weekend)
1/2 Cart Fee: $15 (weekend)

Tees	Men's	Women's	Yards
Red		69.8/122	4998
Gold	64.4/117		5365
White	69.8/129		6166
Blue	71.0/130		6409
Black	72.3/133		6703

Blueberry Pines Golf Club in Menahga, Minnesota, designed in 1991 by Joel Goldstrand, takes advantage of the natural beauty of the former Christmas tree farm from which it's carved. You'll start your day at the immense log cabin clubhouse, which combines the pro shop, lounge, restaurant and event facility. The networked GPS system on the carts will provide you with updated distances to all pertinent shot locations: pin, front and back edges, lay-up area, hazards and locations of other carts on the hole. You can even preorder a sandwich or snack from the 9th tee.

Blueberry Pines' layout gives the average golfer a generously open landing area from the tee, leading to soft, lush greens bordered by sand, marshes and natural water hazards. Five tee boxes offer a different look and a variety of challenges in traversing this landscape. After becoming comfortable with the opening holes, signage will alert you to the "Death Valley" trio (#5, 6 and 7), where the fairways are narrower, the water more plentiful and the tee shots more challenging. A special feature of the 7th hole is the presence of two parallel tee areas and fairways, offering either an open drive to a dogleg or a straight shot that must carry the marsh and water hazard fronting the tee area. Other delights will present themselves, including wildlife views, a family of trumpeter swans, covered bridges and the beautifully maintained grounds.

A full bar and varied menu is available at the clubhouse, and a buffet breakfast is available until 1 pm on Sundays. Food service is prompt and affordable, and the facilities are welcoming and comfortable. Stop at the well-appointed pro shop, talk to PGA pro Jim Carlson about instruction or swing analysis, or make use of the practice range and putting green as you continue to improve your game Blueberry Pines' excellent website includes aerial photos and course layout, rates and information on events and lessons. You can also book tee times and purchase merchandise, gift certificates or packages. Try Blueberry Pines...you'll like it.

BLUFF CREEK

1025 Creekwood
Chaska, MN 55318
Clubhouse: 952-445-5685
Golf Shop: 952-445-5685
Type: Public   Par: 72

www.bluffcreek.com

Tees	Men's	Women's	Yards
Red		71.1/125	5629
White	71.0/122	76.7/137	6398
Blue	71.9/124		6641

Region: Twin Cities

Course Rating

HOSPITALITY   7.15
PLAYABILITY   6.95
USABILITY   6.96
FACILITY   6.94
VALUE   5.44

OVERALL SCORE
785

Greens Fee: $42.00 (weekend)
1/2 Cart Fee: $15.00 (weekend)

Bluff Creek Golf Course in Chaska, Minnesota, might be considered a hidden gem and it tries hard to stay that way. If you didn't know it was there you'd miss it. If you are lucky enough to find the sign and do make the turn, you'll drive along what appears like a residential blacktop and even when you pull into the parking lot, you'll have to walk right up to the building to make sure you are at the right place.

Once there, you might be fooled when seeing the clubhouse for the first time. It is quite plain and doesn't hint at the airy, modern interior. After checking in, you find your cart just outside the door, the driving range nearby and a nice undulating putting green that will foreshadow the greens you'll find on the course.

The course itself is beautifully situated in the rolling hills and colorful hardwoods of Chaska. It is not really a walker's course because of the significant elevation changes. Although the holes are fairly straight with wide fairways, the greens don't do a golfer any favors because of the undulations. If you are not careful, they could easily add 4 to 5 strokes to your score. You won't find a lot of water, but you'll have to hone your sand skills because bunkers are often strategically tucked around the greens.

The course's strong suit is its setting, especially later in the year. It is a good course for hackers with equal opportunities for risk/reward and an average golfer has a chance to score well. Where it seems weak is the cost/value because the pricing seems a bit high for what you get and with its remote location you don't have many food/drink options nearby and are stuck with standard course fare.

If you are looking for a fair test, Bluff Creek is the kind of course that is good for the average player. If you are looking for a place to celebrate after your round, be sure to stop by Lion's Tap on Flying Cloud Drive, only a two-mile drive from the course. It is known for serving some of the best burgers in the Twin Cities.

ID: 5531808MN

BOULDER POINTE

Region: Twin Cities

9575 Glenborough Drive
Elko, MN 55020
Clubhouse: 952-461-4900
Golf Shop: 952-461-4900
Type: Public   Par: 71

www.boulderpointegolf.com

Course Rating

HOSPITALITY	5.60
PLAYABILITY	7.50
USABILITY	7.43
FACILITY	7.01
VALUE	6.21

OVERALL SCORE
681

Tees	Men's	Women's	Yards
Red	64.7/118	69.0/122	4794
Gold	67.6/123	72.5/129	5426
White	69.5/126		5833
Black	71.2/131		6224

Greens Fee: $34.00 (weekend)
1/2 Cart Fee: $15.00 (weekend)

Boulder Pointe Golf Club, located in Elko, Minnesota, a couple miles west of Interstate 35W, is a very picturesque course with nice elevation changes and lots of great scenery. If you hit the ball well and keep it in play this can be an enjoyable course. However, if you have a tendency to spray your ball a little bit or slice or hook it, you could be in for a long afternoon.

Generally speaking, the course was in excellent shape, with the exception of a few of the tee boxes that needed a little work. The fairways were nice and the rough was not too difficult to play out of. The greens played very true, although with lots of undulations they can be quite tricky. This is definitely a golf course that calls for course management. Club selection is the key. For the first timer this course can cause some problems. Lots of hazards and trouble to get into here.

One thing that was especially helpful was the GPS on all the golf carts. This made club selection much easier. Another nice feature of the GPS was that it showed where the group ahead of you was, and how far away they were (nice feature for those of us who may have a tendency of not knowing if we can hit away).

Boulder Pointe also had a great clubhouse. It has a nice little pro shop with an assortment of balls, clubs, shoes, and apparel. It also has a very nice restaurant that serves appetizers, soups, salads, burgers, sandwiches, pastas, and pizza. There is also a full bar serving mixed drinks, tap and bottle beer, and wine.

One of the greatest things about this course was its staff. Very friendly, professional, and genuinely interested in your having a good time. In particular was one young man working in the pro shop. As we were about to leave, our friend must have left his lights on and so his car would not start. The man behind the counter offered to give us a jump, and we were soon on our way.

All in all, our group enjoyed our golf outing at Boulder Pointe. It is certainly not the easiest course to play, but if you are up for a challenge, want to see a beautiful course, and enjoy a nice day of golf, we would recommend this one.

ID: 5502008MN

BRAEMAR

6364 John Harris Drive
Edina, MN 55439
Clubhouse: 952-826-6791
Golf Shop: 952-826-6799
Type: Public   Par: 36/36/36
www.braemargolf.com

F

Course Rating

HOSPITALITY	8.49
PLAYABILITY	8.53
USABILITY	8.70
FACILITY	8.99
VALUE	7.03

OVERALL SCORE
847

Greens Fee: $36.00 (weekend)
1/2 Cart Fee: $16.00 (weekend)

Tees	Men's	Women's	Yards
Castle/Hays - Red	67.5/118	73.1/126	5702
Castle/Hays - White	70.4/124	76.7/133	6341
Hays/Clunie - Red	66.3/117	71.6/122	5706
Hays/Clunie - White	69.1/123	75.0/129	5972
Clunie/Castle - Red	67.5/121	73.0/128	5579
Clunie/Castle - White	71.2/129	77.6/137	6401

Braemar Golf Course is owned and operated by the City of Edina, Minnesota, and features 27 regulation holes, a 9-hole executive course, banquet facilities, meeting rooms, and a grill that serves breakfast, sandwiches, beer and wine.

Braemar is probably the most unique and diverse course in the Twin Cities area. It has hosted PGA Tour events, amateur championships, numerous Minnesota Golf Association tournaments; has men's leagues, junior golf leagues, 12 women's leagues; and the Sister Kenny Institute holds a golf league for golfers with disabilities. Braemar also is a member of the Cooperative Sanctuary Program of Audubon International. The driving range is probably the heaviest used range in the Twin Cities. Next to the driving range is a large putting green that you can putt or chip.

The front nine (Castle 1-9) is the longest of the three courses. We would recommend the red tees for mid to high handicaps as there are four holes over 400 yards from the white tees. The second nine (Hays 10-18) has a more interesting terrain than the Castle and is also relatively flat except the Par-3 #12 with the tee near the top of a hill. The Castle and Hays nines are the original 18 holes. Their fairways are generous in width, the greens moderately undulating, quite large and in excellent condition. They are also well bunkered, but there is often an opening to run the ball up.

The third nine (Clunie 19-27) is the newest course. The Minnesota Department of Natural Resources (DNR) had significant input on this course's design as it wanders through a number of natural hazards and dense wooded areas. Clunie might be too difficult for the higher handicap player. Others will find it fun and challenging. Clunie is much more difficult to walk as there are three long uphill climbs from green to tee. The condition of Clunie was similar to the original course except the fairways weren't in quite as good condition with some bare spots.

Centrally located, Braemer is a very busy place that is well managed, well maintained and has everything you would want from a full-service golf course.

ID: 5543908MN

BREEZY POINT
(Traditional Course)

9252 Breezy Point Drive
Breezy Point, MN 56472
Clubhouse: 800-950-4960
Golf Shop: 218-562-7166
Type: Public   Par: 68

www.breezypointresort.com

Region: NorthWest

U

Course Rating

HOSPITALITY	8.38
PLAYABILITY	6.60
USABILITY	9.31
FACILITY	7.19
VALUE	5.41

Tees	Men's	Women's	Yards
Red		70.3/113	5127
White	65.7/114		5192

OVERALL SCORE
756

Green Fee: $36.00 (weekend)
1/2 Cart Fee: $16.00 (weekend)

The Traditional is a great name for this 5192-yard resort course because it's steeped in tradition. Located within the Breezy Point Resort complex, which is basically most of Breezy Point, Minnesota, its name really tells the story.

The land was first acquired in 1921 by millionaire publicist Wilfred Hamilton "Captain Billy" Fawcett, the flamboyant owner of Fawcett Publishing and creator of the famous *Captain Billy's Whiz Bang* magazine. Through his many contacts in the publishing and motion picture industry, Breezy Point soon became a mecca for the rich and famous during the Roaring 20s era, drawing such stars as Clark Gable, Carole Lombard, Tom Mix and Jack Dempsey. It's a great respite after playing Whitebirch or neighboring Deacon's Lodge. Short and easy to navigate, the Traditional is fun for hackers, beginners and shot-makers alike.

Like other older courses, The Traditional has hosted some Minnesota golfing luminaries like Patti Berg and Les Bolstad. Walter Hagen called it one of the elite courses of its day.

Priced higher than similar courses, but less than the premier courses in the area, the Traditional is easy to walk and rarely calls for a driver off the tee. The course lacks some of the typical amenities found at its sister course, like more than two tee boxes, better practice areas and a club pro. It's pretty straight-forward, although the narrow fairways may cause you to hear that charming sound of your ball caroming off a dozen trees—which is part of the fun.

Breezy Point is a huge, multi-faceted and full-service resort, which offers its guest a cornucopia of activities to enjoy. The Traditional is one of those ame-nities and proves to be a fun way to kill a few hours up north, especially at $36 for a weekend round. Remember it's an older-style resort course, but it's a great course to hone your skills before taking on one of the bigger dogs.

68

ID: 56472A09MN

BREEZY POINT
(Whitebirch Course)

9252 Breezy Point Drive
Breezy Point, MN 56472
Clubhouse: 800-950-4960
Golf Shop: 218-562-7177
Type: Public   Par: 72

www.breezypointresort.com

Tees	Men's	Women's	Yards
Red		67.3/114	5718
White	68.2/124	73.9/131	5852
Blue	70.4/128		6342
Black	72.2/132		6730

Region: NorthWest

U

Course Rating

HOSPITALITY	8.83
PLAYABILITY	8.39
USABILITY	9.31
FACILITY	8.26
VALUE	7.62

OVERALL SCORE
859

Green Fee: $52.00 (weekend)
1/2 Cart Fee: $16.00 (weekend)

The Whitebirch course at Breezy Point Resort is one of two courses operated by the resort. Located in Breezy Point, Minnesota, The Traditional course is within the grounds of the resort and White Birch is on County Road 11, about one mile west of the Breezy Point main gate. White Birch is easy to find and, compared to many other championship courses in the area, is less expensive to play. Play and Stay packages, guest rates and twilight opportunities make it even more affordable. The clubhouse is attractive and well stocked with a large pro shop and the beautiful adjoining Antlers Restaurant. The clubhouse staff is reduced in the fall and seemed a bit abrupt and matter-of-fact when we visited, but otherwise they were efficient and courteous.

You'll find the course well maintained and scenic. The front and back nines are different, with the back being longer and more picturesque. The fairways and greens were in good condition and there are four tee boxes to choose from. Many of the greens are severely sloped and pin placement is very important—three putts are not unusual. In late fall when we visited, there was no starter, ranger or beverage cart and the portable bathrooms were few and far between, but in the peak summer season these things are readily available.

Aside from the golf, Breezy Point Resort is famous for its expansive grounds, an impressive beach that fronts Pelican Lake, a big marina, tennis courts and an ice arena about a mile away. In winter, the resort is transformed, with skiing, skating, tubing, ice fishing and other outdoor activities in abundance.

Rolling terrain and water features (both natural and man-made) create some beautiful holes and the course itself is very playable for a hacker. While Whitebirch can't match the level of design and maintenance of some of the neighboring courses, it is a reasonable and enjoyable alternative. The Play and Stay packages make Breezy Point Resort a great home base from which to explore the many golf courses along the Paul Bunyan Trail.

ID: 56472B09MN

BROOKTREE

Region: SouthEast

1369 Cherry Street
Owatonna, MN 55060
Clubhouse: 507-444-2467
Golf Shop: 507-444-2467
Type: Public   Par: 71

www.ci.owatonna.mn.us

Tees	Men's	Women's	Yards
Red		72.6/124	5534
Gold	70.3/122	76.0/131	6143
White	71.4/124	77.3/134	6373
Blue	72.8/127		6684

Course Rating

HOSPITALITY	8.67
PLAYABILITY	7.00
USABILITY	7.71
FACILITY	8.00
VALUE	7.17

OVERALL SCORE
773

Green Fee: $31 (weekend)
1/2 Cart Fee: $14 (weekend)

This Owatonna, Minnesota, municipal track has strong visual appeal and Brooktree Golf Course provides a golf experience that accommodates many skill levels. First-time patrons should take note of the stream and bridge just to the left of the parking lot and tuck it away for later reference.

The clubhouse is small but well maintained. There is a compact but adequate pro shop and a diner-style grill area with a friendly staff available to provide a burger, sandwich or hot dog. A spacious dining room provides ample seating for leagues and larger groups. Brooktree has no driving range, however, and practice facilities are limited to two small but well-maintained practice greens. Access to the front nine, which is a more recent addition to the facility, is remotely located from the clubhouse and is accessible roughly 150 yards up a hill and through the woods. This is a minor hindrance for walkers, but generally the course is walker-friendly.

This course has two distinct identities. The hacker-friendly front nine has wide fairways and even wider roughs. The typical 20-handicapper can spray the ball liberally and, as long as a healthy distance is maintained, he or she wouldn't be in too much trouble. The bluegrass fairways and roughs combine to create that perfect combination of lush green and firmness that provide for extra roll from a less-than-perfectly-struck shot. The sizable bunkers are made of dark, hard-packed sand that offer little resistance in slowing the ball. The front nine greens are large, well-maintained and roll surprisingly true, especially for a municipal course.

On the back nine, however, the course begins to test the average golfer. Tighter fairways, smaller greens, more frequent out-of-bounds, thicker tree lines, blind shots and of course the aforementioned stream weaves like a ribbon throughout the entire back nine. The saving grace here is that at a distance of just under 3000 yards, this nine can be quite scorable, especially for short/straight hitters.

70

ID: 5506009MN

BROOKVIEW

200 Brookview Parkway
Golden Valley, MN 55426
Clubhouse: 763-512-2300
Golf Shop: 763-512-2330
Type: Public   Par: 72

www.brookviewgolf.com

Tees	Men's	Women's	Yards
Red		71.1/122	5328
Gold	67.1/123	72.4/125	5569
White	69.6/129	75.5/131	6123
Blue	70.8/131		6387

Course Rating

HOSPITALITY	7.74
PLAYABILITY	7.34
USABILITY	8.06
FACILITY	7.01
VALUE	6.56

OVERALL SCORE
746

Greens Fee: $34.00 (weekend)
1/2 Cart Fee: $14.00 (weekend)

Brookview Golf Course is in the heart of Golden Valley, Minnesota, and because of its location, is one of the busiest courses in the Twin Cities. Just off of Highway 55, it has an irons-only driving range, a par-3 course and 18 holes of urban golf.

With more than 40,000 rounds played yearly, the course has a large staff to keep the course in good condition. Although it doesn't have many bunkers or man-made hazards, there are just enough water and woods obstacles to make the course more challenging than it appears.

The clubhouse is comfortable with a lot of windows and a nice grill that serves both breakfast and lunch fare. The pricing is reasonable and the service is quick. Golden Valley city rules don't allow for more than beer and wine. Another thing to consider is that the course is smoke free.

Brookview is walkable with some elevation changes. Many of the holes are pretty flat, but water and swampy areas do come into play with certain holes requiring a layup. One weakness that often is found at similar courses is signage and the course can use a little help here. Directional signage to point you to the next hole and distance markers are sometimes hard to see. If you've played the course before it shouldn't be a big problem, but if it is your first time then you might pull out the wrong club or make the wrong turn.

The course has just enough challenge for hackers so don't be surprised by the loss of a few balls during your round. For a city course Brookview holds up well. It doesn't have the cachet of fancier courses, but it provides enough risk/reward that an average player has chances to score well.

For those in the city, Brookview is priced reasonably for a weekend round, and you don't have an hour of driving time to get there. If you want to warm up your driver, the range's lawyers won't let you do that because you might bean someone driving along Highway 55. If you want the 19th hole, the Brookview Grill is nice, but there are a number of nicer watering holes nearby that are a more fitting end to your day.

ID: 5542608MN

BULRUSH

605 Brookside Parkway
Rush City, MN 55069
Clubhouse: 320-358-1050
Golf Shop: 320-358-1050
Type: Public   Par: 72

www.bulrushgc.com

Tees	Men's	Women's	Yards
Red		70.9/121	5234
Green	69.0/124	74.4/128	5871
White	72.1/131		6573
Blue	73.7/134		6929

Region: NorthEast

Course Rating

HOSPITALITY	8.78
PLAYABILITY	7.88
USABILITY	7.33
FACILITY	8.43
VALUE	5.62

OVERALL SCORE
785

Green Fee: $32 (weekend)
1/2 Cart Fee: $13 (weekend)

Bulrush Golf Club in Rush City, Minnesota, is 45 minutes north of the Twin Cities Metro area.

We were expecting the course to be fairly open and straightforward, but it definitely was not! Most of the holes have doglegs, hilly fairways, woods on the side and wetlands. The woods and wetlands assure you that a lost ball really is lost. Every hole has a different, interesting variation to keep a golfer thinking.

The fairways are in good shape. There are four tee boxes per hole with distances from 5234 to 6929 yards, allowing for a wide range of abilities. While it was fairly easy to find our way around the course, the local we caught up with on the 4th hole helped guide us and suggested options for playing each hole.

Hole #6 was a par 3 over the wetlands. The green was in really good shape—smooth and quick. In fact all greens were excellent. The local we were playing with named hole #13 the Hacker Special! It is a 181-yard par 3; you tee off from the top of a hill, then go over a stream and marsh at the bottom to the green on the side of another hill. On this green the ball rolls randomly (a four-foot putt can miss every time). The course was tough, but with care one can do well. There are no easy holes.

Is the course walkable? Well, the distance from the clubhouse to the 1st tee plus the distance from the 18th green to the clubhouse is about one mile! So it is walkable, but a cart is close to a requirement. We talked with the owner, three staff people, the groundskeeper and several members. They are all proud of the course. It is about 10 years old and under new management, and they are working to improve an already good course. The course has beautiful terrain, wooded areas and wetlands and is one of the best-kept secrets in Minnesota. We had a very pleasant experience at Bulrush, and it's worth playing again.

ID: 5506909MN

BUNKER HILLS

12800 Bunker Prairie Road
Coon Rapids, MN 55448
Clubhouse: 763-755-4141
Golf Shop: 763-755-4141
Type: Public   Par: 36/36/36

www.bunkerhillsgolf.com

P

Course Rating

HOSPITALITY	8.06
PLAYABILITY	8.73
USABILITY	8.46
FACILITY	8.18
VALUE	6.88

OVERALL SCORE
824

Greens Fee: $38.00 (weekend)
1/2 Cart Fee: $14.00 (weekend)

Tees	Men's	Women's	Yards
North/East - White	69.7/130	75.6/137	6159
North/East - Blue	71.5/133	77.8/142	6558
East/West - White	70.6/128	76.7/137	6321
East/West - Blue	72.1/130	78.5/140	6648
West/North - White	70.5/133	76.5/140	6278
West/North - Blue	72.4/137	78.8/145	6700

Looking for an exceptional course? Then head to Bunker Hills Golf Course in Coon Rapids, Minnesota, located just west of Highway 65 on Highway 242. The course sports 27 holes of golf, simply named West, North and East. The course has been host to a wide array of tournaments from the Senior PGA Tour, to Minnesota High School state boy's and girl's tournaments.

Once you start playing you can see that although they have a lot of trees, they are trimmed fairly high and the grass in the open area is mowed to a very playable length. When you get to the greens you'll find that they are large, sloped and very fast. The greens will test you, especially if you find yourself on the high side. As in the name of the course, you'll also find they put in lots of bunkers. If you land in one, they are filled with some of the nicest sand that you can play out of. One thing you will find is that they can be reached on a lot of the holes with a driver, so be aware of your options. Throughout the course you will find that the tee boxes are well set up, with benches for a quick rest, trash bins and ball washers. They also have good locations for the restroom facilities.

This would be a great course for anyone to walk, with holes close by each other and with the gentle roll of the fairways. The pro shop has everything you will need, at the price you would expect at such a course. They have a nice driving range, as well as a good putting green located right next to the first tee box, so if you want to do some practicing before your round, you won't have far to go when the starter calls you.

There are GPS on the carts for distances, but if you are walking you'll have to look for sprinkler heads for your information. The clubhouse has a bar and grill as well as a restaurant. It also has a lot of history on its walls inside so take time to look around after your round. Bunker Hills is a great facility, the service and people are friendly and helpful, and you will see they take pride in their course the moment you get there.

ID: 5544808MN

CANNON

8606 295th Street East
Cannon Falls, MN 55009
Clubhouse: 507-263-3126
Golf Shop: 507-263-3126
Type: Public   Par: 72

www.cannongolfclub.com

Region: SouthEast

Course Rating

HOSPITALITY	8.00
PLAYABILITY	7.92
USABILITY	7.64
FACILITY	7.00
VALUE	7.50

OVERALL SCORE
771

Green Fee: $36 (weekend)
1/2 Cart Fee: $12 (weekend)

Tees	Men's	Women's	Yards
Red		70.3/126	5136
Gold	67.0/126	71.9/129	5421
White	76.1/138	70.4/133	6186
Blue	72.0/136		6527

Cannon Golf Club in Cannon Falls, Minnesota, is located just a short 30-minute drive from downtown St. Paul, just a minute or two off Highway 52. It's easy to find via the course's signage.

When we played this course on a beautiful Monday morning in early June, we were welcomed by a brand-new (2006), fully appointed clubhouse, well-stocked pro shop and full restaurant. The facilities are extremely well kept, and the staff is friendly, helpful and abundant. There is a putting green with adjacent sand area for hazard practice, the normal chipping areas and also a grass driving range. Electric carts are available, and while we chose to use them, this would be a relatively easy course to walk, at just under 6200 yards from the white tees. The three sets of tee boxes, various leagues and special senior rates are just the start of the variety of offerings for golfers.

Of all the courses played recently, this was one of our favorites. This course is very hacker friendly, which is embodied by its overall length, mostly wide-open fairways and large, flat greens. Although the course has a significant amount of mature trees and a couple narrow fairways, we found it forgiving for the occasional errant shot. The course is very scenic with vistas and Cannon River and prairie views. We enjoyed the traditional layout and never felt like we were playing the same hole over and over again. The scorecard's illustrations of the hole layouts helped us to navigate holes for ideal shot placement. All in all, the average golfer has a good chance to score well at this course. You do not need to consistently drive the ball 250+ yards to have a realistic shot at par. The course is scenic and varied enough to keep your interest, and the facilities are top notch, clean and very well kept.

We would return any time, and we feel confident in recommending this course as an excellent choice for a great day of golf. The 19th hole would be a great venue for lunch, dinner or a beverage or two of your choice.

ID: 5500909MN

CEDAR CREEK

5700 Jason Avenue
Albertville, MN 55301
Clubhouse: 763-497-8245
Golf Shop: 763-497-8245
Type: Public   Par: 71

www.cedarcreekmn.com

Tees	Men's	Women's	Yards
Red	62.9/115	66.9/114	4725
White	67.3/123	72.4/125	5715
Blue	68.8/127	74.3/129	6060

U
V

Course Rating

HOSPITALITY	7.68
PLAYABILITY	8.39
USABILITY	9.00
FACILITY	7.02
VALUE	7.71

OVERALL SCORE
806

Greens Fee: $36.00 (weekend)
1/2 Cart Fee: $14.00 (weekend)

Attention hackers, play it now and score well, wait five years and your score will certainly go up! This environmentally friendly golf course is located in Albertville, Minnesota, just two miles from Interstate 94 and just south of the Albertville Outlet Mall.

Opened in 1999, this 18-hole course with driving range and two practice greens is still in its youth. The course's length is short, playing only 5715 yards from the white tees and 6060 from the blues, although the course's layout has a professional design feel to it. Using natural wetlands to line some of the fairways and also forcing you on some holes to tee off over the wetlands, it makes for a stiff challlenge. The lush fairways are tree-lined, but the trees are small, and the rough is very forgiving. To test your accuracy, it seems every hole has strategically placed sand traps that will catch your errant drives or snag your approach shots to the nicely sized greens.

The pro shop with two pros on staff and a wide range of accessories is very well equipped. There is food and bar service in the clubhouse. It has a great lunch menu and a large patio overlooking the 18th green. The course has five different leagues: men's, women's, senior and junior leagues, as well as a couple's league on Friday.

Put this course near the top of your must-play list and with five more years of maturity, Cedar Creek Golf Course will challenge even the top golfers.

Tim Herron's grandfather Carson Lee Herron, played in the US Open in 1934 and his father, also named Carson, played in the US Open in 1963.

75

ID: 5530108MN

CEDAR RIVER

14927 State Highway 56
Adams, MN 55909
Clubhouse: 507-582-3595
Golf Shop: 507-582-3595
Type: Public   Par: 72

www.cedarrivercountryclub.com

Tees	Men's	Women's	Yards
Red		72.3/121	5582
Gold	67.4/120	72.5/122	5618
White	69.4/125	75.0/128	6076
Blue	70.4/126		6278

Course Rating

HOSPITALITY	8.33
PLAYABILITY	7.70
USABILITY	8.10
FACILITY	6.84
VALUE	7.03

OVERALL SCORE
774

Green Fee: $25 (weekend)
1/2 Cart Fee: $13 (weekend)

Cedar River Country Club is located off State Highway 56 in Adams, Minnesota. This southeastern part of the state seems quiet and laid back, and the course follows suit. It was not too busy the day we were there, and the staff was very friendly. The parking is great, and both the putting green and the driving range are nearby, so you do not have to go far to get warmed up.

The clubhouse is very inviting, but the pro shop is small and has only a few apparel items for sale. The food is standard: hot dogs, burgers, pizza, soda and beer. They do not have a golf pro here at Cedar River, so lessons are not available. But the overall experience of the clubhouse is great.

We thought the layout of the first few holes was boring, but as we got farther into the course, we discovered some truly beautiful holes. There are some tight fairways lined with trees that will suck your golf ball in, never to be seen again. Hole #9 is fun to play, as the approach to the green is just in front of the clubhouse. The rough around that green is pretty difficult to hit from and makes for a tougher-than-average 3rd or 4th shot. There are also some hidden water hazards that come into play throughout the course. The fairways are in good condition but the tee boxes are a bit worn—full of divots and not very attractive. We were pleasantly surprised with the condition of the greens. They are not super fast, but they do hold a ball nicely and are mowed to a good length.

The signage on the course is not great, and getting from one hole to the next is sometimes cumbersome and frustrating. There are also no cart paths to speak of. The gas-powered carts work well, though. It seems that Cedar River is more of a social hangout than anything, as they have regular card-playing days in the clubhouse. The course is okay—if you live in the area it is certainly worth playing. The prices are good, and walking this course is a definite option. We had a nice time with the locals and the staff, and we came away with a good feeling overall.

76

ID: 5590909MN

CEDAR VALLEY

25019 County Road 9
Winona, MN 55987
Clubhouse: 507-457-3241
Golf Shop: 507-457-3129
Type: Semi-Private Par: 36/36/36
www.cedarvalleymn.com

Course Rating

HOSPITALITY	6.16
PLAYABILITY	8.05
USABILITY	7.49
FACILITY	7.37
VALUE	6.57

OVERALL SCORE
722

Tees	Men's	Women's	Yards
TIsland/GMonster (white)	69.8/129	75.9/136	6023
TIsland/GMonster (blue)	72.0/133		6505
TroutsRun/GMonster (white)	70.8/131	77.3/139	6366
TroutsRun/GMonster (blue)	72.7/135		6785
TroutsRun/TIsland (white)	68.7/126	74.3/131	5861
TroutsRun/TIsland (blue)	68.7/126		6256

Green Fee: $26 (weekend)
1/2 Cart Fee: $13 (weekend)

If you're looking for great golf, check out Cedar Valley Golf Course in Winona, Minnesota. But if you're looking for great service, go elsewhere. We visited the course on three different occasions and were "greeted" each time with the same cold, unwelcoming demeanor. But don't let that keep you from coming here. The borderline rude behavior indoors is no indication of what awaits you outdoors.

Cedar Valley is a golfing marvel. This phenomenal 27-hole course has three very different nine-hole courses, each providing three sets of patriotic tees, so you could play here daily for years and never tire of the variety. Trouts Run, the first nine, tees off and drops off from the clubhouse, and continues to provide an array of fun in holes 2, 3 and 4. The fairways and bunkers are well kept, but the greens are a little rough in low areas. This nine is the simplest and easiest; it is the kindest to walkers and caters far more to accuracy than distance from the tee.

The 2nd nine, Treasure Island, has the beauty of fool's gold. This nine will pillage your golf balls and make you walk the plank on 18. With no two holes alike, every hole is an adventure worthy of a Robert Louis Stevenson book. The elevation changes and hole contours are dramatic. Pars can be had, but so can 10s. This nine is neither for the faint of heart nor for those without a cart. Cedar Valley's 3rd nine, the Green Monster, is the newest, and it's a beast. You'll need to get out the big sticks now. Water comes into play on the first five holes. Hole 6 is one of a kind: You hit a downhill shot over a mountain in the middle of the fairway. Got that? Using your driver on #8 is ill-advised, and #9 makes you want to play 27 more. The practice facilities are basic but adequate. The clubhouse has a restaurant and patio from which you can eat reasonably priced good food and watch the golfers find water on the adjacent island green. Green fees are a little high, but the course is stunning and fun, and that's what you should care about the most.

77

ID: 5598709MN

CHASKA TOWN

3000 Town Course Drive
Chaska, MN 55318
Clubhouse: 952-443-3748
Golf Shop: 952-443-3748
Type: Public   Par: 72

www.chaskatowncourse.com

Tees	Men's	Women's	Yards
Red		69.4/119	4853
Red/White		71.6/124	5246
White	70.0/132	75.6/132	6038
Green	71.9/136	78.0/137	6397
Green/Black	72.5/137		6531
Black	73.8/140		6817

P
U
F

Course Rating

HOSPITALITY   8.21
PLAYABILITY   8.81
USABILITY   9.22
FACILITY   8.71
VALUE   5.92

OVERALL SCORE
844

Greens Fee: $58.00 (weekend)
1/2 Cart Fee: $16.00 (weekend)

The Chaska Town Course is owned and operated by the City in Chaska, Minnesota. There are four sets of tees ranging from 4853 yards to 6817 yards. Chaska has done something unique in that the scorecard shows six different distances. In addition to the four tees, they have a black/green distance which is a combination of the two longest tees. At the other end of the spectrum is the red/white distance which is a combination of the two shortest tees.

We found the secret was to pick the correct tees. We chose the white tees at 6038 yards which had a course rating of 70.0 and a slope of 132. It turned out to be the correct choice and it provided a good challenge and an enjoyable round.

The fairways were all very generous in their width. The rough was a consistent two inches, the bunkers were the best we've played, but the greens had a number of ball mark bruises that didn't heal very well.

The front nine was interesting as you went from a 408-yard second hole to the third hole of 254 yards with a big tree in the middle of the fairway about 50 yards from the green. The back nine was the tougher of the two with #11 at 410 yards the toughest hole on the course. After your drive you have to negotiate trees on the right and a pond on the left that ran up to the green. The course layout is excellent with the cart paths and signage very good. There was water available every other hole and more restrooms than any course we've played. The golf carts were unique in that the GPS was built into the dashboard. The practice area is first class and in wonderful shape.

The clubhouse is average size with a nice pro shop, a friendly staff, and the Chaska Town Course Grille that has the usual menu and bar. The Grille seating area is a little small and can probably seat 50 to 75 people.

Chaska Town Course will give you an upscale experience at half the cost where golfers of all skills can have an enjoyable experience.

ID: 5531808MN

CHISAGO LAKES

12975 292nd Street
Lindstrom, MN 55045
Clubhouse: 651-257-1484
Golf Shop: 651-257-1484
Type: Semi-Private   Par: 72

www.chisagolakesgolf.com

Region: NorthEast

Course Rating

HOSPITALITY	8.61
PLAYABILITY	8.26
USABILITY	8.29
FACILITY	8.26
VALUE	7.48

OVERALL SCORE
827

Green Fee: $32 (weekend)
1/2 Cart Fee: $14 (weekend)

Tees	Men's	Women's	Yards
Red		71.5/125	5333
White	68.2/119.	73.1/129	5701
Blue	70.5/124	76.0/135	6225
Gold	72.0/127		6545

Chisago Lakes Golf Course's website gives you an excellent sense of what you will find at this fun track in Lindstrom, Minnesota. Located just outside the Metro area, it is an easy drive from the Twin Cities. The course offers deals for juniors and seniors, and the website has coupons that make it even more reasonable.

When you arrive, walk to the deck that serves the pro shop and restaurant, and everything you need is there. An ample putting green with a large bunker and chipping area accurately replicate what is on the course. The 12-station driving range has a number of well-marked targets, and the 1st and 10th tees are in sight. The pro shop is well stocked and the personnel are well dressed, knowledgeable and very friendly.

The first thing you notice is that this is a clean course. The tee boxes are attractive and well maintained, and you will struggle to find a rock or debris in the well-groomed bunkers. The turf appears freshly and consistently mowed. Each hole bears excellent signage that includes an aerial photo of the hole with distances marked to hazards and doglegs. High handicappers need to swallow some pride as the shortest men's tees are uncomfortably close to the forward tees. The hazards, in the form of water, sand and an abundance of trees, are out there, but they can be avoided if you play the distance that is appropriate to your game.

Chisago Lakes is a picturesque course. Trees and ponds and a general up-north atmosphere coupled with the hilly terrain make you forget you are so near the Cities. It is difficult to get lost or thirsty as the ranger and beverage cart are never far away and visit often. Pace of play may be impacted because the course allows fivesomes, and there are also a lot of walkers. Reasonably priced, accommodating and very playable while still offering plenty of challenge, Chisago Lakes is a great option for hackers.

ID: 5504509MN

CHOMONIX

700 Aqua Lane
Lino Lakes, MN 55014
Clubhouse: 651-482-8484
Golf Shop: 651-482-7528
Type: Public   Par: 72

www.chomonix.com

Tees	Men's	Women's	Yards
Red	66.6/117	71.8/124	5445
White	70.8/129		6325
Blue	72.0/131		6596

Region: Twin Cities

Course Rating

HOSPITALITY   6.59
PLAYABILITY   6.31
USABILITY   7.61
FACILITY   6.25
VALUE   6.78

OVERALL SCORE
668

Greens Fee: $27.00 (weekend)
1/2 Cart Fee: $13.00 (weekend)

A twenty five minute jog to the northeast of the cities on Interstate 35 will get you to the city of Lino Lakes, Minnesota, where Chomonix Golf Course sits about two miles off the highway.

Part of a regional park reserve, it is clear throughout your round that Chomonix was built into the existing environment. Tall, mature trees constitute the biggest defense against those who spray the ball, while water works its way into play on a very manageable 7 of the 18 holes.

The course does a great job off the bat of giving golfers a chance to build up a head of steam playing the first few tees. Number one plays as a very straight-forward and scoreable par 4, which leads into a subtle dogleg par 5 with a very attackable putting surface. If golfers can start out with a couple decent holes, he/she should be able to carry themselves through the rest of the front nine. Golfers can expect whatever number ends up getting posted on that front will increase on the back.

Playing to a total just less than 6600 yards, Chomonix presents itself very fairly as far as distance goes. Eight out of the ten par 4s come in at under 390 yards, and no par 5s are overbearingly long.

As a hacker-friendly course should, the majority of the time, Chomonix offers golfers a safe out for most shots. No 240-yard carries over water can be found, and real estate to the other side of the fairway seems to come more freely when water does come into play.

Bottom line, Chomonix plays like a city course should, and that is right up the alley of an average golfer. Scoring is fair, the prices are right, and the course isn't going to punish any more than you allow it to. As far as getting in your strokes at a comfortable level of play goes, there isn't a whole lot of bad to say about Lino Lakes Chomonix Golf Course.

ID: 5501408MN

COFFEE MILL

180 Coffee Mill Drive
Wabasha, MN 55981
Clubhouse: 651-565-4332
Golf Shop: 651-565-4332
Type: Semi-Private   Par: 71
www.coffeemillgolf.com

**H
P
F
V**

Course Rating

HOSPITALITY	8.98
PLAYABILITY	8.84
USABILITY	8.26
FACILITY	8.83
VALUE	7.98

OVERALL SCORE
867

Tees	Men's	Women's	Yards
Red		69.5/120	5127
Gold	6.2/121	70.5/123	5317
White	69.6/128	74.7/131	6072
Blue	71.2/131		6412

Green Fee: $28 (weekend)
1/2 Cart Fee: $14 (weekend)

The drive to Coffee Mill Golf and Country Club in Wabasha, Minnesota, can be a long one from the Metro area, but the course is easy to find and the views along the way are amazing. When we drove into the parking lot, we were awed by the perfectly manicured fairways and the beautiful clubhouse.

This course was built in 1966 as a nine-hole course and expanded to 18 in 2003. The course's layout is wonderful. With the putting green next to the 1st tee, it's convenient to warm up while waiting for your tee time. The driving range is somewhat short but more than adequate. Well-marked signs at every tee box lay out the hole so you can see what obstacles are waiting. Distances to the various hazards are also marked, making club selection much easier. The fairways are tight in some areas, so losing balls may be a common occurrence. But we don't think anyone would mind losing a few balls on this scenic golf course. The beautiful bunkers surrounding the greens are actually fun to hit out of—the sand is soft and well-raked. The bent-grass greens hold most of the shots extremely well; they gave us the feeling of a much more expensive course. Yes, they were fast! The bunkers combined with the beautiful water features make each hole unique and special. Shooting a good score is possible here if you can avoid the lost balls. The gas-powered carts are loud; electric carts would be much more desirable in this setting. The cart paths are excellent throughout the course. We saw the beverage cart two times, but in fairness, it was a cooler day.

The course's restaurant has everything from sandwiches to steak and chicken, plus an excellent salad bar. The food is very good with reasonable prices. There is a fantastic deck overlooking the 18th green. Did we mention the excellent views on this course? Hanging around after your round is easy. Catering is also available for special events. Make this course a priority on your list of courses to play. And with all the river towns nearby, there are many fun stops for your way home. You will not be disappointed with Coffee Mill.

ID: 5598109MN

COLUMBIA

3300 Central Avenue NE
Minneapolis, MN 55418
Clubhouse: 612-789-2627
Golf Shop: 612-789-2627
Type: Public   Par: 71

www.minneapolisparks.org

Tees	Men's	Women's	Yards
Red		69.8/121	5152
White	69.5/122	75.2/132	6121
Blue	70.6/124		6371

Course Rating

HOSPITALITY	7.02
PLAYABILITY	7.42
USABILITY	6.68
FACILITY	5.59
VALUE	4.93

OVERALL SCORE
665

Greens Fee: $30.00 (weekend)
1/2 Cart Fee: $14.00 (weekend)

Columbia Golf Course, located in northeast Minneapolis, is actually the second oldest course in the Minneapolis park system. Founded in 1919, it has evolved over the years and continues to be a very busy and popular golf course. At 6371 yards from the tips, it is well within the capabilities of most golfers.

Shoehorned by the city, the course tries to overcome its limited length with mature trees, strategically placed bunkers, hazards and changing elevations. On certain holes, hitting into the side of a hill isn't necessarily a bad thing. Although very compact, there are still some decent walks that must be made between a few holes, reminding you that you should have rented a cart.

The clubhouse has a country club feel with a small pro shop and a nice eating area with flat screen TVs. The facility is nicely organized with parking only a short distance from the first tee. One major drawback is that although they have a nice practice center (Columbia Driving Range), it is not within walking distance and is situated on the opposite side of the course. A golfer who wanted to hit a few balls before his round would need to add at least 30 minutes to his day.

Unlike many overly busy urban courses, the staff, from the food counter to the starter, were all very pleasant and efficient. Where the course seemed to need some help was maintenance. Although the day the course was rated the weather had been dry, the course seemed to have a number of fairways and a couple of greens with brown or dead spots. This could be partially attributed to the weather, but other courses rated at the same time didn't seem to have this problem so it doesn't appear that this is the only reason.

For the average golfer, you can't beat the value. At $30, you can play this urban course and not have to make an hour's drive to get there. The course seems to mirror its working-class urban location, so if you are looking for a fancy, well-manicured track, this isn't your course. If you are looking for a chance to score well where the staff is pleasant, the course should give you a shot at lowering your score.

ID: 5541808MN

COMO

1431 North Lexington Parkway
St. Paul, MN 55103
Clubhouse: 651-488-9679
Golf Shop: 651-488-9673
Type: Public   Par: 70
www.golfstpaul.org

Tees	Men's	Women's	Yards
Red		69.8/121	5077
White	67.5/122		5581
Blue	68.6/124		5842

Course Rating

HOSPITALITY	6.18
PLAYABILITY	6.02
USABILITY	6.37
FACILITY	5.37
VALUE	5.93

OVERALL SCORE
602

Greens Fee: $30.00 (weekend)
1/2 Cart Fee: $14.00 (weekend)

Nestled within the extensive Como Park, St. Paul's Como Golf Course has been a fixture in the city since 1929. Initially opened as a 9-hole course, it was extensively redesigned in 1988, with new a layout, clubhouse and cart storage area.

The facility is compact, with the parking just steps from the clubhouse and the power cart corral. The clubhouse is pretty bare bones, but does have a nice grill with the standard food and drinks at the turn. The sitting areas have an excellent view of the course from the elevation of the clubhouse, but the inside seating is not meant to keep you there very long.

Although the grill service was good and attentive, the pro shop, cart tender and on-course service was a bit spotty. It might have been because we visited on a Thursday afternoon, but the facility seemed to be a bit understaffed that day.

The course tries hard to overcome its lack of length and is only partially successful. It does have three picturesque ponds, but few hazards come into play except for an imposing par-5 #8 with the green tucked behind one of those ponds. The course, like a lot of city courses, has seen a lot of use. There were a number of "under construction" areas, its fairways were a bit overdry and the greens often had brown spots on their surfaces. Signage was also very poor with directional information spray painted in white on the asphalt cart paths. Also, if there were tee box distance signs, they were well hidden. The course also lacks a driving range because there is no place to put it.

For value-priced golf, Como is quite economical at $30 for 18 holes. If you are looking for a fast round in the City of St. Paul, Como Golf Course should be considered an option but just remember, it plays more like a long executive course than it does a regulation par-72. After your round, for better food, just walk down the hill to the Lakeside Pavilion and stop in at the Black Bear Crossings coffee shop.

ID: 5510308MN

COUNTRY AIR Exec. 18

404 Lake Elmo Avenue North
Lake Elmo, MN 55042
Clubhouse: 651-436-7888
Golf Shop: 651-436-7888
Type: Public   Par: 54

www.countryairgolfpark.com

Tees	Men's	Women's	Yards
Red	54.0	54.0	1042

Region: Twin Cities

Course Rating

HOSPITALITY	8.19
PLAYABILITY	5.76
USABILITY	7.94
FACILITY	6.17
VALUE	7.17

OVERALL SCORE
701

Greens Fee: $15.00 (weekend)
1/2 Cart Fee: no carts available

Country Air Golf Park, located just south of Interstate 94 in Lake Elmo, Minnesota, has something for everyone. For one thing, it has a heated driving range that is open year round. Another portion of the driving range provides choices of hitting off natural grass or artificial turf, and a large practice putting green and bunker. It seems the main attraction is the 18-hole pitch and putt course.

The course is a jaunt from the clubhouse, and it's easy to think the tenth hole is really the first hole. The holes are labeled by the flags on the greens, but if there isn't a wind, it may be difficult to determine the hole number. Small signs point from one hole to the next, so it's a good idea to follow the scorecard layout. Since the holes crisscross in close proximity, one may want to be on the lookout for errant golf balls if the course is busy. The length of the holes range from 40 to 75 yards making Country Air the perfect spot to practice one's short game. In fact, the manager suggests that one needs to use only a pitching wedge and putter to play the course.

Families with young children find it an ideal spot to bring the kids who are transitioning from miniature golf to an actual 18-hole format. Adults will also enjoy the setup while working to improve their shorter shots and putting. Most of the holes have at least one sand trap, although none contain a rake. The fairways provide slight hills and twists which lead to greens that are nearly perfectly groomed. A small creek meanders through the nicely landscaped course.

Country Air offers lessons for both juniors and adults, along with leagues, tournaments, and events. The clubhouse presents few amenities except for some snacks and beverages. It's a great spot to bring younger golfers, and parents could practice their short game at the same time.

ID: 5504208MN

CRAGUN'S

(Bobby's Legacy)

11000 Cragun's Drive
Brainerd, MN 56401
Clubhouse: 800-272-4867
Golf Shop: 218-825-2800
Type: Public   Par: 73

www.craguns.com

Course Rating

HOSPITALITY	8.87
PLAYABILITY	9.09
USABILITY	8.75
FACILITY	9.03
VALUE	4.99

H
P
F

OVERALL SCORE
855

Green Fee: $125 (weekend)
1/2 Cart Fee: included in fee

Tees	Men's	Women's	Yards
Red		70.1/122	4903
Gold	67.7/135	72.5/127	5344
White	69.9/139	75.2/132	5817
Blue	72.3/144		6348
Black	74.4/149		6807

If you are convinced that you have experienced the best and most beautiful Minnesota golf after playing The Preserve, Deacon's Lodge and similar premier courses on the Brainerd Golf Trail, you may have a surprise in store because it only gets better. Bobby's Legacy at Cragun's Resort brings you to the upper tier of the golf hierarchy in this storied area. This Robert Trent Jones design is awe-inspiring in the way it looks, the way it plays and the way it makes you feel. Golf Digest made no mistake when they bestowed their rare 5-star rating to Bobby's.

You are greeted to this resort course by a beautiful clubhouse that is staffed by a crew that does everything they can to make your day enjoyable. The carts are newer and equipped with state-of-the art GPS. The clubhouse is massive, well stocked and hospitable, and boasts a large deck that overlooks some pretty spectacular landscape. Don't be dissuaded by the Mercedes, Porsches and Jaguars in the parking lot—the folks at Cragun's are equal-opportunity pleasers.

The golf course itself is intimidating at first glance. It is impeccably groomed, long and fraught with hazards of every nature. But it is also very playable if you have selected the appropriate set of tees from the five that are available. Everything is in front of you and the GPS takes a lot of the guesswork out of navigating each hole. If you use the extensive putting, chipping and driving areas, you will already have a great feel for the course. The greens are fast and contoured and a pleasure to play. Tee boxes are flat, even and ample for any game. The one criticism we have of Bobby's Legacy is that it is hard to concentrate on; it's difficult to get too serious about your game when you are surrounded by such natural and man-made beauty. Certified by the Audubon society, highly rated by Golf Digest and intelligently designed and managed, Bobby's is worth the high price you pay even if you can only afford to do it once.

CRAGUN'S
(Dutch's Legacy)

11000 Cragun's Drive
Brainerd, MN 56401
Clubhouse: 800-272-4867
Golf Shop: 218-825-2800
Type: Public   Par: 73

www.craguns.com

H
P
F

Course Rating

HOSPITALITY	8.98
PLAYABILITY	9.05
USABILITY	8.42
FACILITY	9.05
VALUE	5.76

OVERALL SCORE
858

Tees	Men's	Women's	Yards
Red		69.2/123	4799
Gold	67.2/132	72.4/130	5391
White	68.6/135	74.2/134	5699
Blue	71.0/139		6225
Black	71.0/145		6879

Green Fee: $125 (weekend)
1/2 Cart Fee: included in fee

The Dutch Legacy course in Brainerd is part of the 54-hole Legacy Course at Cragun's Resort. This course is beautiful and has long been considered one of the top public courses in Minnesota. The course plays well for someone who can hit the ball straight and find the fairway off the tee, although if you play from the black tees, you may have to carry your drive over 200 yards.

Overall this course is in immaculate shape. The tee boxes are clean and have very few divots. Fairways are in excellent shape and are taken care of like a championship course. The greens are very quick and the bunkers are filled with soft sand that is easy to hit from. Bunkers and water hazards are plentiful and challenging, and both can come into play often. Practice facilities include a driving range and a putting green, the latter of which rolls really fast, making it difficult to hold your chips on the green if you aren't careful, but it's good practice for what the greens are like on the course.

GPS systems, standard with every cart, show the pin placements and where other golfers are located on the course. You can also order food from the GPS so it is ready when you get back to the clubhouse. The signature hole, if you have to pick one, would probably be #5. It requires a long uphill tee shot that requires avoiding a tree on the left side of the fairway, and the green is protected by three bunkers and a marsh area.

The clubhouse has a nice dining area along with a full-service bar and restaurant. The pro shop and clubhouse are located in the same building. The beverage carts on the course come around often, and they have a good selection of food and drinks.

Our overall impression of this course is that it is one of the nicest and most enjoyable experiences that we have had on a golf course. The course was in immaculate shape and the staff was friendly and always willing to help or answer any questions you have.

ID: 5640109MN

CREEKSBEND

26826 Langford Ave
New Prague, MN 56071
Clubhouse: 952-758-7200
Golf Shop: 952-758-7200
Type: Public   Par: 70
www.creeksbendgolfcourse.com

Course Rating

HOSPITALITY	8.13
PLAYABILITY	6.80
USABILITY	7.26
FACILITY	6.61
VALUE	5.15

OVERALL SCORE
703

Green Fee: $31 (weekend)
1/2 Cart Fee: $15.50 (weekend)

Tees	Men's	Women's	Yards
Red		68.6/121	4866
Gold	66.6/125	71.7/128	5417
White	68.7/129	74.2/134	5884
Blue	70.7/133		6326

Creeks Bend Golf Course is located just outside the southwest Metro area in New Prague, Minnesota. The course, opened in 1995, is situated on 230 acres and offers a geographical taste of Minnesota, with its rolling hills and native prairie combined with over 80 acres of ponds and wetlands. The clubhouse, a converted barn dating back to the 1930s, now contains the pro shop and facilities for sit-down dining and banquets. There is a practice green and a driving range, and carts are available (and recommended). Of the four sets of tees, the distance is 5884 yards from the most often used whites. The longest blues play to 6326 yards. The pricing structure offers only a couple specials—which we thought were too high. The pro shop has complimentary ball markers and divot repair tools, which is a nice touch.

We played on a Wednesday in mid-September and found the course to be wide open for play. But from a hacker's perspective, the course has left a bit to be desired. While we cannot say we did not enjoy our round (due more to the great weather perhaps), this Joel Goldstrand-designed course is not one of his better efforts. The holes leave no lasting impression; we struggled to remember any holes, other than #14, which we all agreed was a design nightmare. The water hazards and bunkers do not seem to be a major factor in play. The hacker will appreciate that the greens are of good size, mostly flat, and roll fairly nicely. The condition, through no fault of the course, was average. It seems that a little care by other golfers would improve the greens' playability. On several holes we had to ride ahead to check out the green location, and many of our 2nd shots were to a target we could not see.

In our opinion, the course needs to review its pricing structure and offer better incentives to play. There are some courses offering some great deals, and this is not one of them. Would we go there again? Only if we saw lower pricing and better specials to retain current regulars and entice new business.

ID: 5607109MN

CROSSWOODS

35878 County Road 3
Crosslake, MN 56442
Clubhouse: 218-692-4653
Golf Shop: 218-692-4653
Type: Public   Par: 71

www.crosslakegolf.com

U

Course Rating

HOSPITALITY	8.67
PLAYABILITY	8.68
USABILITY	9.16
FACILITY	8.38
VALUE	7.47

OVERALL SCORE
861

Green Fee: $27 (weekend)
1/2 Cart Fee: $13 (weekend)

Tees	Men's	Women's	Yards
Yellow		59.5/99	3283
Red	63.2/111	66.0/112	4449
White	67.0/118	71.2/124	5398
Blue	69.1/122		5862
Black	70.2/124		6113

Their website's boast that they're the best golfing value in the Lakes Area is more than marketing. From this group's eyes, it is a true statement. With the green fee starting at $25 (weekday), golfing at Crosswoods Golf Course in Crosslake, Minnesota, is one of the best deals in the Brainerd Lakes Area. Conveniently located at the edge of Cross Lake, Crosswoods is an easy 2 ½-hour drive from the Metro area, or 20 minutes north of Brainerd. The signage to get there is easy to follow. The pro shop sells top-of-the-line golf equipment, and they even price match any big-box retailers for that year's merchandise.

The Crosswoods Grill, new in 2008, has plenty of seating area both inside (with flat-panel TVs and a fireplace) and outside (overlooking the waterfall garden and the golf course). They have an extensive menu of burgers, sandwiches and hot dogs, and the bar offers soft drinks, beer, wine and setups. The prices in the restaurant are reasonable.

Besides a driving range and putting green, Crosswoods has a nice 18-hole pitch and putt to warm up on before you play your round. But wait until you see the beautiful course! It's cut from the native woods, giving it a secluded, natural setting. There are plenty of trees to get you into trouble, but the fairways are wide enough so that even a hacker can score well. The tee boxes are in great shape and offer five different tees for differing abilities. It isn't a long course (just over 6100 from the tips), but it is challenging enough. Don't fly by the 6th hole—it was featured by Minnesota Golfer Magazine as a "hidden gem." The fairways are perfectly cut and in great shape. The greens are perfect for resort golf: relatively flat, large and cut a little long. The scenery is great. You have some water, a few bunkers and lots of trees. You hardly ever see golfers on the next hole. We decided that this course is one of the best values we've ever played, and we'd recommend it as much as any of the other courses we enjoy playing.

ID: 5644209MN

CROW RIVER

915 Colorado St NW
Hutchinson, MN 55350
Clubhouse: 320-587-3070
Golf Shop: 320-587-3070
Type: Semi-Private   Par: 71
www.crowrivergolf.com

V

Course Rating

HOSPITALITY	7.45
PLAYABILITY	7.80
USABILITY	8.37
FACILITY	7.65
VALUE	7.75

OVERALL SCORE
780

Tees	Men's	Women's	Yards
Forward		70.4/122	5239
Regular	69.7/123	74.8/131	6024
Membership	72.0/127	77.5/137	6507
Professional	73.4/130		6820

Green Fee: $41 (weekend)
1/2 Cart Fee: included in fee

Crow River Country Club in Hutchinson, Minnesota, is a very scenic course. It overlooks a river/lake (or combination thereof) and has many mature trees and numerous well-tended flower beds. The scorecard even states that you must take total relief from them!

The clubhouse is big and has room for banquets, weddings, etc. The staff told us that the building is old and in need of repair, and they are very excited about a completely new building next year. The pro shop treated us like VIPs. We met the general manager and the pro, both who were very accommodating. Lessons for young children were going on at the time, but they don't have organized leagues for men or women. The pro shop offers a lot of merchandise—mostly for men, but some for women—at reasonable prices. Both the membership and green fees are competitive.

The course is scenic, hilly and well-cared for. The tees are professional (black), membership (blue), regular (white) and forward (red), with flags to mark pin placement. The markers in the fairways (175, 150 and 100) include yardage for front, middle and back. The first seven holes have out-of-bounds close enough to come into play, and there are huge trees to contend with, but the bunkers have nice sand to play from. We found the greens very difficult. They were extremely quick and it was hard to stop the ball, even when putting. Maybe it was just us, but two-putts were rare.

The kitchen was closed the day we were there, but the beer was cold and served in chilled mugs. The only food available was chips or pretzels. In their defense, it was a quiet Monday and we were the only ones in the bar. They do have food and a beverage cart on the nights they're busy. Overall we thought Crow River had more of a community feel than a country club feel. Located just 60 miles west of Minneapolis, Crow River Country Club is worth the drive.

ID: 5535009MN

CRYSTAL LAKE

16725 Innsbrook Drive
Lakeville, MN 55044
Clubhouse: 952-432-6566
Golf Shop: 952-432-6566
Type: Public   Par: 71

www.crystallakegolfcourse.com

F

Region: Twin Cities

Course Rating

HOSPITALITY	7.61
PLAYABILITY	8.33
USABILITY	7.91
FACILITY	9.01
VALUE	6.83

OVERALL SCORE
802

Tees	Men's	Women's	Yards
Front	64.0/118	68.3/119	4805
Middle	68.7/127	74.0/131	5825
Back	70.8/132		6306

Greens Fee: $40.00 (weekend)
1/2 Cart Fee: $15.00 (weekend)

Crystal Lake Golf Course is located in Lakeville, Minnesota, and is a tale of two different nines. The front nine rambles through a residential area with gentle rolling hills. The back nine is flat and meanders among natural wetlands. The course is walkable but the front nine has a number of medium to long walks between greens and tees. The walk from the first green to the second tee and the eighth green to the ninth tee requires a walk over a street bridge.

The clubhouse has a pro shop, banquet facilities, and snack shop with a variety of food choices, beer and even cigars. It is small and compact, but well stocked, very friendly and helpful. There is also a nice patio overlooking the driving range. The driving range is in back of the clubhouse and very spartan. The tee area grass is barely adequate and the range consists of a field bordered by wetlands and no flags or distance markers. The putting green was large and rolling and in excellent condition.

We found all aspects of the course in excellent condition. The greens had been aerated a couple of weeks previous, but were smooth and much faster than the putting green. The greens were undulated and most tilted back to front which made putting very difficult in any position other than directly below the hole. The rough was about two inches high, but the ball would settle down and was difficult to find and even more difficult to hit a quality shot. The cart paths are a combination of blacktop, concrete and gravel and are well routed around the course. The golf carts are electric with GPS. We weren't impressed with the GPS as it displayed ads between each hole and most of the time you had to manually press the buttons to get to the next hole. The distances in the GPS to the green were to the front and the center, not to the flag.

Even though the course was in excellent condition the overall golfing experience didn't excite us. Some holes seem a bit ill-conceived with blind approaches to the green, and for hackers wary of water, there are three holes with carries of 90 to 125 yards over wetlands.

ID: 5504408MN

CUYUNA

24410 State Highway 210
Deerwood, MN 56444
Clubhouse: 218-534-3489
Golf Shop: 218-534-3489
Type: Semi-Private   Par: 72

www.cuyunacountryclub.com

Tees	Men's	Women's	Yards
Red		74.0/132	5686
Gold	68.6/130	74.5/133	5766
White	70.6/133	769/138	6190
Blue	71.5/135		6407

Course Rating

HOSPITALITY   8.72
PLAYABILITY   7.46
USABILITY   7.82
FACILITY   7.61
VALUE   6.45

OVERALL SCORE
777

Green Fee: $39 (weekend)
1/2 Cart Fee: $17 (weekend)

The Cuyuna Country Club is located north of Highway 210 about a half mile east of Deerwood, Minnesota—right in the heart of central Minnesota's lake country. As we drove into the parking lot adjacent to the clubhouse, we saw what appeared to be an open, tree-lined course, and we saw golfers of all ages—seniors, men, women, and teenagers and younger.

The clubhouse overlooks the 9th hole and has a wide variety of golf apparel and equipment for sale. They also offer a full bar and menu. The staff is friendly and helpful (as are the locals).

We signed in and got right on the course. The first hole is fairly straightforward. The fairway is in good shape and the rough is almost like a fairway. The 1st green is also in excellent shape (as are all the greens). The tee boxes have ball washers, garbage cans and benches, and they are all nicely landscaped with beautiful flowers. The good signage at every tee box is helpful.

After the first few laid-back holes the real course became apparent! The course is carved out of the woods, and no attempt was made to flatten out the large hills or to fill in the ponds (swamps). The fairways follow the natural contours of the land, with 20- or 30-foot changes of elevation several times per fairway. Because of the many doglegs, you can't often see the greens from the tees or even from the fairway itself. The fairways are surrounded by woods and the rough is so thick that lost balls are really lost. The back nine is particularly challenging, and it requires a good knowledge of how you hit your clubs and a strong ability to hit uphill shots. The putting greens on the back nine are also particularly challenging.

In short, the course is very scenic with rolling hills surrounded by woods, ponds and swamps. It is a tough course but truly enjoyable to play because of the challenge of a wide variety of obstacles! We look forward to playing this course again.

91

DACOTAH RIDGE

31042 County Highway 2
Morton, MN 56270
Clubhouse: 507-697-8050
Golf Shop: 507-697-8050
Type: Public   Par: 72

www.dacotahridge.com

P

Course Rating

HOSPITALITY	8.43
PLAYABILITY	9.05
USABILITY	7.49
FACILITY	7.83
VALUE	5.02

Tees	Men's	Women's	Yards
Forward		70.2/130	5055
Intermediate	68.4/133	73.7/137	5668
Regular	70.8/138	76.8/143	6217
Championship	72.7/141		6642
Tournament	74.9/146		7109

OVERALL SCORE
799

Green Fee: $65 (weekend)
1/2 Cart Fee: $20 (weekend)

Morton is an oasis in southwestern Minnesota for both the golfer and the gambler. Dacotah Ridge Golf Club partners with Jackpot Junction Casino Hotel for quite the 1, 2 wallet punch. The $50 donation to Mr. Blackjack was expected. However, the $85 round of golf at Dacotah Ridge, was not. It is, however, an aesthetically spectacular course and meticulously groomed—a needle in a haystack. You would not expect to see what you do when you get there.

This little course on the prairie has breathtaking panoramic views from the clubhouse and the #1 and #10 tee boxes. It probably wouldn't hurt you to sneak 27 different clubs (and balls) into your golf bag, as you could use every one. There isn't a shot you'll see twice on the course. You need to hit right, left, high and low. You'll battle wind, bunkers, trees, shanks, slices, hooks, fescue, and a very hungry Wabasha Creek. Then you'll get to the 2nd tee. But don't let that discourage you. If you can honestly break 100 at your local course, you can break 100 here.

The guest service at this course is good but falls short of exceptional. There is also considerable sticker shock in the snack prices and little pocket relief besides the complimentary range balls. There's no question that for what you pay here, there should be GPS on the carts or you should receive a complimentary yardage book with a full-price green fee. GPS would make a huge difference here. The yardage book definitely does. Dacotah Ridge is a convenient and short trip from the Twin Cities and/or Mankato. There is a collection of signature holes here. Hole #1 is a phenomenal opener. Captain hook often makes an appearance on beautiful #4. Five defines risk and reward. Nine is spectacular, fun and very hard. Everyone loves the par-3 over-the-water #11. Thirteen is too easy. Fourteen is too hard. And then there's #18 and its 210-yard difference between the black and red tees. Yes, we found plenty to love about this course…. We'd just love it more for $30 less.

ID: 5627009MN

DAHLGREEN

6940 Dahlgreen Road
Chaska, MN 55318
Clubhouse: 952-448-7463
Golf Shop: 952-448-7463
Type: Semi-Private   Par: 72

www.dahlgreen.com

Tees	Men's	Women's	Yards
Red		69.9/126	5108
Gold	69.3/128	73.9/135	5831
White	72.4/134	77.8/143	6527
Blue	73.5/136		6761

Region: Twin Cities

Course Rating

HOSPITALITY	7.65
PLAYABILITY	7.12
USABILITY	7.74
FACILITY	7.29
VALUE	6.46

OVERALL SCORE
733

Greens Fee: $42.00 (weekend)
1/2 Cart Fee: $15.00 (weekend)

If you look on a map, you might think that Dahlgreen Golf Club really doesn't exist because the course claims it is located in Chaska, Minnesota. Yet, it is there right off Highway 212 with a Chaska address. Everything about Dahlgreen is big: the parking lot, the fairways, and the greens. Surrounded by farms, the course is like a visit to the country and if the wind is blowing in the right direction, you'll know that a dairy farm is just next door.

With the completion of Highway 212 a few years ago, the time to get to the course has been shortened by at least 15 minutes for those coming from the Twin Cities. To give you an additional reason to visit, the course offers a 50-cents/mile discount (up to 30 miles) if you are coming to the course. That is usually equivalent to a free cart.

The course first opened in 1968 and has grown to become a sprawling 6761 yards with broad fairways and large gradually sloped greens. Although large, these greens are also very fast so you will have to have a light touch to find the hole. Course hole signage is good with a picture of the hole just under the listed yardages, but the on-course distance markers only show the 150-yard marks with other distances difficult to find. If you are taking a cart, your distance worries will be for naught because they have a very simple GPS system that is easy to use and doesn't block the cart windshield.

The course's only real weakness is that it ends with a par-4 final hole that has an awful approach onto an elevated green. That might not be bad, but it probably has at least a 100-foot elevation change and if you hit to the right you'll find your ball down a very steep hill and will need mountaineering gear to get up and down.

The clubhouse is a bit dated with 1970s era paneling, but it does have a nice bar and the Willows Bar & Restaurant is an inexpensive stop for the 19th hole. If you're on your way to Mankato or St. Peter, consider Dahlgreen on your way out of town.

ID: 5531808MN

DAYTONA

14730 Lawndale Lane
Dayton, MN 55327
Clubhouse: 763-427-6110
Golf Shop: 763-427-6110
Type: Public   Par: 72

www.daytonagolfclub.com

Tees	Men's	Women's	Yards
Red		71.0/121	5365
Gold	66.9/116	72.4/124	5614
White	70.4/124	76.9/135	6377

Region: Twin Cities

Course Rating

HOSPITALITY	7.05
PLAYABILITY	5.63
USABILITY	6.37
FACILITY	5.01
VALUE	4.62

OVERALL SCORE
594

Greens Fee: $34.00 (weekend)
1/2 Cart Fee: $14.50 (weekend)

Surrounded by corn fields, Daytona Golf Club, located in Dayton, Minnesota, is a country club, with the emphasis on country. A bit off the beaten path, it also has an indoor tennis facility with a metal roof that appears to be used more extensively in the cooler months.

The two-story clubhouse is nicely appointed with a pro shop, full oak bar, a number of flat screen TVs and a grill with a nice selection of entrees. Its layout flows nicely onto the course and the first tee is only steps from the pro shop where you check in and golf carts are just outside the door. One thing missing was a driving range, even though something called a driving range appears to be located on land adjacent to the facility.

Listed at 6377 yards from the tips, all the holes do not boast tees at that length so it really plays about 6100 yards. Some courses play longer than their length, but this course really feels shorter attesting to the listed rating of par 72, but the USGA only scoring it at par 70.4. Also, because it has very few hazards and trees, most holes are wide open with large areas to land an errant tee shot, making this a very easy course to play. Although the yardage markers were good, the course signage as well as the cart paths were very poor. Other weaknesses are that the course has no water coolers and we counted only two portable bathrooms.

The golf course conditions show that it needs some attention and maintenance. Everywhere could be found evidence that the course is rarely if ever watered. With the exception of the greens, which were in very nice shape, the rest of the course from the tee boxes to the fairways was dry and the ground was hard, making a ball roll a good distance before stopping. The layout also could use some improvement by adding water, rough and more sand bunkers. Right now it is relatively unimaginative with only a couple of doglegs breaking up the monotony.

This facility's strongest suit is the clubhouse. If you are looking for a nice, mid-priced meal after your round, its a nice place to linger. As to the course, it needs a facelift and is not a great value for the money.

ID: 5532708MN

DEACON'S LODGE

9348 Arnold Palmer Drive
Breezy Point, MN 56472
Clubhouse: 218-562-6262
Golf Shop: 218-562-6262
Type: Public   Par: 72

www.grandviewlodge.com

Tees	Men's	Women's	Yards
Winnie		68.6/119	4766
Lodge	66./5/132	71.9/126	5364
Deacon	69.7/138	75.8/134	6067
King	72.1/143		6541
Palmer	73.8/146		6964

Region: NorthWest

Course Rating

HOSPITALITY	8.17
PLAYABILITY	8.70
USABILITY	7.07
FACILITY	5.59
VALUE	6.02

OVERALL SCORE
796

Green Fee: $114 (weekend)
1/2 Cart Fee: included in fee

If you are a hacker and are playing Deacon's Lodge Golf Course in Breezy Point, Minnesota, for the first time, you are not going to be a particularly happy camper. This championship course offers no hints to help you navigate the many forced carries, risk/reward holes, doglegs and hazards unless you add $2 to the already high green fee and buy a course book. There are no signs on tee boxes or hints on the scorecard to tell you how much you can cut off or what club you need to hit a fairway without driving through it. Standing on most of the tee boxes still does not give you a good sense of distances or undulations in the fairway.

The course, managed by Grandview Resort, is one of four courses that can be included in the Grandview stay-and-play packages. Each of the four courses (The Pines, The Preserve, The Garden Course and Deacon's Lodge) offers different levels of playability, and each is beautifully designed. Deacon's is beautiful and the staff is hospitable and friendly. The practice facilities are ample and well groomed, and the sand and putting green replicate what you find on the course. The vistas are beautiful and the course takes care to keep the environment safe and natural. Trees, water, sand and wildly rolling fairways all blend in well in this north woods atmosphere. Add to that a clean and well-equipped clubhouse and café and you could have a great day at Deacon's—if you didn't have to play golf.

For a premium-priced course, the fairways are not well maintained. Unfilled divots guarantee a number of bad lies; guests apparently do not see a need to repair ball marks on the greens. The beverage cart and ranger are conscientious and always close by, but they can't hit your shots for you. If your handicap is 10 or under and you are familiar with the course, you will love Deacon's Lodge. If you are a hacker and play a course of this caliber infrequently, you will be better off playing two rounds at a less expensive course. You will play better and more golf and you will have enough money left over for lunch.

ID: 5647209MN

DEER RUN

8661 Deer Run Drive
Victoria, MN 55386
Clubhouse: 952-443-2351
Golf Shop: 952-443-2351
Type: Semi-Private   Par: 71

www.deerrungolf.com

F

Course Rating

HOSPITALITY	8.49
PLAYABILITY	8.61
USABILITY	8.75
FACILITY	8.97
VALUE	7.13

OVERALL SCORE
851

Greens Fee: $54.00 (weekend)
1/2 Cart Fee: $15.00 (weekend)

Tees	Men's	Women's	Yards
Red		69.3/118	5040
Gold	65.9/118	70.6/120	5273
White	69.8/126	75.5/131	6146
Black	70.5/128		6292

If you are tired of playing a round that seems to take hours at your local course, you might want to try to book a tee time on a "Fast Play Friday" at Deer Run Golf Club located in Victoria, Minnesota. On "Fast Play Fridays" if your group doesn't finish the front nine in the required 1 hour and 55 minutes you are given a rain check and asked to leave the course. The starters and rangers are present and watchful, but not intrusive. On the Friday that we played, this policy made for a very pleasant round that did not feel rushed or hurried. The policy alone might be enough to recommend Deer Run; however, there is much more to this course than a fast round.

Deer Run is a beautiful and extremely well-maintained course set amidst lovely homes in the western suburbs. The condition of the course was ideal with lush green fairways and well-manicured greens that proved to be both fast and challenging. Most of the holes involve quite sloping fairways which made for numerous second shots from less than level lies, but the fairways were fairly forgiving so even high handicappers have the opportunity to keep the ball in play and achieve a decent score—that is, if your short game and putting are on that day.

In addition to a professionally groomed course that plays well, Deer Run has other amenities. All of the carts have a cleverly mounted book with individual pages for each hole showing the layout, hazards and distances. In addition, most carts are equipped with a GPS device showing distance from the cart to the green. This was certainly easier and faster than having to search for a sprinkler head to determine your yardage. There are good practice facilities with a driving range, two putting greens, and fairway and greenside bunkers. The clubhouse, which is a converted 100+ year old farmhouse, has a small pro shop and a nice pub/restaurant at which we had an excellent lunch.

Although Deer Run Golf Club may be a bit of a drive from some areas of the Twin Cities, we would highly recommend giving this beautifully kept course a try. It will provide a challenging, but satisfying, round for golfers of all levels.

DETROIT

(Pine to Palm)

24591 County Highway 22
Detroit Lakes, MN 56501
Clubhouse: 218-847-5790
Golf Shop: 218-847-5790
Type: Public   Par: 71

www.detroitcountryclub.com

Tees	Men's	Women's	Yards
Green	65.0/118	69.2/120	4966
White	68.9/126	72.6/127	5839
Blue	69.9/132		6106

Course Rating

HOSPITALITY	9.01
PLAYABILITY	8.49
USABILITY	8.53
FACILITY	8.09
VALUE	6.63

H

OVERALL SCORE
838

Green Fee: $40 (weekend)
1/2 Cart Fee: $15 (weekend)

Detroit Country Club and its Pine to Palms course are steeped in history. Located just south of Detroit Lakes, Minnesota, it was founded in 1916 and is the oldest public golf course in Minnesota. Its true country club feel is obvious from the fence-lined drive entrance to the woodsy clubhouse.

The course's name comes from a historic railroad that used to run from Minnesota to Texas. Famous for its Pine to Palms amateur pro-am tournament held each August (started in 1931), it is ground zero for local amateur and semi-professional golf events from the Happy Hackers to the Wiff n Poofs. The course is a 6106-yard par 71, but don't think that it isn't up to the challenge. Rolling hills, raised greens, mature trees and blind shots all make for a great golf. According to the pro Mark Holm, it is the ultimate risk/reward course, making it very popular for match play tournaments.

The inviting clubhouse is warm and inviting with both an indoor and outdoor bar area, a full-service restaurant called the Big Easy Bar & Grill, locker rooms and an outdoor patio. Being the oldest public golf course in Minnesota, historic photos and ancient winners' trophies hang on the walls and are perched on shelves in the pro shop. Course maintenance is very good, with tee boxes and greens showing little wear even at the end of the season. Yardage markers are easy to find at 200, 150 and 100 yards, with vertical markers also every 150 yards. Some non-course aspects could use a bit of an upgrade: golf carts definitely look their age and some cart paths may rattle your teeth. Tee box signage looks tired, but an upgrade is planned for 2010.

This is a must-see stop for area golfers. Part of the newly christened Minnesota Golf Trail (a collection of nine area courses), Pine to Palms is unique to the area and has all the feel of a country club without the pretension. You'll come for the golf, but will want to stay for the restaurant and bar.

DODGE

18187 County Road 34
Dodge Center, MN 55927
Clubhouse: 507-374-2374
Golf Shop: 507-374-2374
Type: Semi-Private   Par: 71

www.dodgecountryclub.com

Tees	Men's	Women's	Yards
Red		69.7/114	5151
Gold	68.2/116	73.1/122	5776
White	70.0/119		6176

Course Rating

HOSPITALITY	8.44
PLAYABILITY	7.90
USABILITY	6.60
FACILITY	7.48
VALUE	7.57

OVERALL SCORE
768

Green Fee: $30 (weekend)
1/2 Cart Fee: $13 (weekend)

Dodge Country Club in Dodge Center, Minnesota, is about 70 miles from the south Metro. We found the course difficult to find, as signage isn't obvious until you get to the entrance of the course. The staff are very friendly and knowledgeable and it is a pleasure to deal with them. The clubhouse restaurant has a decent menu, and a nice deck overlooks the 18th fairway and green (their signature hole).

There is plenty of parking nearby, and the driving range near the clubhouse is very close to the 1st tee. Gas carts are available and are in good condition, but this is a great course to walk. There are plenty of trees and beautiful views, especially if you look back toward the tee boxes from the greens. Nice landscaping runs throughout the course, and overall it is very well kept. A few of the holes could use some signs directing you to the next hole to make things a bit more clear, but it is not too bad. Coming from the green on #9 to the clubhouse is a good walk, but it is well marked. There is not a beverage cart except for during tournaments.

The course is friendly to the average golfer, as it is only 6176 yards from the white tees. There are a lot of trees throughout the course, which adds to its natural beauty, but it also adds some challenges if you are prone to slice the ball. The handful of bunkers are in good condition, and water hazards show up on four or five holes. The tee boxes are great as are the fairways, which get mowed twice a week. The biggest surprise for us was the greens. They are beautiful and fast, and putts seem to role true with mild undulations. The red, white and blue flags on the greens are helpful with pin location. The course is fully irrigated and the greens are plugged and sanded, so even in a hard rain there is no standing water. Dodge Country Club is an excellent value, especially if you live near the area. They do not take tee times, which you think might be bad, but our experience at 7:30 on Saturday morning was great.

ID: 5592709MN

DWAN

3301 West 110th Street
Bloomington, MN 55431
Clubhouse: 952-563-8702
Golf Shop: 952-563-8702
Type: Public   Par: 68

www.ci.bloomington.mn.us

Tees	Men's	Women's	Yards
Red		65.4/110	4518
White	64.9/113	69.6/119	5275
Blue	65.8/115	70.8/121	5485

Region: Twin Cities

Course Rating

HOSPITALITY	7.58
PLAYABILITY	7.32
USABILITY	6.99
FACILITY	7.26
VALUE	5.11

OVERALL SCORE
709

Greens Fee: $28.00 (weekend)
1/2 Cart Fee: $16.00 (weekend)

Established in 1970, Dwan Golf Course is a municipal course located in a quiet residential neighborhood in south Bloomington. Dwan has an abundance of mature trees that line the fairways and dot the course so one is seldom aware of the homes that surround it. The trees are interspersed with wildflower plantings, raised flower beds, a few ponds and a number of well-placed bunkers. The course is very attractive visually and everything was beautifully maintained.

While Dwan's relatively short length (5485 yards from the tips) and six par-3 holes may make it look easy on the scorecard, it proved to be a challenge for all the golfers in our foursome. We found it provides a good challenge but not to the point of frustration. The fairways are not overly wide; however, most errant drives remain in play although not always with a clear shot to the green. They are also quite rolling which means a number of second shots will be from a less than level lie. The rough is very manageable and allows for plenty of opportunity to advance the ball. The greens are firm and fast and, as we discovered, not always easy to read.

The clubhouse is adequate but nothing to write home about. You can purchase balls and tees but that seems to be the extent of the pro shop. There is a snack bar with the usual items for both breakfast and lunch. The staff members we came in contact with were friendly and helpful including the marshal who let us know in the nicest way on the 10th tee that we were about 5 minutes behind the pace and could we pick it up a little. There is no driving range and the area to practice chipping is some distance from the clubhouse. On the day we played, this area was much in need of some mowing and attention to the practice green there. The putting green near the clubhouse was in beautiful shape and gave one a good feel for the actual greens on the course.

This course is fun for the hacker but also has enough challenge for the lower handicap golfer. Fees are reasonable, particularly if you walk since the cart fee seems a bit high. The course is very walkable and should provide an enjoyable round of golf.

EAGLE CREEK

1000 26th Avenue NE
Willmar, MN 56201
Clubhouse: 320-235-1166
Golf Shop: 320-235-1166
Type: Semi-Private   Par: 72

www.willmargolf.com

Tees	Men's	Women's	Yards
Red		70.6/129	5208
Gold	68.2/125	73.2/135	5683
White	70.1/130	75.6/139	6098
Blue	71.3/131		6349

Region: WestCentral

Course Rating

HOSPITALITY	8.46
PLAYABILITY	8.55
USABILITY	8.60
FACILITY	8.43
VALUE	7.85

OVERALL SCORE
845

Green Fee: $31.50 (weekend)
1/2 Cart Fee: $16 (weekend)

Eagle Creek Golf Course has the setting of a private country club. Overlooking Willmar Lake in Willmar, Minnesota, it is very beautiful and quite impressive. Some road construction (hopefully temporary) mars the view, but it still has the atmosphere of a private and expensive club.

The golf pro is really nice and very accommodating. He explained that there would be no beverage cart because much of his help has returned to college when we were there in the late fall, but there are water coolers all along the course. Prices for both the private and group lessons are very reasonable. The pro shop has a lot of merchandise that is well displayed and reasonably priced.

The restaurant is huge and nice, and many golfers and non-golfers were there enjoying the Sunday brunch. The restaurant also advertised daily specials and happy hour items, and there is a banquet room that can fit up to 200 people.

The course itself is top-notch. Each tee box offers four different markers so golfers of any level will find their proper challenge. The tees are in good condition, and each one has benches and ball washers.

Some of the holes are quite intimidating with the many water hazards and trees. The trees come into play more often than the water, but that may have been just us (hackers for sure). The cart paths are well marked and there are some fancy bridges and turnarounds on some holes. There are also many signs with time warnings to keep the pace. The play was a little slow, but we still finished within four hours.

This is a course that is a little harder than it looks, so playing it on a regular basis would help. Staff told us that most of the golfers are members, and the golfers we talked with were very friendly and helpful. If we lived closer, we would definitely play it again.

100

ID: 5620109MN

EAGLE RIDGE

1 Green Way
Coleraine, MN 55722
Clubhouse: 218-245-2217
Golf Shop: 218-245-2217
Type: Public   Par: 72
www.golfeagleridge.com

Region: NorthEast

Course Rating

HOSPITALITY	8.88
PLAYABILITY	8.13
USABILITY	8.54
FACILITY	8.18
VALUE	6.86

H

Tees	Men's	Women's	Yards
Red		70.3/119	5220
Gold	66.9/121	72.5/124	5624
White	69.7/128		6254
Blue	72.1/132		6772

OVERALL SCORE
828

Green Fee: $32 (weekend)
1/2 Cart Fee: $10 (weekend)

Eagle Ridge, a municipal golf course in Coleraine, Minnesota, is about seven miles northeast of Grand Rapids and overlooks the beautiful Trout Lake. The course has some housing development around it, but the housing does not give the course a closed-in feeling.

The snack bar serves burgers, hot dogs and snacks, and there is a bar for after-round drinks. The service is top-notch and very friendly. The small pro shop has an assortment of clubs and apparel, and pricing is quite competitive. Lessons, instructions and equipment repair are available from the club pros.

The practice facilities are conveniently located by the clubhouse and 1st tee. The practice green is quite large and in great condition. They do allow chipping and short pitching onto the practice green. The driving range has grass hitting areas and good distance marking. The practice bunker has fairly hard sand in it, but it has the same feel as the bunkers on the course.

General course conditions are superb. The fairway grass is lush and well manicured. The greens are in great shape and have good contouring. Because the course was built on top of old iron mining overburden dumps, in some areas the rock from the dumps comes into play when you are in the rough.

With four sets of tee boxes, you can find the correct tees to fit your game. There are no long carries required off the tees or onto greens. Most holes are forgiving of slightly errant shots. Several areas of woods and deep rough are marked as lateral water hazards, so you can take advantage of the two club lengths sideways from the hazard line relief option. Hole #6, a par 5, needs a fairly accurate second and third shot due to the water on both sides of the fairway coming into the green. Most of the large greens slope back-to-front, so they are receptive to approach shots. Greens are well bunkered, but all of them are open in front for bump and run approaches.

ID: 5572209MN

EAGLE TRACE

1100 Main Street
Clearwater, MN 55320
Clubhouse: 320-558-4653
Golf Shop: 320-558-4653
Type: Public Par: 70

www.eagletracegolf.com

Tees	Men's	Women's	Yards
Red		69.8/123	5059
White	68.0/122		5715
Blue	69.6/125		6034

Region: WestCentral

Course Rating

HOSPITALITY	8.24
PLAYABILITY	8.21
USABILITY	7.49
FACILITY	7.73
VALUE	7.11

OVERALL SCORE
789

Green Fee: $35 (weekend)
1/2 Cart Fee: $13.50 (weekend)

Eagle Trace Golfers Club in Clearwater, Minnesota, is just a 45-minute drive on I-94 west of the Metro area. Before even seeing the course we were impressed with its great website, where you can tour the course, book tee times and check rates, among other things. We booked our tee time online and received a confirmation right away.

The course is easy to find and has ample parking. The electric carts are clean, and the pro shop staff is young and friendly. The rates to play are very reasonable. The pro shop does not offer a lot of merchandise, but the prices are reasonable. The locker rooms are big and clean.

You can choose to walk, but we thought walking the course would be difficult since there are long distances from some greens to the next tee. The 1st tee is a long way down a dirt road—past the driving range. The electric carts the course offers are clean and easy to use. The ranger was very helpful when we told him it was our first time there. The scorecards are also informative—they include a description of each hole and some hints to stay out of trouble. Distance markers are at 300, 200, 150 and 100, but we did not see any pin placement flags. The par 3s are long and difficult, so it is hard to make up strokes there. The greens are in good condition. The course has a lot of water and woods, especially along the river, so bring a lot of balls!

We found the back nine to be quite tight, with holes playing back and forth parallel to each other, but hitting the wrong fairways didn't seem to be a problem, even for a Saturday. A snack gazebo on the course is accessible on #2, #4 and #9, and hamburgers and hot dogs are available, as well as beverages (including alcoholic beverages). The bar and grill is open daily and has a big menu: breakfast, sandwiches, etc. Club members and residents can also use the outdoor pool. Prices for family memberships are not unreasonable, and kids seem welcome.

EAGLE VALLEY

2600 Double Eagle Lane
Woodbury, MN 55129
Clubhouse: 651-714-3750
Golf Shop: 651-714-3750
Type: Public   Par: 72

www.eaglevalleygc.com

Tees	Men's	Women's	Yards
Red		69.7/119	5207
White	69.7/124	75.0/130	6165
Blue	71.5/128	77.2/135	6570
Black	73.1/131		6907

Region: Twin Cities

Course Rating

HOSPITALITY   8.45
PLAYABILITY   8.10
USABILITY   8.15
FACILITY   7.08
VALUE   6.69

OVERALL SCORE
790

Greens Fee: $40.00 (weekend)
1/2 Cart Fee: $16.00 (weekend)

Eagle Valley Golf Course, off Interstate 94 in Woodbury, is our nominee for "Retired Guy Who Has the Job I Want/Ranger of the Year" award. From a cordial welcome at the first tee, to telling stories of ridiculous golfers he's seen on the course, to a few check-ins throughout the rest of the round—every course should have employees who exhibit this type of service. He even brought a playing partner's wedge up to him from a previous hole before he had time to realize he had left it behind.

The conditions of the course are nearly as pristine as the service. There is a great collection of doglegs and holes with hidden greens that are set up perfectly. You'll need to go over water on some of the holes, avoid large traps on others and stay out of the trees on a few more but the fairways are relatively wide leaving you lots of room to land your drive. The par 3s are relatively short including the 120-yard fifth hole which is easily parable. The back nine starts with a relatively easy par-5 but seems to be a bit more difficult than the front.

As you finish the front nine, take advantage of the walkie-talkie in the mailbox to "call in" your food order for the turn. It's pretty slick and a nice amenity that keeps play moving. Whether you go pizza or hot dog, it's great food and the service in the clubhouse and on the course is top notch.

Eagle Valley does a great job of marking distances on the course. You'll rarely have to walk far to find your yardage as they have put distances on all sprinkler heads and also have regular yardage markers on every hole.

We think Eagle Valley is a gem, combining a beautiful layout with leniency for the ever occasional erratic shot. They package service and amenities at a great price point that leaves golfers wanting to return for another round.

We stopped the white-haired, yet spry, ranger as we were leaving and told him how much he meant to our golfing experience. Then we asked him to keep it up for another 40 years so we can have his job when we're ready to retire.

ID: 5512908MN

EAGLE VIEW Exec. 18

24988 US 71
Park Rapids, MN 56470
Clubhouse: 218-732-7102
Golf Shop: 218-732-7102
Type: Public Par: 63
no website

Tees	Men's	Women's	Yards
Red		58.5/92	3379
White	59.2/90		3636

Region: NorthWest

Course Rating

HOSPITALITY	8.24
PLAYABILITY	6.72
USABILITY	7.43
FACILITY	7.69
VALUE	6.70

OVERALL SCORE
739

Green Fee: $19 (weekend)
1/2 Cart Fee: $11.25 (weekend)

For anyone visiting the Park Rapids, Minnesota area, golfing at Eagle View should definitely be part of the plan. At about five miles out of Park Rapids on Highway 71, the course is easy to find; you can't miss the big sign at the entrance. The course is simply designed using the rolling hills for the well-maintained fairways, which are mainly lined with mature birch, oak and pine trees. Greens are well placed without being too big or too small, and all are in great shape. While there is some highway noise on several holes, it is minimal and we barely noticed it due to the lovely surroundings.

Walking nine holes may be a workout because of the hills, but due to the number of short holes, it is a nice walk in the woods. Signage is well placed, and it is easy to follow the layout of the course. Benches and ball washers are at nearly every tee box, as well. The beverage cart came around regularly and we saw at least two Satellites on the course.

If we have any complaints it would be that there are too many par 3s and not enough par 4s to really smack the ball. The only par 5 on the course was well placed for the white tee but too short for the red tee. Otherwise scoring seemed right for all the holes. The clubhouse staff could not have been nicer. The clubhouse is well maintained and surrounded by flower baskets. There is a basic menu of brats, hot dogs and chips along with a soup and sandwich special each day, so if you're hungry and thirsty after your round, food and drink are available at very reasonable prices.

Eagle View does not take tee times, but they assured us that getting on the course is not a problem. During the busiest holidays and weekends, extra staff is brought in to help golfers start off and get adequately spaced. All in all we loved this course. The reasonable prices are the same seven days a week, with a discount in the spring and fall. Basically, Eagle View is a grown-up par 3 with few hazards, no attitude and beautiful scenery.

ID: 5647009MN

EAGLE'S LANDING

Region: WestCentral

14825 263rd Street
Fort Ripley, MN 56449
Clubhouse: 320-632-5721
Golf Shop: 320-632-5721
Type: Public   Par: 72
www.eagleslanding-golf.com

Course Rating

HOSPITALITY	8.80
PLAYABILITY	8.72
USABILITY	8.93
FACILITY	8.36
VALUE	8.15

U
V

OVERALL SCORE
867

Green Fee: $22 (weekend)
1/2 Cart Fee: $11 (weekend)

Tees	Men's	Women's	Yards
Red		68.3/111	5098
Gold	67.4/108	72.1/119	5783
White	70.0/112		6347
Blue	72.5/119		6871

Eagle's Landing Golf Club in Fort Ripley, Minnesota, is a great surprise. It's safe to say that we were wowed by it! The clubhouse and staff of this golf course in the Brainerd/Cross Lake area are extremely friendly and helpful.

It was only 46 degrees late in the season when we started, but the course was quite busy for a late-season weekday, but it played at a nice pace. The pro shop has nice merchandise, most of which was on sale due to the late season.

Cart paths, tee boxes and signs are all top-notch and well kept up. Since we played on a fall day and there were leaves everywhere, it wasn't always easy to find your ball—but hitting in the fairway would help in the first place! Fairways are nicely mowed and easy to see. Bunkers are everywhere but they don't seem to be a problem. The very few water hazards didn't come into play, either.

Overall, it seems to be a very forgiving course. Flags mark the pin placements, but we didn't see any other markings other than the 200, 150 and 100. There are four tee boxes, with the forward tees being especially forward and very friendly.

The greens are huge (maybe double the size of other greens) and undulating with many hills, valleys, curves, and they are in good shape. Because of the size of the greens, we had some very long and curvy putts that were challenging but still fun. A couple of the greens have downslopes so the balls just keep on rolling. Yet other times a too-short putt might come right back to you!

The restaurant was closed for the season when we were there, but they had some hot snacks, beer and a very comfortable bar area. The in-season menu looks reasonable and varied. There is also a big patio area, but it was too cold to try it out.

ID: 5644909MN

EASTWOOD

3505 Eastwood Road SE
Rochester, MN 55904
Clubhouse: 507-281-6173
Golf Shop: 507-281-6173
Type: Public Par: 71
www.rochestermn.gov

V

Region: SouthEast

Course Rating

HOSPITALITY	8.58
PLAYABILITY	7.62
USABILITY	7.25
FACILITY	6.75
VALUE	7.96

OVERALL SCORE
769

Green Fee: $24 (weekend)
1/2 Cart Fee: $13 (weekend)

Tees	Men's	Women's	Yards
Red		67.4/116	4723
White	67.4/123	71.8/125	5501
Blue	70.5/130		6192
Black	72.2/133		6572

Eastwood Golf Club is the 2nd oldest of three city-owned golf courses in Rochester. Located off Eastwood Road, the signage makes the course relatively easy to find. The golf pro and staff are incredibly helpful and friendly. Eastwood is a combination of all the elements a golfer looks for in a course. This course's "rule of thumb" is to aim your first shot at the 150-yard marker in the center of the fairway and your second shot at the pin. Distance markers line the fairways at 25-yard intervals from 200 to 100 yards out.

The practice green is right next to hole #1, but the driving range is a bit farther away. But really, this course is the tale of two nines. The front nine is a nice layout with great rolling terrain, but the tees are long and the bunkers are untouched and not much fun to hit out of. The whole front nine just seems a bit run down. But then comes the back nine: You'll find tear-inducing tiered greens, cavernous bunkers, tall ball-eating grass, wildlife audiences and a par-5 14th hole that should be a par 6. Hole #17 is an amazing uphill par 3 that is intimidating and fun. You have to see this nine to believe it, and even then you probably still won't. But before you call your friends and tell them to book a tee time at Eastwood, one more thing: hole #11. Don't go for it in two unless you're a scratch golfer playing from the whites. And if you're a scratch golfer, why are you playing from the whites? Lay up and you could birdie or par the hole. Go for it, and your septuple-bogey will haunt you.

The pro shop has a great selection of items with better-than-average prices. With the abundance of women's golf items and apparel for sale combined with the women's tournament coming the next day, we'd say this course reaches out to women golfers nicely.

The restaurant has great food items from sandwiches to burgers, wings and even breakfast items. The prices are very good. The seating area is plenty big for this course and has a wonderful deck area to sit and catch a drink after.

EDINBURGH USA

8700 Edinbrook Crossing
Brooklyn Park, MN 55443
Clubhouse: 763-315-8500
Golf Shop: 763-315-8550
Type: Public   Par: 72

www.edinburghusa.org

Course Rating

HOSPITALITY	7.06
PLAYABILITY	7.65
USABILITY	6.57
FACILITY	7.54
VALUE	5.19

Tees	Men's	Women's	Yards
Red		71.6/133	5255
White	69.7/135	74.5/139	5858
Blue	72.1/139		6383
Black	74.2/149		6867

OVERALL SCORE
702

Greens Fee: $50.00 (weekend)
1/2 Cart Fee: $17.00 (weekend)

Approaching the clubhouse at Edinburgh USA, you may feel like you are entering a plush country club atmosphere in the heart of Brooklyn Park. Luckily, Edinburgh USA is reasonably priced and was constructed with public funds. It is also consistently rated as one of the top 100 public courses in the USA. The huge, stone clubhouse contains conference rooms, banquet rooms, a pro shop, locker rooms, bar and restaurant. The bar features good happy-hour specials and great appetizers as well as a full menu. You can order lunch from a phone system located at the 9th hole and have it ready for you when you arrive at the clubhouse.

This is one of the most challenging courses one can expect to play. Accuracy is key and strategy a must. There are five lakes on the course and somewhere between 70–80 traps. Trees protect the edges of the fairways on many holes. Bring plenty of balls when you come to play and consider yourself fortunate indeed if you don't need them.

As the course is considered a championship course, there are four sets of tee boxes on each hole. The fairways, greens and traps are in excellent shape and the cart paths and signage are adequate for finding your way from one hole to the next.

The course is within the hacker's budget and the food and beverages are reasonably priced. There are clocks set up around the course to time your progress and encourage those that may be slow to speed up their games. The ranger is quite regular in his rounds to ensure proper course conduct and play speed. If you are a walker, the course should still play about the same time as it is gently rolling and not too exhausting to walk.

We found the staff to be very friendly and cooperative and other golfers well mannered. The only problem encountered was with the workers on the fairways and tee boxes continuing to work while we were teeing off. Seeing as they were laying sod in the middle of the fairway, we can only assume that they felt unthreatened by our tremendous drives.

ID: 5544308MN

ELK RIVER

Region: Twin Cities

20015 Elk Lake Road
Elk River, MN 55330
Clubhouse: 763-441-4111
Golf Shop: 763-441-4111
Type: Semi-Private   Par: 72

www.elkrivercc.com

U
V

Course Rating

HOSPITALITY	7.66
PLAYABILITY	8.65
USABILITY	9.16
FACILITY	7.86
VALUE	7.71

Tees	Men's	Women's	Yards
Red		72.7/123	5590
White	70.1/123	75.7/130	6140
Blue	71.6/126		6480

OVERALL SCORE
829

Greens Fee: $33.00 (weekend)
1/2 Cart Fee: $13.15 (weekend)

Blind tee shots, doglegs and small, fast greens! If you want to challenge your short game, Elk River Country Club in Elk River, Minnesota, is the course to give it to you. Located a half-hour drive north of the Twin Cities just off of Highway 10, Elk River Country Club has it all, from a professionally run pro shop along with a teaching pro to help you on their driving range.

The course staff were very friendly as were the other golfers. We decided to play from the back tees, as looking at the scorecard 6480 yards seemed somewhat short from these tees. The course does play short, as with a good drive, 220–260 yards, you have a short iron shot to all of the par-4 greens. The obstacle was making a good drive! We seemed to be faced with a lot of blind tee shots and doglegs while standing at the tee box. Hint #1—don't play for money if playing someone with course knowledge!

The course, tees, fairways and greens were in great shape. You can easily see your ball in the rough, and the trees are trimmed up allowing for an easy recovery shot. Being that the holes played short there had to be a catch and it is the small, fast greens. The greens do not have many slopes to them but they are small and they are fast! Hint # 2—practice the bump and run and your short chip shots.

For the golfer that enjoys the game when they walk, this course is very favorable. There are only a couple holes with a major change in elevation from tee to green; and the next hole's tees are not that far from the previous green. Also we never experienced everyone else's errant shots from other fairways due to the large trees that line each hole.

On-course facilities were a bit slim, as it wasn't until after the 7th hole that a porta-potty and drink machine were located. Finishing our round in a fast four hours, we easily found a table on the shaded patio of the clubhouse. The restaurant staff was very pleasant and the food was quick, plentiful and very tasty. If you want to challenge your short game or entertain the whole family, Elk River Country Club will fulfill all of your needs.

ID: 5533008MN

ELM CREEK

19000 Highway 55
Plymouth, MN 55446
Clubhouse: 763-478-6716
Golf Shop: 763-478-6716
Type: Public   Par: 70

www.elmcreekgc.com

Tees	Men's	Women's	Yards
Red		68.0/117	4728
Yellow	66.0/120	70.9/123	5245
White	67.5/123	72.7/127	5577
Blue	69.0/125		5891

Region: Twin Cities

Course Rating

HOSPITALITY   7.26
PLAYABILITY   7.27
USABILITY   7.89
FACILITY   7.29
VALUE   6.08

OVERALL SCORE
728

Greens Fee: $32.00 (weekend)
1/2 Cart Fee: $14.00 (weekend)

If you played Elm Creek Golf Course five years ago, you might have remembered it as one of those courses that was the first to open and the last to close in an attempt to squeeze every dollar from the golf season. Well, things have changed.

According to the course's general manager, since new owners took over in 2004, they have continued to improve both the on- and off-course experience with a methodical investment leading to better manicured fairways and greens. You also won't find them open late into November any longer so they are able to preserve the course for the following year.

Traveling on Highway 55, Elm Creek Golf Course, just on the Western edge of Plymouth, Minnesota, is only accessible from the east. The layout of the facility is very compact and you can hit the front door and find your cart in just a few steps. The course, because it has nowhere to expand, unfortunately doesn't have a driving range, but does have a nice putting green.

Elm Creek, from which the course gets its name, makes its presence known at a handful of holes where the creek snakes alongside or through the fairway. Although the course is relatively short at 5891 yards, it makes up for it with wickedly difficult fairways and challenging approach shots that might tempt you to try and drive the green. This is not a "grip it and rip it" course; it is all about course management and shot selection.

Like all courses, Elm Creek has its own quirks. Since some of the holes cross each other, the signage can be a bit confusing so make sure you check out the map before venturing out. Also, yardage markers are a bit hard to see in spots and because of significant elevation changes on some holes, it will be important to know when you have a blind approach shot.

With close proximity to the Twin Cities as well as excellent pricing, the course is very popular with groups and has a nice clubhouse that allows for catering and an open patio for barbecues. It also is priced right with rates from $19 to $32 depending upon the time and day.

109

ID: 5544608MN

EMERALD GREENS
(Bronze/Gold)

14425 Goodwin Avenue
Hastings, MN 55033
Clubhouse: 651-480-8558
Golf Shop: 651-480-8558
Type: Public   Par: 72/72

www.emeraldgreensgolf.com

Tees	Men's	Women's	Yards
Red		71.4/118	5493
Gold	67.6/114	72.6/120	5704
White	70.6/119	76.3/129	6361
Blue	71.6/122		6585

Distances specific to this hole combination only.

Course Rating

HOSPITALITY	8.23
PLAYABILITY	7.62
USABILITY	8.63
FACILITY	6.55
VALUE	7.19

OVERALL SCORE
777

Greens Fee: $51.00 (weekend)
1/2 Cart Fee: $15.00 (weekend)

Emerald Greens is a 36-hole complex located in Hastings, Minnesota. It is a large facility with four different 9-hole courses all on one property. They have a good sized practice range, two putting greens with one having a practice bunker, grill service, full bar, cart service, and banquet room. And during the busy season they have a "grill shack" at the turn to get a decent hamburger.

Pulling up to the clubhouse during the summer, do not be swayed by the sheer volume of cars parked on the lot. Emerald Greens takes pride in its ability to host tournaments AND have daily fee golf all in the same day. The Bronze/Gold combination is 6361 yards with a rating of 70.6 and slope 119. The Bronze course is the weakest of the four courses and it shows. While the overall conditions of the course is on par with the other three as it pertains to fairways and greens, it just seems like this nine does not get as much maintenance attention as the others and the layout is slightly haphazard.

They have a lot of signage and it's needed since you often cross by other holes on your way to your next hole. The only lack of signage was on the Bronze course. Cart paths could have been in better shape, most being a gravel path and on occasion they were rutty.

Sand traps were generally raked but the edges looked ratty and in need of some grooming. The quality of the sand was grainy and of the typical "playground" type of grainy sand we find on Minnesota courses. This course is playable and you rarely get in too much trouble with errant shots. It's a little harder in the summer since they let some of the wild grasses grow tall that are between adjacent holes and hitting out of or finding your errant ball is more difficult.

Carts are older and are of the gas type. They really need to get some newer electric carts with GPS, but we can understand their hesitation since they have a fairly large fleet of carts. Yardage markers are plainly marked at 200, 150 and 100 yards. Overall impression is that it is a large course with a multitude of different combination of nines to choose from. For typical golfers it is playable and scoreable.

ID: 55033A08MN

EMERALD GREENS
(Silver/Platinum)

14425 Goodwin Avenue
Hastings, MN 55033
Clubhouse: 651-480-8558
Golf Shop: 651-480-8558
Type: Public   Par: 72/72

www.emeraldgreensgolf.com

Region: Twin Cities

Course Rating

HOSPITALITY	7.29
PLAYABILITY	7.98
USABILITY	8.99
FACILITY	7.09
VALUE	7.10

U

OVERALL SCORE
779

Greens Fee: $51.00 (weekend)
1/2 Cart Fee: $15.00 (weekend)

Tees	Men's	Women's	Yards
Red		73.2/128	5789
Gold	70.4/126	76.2/134	6326
White	72.5/130	78.8/139	6792
Blue	74.2/133		7163

Distances specific to this hole combination only.

Emerald Greens is found at the corner of Highway's 55 and 42 in Hastings, Minnesota. It has four 9-hole courses, a great practice area and a plain but very functional clubhouse. The clubhouse has a small snack area where you can get a hot dog, bratwurst, hamburgers, and soup. Downstairs there are banquet facilities to accommodate 175 people.

The four courses are the Bronze, Silver, Gold, and Platinum. A majority of the time the 18-hole configuration is Bronze/Gold and Silver/Platinum. On this day we played the gold tees on the Silver/Platinum courses.

Overall the whole course is in excellent condition. The owners have done a tremendous amount of work planting trees, landscaping, building beautiful stone bridges, and building elevated tees with large boulders. The tees, fairways, short rough, and greens are well maintained. We were disappointed in the bunkers. They contained playground sand and a large number of them had footprints of players who had failed to rake when leaving. The cart paths are only around the tees and greens. They consisted of badly deteriorated blacktop and gravel, but were functional. Getting from greens to tees was well defined.

Both these nines are relatively flat and easy to walk with the Platinum having a couple of small hills. Being relatively an open course makes it difficult to play in wind, but in the fall it is a good place to play as there are few leaves. They have planted many small trees that will completely change the nature of the course in a few years. The Silver course has a par-3 with a very nice elevated tee to an island green. The Platinum course has a par-5 dogleg that plays 536 yards from the gold tees and 632 yards from the blue tees—very difficult even downwind.

We played on a cool windy day and managed to get around in less than four hours and had little trouble with sprayed shots. We thought that the Silver/Platinum combination played a little long for the higher handicap player. Golfers may find a combination of the other courses to be more enjoyable but challenging due to the shorter lengths.

111

ID: 55033B08MN

EMILY GREENS

Region: NorthEast

39966 Refuge Road
Emily, MN 56447
Clubhouse: 218-763-2169
Golf Shop: 218-763-2169
Type: Public   Par: 69

www.emilygreens.com

Course Rating

HOSPITALITY	7.60
PLAYABILITY	7.03
USABILITY	8.00
FACILITY	6.92
VALUE	7.50

Tees	Men's	Women's	Yards
Red		66.2/114	4399
Gold	63.5/107	67.3/116	4595
White	66.3/114		5168
Blue	66.9/115		5299

OVERALL SCORE
740

Green Fee: $26 (weekend)
1/2 Cart Fee: $13 (weekend)

The family- and hacker-friendly Emily Greens Golf Course in Emily, Minnesota, is a privately-owned public golf course on the north side of the Brainerd Lakes area. The green fees are very competitive and there are usually coupons and specials available.

The pro shop has a limited amount of merchandise, but it is fairly priced. Food service consists of only drinks and a few snack items. A teaching pro is available for groups and by appointment. The practice facilities are convenient and are kept in good condition. The driving range is well marked for distance but is a little narrow. The practice green is in great condition, and there is good area for chipping practice.

The original nine is 2005 yards and plays to a par of 33. It is fun and yet challenging if you try to reach some of the shorter par 4s with your drive. The back nine is a newer championship-style course. It is 3294 yards from the back tees and plays to a par of 36. We found a few holes where familiarity of the course would have been helpful. There are a few blind shots and doglegs to contend with, but there are only six bunkers on the entire course and water does not really come into play. The championship nine has some challenge from the back tees, but there are four separate tees on most holes. The forward tees make it a family- and hacker-friendly course. Conditioning of the course is quite good. The fairways and greens are very well maintained, though the bunkers are a little ragged and have hard sand. Some sections of the cart paths have washout and erosion problems due to the terrain.

Emily Greens boasts a commitment to family-friendly golf. That combined with its value and playability makes Emily Greens a great destination for families and hackers. The management is customer-friendly and works hard to make sure everyone's day is a great one.

ID: 5644709MN

ENGER PARK

1801 W Skyline Boulevard
Duluth, MN 55806
Clubhouse: 218-723-3452
Golf Shop: 218-723-3451
Type: Public   Par: 36/36/36

www.golfinduluth.com

Region: NorthEast

Course Rating

HOSPITALITY	7.11
PLAYABILITY	6.83
USABILITY	6.33
FACILITY	6.62
VALUE	6.05

OVERALL SCORE
669

Green Fee: $29 (weekend)
1/2 Cart Fee: $14.50 (weekend)

Tees	Men's	Women's	Yards
Front/Middle - Gold	67.9/131	73.1/128	6554
Front/Middle - White	70.2/135	75.9/134	6145
Middle/Back - Gold	68.0/132	73.8/129	5691
Middle/Back - White	69.7/135	75.8/134	6060
Back/Front - Gold	68.9/128	74.3/127	5841
Back/Front - White	70.7/131	76.4/132	6231

Enger Park Golf Course is one of two golf courses run by the city of Duluth. It has been around a while, and its age shows itself in several areas. The clubhouse is old and did not have air-conditioning, which would have been welcome on the hot day we were there. We're unsure if the A/C was not working or if they just don't have it.

This course has three nines, each with four sets of tees. Blue tees are 6700 yards, whites are 6100, golds are 5600 and reds are 5100. One woman we talked with said she didn't think the course was very female-friendly because the red tees are fairly close to the others. There is approximately 1000 yards difference between the red and white tees.

Enger Park has a very hilly layout, and it seems prone to having soggy areas. Walkers are the exception on this course. Most of the holes are fairly generous from the tees with only a few holes with hazards to clear. If you don't hit huge slices or hooks, you will generally be okay off the tee. There are a lot of trees and a number of water hazards and bunkers. The water hazards mostly come into play only if you have wild shots, but the bunkers, on the other hand, are plentiful and strategically placed. The bunkers were in very nice condition the day we played, even though it had rained the night before. The greens were also in nice condition—they roll true and don't have a lot of ball marks. The fairways and tees are not nearly as nice as the greens and bunkers.

The entire course is beautiful. There are several holes that are completely lined with trees, making it impossible to see other holes, and you shoot to generous and well-kept greens. Unfortunately, there are also holes that have a soggy ground or beat-up fairways and tees.

All in all, this course is a good hacker's course. If they fix some fairways and tee boxes and upgrade the clubhouse and pro shop it would be a great course.

ID: 5580609MN

FAIR HAVEN

13404 149th Avenue
Menahga, MN 56464
Clubhouse: 218-732-0519
Golf Shop: 218-732-0519
Type: Public   Par: 71

www.fairgolf.com

Region: NorthEast

Course Rating

HOSPITALITY	8.02
PLAYABILITY	5.45
USABILITY	7.78
FACILITY	6.86
VALUE	6.85

OVERALL SCORE
691

Tees	Men's	Women's	Yards
Red		65.8/103	4459
Yellow	65.4/107	69.9/112	5207
White	68.7/113		5922

Green Fee: $25 (weekend)
1/2 Cart Fee: $12 (weekend)

Fair Havens Golf Course is a privately-owned course in Menahga, Minnesota, just south of Park Rapids. It is a ten-year-old course that is continually doing work to improve and extend the length of the course.

The clubhouse is a conveniently located log structure that has drinks and a few snack items available. But keep in mind that there are no other food services available. There is also not a pro shop with equipment or accessories for sale, and there are no practice facilities of any kind here.

Without any practice swings you start out on the course with a fairly tight par 5. It is not very long, but the narrowness makes it a harder 1st hole. The 1st green seems to be the largest green on the whole course. Most of the greens are quite small, but the conditioning of the greens is very good. They do seem to be pretty easy to hit and stick on, despite their small size. The middle holes of the front nine are mostly wide open and forgiving. Due to the newer tee boxes on some holes, some of the yardages on the scorecard and signs don't match up accurately. On the par 3s you have to do some calculating to get the yardage right.

The back nine has several short par 4s that have doglegs and large pine trees to contend with. The holes are still very playable and forgiving, but if you try to challenge the hole because it is short, it may cost you more strokes than you were trying to save.

Overall this course is kept in very good condition and is fun to play. Knowing how the hole is laid out, especially on the doglegs, would be helpful. Join up with one of the friendly locals and use them as your guide. It is hard to beat the value of the green fees here. The friendly staff will work to make your outing a pleasant and affordable one.

ID: 5646409MN

FALCON RIDGE

33942 Falcon Avenue North
Stacy, MN 55079
Clubhouse: 651-462-5797
Golf Shop: 651-462-5797
Type: Public Par: 71

www.falconridgegolf.net

Tees	Men's	Women's	Yards
Red		69.4/120	4976
White	68.1/113	72.7/127	5566
Blue	70.1/118		6011

Region: NorthEast

Course Rating

HOSPITALITY	7.46
PLAYABILITY	5.32
USABILITY	7.16
FACILITY	5.47
VALUE	6.15

OVERALL SCORE
633

Green Fee: $25 (weekend)
1/2 Cart Fee: $14 (weekend)

Located an hour north of the Twin Cities, Falcon Ridge Golf Course sits along I-35 in Stacy, Minnesota. The website is user-friendly and the course is easy to find. Arriving at the golf course, the unkempt parking lot and sparse pro shop do not do the course justice. The pro shop is small and carries basics, but not much more. All beverages are either in cans or plastic bottles, and the food selection is better at any Holiday gas station. The staff is friendly and helpful; the beverage cart came by at least three times per nine.

The carts are cheap both in price and appearance: they're gas-powered with no GPS, divot fill bottles or coolers. The practice facilites, however, are quite nice. The practice green holds two distinct cuts of grass with several holes to choose from. The all-grass driving range is well-defined, with game-like targets of varying distances to choose from. Golf lessons range from start-from-scratch lessons for the new golfer to the trying-to-become-scratch option for the low handicapper.

The course itself is fun to play. It's not too long and it provides the golfer with more than a few risk/reward situatons. Notable holes include the 541-yard dogleg-right par-5 #2 and an obtrusive fairway oak on the 506-yard par-5 #18. With only a couple dogleg-left holes and a lot of open land to the right, this is a slice-friendly course. The par 3s have a huge varity of distances (125 to 220 yards), and the three different tee boxes cater to every ability level.

Course condition is the best attribute of Falcon Ridge. The greens are very well-maintained with two distinct cuts of grass and a manicured rough. Fairways are well-defined and easily picked out from any tee box; the rough is consistent for the boundaries of the hole. Three pairs of distance stakes (200, 150, 100) are on every applicable hole and they're always easy to see.Overall, Falcon Ridge is a terrific value. While it may not be a destination course, it's one of the most convenient and value-packed choices along the I-35 corridor.

ID: 5507909MN

FALLS

4402 County Road 152
International Falls, MN 56649
Clubhouse: 218-283-4491
Golf Shop: 218-283-4491
Type: Semi-Private Par: 72

www.fallscc.com

Course Rating

HOSPITALITY	8.81
PLAYABILITY	8.84
USABILITY	8.70
FACILITY	8.42
VALUE	7.31

P

Tees	Men's	Women's	Yards
Red		69.4/114	5141
Gold	68.0/114		5795
White	70.0/118		6233
Blue	72.2/129		6632

OVERALL SCORE
859

Green Fee: $35 (weekend)
1/2 Cart Fee: $13 (weekend)

Nestled along the Rainy River on the edge of International Falls, Minnesota, Falls Golf Club was a very pleasant surprise. This Joel Goldstrand-designed course is only 6,632 yards, but has a 129 slope, easily making up for its modest length. The course also has a nice practice area to warm up at before your round. We had heard it was a nice course, but didn't expect to find it to be so well kept.

When we arrived for our tee time, it was raining so we sat in the clubhouse for almost an hour drinking coffee (they only charged us for 1 cup and we had 3) waiting for it to stop. When we did get out, the pro paired us up with a local player as we had never played the course before. We found him to be a very friendly guy who provided us with some valuable course knowledge.

The day we played the temperature was in the 40s and it had rained a lot a few days prior to our visit. Despite all of the rain, the greens still were rolling very fast and true. The fairways were well tended. The course has a woodlands feel to it. There are a couple of holes along the Rainy River that really add to the aesthetic experience. It is a course that rewards a good shot and can be punitive on a poor one. It is how a course should be.

The clubhouse was very comfortable with a large fieldstone fireplace. The people were very friendly and hospitable. We didn't get a chance to eat there, but they appeared to have a nice variety of food options available. The food is fairly-priced and if you want to really work on your game, an all-day lesson (including lunch) can be had for less than a round at a fancy resort course. Although Falls Golf Club isn't the northern most course in Minnesota (that is reserved for Warroad Estates in Warroad), it is a reasonably-priced course, on the Minnesota/Canadian border with just enough challenge to make you want to return on your next vacation. If you are planning a trip to Rainy Lake or Voyageurs National Park, don't forget to pack your clubs.

ID: 5664909MN

FARIBAULT

1700 NW 17th Street
Faribault, MN 55021
Clubhouse: 507-334-5559
Golf Shop: 507-334-3810
Type: Semi-Private Par: 72
www.faribaultgolf.com

Region: SouthEast

Course Rating

HOSPITALITY	8.13
PLAYABILITY	7.16
USABILITY	8.23
FACILITY	6.74
VALUE	6.77

Tees	Men's	Women's	Yards
Red		71.4/125	5468
White	69.8/127	75.8/134	6252
Blue	70.7/129		6447

OVERALL SCORE
751

Green Fee: $32 (weekend)
1/2 Cart Fee: $15 (weekend)

Faribault Golf Club in Faribault, Minnesota, was established in 1910, but the original nine-hole course was redesigned in 1956 and a second nine was added in 1966. The semi-private golf course is about a 35-minute drive south of the Twin Cities. Our first impression of the course was that it was flat and tree-lined with most of the holes between 300 and 385 yards and some long par 5s. But after a couple of holes our impressions changed quite dramatically. The fairways are generous, as are the number of trees. Any shot that wanders into the trees is a minimum of one lost shot. The greens are smooth, fast and humpbacked. Approach shots don't hold very well; if they land in the wrong spot they tend to roll off the green. The greens are difficult but fair. Ten of the non-par-3 holes are doglegs that require good placement of your tee shot, or else you'll have a difficult shot into the green.

As stated, the course is flat with the greens and tees quite close together. There are few bunkers, but they are strategically placed. The rough is 1 – 2 inches, but along the fairway where it is watered it is heavy and thick. This course is in excellent condition compared to many other courses. We walked and completed play in 3 hours and 40 minutes.

It appears that much hasn't changed since the final nine holes were completed in 1966. The tee boxes are well-maintained but small. The blue tees are only 195 yards longer than the whites. On most holes the difference between the white and blue tees is only about 10 yards. The greatest distance is 25 yards. There is a putting green and driving range between the 1st and 10th holes, and the clubhouse is just a few yards away. The staff is very accommodating and helpful. The clubhouse has a small pro shop and a bar with a dozen tables. Food is very basic, but the hot popcorn is a nice touch. Faribault Golf Club is a good test of golf in a relaxed atmosphere, and we would highly recommend giving it a try.

ID: 5502109MN

FIDDLESTIX

1081 395th Street
Isle, MN 56342
Clubhouse: 320-676-3636
Golf Shop: 320-676-3636
Type: Public   Par: 71

www.golffiddlestix.com

F

Course Rating

HOSPITALITY	8.72
PLAYABILITY	8.51
USABILITY	7.74
FACILITY	8.75
VALUE	6.12

OVERALL SCORE
820

Tees	Men's	Women's	Yards
Red		69.5/123	5032
White	68.2/124	73.3/131	5709
Blue	69.8/127		6055

NOTE: website was not working at presstime (Jan-2010) so greens fees are estimated.

Green Fee: $34 (weekend)
1/2 Cart Fee: $14 (weekend)

Fiddlestix Golf Course is three miles south of Lake Mille Lacs in Isle, Minnesota, and it seems a little out of place there. You would expect the attractive clubhouse with its full-service restaurant and bar and the carefully groomed golf course to be just as comfortable in the Gull Lake area. This is like a secret that the folks on Lake Mille Lacs want to keep to themselves. In spite of the flat farmland that surrounds it, The Stix is what we hackers like: a challenge that we can overcome on our best days.

Trees, ponds and sand abound. Twelve of the holes have some water, and several trees are in very uncomfortable positions at the edges of the fairways, with their boughs filling the air space that is desperately needed on those errant shots. Nature surrounds you at The Stix. We even had to yield the right-of-way to a doe and her fawn as they took their time foraging around the 3rd green. It is near futile to tell a hacker that they should lay up or skirt hazards and aim for the fat part of the fairways and greens, but that is exactly what you need to do here. With some intelligent play it is very easy to shoot bogey.

Most impressive at this course is the care given by the grounds crew. Bunkers are raked and clear of rocks. Fairways are well groomed and the rough (our fairway) is kept at a playable length. The greens are carefully cut and the man on the mower has a plunger to repair the ball marks left by some of our inconsiderate friends. Course signage and cart paths are in good condition (we only got lost once), and the tee boxes are also well attended. There is some leg power involved if you are walking. Although the course is relatively flat, there are some significant green-to-tee walks. The long trek from the clubhouse to the 1st tee was enough to make us glad we were riding. There are a lot of specials available, but even the standard rates are reasonable for this course. All in all, The Stix is well worth the drive. It is a championship course that is interesting, attractive and fun to play.

ID: 5634209MN

FOREST HILLS

22931 185th Street
Detroit Lakes, MN 56501
Clubhouse: 218-439-6930
Golf Shop: 218-439-6400
Type: Public   Par: 72

www.foresthillsgolfrv.com

Tees	Men's	Women's	Yards
Silver		68.2/125	4939
Gold	68..1/124	72.9/135	5789
Black	70.3/127		6244

Course Rating

HOSPITALITY	8.86
PLAYABILITY	8.07
USABILITY	7.42
FACILITY	7.21
VALUE	6.85

OVERALL SCORE
789

Green Fee: $34 (weekend)
1/2 Cart Fee: $14 (weekend)

The golf course at Forest Hills Golf and RV Resort is conveniently located just a few miles west of Detroit Lakes on Highway 10. Over half of the course is cut through woods both thick and sparse. Fewer than half the holes find their way onto the hills and prairie, highlighting the natural diversity that makes this part of the state a real treasure. One can move from pine to hardwood to prairies in literally a matter of miles, and Forest Hills takes great advantage of this natural beauty.

While the course itself is easy to find, it can be a bit more difficult to navigate while on the course and avoid the blind hazards. Take advantage of the help offered at the pro shop, for a finely hit shot can easily find its way into a pond or wood if you don't know where the hazards are. If you are on a cart (which is recommended because of some distances between green and tee), it is a good idea to drive ahead to see where a pond lurks below a hill or where woods sneak inside a dogleg. Watch for the blind water hazards on holes 4, 7, 8, 12, 13 and 18, as well as blind dogleg shots on holes 6 and 15. It is a good idea to keep your driver in the bag for the first five holes and the final two; the short lengths are offset by sometimes incredibly narrow fairways or landing areas. Some preliminary work on the driving range, located a lengthy cart drive from the clubhouse, will help you get that slice or hook out of your system.

Good course management and shot selection will yield better scores and allow you to truly enjoy the woods and water. Look for improvements in the coming year or two, including a new green layout on #15 (which eliminates a dogleg sharper than a U-turn) and a rumored flip-flop of holes 9 and 18. The trip to Forest Hills is not complete without a visit to Izzo's, a full-service restaurant where the spicy buffalo chips are a welcome change to a side of French fries. A weekend in the Detroit Lakes area should include a round at this somewhat quirky and fairly well-maintained course.

119

ID: 5650109MN

FOUNTAIN VALLEY

2830 220th Street West
Farmington, MN 55024
Clubhouse: 651-463-2121
Golf Shop: 651-463-2121
Type: Semi-Private   Par: 72
no website

Tees	Men's	Women's	Yards
Red		73.7/127	5797
White	70.7/128	76.6/133	6318
Blue	71.9/130		6560

Region: Twin Cities

Course Rating

HOSPITALITY   6.63
PLAYABILITY   5.92
USABILITY   6.84
FACILITY   5.69
VALUE   6.39

OVERALL SCORE
629

Greens Fee: $29.00 (weekend)
1/2 Cart Fee: $15.00 (weekend)

Golfers tend to categorize golf courses based on their reputation, type or location. Fountain Valley Golf Course, just south of the Twin Cities in Farmington, Minnesota, is a country course. It's not fancy, it's not expensive and it isn't difficult to play. All the basics are there—course, clubhouse, driving range, golf carts—but that is the extent of it.

Carved out of former farm fields, the course is relatively flat with trees that appear to be planted in the last decade so they aren't very large yet. The fairways are wide open with few hazards to speak of until the back nine. Overall condition of the course was average, with tee boxes and fairways holding up well. The putting surface was fast and in excellent condition, but most are billiard table flat with few undulations. Putts roll true so long as you have good aim; they should usually find their destination.

Cart paths, what there are of them, are an afterthought. Distance markers are the standard 200, 150, 100 yards, so you can dial in your distances, but tee box signage is weak, sometimes making the search for the next hole a bit more difficult than necessary.

The facility's layout is compact with a small parking lot just steps from the driving range and clubhouse. A brick patio surrounds the large modern clubhouse and inside is an open area with check-in, a small food counter and a seating area that could accommodate events of at least 150 people. After putting out at the 18th hole, you might consider grabbing a refreshment and bringing it to the patio to watch as other golfers finish up their rounds, but dinner afterwards would have to be found elsewhere.

As a golf experience, this is a no frills, workman-like course. It has all the basics you'd expect, but nothing fancy. Don't expect umbrellas in your mixed drinks or fancy food at the clubhouse. This is a course designed for an easy round of golf that won't stress out you or your wallet. For less skilled players, it is a course that will build confidence. For better players, this is not the track for you.

ID: 5502408MN

FOX HOLLOW

4780 Palmgren Lane NE
St. Michael, MN 55376
Clubhouse: 763-428-4468
Golf Shop: 763-428-4468
Type: Semi-Private   Par: 36/36/36

www.foxhollowgolf.net

Tees	Men's	Women's	Yards
Red		73.7/127	5797
White	70.7/128	76.6/133	6318
Blue	71.9/130		6560

Region: Twin Cities

Course Rating

HOSPITALITY   6.74
PLAYABILITY   7.25
USABILITY   8.15
FACILITY   6.69
VALUE   5.98

OVERALL SCORE
709

Greens Fee: $42.00 (weekend)
1/2 Cart Fee: $15.00 (weekend)

Located about a mile off Interstate 94 in St. Michael, Minnesota, Fox Hollow is a collection of 27 holes that provide a string of challenges for the consummate hacker.

They have an original 18 and a new "Black /Gold 9" on the other side of County Road 36 that apparently can be played in both directions.

The original 18 is a challenging collection of holes which starts deceptively easy and gets tougher. The third hole, par 3, is 156 yards over the Crow River, which isn't too tough—if you can tell yourself the river isn't there. On the back nine is an even shorter par 3 at 131 yards that is down a wicked hill and blind from the tee box. You need to hit a club you believe in. The par 5s are laid out pretty simple and provide a good chance to score well.

As far as conditions go, the tee boxes were soft and the greens rolled true but the fairways needed some serious help. Several of the fairways were covered in ant hills—picture an 8 year old with chicken pox. We asked the ranger about it and got the cordial reply, "I don't know—must be that time of season." we didn't know there was an "'ant hills pop up all over the fairway time of season. We hope they get it fixed because it really ruined a few fairways.

And that brings us to service. The life of a ranger, on the course that is, can't be too tough. He is likely retired, gets to ride around on a golf cart all day and meet what you have to believe are generally nice people. A good ranger can do a lot for a golfer's experience. Well, the aforementioned ranger had to be the most unfriendly and disgruntled man we have ever met on a course. He barely said hello and wandered around the edge of a creek for a while in a world of his own. Service in the pro shop and clubhouse was fine but not exceptional.

Fox Hollow is a nice course that can be a great course if they can eliminate the ant hills and put a big permanent smile on that ranger's face!

ID: 5537608MN

FRANCIS A. GROSS

2201 St. Anthony Boulevard
Minneapolis, MN 55418
Clubhouse: 612-789-2542
Golf Shop: 612-789-2542
Type: Public   Par: 71

www.minneapolisparks.org

Tees	Men's	Women's	Yards
Forward		67.6/112	4939
Gold	63.5/107	68.0/113	5022
Standard	69.6/118	74.9/128	6348
Long	71.0/120		6631

Region: Twin Cities

Course Rating

HOSPITALITY	6.94
PLAYABILITY	6.30
USABILITY	7.78
FACILITY	5.72
VALUE	6.73

OVERALL SCORE
671

Greens Fee: $32.00 (weekend)
1/2 Cart Fee: $14.00 (weekend)

In the heart of northeast Minneapolis, Francis A. Gross Golf Course, also known as Gross National Golf Club, has been a fixture since 1925. Conveniently located just off of Interstate 35W, it is easy to get to and easy to play.

Like many urban courses, it is landlocked and what it lacks in length needs to be made up by adding traps, water and trees. The scorecard says the course is 6574 yards, but since many holes didn't even have the blue tees marked, it really plays from 6348 yards. Yet, for an average golfer, this length is perfect with a couple of 500+ yard par 5s and a couple of 180+ yard par 3s. Just enough length to goad you into trying to hit your irons too far.

As to interest, Gross really doesn't do as great a job. Yes, the course has mature trees and some sand bunkers and almost every hole provides the golfer a safe landing area. The course also limits the number of "lost ball" hazards like unruly rough and open water, but there is a sense of sameness to the layout with a lot of the par 4s with similar lengths and design.

A strength of this course is that it understands what hackers need on-course: bathrooms, benches and frequent visits from the food cart. Each hole had a ball washer and a bench, even for the ladies' tees, and about every third hole, a bathroom. Even more amazing, the cart person was there every third hole like clockwork. Inside the clubhouse, they have the standard food offerings, but you can order sandwiches to go and they are ready in short order.

Francis Gross reflects its working class roots so don't expect fancy trappings on or off the course. You'll probably notice that the course needs a bit of tending and if it is dry, your ball will roll for miles. Yet, what they save on maintenance is reflected in the prices. Gross is one of the best overall values in the Twin Cities and even the food is at working class prices with a hot dog only $2.50 and made-to-order sandwiches for only $3.75.

ID: 5541808MN

GEM LAKE HILLS Exec. 18

Region: Twin Cities

4039 Scheuneman Road
White Bear Lake, MN 55110
Clubhouse: 651-429-8715
Golf Shop: 651-429-8715
Type: Public   Par: 57

www.gemlakehillsgolf.com

Tees	Men's	Women's	Yards
Red		57.0	2911
White	57.0		3366

Course Rating

HOSPITALITY	8.43
PLAYABILITY	6.06
USABILITY	8.00
FACILITY	5.63
VALUE	6.63

OVERALL SCORE
703

Greens Fee: $22.00 (weekend)
1/2 Cart Fee: $10.00 (weekend)

Gem Lake Hills Golf Course, located in White Bear Lake, Minnesota, is worth the search to find it. It's just east of Highway 61 and County Road F, but you may want to bring your Google map with you since there aren't any local signs directing one to the course. Gem Lake Hills is a great course for beginners, seniors, and those who want to complete a quick 9 or 18 holes. Playing both the par-3 and executive-9 courses is just over 3300 yards and is easily walkable for most golfers. The course offers a number of junior leagues with or without lessons, and there are quite a few adult leagues. The clubhouse doesn't have a pro shop, but it does have friendly, helpful staff along with a good selection of snacks and popcorn.

A large, well-maintained putting and chipping green is close to the clubhouse. Those who wish to warm up at a driving range will have to be satisfied with hitting balls into a large netted area. Since most of the holes average about 170 yards for men, one may want to spend more time on the putting green. Fees are reasonable for either 9 or 18 holes, and the front nine is quite level for those who like to walk. Cold water is available every 2–3 holes, and the beverage cart comes around frequently.

There are few hazards on the course. Golfers encounter one hole where the ball must be driven over a slough, and there are some holes where an errant ball may be lost to water areas. There aren't any sand traps, and trees line some holes, but for the most part trees are only a problem if one drives quite a bit off center or overshoots the green. The fairways and greens are in good condition, while the tee boxes are a bit worn by summer's end. Geese often gather by the 17th and 18th holes. Most players won't need to use their drivers often at Gem Lake Hills. A decent first shot and a fairly good chip will bring golfers into putting range on the par-3 holes. The cup placement on some of the holes will make achieving a par more difficult than it appears at times. A foursome can easily walk and complete 18 holes in just under four hours on most days. All in all, Gem Lake Hills provides a pleasant golf experience without the challenge of dealing with too many hazards.

ID: 5511008MN

GENEVA

4181 Geneva Golf Club Drive
Alexandria, MN 56308
Clubhouse: 320-762-7089
Golf Shop: 320-762-7089
Type: Public   Par: 35/36/37

www.genevagolfclub.com

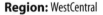

H

Course Rating

HOSPITALITY	8.92
PLAYABILITY	8.11
USABILITY	7.76
FACILITY	7.83
VALUE	6.58

OVERALL SCORE
805

Green Fee: $53 (weekend)
1/2 Cart Fee: included in fee

Tees	Men's	Women's	Yards
Ponds/Marsh - gold	67.9/129	72.8/125	5630
Ponds/Marsh - white	70.5/134	76.1/131	6210
Marsh/Island - gold	69.6/126	74.6/129	5932
Marsh/Island - white	71.9/131	77.4/135	6434
Island/Ponds - gold	68.5/122	72.9/124	5676
Island/Ponds - white	70.9/127	75.9/130	6206

"This course compares favorably with some of the best resort courses in Minnesota." ~Joel Goldstrand. That quote, by the course designer, is found on the Geneva Golf Club's website. Having played Geneva as well as many other resort courses in Minnesota, we would certainly agree, especially when you compare the golf value. In fact, we would say that Geneva is a golf gem in the Alexandria area.

Geneva is set up as three nine-hole courses: Ponds, Island, and Marsh. What this in fact gives you is three distinct 18-hole courses, and of course the option of playing all 27. We played the "Ponds/Island" combination. Now, we know that looking at those names could make the average hacker a bit nervous. But while there is quite a bit of water, including a number of forced carries, it really isn't that bad. A person should be able to score fairly well here, but good course management is a must. Don't try for miracles—you're not Tiger Woods. Play smart.

The courses are well laid out, and there's a good use of the overall landscape and terrain. There are multiple tee boxes, and tee-to-green course conditions are very good. Despite the amount of water around the course, landing areas are very generous. Depending on which layout you play, the courses can range from nearly 7000 yards from the back tees to under 5000 from the forwards. Other pluses include GPS distance to center of green in all carts, and a yardage book with playing hints mounted in all carts. Drop areas are indicated in the book. The staff is friendly and seems efficient. The clubhouse is fairly new and has a nice bar and grill, The Geneva Grill. We did not see a beverage cart on the course; however, there are pop machines located by the restroom where all three courses intersect. The biggest drawback of the course is on-course signage. There are several places where the courses intersect, making it confusing to know where to go. All in the all, our experience at Geneva was a good one. Once you play a round here you'll probably agree.

ID: 5630809MN

GIANT'S RIDGE

(The Legend)

6325 Wynne Creek Drive
Biwabik, MN 55708
Clubhouse: 800-688-7669
Golf Shop: 800-688-7669
Type: Public   Par: 72

www.giantsridge.com

P

Course Rating

HOSPITALITY	8.85
PLAYABILITY	8.91
USABILITY	7.78
FACILITY	8.38
VALUE	6.91

Tees	Men's	Women's	Yards
Red		70.3/126	5084
White	70.1/126		6112
Blue	71.9/129		6528
Gold	73.7/133		6930

OVERALL SCORE
839

Green Fee: $89.00 (weekend)
1/2 Cart Fee: included in fee

The Legend, part of Giants Ridge resort and located just outside of Biwabik, Minnesota, has long been regarded as one of the best ski resorts in Minnesota. In the late 1990s Giants Ridge constructed The Legend golf course to offer year-round sporting entertainment. Later, they built The Quarry as its complement. Both courses are consistently at the top of numerous lists of best golf courses in the country.

The Legend is a startlingly beautiful golf course comprised of steep ridges, deep ravines and hazardous waterways. The challenges begin at the 1st tee box with a 150-yard carry over a cavernous gorge, leading up a steep fairway. The following hole, a par 3, requires another carry over an imposing body of water. The 3rd, a lengthy par 5, presents a short and extreme dogleg off the tee that also requires golfers to negotiate a giant footprint bunker. The difficulties are endless, even on seemingly straightforward shots. Challenging though it might be, The Legend is a fantastic golf experience for anyone who enjoys the game. It provides average golfers with the unique opportunity to enjoy a true championship-level course, just like the pros. And like the pros that play TPC Sawgrass, you too will be humbled by The Legend's signature hole, a 200-yard par 3 on an island green.

This course offers a unique golf experience with fine hospitality. It offers free range balls and allows golfers to purchase refreshments on the course and pay at the conclusion of the round. Also, the staff offers complimentary club cleaning. Giants Ridge provides year-round lodging with an assortment of activities for outdoor enthusiasts. However, Giants Ridge does fall short with some amenities that could make The Legend much more enjoyable for the first-timer. For instance, the golf carts lack GPS devices. Cart paths are generally unpaved and the signage is poor, which makes it easy to get lost especially with the long distances between holes. Nevertheless, Giants Ridge has earned its stellar reputation as home to two of the state's best golf courses.

ID: 55708A09MN

GIANT'S RIDGE

(The Quarry)

6325 Wynne Creek Drive
Biwabik, MN 55708
Clubhouse: 800-688-7669
Golf Shop: 800-688-7669
Type: Public   Par: 72

www.giantsridge.com

Course Rating

HOSPITALITY	8.79
PLAYABILITY	8.96
USABILITY	7.95
FACILITY	8.58
VALUE	6.91

P

OVERALL SCORE
845

Tees	Men's	Women's	Yards
Red		70.8/125	5119
White	70.5/132		6101
Blue	73.1/138		6696
Gold	75.6/146		7201

Green Fee: $89.00 (weekend)
1/2 Cart Fee: included in fee

Giants Ridge, located just outside of Biwabik, Minnesota, is a destination for both skiiers and golfers alike. After receiving critical acclaim for The Legend, Giants Ridge matched its first endeavor by building the equally magnificent Quarry in 2003.

Minnesota's Iron Range is home to some of the some of the best golf courses in the state. The Quarry is a majestic golf course that embodies the spirit and native topography of the region. Its fairways curve along narrow valleys that cut through jagged rocks and evergreen trees. To conquer this terrain, golfers must be prepared to cut, chop and blast their way through, just as the pioneers did almost 200 years ago.

The Quarry is more playable than the other Giants Ridge course, The Legend, but there is little solace in that fact. This is still a very difficult course that is littered with crags, sand traps, rolling mounds and waste bunkers. Likewise, the rippled and multi-tiered greens are fascinating and punishing.

The Quarry also highlights northern Minnesota's lakes and rivers, but much of the water on this course is aesthetic rather than imposing. The signature element and predominant challenge at The Quarry are its pocketed fairways. Nearly all of the fairways are at some point interrupted by unplayable rough, splashes of rock or large waste bunkers. These features require accurate and precise shots at the golfer's peril. The Quarry is an amazing golf experience that will test your patience and fortitude.

The course is a bit spendy, but everything is included in the fee making this a top-notch experience that you'll want to try at least once a summer.

ID: 55708B09MN

GLENCOE

1325 East 1st Street
Glencoe, MN 55336
Clubhouse: 320-864-3023
Golf Shop: 320-864-3023
Type: Semi-Private   Par: 71
www.glencoecountryclub.net

Tees	Men's	Women's	Yards
Red		68.7/117	4940
White	66.7/125		5734
Blue	68.5/129		6094

Course Rating

HOSPITALITY   7.09
PLAYABILITY   6.83
USABILITY   7.29
FACILITY   6.09
VALUE   6.34

OVERALL SCORE
683

Green Fee: $28 (weekend)
1/2 Cart Fee: $14.50 (weekend)

Glencoe Country Club is located in Glencoe, Minnesota, approximately 60 miles southwest of Minneapolis. The course is 18 holes, each with three sets of tees. The full yardage is 6094 from the blue tips. The course also offers a junior set of tees for younger players. The golf course is relatively flat, has many trees and a river and creek to make it challenging. Although a familiarity with the golf course would improve your score, you will still enjoy a round here.

The pro shop is located on the lower level of the clubhouse, with a restaurant/bar on the upper level. There is an adequate driving range and putting green, and although the course is walkable, we would suggest using a cart, as there are some distances between green and tee box that can slow you down. The course is user-friendly with good signage, paved cart paths, well-marked hazards, etc. Appropriate fencing is used to guard tee boxes from errant golf shots from fairways.

The golf course is suited to players at all levels. Because it is flat and has minimal blind shots, any level of golfer will appreciate the overall layout. We think the course would fit any hacker's interest. We played Glencoe on a Sunday afternoon, and even though it wasn't very crowded, play did slow down a number of times. This is because Glencoe does not require foursomes. There were a few twosomes and singles who should have been paired up at the beginning of their round. The head professional didn't appear to be at the course, but some direction to the person in the pro shop would have been helpful. Also, there was no sign of a beverage cart—which is typically important to golfers.

Because the golf course is located outstate but relatively close to the Twin Cities Metro area, you can play Glencoe Country Club at an affordable price without having to drive a great distance. This is of particular interest to those who live on the fringe of the Metro area.

127

ID: 5533609MN

GOLDEN EAGLE

16146 W Eagle Lake Road
Fifty Lakes, MN 56448
Clubhouse: 218-763-4653
Golf Shop: 218-763-4653
Type: Public   Par: 72

www.golfgoldeneagle.com

Course Rating

HOSPITALITY	8.49
PLAYABILITY	8.79
USABILITY	7.86
FACILITY	9.19
VALUE	6.78

P
F

OVERALL SCORE
839

Tees	Men's	Women's	Yards
Red	65.7/123	70.5/125	5097
White	69.3/131	74.9/134	5898
Blue	71.5/135		6359
Gold	73.3/140		6745

Green Fee: $84 (weekend)
1/2 Cart Fee: included in fee

It was hard to find anything we didn't love here. The word "Brainerd" is synonymous with "amazing golf." Mention that you played Madden's, Cragun's or Deacon's and everyone knows how blessed you are. But Golden Eagle should also be in that same grouping. A comparable experience (it's about 40 miles north of Brainerd) at a more affordable price, Golden Eagle is an isolated, serene beauty of a course. But it's well worth the drive, and it plays as perfectly in October as it does in May. The design is spectacular, using the contours of the land to the greatest capacity. The elevation changes provide great views and, combined with wide-open fairways, they allow for maximum forgiveness off most tees. The greens are nearly perfect in firmness and condition, allowing for a true test of your putting skills. The tee boxes are a little beat up, but the fairways and greens are borderline immaculate. The pro shop service is a little sub-par, but at the end of the Minnesota golf season we're a little grumpy, too, so we'll cut them some slack.

At Golden Eagle you are surrounded by hills, valleys, lakes, marshes, rivers and forests, and you play over and through them on every hole. Every par 3 is reachable and reasonable. There are bunkers scattered everywhere, but they stay out of the way of good shots. Holes 1 and 2 are par 5s, both reachable in two with a decent straight drive off the tee. Only #5 and #9 really threaten you on the front. Play the distance on #4; don't go down a club. (Loved the menu phone at the #9 tee box. We wish every course did this!)

The back nine is a different animal, with a bite to match its bark the first time you play it. Ten and 11 are stern tee shot tests, but 12 and 13 ("signature holes") are as magnificent and fun as golf gets. A fear of the unknown is well merited the rest of the way. The second shot on #14 isn't really fair; neither is the tee shot on #17. Expect to lay up on #14 and hate it. Better lay up on #17 or hate it. And #18 isn't a good finishing hole. That may sound a little harsh, but we loved everything else.

128

GOODRICH

1820 North Van Dyke Street
Maplewood, MN 55109
Clubhouse: 651-748-2525
Golf Shop: 651-748-2525
Type: Public   Par: 70

www.ramseycountygolf.com

Tees	Men's	Women's	Yards
Red	64.9/111	69.9/119	5125
White	68.4/118		5914
Blue	69.9/121		6235

Region: Twin Cities

Course Rating

HOSPITALITY	7.66
PLAYABILITY	7.48
USABILITY	8.30
FACILITY	7.10
VALUE	6.75

OVERALL SCORE
756

Greens Fee: $26.00 (weekend)
1/2 Cart Fee: $17.00 (weekend)

Much could be said about a golf course that has the words "good" and "rich" in its name. The good news is that you need to be neither good nor rich to enjoy a round at this hacker-friendly course on the east side of St. Paul. In fact, Goodrich Golf Course is one of the most accessible and playable of the golf courses owned and operated by Ramsey County.

The signature element of Goodrich Golf Course is its indoor golf dome. This multi-level golf facility is open year-round to hone your stroke before a round and to keep sharp in the cold months when golf is nothing more than a distant memory or the product of winter dreams. The course also offers such amenities as outdoor putting and chipping greens, a small patio, on-course beverage service and a pro shop with golf equipment and a small menu of food and beverages. Lessons are available for the novice and the avid golfer alike, and, at under $30 per round, the value is unmistakable.

Although Goodrich is an enjoyable and playable course, it finds itself in tough company. With Keller Golf Course and Manitou Ridge Golf Course (both operated by Ramsey County) within three miles, the seasoned golfer may prefer to play the more extravagant and challenging courses. However, Goodrich is not without its own charm. The course is rarely busy, which makes tee times readily available and the pace of play steady and fast. Because it is not as difficult as other local courses, Goodrich is a good place for the novice golfer to learn the game. The 6200-yard course provides fairways ranging from 140 yards in length to 475 yards. With mature tree lines, the copious pines are the primary hazards, although sand traps are scattered along the fairways with the occasional water trap.

Goodrich is a fairly navigable golf course and has water stations every four holes. Its attendants know the course well, although their customer service leaves something to be desired. In sum, Goodrich is a great course for the novice golfer and a nice place to play for a quick and uninterrupted round. And don't forget the indoor golf dome for those harsh winter months!

ID: 5510908MN

GOPHER HILLS

26155 Nicolai Avenue
Cannon Falls, MN 55009
Clubhouse: 507-263-2507
Golf Shop: 507-263-2507
Type: Public Par: 72

www.gopherhills.com

Tees	Men's	Women's	Yards
Red		69.5/109	4913
Gold	67.6/111	72.6/116	5464
White	70.6/116	75.2/122	5995
Blue	71.6/119		6355

Region: SouthEast

Course Rating

HOSPITALITY	8.35
PLAYABILITY	8.07
USABILITY	6.94
FACILITY	7.62
VALUE	6.69

OVERALL SCORE
771

Green Fee: $26 (weekend)
1/2 Cart Fee: $13 (weekend)

Gopher Hills Golf Course in Cannon Falls, Minnesota, is not called Gopher Plains Golf Course for a reason—the hills outnumber the holes about two to one. Located 15 minutes off Highway 52, Gopher Hills is a gem of a course providing top-notch amenities, beautifully manicured landscape and a challenging mix of uneven terrain and native grasses.

The main entry to the clubhouse takes you into a beautifully decorated banquet center, which would be a great place for a wedding reception or for hoisting a championship golf trophy, but finding the pro shop is a tad confusing. A sign on the front of the building would make things much clearer for visitors. Service in the pro shop is great; we were out and settled into our gas cart in no time. There is a more-than-adequate driving range and putting area between the clubhouse and the 1st hole.

Built in 1999, the front nine is not the original, but it is a welcoming nine holes to start your round. There are very few trees, and if you can keep your ball out of the natural, knee-high grasses that line the fairway, you should be scoring pretty solid as you get to the back nine—which is the original front nine. Still with us?

The par 3s on this course are great for hackers. None of them are over 171 yards if you play the whites—which you should be playing. They're slightly challenging but not because of distance, a stumbling block that can get into any hacker's head. A couple of our favorite holes on the course include the par-5 #7, where the fairway appears to be about 25 yards wide. Try your 3-wood. The 323-yard #15 is a sharp dogleg left and is beautifully sculpted out of the trees. Again the driver will tempt you, but stick to a safer shot with a fairway wood. Overall, this is a fantastic course with friendly golfers and staff. It's not very far from the Twin Cities and provides some challenges due to a landscape that you don't see on many courses in the Metro area.

ID: 5500909MN

GRAND NATIONAL

305 Lady Luck Drive
Hinckley, MN 55037
Clubhouse: 320-384-7427
Golf Shop: 320-384-7427
Type: Public   Par: 72

www.grandnationalgolf.com

Tees	Men's	Women's	Yards
Red		69.2/122	5100
White	72.0/131		6149
Blue	72./134		6530
Black	73.6/137		6894

Region: NorthEast

Course Rating

HOSPITALITY	7.49
PLAYABILITY	7.77
USABILITY	8.20
FACILITY	8.40
VALUE	7.34

OVERALL SCORE
784

Green Fee: $35 (weekend)
1/2 Cart Fee: $18 (weekend)

First impressions would lead you to believe that Grand National Golf Course in Hinckley, Minnesota, is flat and boring, but that is not the case. Once you tee off you'll discover hills, woods, water and sand in abundance. Grand National, a respectable 70-minute drive from the Metro area, was a privately owned course that was recently purchased by the Mille Lacs Band of Ojibwe. Changes are already visible but not significant, so don't expect to find a track that is any threat to Dakotah Ridge or the Wilderness at Fortune Bay. But you will not find their prices here, either.

Clubhouse personnel are friendly and helpful, but there are no PGA-affiliated employees on staff. Food comes in the form of sandwiches delivered by the casino catering staff. The beautiful deck looks down on an expansive putting green and well-maintained and marked driving range. Your green fee includes unlimited range balls and a cart. The tees are well-marked and well-maintained, and each bears signage that lays out the design of the hole as well as the pin placement of the day. A chart at the first tee helps you decide which set of tees you should use; the four choices range from 5100 to 6894 yards.

The greens are generally large and receptive, but they were cut long, so expect to pound putts to get them to the hole. The fairways are clean and the entire golf course is visually attractive. You will have to work hard to find a square foot of brown turf on this course. Water appears on 12 of the 18 holes, and there are plenty of raked but slightly rocky bunkers on nearly every hole. Fairways are fair and some are narrow, and the trees are avoidable without having to hit perfect shots. While the white 150-yard stakes are clearly visible, you may have trouble locating the smallish discs that mark the 200- and 100-yard points. Grand National is worth the trip north if you aren't fussy about amenities and are just looking for a well-maintained and thoughtfully designed golf course.

ID: 5503709MN

GRANDVIEW LODGE
(The Pines)

23521 Nokomis Avenue
Nisswa, MN 56468
Clubhouse: 218-963-8755
Golf Shop: 218-963-8750
Type: Public   Par: 36/36/36
www.grandviewlodge.com

F

Region: NorthWest

Course Rating

HOSPITALITY	8.21
PLAYABILITY	8.64
USABILITY	8.67
FACILITY	9.08
VALUE	6.10

OVERALL SCORE
835

Green Fee: $104 (weekend)
1/2 Cart Fee: included in fee

Tees	Men's	Women's	Yards
Lakes/Woods - Gold	68.7/132	73.7/135	5745
Lakes/Woods - White	70.5/136	76.0/140	6152
Woods/Marsh - Gold	67.8/132	73.0/131	5625
Woods/Marsh - White	70.2/136	76.0/137	6159
Marsh/Lakes - Gold	68.3/130	73.5/137	5658

The Pines at Grandview Lodge in Nisswa, Minnesota takes full advantage of the natural Minnesota terrain in 27 beautiful holes. With three 9-hole courses, each is thematically distinct and representative of the state's topographic features. The aptly named courses (The Lakes, The Woods and The Marsh) utilize those features to create a scenic and challenging golf experience. Although The Pines includes three unique courses, rounds of golf are sold in 18-hole increments. On most weekdays, golfers are free to select the two courses of their choosing. However, on weekends and busy weekdays the pro shop dictates course assignments.

As expected, water comes into play often on The Lakes, which makes this the most interesting and entertaining of the three courses. The 3222-yard course requires a thoughtful approach to the game. Many of the lengthy holes are made more difficult by fairways with sharp doglegs. The shorter holes, where most of the water hazards are found, require accuracy and consideration in shot selection. The Woods is a narrow and unforgiving golf course that is lined with mature pines and harsh brush. Aside from the imposing tree lines, sand traps are the predominate hazards on The Woods. In many instances, the sand traps are clustered in dangerous fairway locations and around the greens. However, the pitfalls of this course are offset by the feeling of serenity that comes from a relaxing hike in the forest.

Most intense of the three courses at The Pines is The Marsh. The wet marshland gives rise beautiful deciduous trees along the fairways and presents unending hazards along the way. A marsh can be a more daunting hazard than even water. Water hazards are generally finite on a golf course, but from a distance it is difficult to decipher where a marsh ends and the rough begins. At $104.00, this is not a cheap round of golf, although the green fee includes a cart, unlimited range balls and access to the practice facilities. However, The Pines is a treat to play and should be starred on a list of destination courses.

132

ID: 5646809MN

GRANDVIEW LODGE
(The Preserve)

5506 Preserve Boulevard
Pequot Lakes, MN 56472
Clubhouse: 218-568-4944
Golf Shop: 218-568-4944
Type: Public   Par: 72

www.grandviewlodge.com

Tees	Men's	Women's	Yards
Red		68.6/121	4816
Gold	68.5/126	73.5/131	5700
White	10.8/131		6204
Blue	72.5/137		6601

Region: NorthWest

Course Rating

HOSPITALITY	8.53
PLAYABILITY	8.96
USABILITY	8.26
FACILITY	9.02
VALUE	6.43

OVERALL SCORE
847

Green Fee: $104 (weekend)
1/2 Cart Fee: included in fee

Managed by Grand View Lodge, The Preserve is a difficult, pricey and very beautiful golf course a hacker can play without becoming embarrassed or overly frustrated. Like Deacon's Lodge, The Preserve is in the Brainerd Lakes area in Nisswa, Minnesota.

In the case of The Preserve, information is key. Feel free to seek out the assistant professionals for advice; they'll point out difficult spots and help select the correct tees for your level of play. The GPS provided in the carts leaves no mystery as to the layout, best route and detailed distances on each hole. The hard-surfaced cart paths make it nearly impossible to get lost. And golfers can get a good idea of what's in store just by standing on the clubhouse deck and looking down at several of the well-manicured and environmentally conscious golf holes. The practice facilities are immaculate and indicative of the speed and contour of the difficult greens you will encounter.

The fairways are cut out of the woods and meander around water. However, they are often wide and with the information on the GPS screen, golfers should be able to stay safe. The greens are very fast and difficult to read, but that only adds to the fun. The environment is beautiful and protected; The Preserve is a member of The Audubon Cooperative Sanctuary. Fellow players at The Preserve take care to fill divots and repair ball and spike marks on the green. The golf course is designed and presented in such a way that you want to protect it for the next group.

Hackers who want to experience what a well-designed, well-maintained and difficult championship-level course is all about should try The Preserve. The expense can be justified by the sheer joy of playing a course that looks like those you see on television on Sunday afternoons. If you have a few extra dollars in your wallet and are looking for great golf then vist The Preserve.

ID: 56472C09MN

GREEN LEA

Region: SouthEast

101 Richway Drive
Albert Lea, MN 56007
Clubhouse: 507-373-1061
Golf Shop: 507-373-1061
Type: Public   Par: 72

www.greenlea.com

H
U

Course Rating

HOSPITALITY	8.88
PLAYABILITY	8.14
USABILITY	8.93
FACILITY	8.21
VALUE	6.81

OVERALL SCORE
836

Tees	Men's	Women's	Yards
Red		69.5/118	5049
White	69.0/117		5991
Blue	70.0/121		6213

Green Fee: $28 (weekend)
1/2 Cart Fee: $14 (weekend)

Green Lea Golf Course in Albert Lea, Minnesota, is a true gem of a course. It's well worth the drive if you live in the Twin Cities and a must-play if you live in the Albert Lea area. The clubhouse is very attractive and a welcoming sight to golf lovers. The inside has a small-town café-like atmosphere. The warm and friendly restaurant has a great breakfast selection as well as hot dogs, burgers, sandwiches, salads and appetizers. There is also a full-service bar. The food is very good. You certainly don't have to be a golfer to enjoy this clubhouse!

The pro shop is one of the nicest we have seen. They have everything from clubs to apparel, all at good prices. The staff took good care of us at the check-in desk and quickly got us on our way. The putting green is near the 1st and 10th tee boxes.

We'll mention the two negatives, and then we'll move on: 1) They do not have a driving range, so warming up is tough, and 2) The golf cart paths are in bad shape throughout the course. But this is only a minor distraction as you are looking at the 1st tee and fairway. What a gorgeous view. The tee boxes are in great condition and the fairways are beautiful. There are plenty of trees throughout this course, so you might lose a ball on occasion, but it's well worth the risk. The rough is long enough to give you a penalty if you miss the fairway, but it's not ridiculous. The greens are as nice as any we have played on all year. They are fast and the putts roll true. Green Lea has some nice bunkers throughout the course, and they were in good condition even after a couple days of rain. The signs for each hole are fantastic and easy to read. Overall, the course is hacker friendly, but it is also a good challenge to those with a lower handicap. The length of the course seems fair at 6200+ from the blue tees, 5990+ from the whites and just over 5000 from the reds. The price to play is very good, and even memberships are reasonable. We drove from the south Metro area and were happy we made the trip, even in the rain.

134

GREENHAVEN

2800 Greenhaven Road
Anoka, MN 55303
Clubhouse: 763-576-2965
Golf Shop: 763-576-2970
Type: Public   Par: 71

www.greenhavengolfcourse.com

Tees	Men's	Women's	Yards
Red		71.0/123	5333
Yellow		75.0/132	6059
Yellow/Gold	69.5//128		6059
Blue	70.5/130		6276

Course Rating

HOSPITALITY	7.84
PLAYABILITY	7.57
USABILITY	7.64
FACILITY	6.63
VALUE	6.98

OVERALL SCORE
745

Greens Fee: $31.00 (weekend)
1/2 Cart Fee: $14.00 (weekend)

Folks traveling along Highway 10 on their way to the lake may miss Greenhaven Golf Course in Anoka. Pigeonholed between a frontage road and railroad tracks in the heart of a developed city, the course is landlocked. Only 6300 yards from the tips, the course does all it can to maximize the playing experience and has used the land to such a degree that you'll find very little rough in which to lose your ball.

Arriving at the course makes you feel you are playing at a country club. The large clubhouse has a full bar, grill, and outdoor seating as well as space to host weddings. Even breakfast is available if you've just finished an early round. One surprise was the brand new golf carts.

Although the course is short, it does its best to try to challenge the typical golfer. Even with these additions, the course still feels tired and limited. Big weaknesses are the cart paths and signage. The cart paths are sporadic and where the asphalt ends and the dirt starts, watch for potholes. On-course signage is quite weak and unless you follow the white lines painted on the course, you might lose your way to the next hole. Another weakness is the practice area were you hit "floater" balls that land in a pond. When we were there the practice range had run out of balls so we were only able to practice our putting.

The course is very walkable and has benches at each hole, but shade is a rare commodity so take sunblock. Also, because of its location within the city of Anoka, the Highway 10 frontage road and a very busy and loud train track line define the edge of the course on two sides. The frontage road is so close that on #17 you can hear drive-through orders being placed at a nearby Taco Bell and if you want, get your own Mexican food fix before you tee off.

If you are looking for an inexpensive round of golf on a course that accommodates short hitters, Greenhaven is your course. If you want a better layout that provides more challenge in a more quiet location, another course might be a better option.

ID: 5530308MN

GREYSTONE

10548 Andrews Drive
Sauk Centre, MN 56378
Clubhouse: 320-351-4653
Golf Shop: 320-351-4653
Type: Semi-Private   Par: 72

www.greystonegc.net

Course Rating

HOSPITALITY	8.88
PLAYABILITY	8.62
USABILITY	8.52
FACILITY	8.37
VALUE	7.85

H
V

OVERALL SCORE
855

Tees	Men's	Women's	Yards
Purple		71.8/127	5395
Platinum	69.3/126		5880
Green	71.6/131		6391
Black	74.5/137		7059

Green Fee: $43 (weekend)
1/2 Cart Fee: $16 (weekend)

Greystone Golf Club, located just north of Sauk Centre, Minnesota, opened its doors in 2000. Designed by Tom Lehman, this course is a premium course rivaling the Brainerd Lakes courses in playability and enjoyment at a significantly more modest cost.

The facility layout is very convenient with the upscale clubhouse next to the putting green area and the driving range. As you move to the 1st tee you are looking over a sea of grass that has 18 uniquely designed holes placed within it. You can choose from four different tee boxes with yardage ranging from 5395 yards to 7059 yards. Being hackers, we chose the platinum tees, which are 5880 yards and carry a slope rating of 126.

Greystone is a Scottish links-style course with water hazards and bunkers dispersed generously around the course. The fairways are liberal, the holes are well-marked and electric carts move you around quickly. Carts are recommended as some holes have lengthy distances between greens and tee boxes. The greens are not exceptionally fast—at least not on the day we played—but they have a variety of contour, and some holes have several levels.

The signature hole is #17. From the elevated tee box you are looking down at a green protected by a moat, which gives no place to bail out for any golfer, let alone a hacker. Our distance was 109 yards; reachability is not the issue. Moving to #18, a 361-yard par 4, you have views of Big Sauk Lake as you work your way down to the final green. Accuracy is a must to score well on all of the holes, but recovery from errant shots is possible because of the open nature of this primarily links-style course.

The semi-private Greystone Golf Club has the feel of a premium course, but the regular prices are very mid-range and specials abound. This course is clearly worth the extra drive; it's one you will want to play again and again.

ID: 5637809MN

HARDWOODS

18517 Captive Lake Road
Garrison, MN 56450
Clubhouse: 320-692-4325
Golf Shop: 800-435-8720
Type: Public Par:

www.millelacsgolf.com

Tees	Men's	Women's	Yards
Red		69.8/116	5041
White	70.1/123		6067
Blue	71.2/125		6291

Region: NorthEast

Course Rating

HOSPITALITY   6.73
PLAYABILITY   4.50
USABILITY   6.99
FACILITY   4.67
VALUE   4.83

OVERALL SCORE
561

Green Fee: $35 (weekend)
1/2 Cart Fee: $16 (weekend)

When you play the Hardwoods Golf Course at the Mille Lacs Resort and Marina in Garrison, Minnesota, you may be able to visualize that it was once an enjoyable and reasonable place for a golf outing. That is, if you can get past what is there now. The empty parking lot that greeted us was an omen of what we would find.

This course, and the area that surrounds it, is not fun to look at. Evidence of maintenance on the course is nearly nonexistent. The fairways are rough with weeds and never recovered winterkill, and the greens are pitted and uneven and nearly impossible to putt because of the dead spots. There are few level places on the tee boxes, and one bunker was filled to the brim with creeping vines.

The course is bordered with housing that runs the gamut from the resort's attractive rental twin-homes to a collection of finished, half-finished and decaying log homes and townhouses. These beautiful structures were built and then abandoned, and at least one of the unfinished homes has walls that have given up and fallen to the ground. As hard as we tried to look away, it was depressing to see this reflection of the tough economy visible on so many of the fairways on the back nine. The clubhouse itself needs paint even if only a quarter of it is being used.

Hardwoods was—and could still be—a fun course for hackers. It is nicely designed and has that up-north look to it. The rolling fairways and interesting doglegs are very playable. Most of the greens are elevated and the tee boxes are situated so you always have a good idea of where to play to avoid the woods and water that are prevalent on many of the holes. The condition of the course may break your heart, but the golf itself will not. This course needs an infusion of cash, customers and caring attention to be back to where it once was. And it once was a nice stop for hackers in the Mille Lacs area.

ID: 5645009MN

HAWLEY

301 Highway 10
Hawley, MN 56549
Clubhouse: 218-483-4808
Golf Shop: 218-483-4808
Type: Public Par: 71

www.hawleygolf.com

Tees	Men's	Women's	Yards
Red		68.6/113	5087
White	67.5/120		5773
Blue	69.0/123		6114

Region: NorthWest

Course Rating

HOSPITALITY   8.04
PLAYABILITY   6.85
USABILITY   8.15
FACILITY   6.66
VALUE   7.38

OVERALL SCORE
743

Green Fee: $16 (weekend)
1/2 Cart Fee: $16 (weekend)

Just off Highway 10 and located smack between Moorhead and Detroit Lakes is Hawley Golf and Country Club. Named for Thomas Hawley Canfield, an officer in the Northern Pacific Railroad, the city of Hawley hugs the Buffalo River, which also winds through part of the course. Coming in off Highway 10 (the only possible way to get there), the course's road signage isn't hard to miss so you won't need a map. It is a modest facility with all you'd expect from a small-town golf course. It has a driving range, a putting green, a two-story clubhouse and outdoor grills on the deck in the summer.

This is what you'd call relaxed golf. The course doesn't have an attitude. It doesn't have fancy trappings, state-of-the-art golf carts equipped with GPS or a driving range with pyramids of practice balls. What it has is cheap golf that is very hacker friendly. Weekend green fees are $16. Yes, only 16 bucks for 18 holes. If you want a cart, the cost goes up to $20 for a twilight rate. Even their driving range costs only $3.50 for a bucket. This course has some of the cheapest rates you'll find anywhere. With such a low rate you'd probably think it has poor conditions. Think again. The course, even late in the season, was in excellent condition. The fairways were nicely mowed, the greens showed little wear and most of the tee boxes looked great.

It's a compact par-69 course (the scorecard will say 71) at only 6113 yards. It isn't a course set up to steal your golf balls because the rough is minimal, the fairways are wide and there are few hazards to contend with. It's a pretty course with rolling hills, and it's a toss-up if a cart is needed.

The pro shop is small with a minimum of products. Check-in is easy and they have a speaker system to announce which group is next off the tee. For skilled players looking for a challenge, there isn't much here to keep their attention. For someone looking for inexpensive golf, a boost to their golfing ego and a place to play on a beautiful summer day in northern Minnesota, Hawley Golf Club is a good choice. **138**

ID: 5654909MN

HAYDEN HILLS Exec. 18

13150 Deerwood Lane North
Dayton, MN 55327
Clubhouse: 763-421-0060
Golf Shop: 763-421-0060
Type: Public   Par: 62

www.haydenhillsgolf.com

V

Course Rating

HOSPITALITY	7.49
PLAYABILITY	6.33
USABILITY	5.85
FACILITY	6.14
VALUE	7.93

OVERALL SCORE
666

Tees	Men's	Women's	Yards
White	56.7/80	56.2/78	3054
Blue	57.6/82	57.9/82	3368

Greens Fee: $22.50 (weekend)
1/2 Cart Fee: included in fee

Need to practice on your short game? If so, Hayden Hills Executive Golf Course in Dayton, Minnesota, is a great course to do so. With one par 5, six par 4s, and twelve par 3s, the course plays to a total of 3368 yards. This is a great walking course (very flat) that features a nice mixture of trees, water and sand to make it a bit of a challenge but also very forgiving. The rough is short and it is difficult to lose balls on this course. The play offers some interesting challenges on doglegs (should I go over the trees for a shot at the green or go down the center of the fairway for an easy approach?) and a couple of holes where a golfer can hit over water or play it safe. The course has a nice screen of trees and shrubbery that enhances the play with very little visibility of the bordering housing subdivisions. Gives you a feeling of a nice walk in the country.

The course is fairly easy to find. It is located off of County Road 121. There is also easy access off of Country Road 81 (Maple Grove) or Highway 169 (Champlin). Keep an eye open for Deerwood Lane as the signage isn't the best and the entrance isn't seen from the road until you get to the end of Deerwood Lane.

The course has a putting and pitching green just outside the dated but clean clubhouse. There is no golf pro and no pro shop for clothing items. The clubhouse features clean restrooms, snack bar and a large community room for seating.   Staff are friendly, players courteous, and the snack bar offers standard fare at reasonable prices. Eighteen holes and cart for $22 is very reasonable.

This is a good course to start the season and get your irons ready for the regulation courses to follow.

COURSE INFO

Town & Country Club, a private golf club in St. Paul, opened in 1893, is the nation's second oldest golf course and has been in continous operation to this day.

139

HEADWATERS

20018 County Road 1
Park Rapids, MN 56470
Clubhouse: 218-732-4832
Golf Shop: 218-732-4832
Type: Semi-Private Par: 72

www.headwatersgolf.com

Course Rating

HOSPITALITY	8.28
PLAYABILITY	7.94
USABILITY	8.29
FACILITY	7.90
VALUE	7.24

OVERALL SCORE
802

Tees	Men's	Women's	Yards
Red		70.3/122	5202
Gold	67.0/117	71.8/125	5478
White	70.2/123	75.7/133	6182
Blue	71.4/126		6482

Green Fee: $38.25 (weekend)
1/2 Cart Fee: $13.75 (weekend)

One of the great things about playing golf in northern Minnesota is that we've yet to play an ugly golf course. Headwaters Golf Club in Park Rapids, Minnesota, is absolutely beautiful. The front nine as well as #10 and #12 are tree-lined but spacious. The course has numerous elevation changes, but they're not too big. This makes it interesting and attractive yet still very walkable. It was late season but the fairways were still in great condition; greens had recently been aerated but we suspect they are normally excellent, too. There are a lot of bunkers—well placed but not overly difficult. Water comes into play in only a very few places.

The course has four sets of tees and plays at a little under 6500 yards from the back tees and only 5202 from the front. It offers something for everyone. The layout makes sense, and a person can find their way around it easily—even if there are no signs—just by following the map on the back of the scorecard. The clubhouse at Headwaters is a relatively modest affair. The pro shop seems a little small but is well organized. Prices are reasonable on clubs, of which they have a surprisingly good selection for a small shop, and clothing items are even a little lower in price than one might expect. Food service is basic grill food in the clubhouse, and the prices are reasonable. The fried fish was excellent. There is a small bar area with several beers on tap, an assortment of canned/bottled beer, as well as wine and spirits. Additionally, during the main season there is a snack bar at the junction of the 5th and 6th, and 8th and 9th holes.

General manager and club pro, Jeff Anderson, is a friendly guy with a warm greeting for everyone who comes through the door. The other staff at the course was busy going about their work and making sure things were in tip-top shape. We didn't see much of them but surely saw the results of their efforts. If you're in the Park Rapids area it is a must play.

ID: 5647009MN

HERITAGE LINKS

8075 Lucerne Boulevard
Lakeville, MN 55044
Clubhouse: 952-440-4656
Golf Shop: 952-440-4656
Type: Public   Par: 71
www.heritagelinks.com

Region: Twin Cities

Course Rating

HOSPITALITY	7.09
PLAYABILITY	7.18
USABILITY	7.03
FACILITY	6.79
VALUE	6.92

Tees	Men's	Women's	Yards
White		71.3/117	5145
Blue	69.7/122	75.7/126	5929
Gold	71.4/126		6320
Black	73.0/130		6672

OVERALL SCORE
704

Greens Fee: $34.60 (weekend)
1/2 Cart Fee: $15.00 (weekend)

Heritage Links Golf Club in Lakeville, Minnesota, is set amongst the low rolling hills of the South Metro's farm country. The first thing you notice when walking up to the clubhouse is the well-designed practice area with putting green and driving range. The large driving range has visible yardage markers and is well maintained to give each golfer a proper practice area.

Inside the upper level of the clubhouse is the pro shop and course dining area. The pro shop has a large selection of golf equipment and apparel with the smaller items such as golf balls, tees, and gloves seemingly fair priced. They have a large selection of golf bags and clubs that are higher priced. The clubhouse has standard food options to grab a quick meal or drink during your round. Check-in for tee times was quick, easy and relatively painless thanks to the reasonably priced greens fees.

The course is a links style layout that plays deceptively longer than its 6672 yards from the back tees. The front nine holes are more wide open and playable with very few trees and limited hazards. The back nine will test your skills and patience with tighter fairways, more water hazards and well protected greens. Heritage Links signature hole is #13, a short 270-yard par 4 with a heavily wooded tee box that leads to a large open area around the green. It is too difficult to pass up and it will tempt even the most disciplined hacker into taking the driver out of the bag. If it is your first time playing the course it is sometimes difficult to determine your distances remaining to the flag because of limited yardage markers. Every fairway has a 150-yard from the pin pole but other than that you are left judging the distance with your eyes frequently.

Heritage Links Golf Club is a fairly priced and challenging course that any hacker would be happy to have in their neighborhood. It is also perfectly suited for the average golfer to shag a bucket of balls at the driving range after work or take advantage of the inexpensive twilight pricing starting after 2 p.m.

ID: 5504408MN

HIAWATHA

4553 Longfellow Avenue South
Minneapolis, MN 55407
Clubhouse: 612-724-7715
Golf Shop: 612-724-7715
Type: Public   Par: 73

www.minneapolisparks.org

Course Rating

HOSPITALITY	6.55
PLAYABILITY	6.64
USABILITY	6.82
FACILITY	7.59
VALUE	7.96

OVERALL SCORE
693

Greens Fee: $32.00 (weekend)
1/2 Cart Fee: $16.00 (weekend)

Tees	Men's	Women's	Yards
Red		69.3/118	5122
Gold	67.1/118	72.4/125	5685
White	69.5/123	75.3/131	6211
Blue	71.4/126		6613

Located one block east of Cedar between Interstate 94 and Crosstown 62, Hiawatha Golf Course in Minneapolis, Minnesota, is an easy course to find and a pleasure to play. The topography is gently rolling and well suited to the player that enjoys walking.

The clubhouse offers the traditional grill and has a limited supply of clothing and golf accessories. Restrooms are clean and well maintained as are the golf carts. There are no restrooms on the course but the clubhouse is centrally located and golfers pass it by every 4 holes. The beverage cart is nonexistent after Labor Day.

The golf fees are competitive and there are good deals for seniors at $26 for 18 holes and a cart. There are junior rates, twilight rates and evening rates as well as patron cards. Lessons are available as are junior golf camps.

This course is very well maintained with lush, green fairways, tees and greens. It does, however, offer a challenge to the average hacker. The fairways are narrow and well guarded by trees. Venturing off to the right or left will leave the hacker a difficult shot through the trees or a punch-out back to the fairway. The greens are postage stamp in size but they are not too difficult.

Overall, hackers will have their share of frustration but the course is well worth your time and it is difficult to lose balls as the course rough is cut short and the grass under the trees is well mowed. The competitive rates and the gently rolling and wooded course make this city course a must even though you may find it a bit difficult for the 20+ handicapper.

Alexandria, Minnesota native and PGA Professional Tom Lehman, winner of the 1996 British Open and 1996 PGA Player of the Year, has his brother Jim Lehman, Jr. as his agent.

ID: 5540708MN

HIDDEN CREEK

4989 East Rose Street
Owatonna, MN 55060
Clubhouse: 507-444-9229
Golf Shop: 507-444-9229
Type: Public   Par: 72

www.hiddencreekmn.com

Tees	Men's	Women's	Yards
White		67.3/116	4554
Gold	68.1/123	73.1/128	5592
Blue	70.9/129	76.6/135	6220
Black	74.5/136		7002

NOTE: website was not working at presstime (Jan-2010).

Region: SouthEast

Course Rating

HOSPITALITY	5.86
PLAYABILITY	6.12
USABILITY	7.25
FACILITY	5.26
VALUE	6.52

OVERALL SCORE
619

Green Fee: $36 (weekend)
1/2 Cart Fee: $14 (weekend)

If you are heading south from the Metro area, you may have to Google or use your GPS to locate Hidden Creek Golf Club in Owatonna, Minnesota. If you bring your compass, you may need to use it on the course, as well. Hidden Creek could easily be renamed Hidden Shot, since there are a few greens you cannot see from your approach shot. The course is located east of downtown Owatonna near Rice Lake State Park.

This course is a birdie in the rough waiting to happen. It's literally a bit rough around the edges, but it's still an expedition to play. It is a fun course to play in a tournament or event with old and new friends. The best part of the club-house is their outdoor deck with a lovely view overlooking the course. Hidden Creek will appeal to the city hackers as well as the more advanced golfer who would like to experience a back-to-nature course. There are holes that make you feel like you are on a real trek with water, bridges and overgrown cart paths.

Be sure to stock up on provisions, especially water, as there are no on-course water stations, and the beverage cart came by only once during our round. The forward tees run about 4500 yards and the back tees range from 6200 to 7000 yards. There is easy check-in and cart availability with a suitable practice facility near the clubhouse.

The fairways are the best part of the course. The greens are medium-sized and cut to a very puttable speed. We have seen some good improvement to the course over the last few years. The bunkers in particular have improved with new sand, and some others are still a work in progress. On-course signage is a plus, and the entrance is easy to find with colorful signage by the road and at the entrance. This course has a chance to return to what it once was. Don't give up on it yet! If you're in the Owatonna area, get out there for an adventurous round and experience the improving Hidden Creek for yourself.

ID: 5506009MN

HIDDEN GREENS

12977 200th Street East
Hastings, MN 55033
Clubhouse: 651-437-3085
Golf Shop: 651-437-3085
Type: Public   Par: 72

www.hiddengreensgolf.com

Tees	Men's	Women's	Yards
Red		71.3/124	5379
White	68.9/121	74.5/131	5954
Blue	70.4/124		6289

Region: Twin Cities

Course Rating

HOSPITALITY	7.51
PLAYABILITY	5.81
USABILITY	8.01
FACILITY	7.58
VALUE	7.08

OVERALL SCORE
707

Greens Fee: $27.00 (weekend)
1/2 Cart Fee: $14.00 (weekend)

Hidden Greens is located just a few minutes south of Hastings, Minnesota, just off Highway 61. Keep your eyes open for their sign on the left about 4 miles south of town. We found the staff we encountered to be friendly and informative. There is a small clubhouse with some basic necessities, and limited menu selections. On weekends they grill burgers and dogs.

They have a grass driving range, and practice green adjacent to the clubhouse and a short distance from the first tee. Carts are available, although this course would be very walkable.

If you like trees, this is the course for you! On nearly every hole, trees can become a scoring/playing factor. This course was cut out of the woods and there is no escaping the abundance of trees and their wrath. On this fall day, the downed leaves were a definite factor, too. We found that the course length, at just under 6000 yards from the white tees, made the greens very reachable overall in regulation. The fairways are not impossibly narrow, but make no mistake: you will pay with strokes if you are not accurate with your drives and second shots.

On the front nine, the fairways seemed to be a bit tighter than the backside. When we did reach the greens we found them to be in excellent condition and quite playable. For the average golfer, the greens were good sized. There are only four or five bunkers on the entire course, and water comes into play on a couple holes, but is easily avoidable.

Because of all the trees, playing this course at other times during the year without falling leaves would have been a better time. Don't get us wrong though, we liked the course and again the greens were as good as we have played in the area and we found it hacker friendly as far as length and playability from the fairways. If you hit straight and relatively short, you should have a great time. If not….bring a few extra balls and be ready to give several strokes away when hitting back to the fairway from among the leaves and trees.

ID: 55033A08MN

HIDDEN HAVEN

20520 NE Polk Street
Cedar, MN 55011
Clubhouse: 763-434-4626
Golf Shop: 763-434-6867
Type: Public   Par: 71
www.hiddenhavengolfclub.com

U

Region: Twin Cities

Course Rating

HOSPITALITY	8.30
PLAYABILITY	7.66
USABILITY	9.06
FACILITY	7.62
VALUE	4.95

OVERALL SCORE
782

Tees	Men's	Women's	Yards
Red		68.8/122	4980
White	68.1/125	73.4/131	5806
Blue	68.9/126		5971

Greens Fee: $30.00 (weekend)
1/2 Cart Fee: $14.00 (weekend)

Hidden Haven Golf Club is closer than you think. Located in the North Metro suburb of Cedar, Minnesota, it's just off Highway 65. It's easy to find, and we found it to be true to its namesake—it really is a "hidden haven." Family owned and operated since 1988, it is open to the public. Tee times are handled by calling the course directly. Riding carts are available. There is a smaller pro shop on site, with a fair assortment of accessories and beverages and limited snacks for you at the turn. The main clubhouse, bar, and banquet rooms are located just across the street as you leave the front nine and proceed to the back nine. It was very well attended on this visit and there is a full menu, large bar, pool tables, games, etc. Happy hour drink specials were dirt cheap.

The course itself is well kept, with interesting holes, and landscaped and cared for quite well. There are several homes in close proximity to the course, so being in the fairway is at a premium. We golfed during the morning, so the course was not crowded at all. Check-in was easy and the staff on site was friendly and helpful. The course itself is great for the hacker. A very walkable course at just over 5800 yards from the white tees. Fairly placed greens that are reachable in regulation make it very user friendly for the average golfer. A negative in our minds were a few holes with out-of-bounds stakes too close to the fairways. We found ourselves making what we thought was a relatively good shot only to find as we approached our ball that we were out-of-bounds. Playing the course regularly would help us to avoid those areas. Greens were okay, but had a noticeable difference in cut length and speed from the front nine to the back. Flags on this day were placed fairly, but the greens do have plateaus and provide some challenge so some green reading is necessary.

All in all we enjoyed our day very much, found the course to be one we would enjoy playing again, and to our surprise (for no other reason than ignorance), it really was a hidden gem!

HIGHLAND NATIONAL

1403 Montreal Avenue
St. Paul, MN 55116
Clubhouse: 651-695-3774
Golf Shop: 651-695-3719
Type: Public   Par: 72
www.golfstpaul.org

Region: Twin Cities

Course Rating

HOSPITALITY	7.32
PLAYABILITY	6.58
USABILITY	7.04
FACILITY	6.35
VALUE	6.41

Tees	Men's	Women's	Yards
Red		69.8/121	5125
Blue	68.7/124	73.8/130	5843
White	70.3/128	75.7/134	6196
Black	72.4/131		6638

OVERALL SCORE
680

Greens Fee: $33.00 (weekend)
1/2 Cart Fee: $15.00 (weekend)

Reopened in 2005 after a $4.3 million facelift, Highland National Golf Course has been a fixture in St. Paul, Minnesota, since 1919, and since it has been around for so many years, it seems a bit neglected and in need of another facelift.

The clubhouse is of a Moorish design with a tiled roof and brick walls, and is starting to look its age. The men's bathrooms are actually down a flight of steep stairs, making it not very accessible, especially for those of us with bad knees. Inside it is just one big room with a fifties-era lunch counter that serves an inexpensive breakfast as well as typical golf course food.

This truly is a hacker's course with wide open fairways, ample greens that roll fast and true, and few hazards that will swallow your golf ball. Water is only a factor on the back nine, and the rough, regardless of where it is on the course, is friendly enough that you can usually find your ball again.

Like all busy urban courses, the staff is efficient, but a bit standoffish. There was no starter or public address system telling you who is next up on #1 or a marshal to rush you along if you are lagging, so you'll have to act like you've been to Highland before because no one is going to hold your hand.

The on-course signage is actually quite good for a popular urban course and finding your way along the cart paths is generally pretty intuitive. The golf course has historically had problems with drainage and if it rained recently, remember to wear the right shoes because water sticks around longer than average. The tee boxes and fairways are well maintained, the rough is not at all unruly, but the greens, although large, seemed a bit pockmarked causing a smartly struck putt to sometimes go a bit off line.

On-course, Highland National does most of the little things right with enough bathroom stops, benches and ball washers. It is just a bit tired and overworked. It could use a facelift and the City of St. Paul appears to recognize some of its issues and is currently renovating the #1 and #10 tee boxes and the main putting green.

146

ID: 5511608MN

HOLLYDALE

4710 Holly Lane North
Plymouth, MN 55446
Clubhouse: 763-559-9847
Golf Shop: 763-559-9847
Type: Public   Par: 71
www.hollydalegolf.com

Tees	Men's	Women's	Yards
Red		69.3/116	5128
Mixed		72.5/123	5666
White	68.8/116	74.0/126	5980
Blue	69.6/118		6160

Region: Twin Cities

Course Rating

HOSPITALITY   7.59
PLAYABILITY   6.92
USABILITY   7.54
FACILITY   6.42
VALUE   7.65

OVERALL SCORE
721

Greens Fee: $29.00 (weekend)
1/2 Cart Fee: $13.00 (weekend)

Hollydale Golf Course in Plymouth, Minnesota, is what would be called a ground-strokes course—a good place to work on your basic shots with little chance of running into any trouble. The 6160-yard course is compact. So compact there is very little need for directional signage. The fairways are wide open with the only hazards being mature trees. There are few if any bunkers and only a couple of holes require hitting near or over water.

Three tee boxes exist on most holes and the course has little if any cart paths. Hole distances are easy to find and the next tee box is only a short distance from the previous green. The greens, although reasonably large, don't require a difficult read because most are very flat with little contour. They were also, at the time of this review, oddly slow and probably in need of aeration.

This is an extremely walkable course because of its lack of length, compact facility and very few elevation changes. The driving range, which sits in the middle of the course, is reasonably priced and the putting area and parking lot are very close to the clubhouse. If you are looking for a fancy place to stop after your round, the clubhouse isn't the place. It is very utilitarian with a small kitchen, sitting area and check-in. The food offerings are very basic and what you expect for golf course cuisine. Check-in is manual and there are no online tee times available from their website.

Unlike area courses that might have a bigger name or are more popular, Hollydale is a little oasis situated in residential Plymouth. Think of a miniature New York's Central Park. It isn't expensive to play here, generally isn't busy and it is close by for those living on the west side of the Twin Cities.

This won't become your favorite course that you play every weekend, but the course is extremely hacker friendly and something you'd want to play on occasion when you want to work on your game. Hollydale prices itself as a good value while still keeping it just enough of a challenge to let the golfer feel good when he/she has finished for the day.

ID: 5544608MN

HYLAND GREENS Exec. 18

Region: Twin Cities

10100 Normandale Boulevard
Bloomington, MN 55437
Clubhouse: 952-563-8868
Golf Shop: 952-563-8868
Type: Public   Par: 54

www.ci.bloomington.mn.us

Tees	Men's	Women's	Yards
Forward	54.0	54.0	2820

Course Rating

HOSPITALITY	7.90
PLAYABILITY	5.99
USABILITY	7.29
FACILITY	6.21
VALUE	6.02

OVERALL SCORE
676

Greens Fee: $23.00 (weekend)
1/2 Cart Fee: $10.00 (weekend)

In less than three hours you should be able to play Hyland Greens Golf Course, a compact executive eighteen. Located in Bloomington, Minnesota, the course is actually two separate 9-hole courses with very fancy names: the long-9 and the short-9. As with any par-3 course, you can leave your driver in the car because the longest hole is just 193 yards.

As you enter the parking lot, you've got a small clubhouse in front of you and the driving range to your right. The range has separate hitting bays, but you'll tee off on permanent mats because there is no option for hitting off the grass. The clubhouse is very simple and you can tell by the few golf carts that this course is very popular with walkers. A small putting green is available just behind the clubhouse and inside the building is just the basics in both the food and sitting area.

The first tee for both courses is just steps from the clubhouse's front door so you can wait for your tee time sipping a beer inside. Interestingly, the long-9 takes reservations and the short-9 doesn't. Also, you can't play all eighteen together. You pay for one course ($13 for the long course), check back in and then pay for the second ($10 for the short course).

The course itself is nicely manicured, if a bit austere. There is very little by way of hazards, except a few holes where you will have to hit around or over water hazards. The holes are pretty straightforward with typical lengths of 135, 174 and 193 yards on the long course and holes as short as 90 yards on the short course. Water is available on the course and there is at least one bathroom for each course. Food in the clubhouse is basic course grub and is quite reasonably priced.

If pace of play is what you are looking for you'll be able to complete the long-9 in 1 ½ hours and the short-9 even faster. If this course ever becomes a 4-hour ordeal then you are wasting way too much time. Leave your woods at home and make this a course where you work on your irons. Once you have solved them at this course, you'll be well on your way to having success with them at a longer course.

ID: 5543708MN

INVER WOOD

1850 70th Street East
Inver Grove Heights, MN 55077
Clubhouse: 651-457-3667
Golf Shop: 651-457-3667
Type: Public   Par: 72
www.inverwood.org

Region: Twin Cities

Course Rating

HOSPITALITY	7.61
PLAYABILITY	7.86
USABILITY	7.64
FACILITY	8.29
VALUE	6.19

Tees	Men's	Women's	Yards
Red		71.0/126	5175
Gold	69.0/125	74.4/134	5795
White	70.8/130		6194
Blue	73.2/144		6724

OVERALL SCORE
765

Greens Fee: $36.00 (weekend)
1/2 Cart Fee: $17.00 (weekend)

The moment that you pull into the Inver Wood Golf Course, you know you're at a course that does things in a big way. From the large parking lot, the huge driving range to the broad fairways, this is a course that means business.

The modern clubhouse facility is alongside one of the biggest driving ranges in the Twin Cities. This range may be a bit more expensive for a bucket, but it goes well beyond just a couple of distance targets, with mock fairways and sand traps to hone your shots. Inside the clubhouse is a nice sandwich grill which goes beyond the typical golf course fare.

When you hit the course, you'd better be ready for a workout because it is very hilly and not very walkable. In addition to being an aerobic workout, it also has a 144 slope which is a testament to both the elevation changes as well as the difficulty. If you take a cart you will never lose your way because the paths are well designed and as long as you stay on them, you'll find the next hole. Another great feature are the distance markers. Markers are embedded in the course every 25 yards from 200 yards in so you will always know what club to pull from your bag.

Overall, this course is well tended, intimidating, long and deceptively hard. It is not for the faint of heart. Although the fairways are large and wide, if you can't keep your drives straight, you will find numerous ways to lose golf balls with tree-lined fairway edges and many areas of deep rough. Also, even after a good shot, don't think that you are completely safe because the course offers a number of strategically placed sand bunkers just waiting to swallow your golf ball.

Inver Wood Golf Course may be a bit more expensive than other local courses, but if you are looking for a real golfing challenge at a high quality facility, it's worth the extra cost.

ID: 5507708MN

IRISH HILLS

6116 Wildamere Drive
Pine River, MN 56474
Clubhouse: 218-587-2296
Golf Shop: 218-587-2296
Type: Public Par: 72

www.pineyridge.com

Tees	Men's	Women's	Yards
Purple			
Gold	Par/Slope Information Unavailable		
White			
Green	67.8/115		5739

NOTE: website was not working at presstime (Jan-2010)
so par/slope and pricing are estimated.

Region: NorthEast

Course Rating

HOSPITALITY 7.83
PLAYABILITY 5.96
USABILITY 6.61
FACILITY 6.22
VALUE 6.99

OVERALL SCORE
670

Green Fee: $29.50 (weekend)
1/2 Cart Fee: $14 (weekend)

Irish Hills Golf Course, located in Pine River, Minnesota, is adjacent to the Piney Ridge resort. This is the kind of up-north resort that you'd imagine: simple cabins, a very small bar/lounge, a postage-stamp-sized pool and 18 holes of golf.

A round of golf at Irish Hills is only $22 plus cart; it is probably the cheapest you'll find anywhere in the Brainerd Lakes area. You don't go to Irish Hills for the accommodations, the nicely manicured greens or the food selection, though. You go for cheap golf. It's not a long course; it plays at just over 6000 yards, and the longest hole tops out at only 511 yards. Most people will play from the middle tees, but you might at well play from the backs because half the hole lengths are almost indistinguishable from each other. The course is surrounded by pine trees, but they generally don't come into play. Water hazards, even in the rainy season, are merely decorative and don't pose a problem. Sand, what there is of it, isn't anything to worry about. When we visited the course late in the season, it had seen limited maintenance and the greens were left long, allowing us to be quite assertive on our putts.

Food selection in the clubhouse is bare bones, but there is a full menu at The Pub at Piney Ridge. One perk is that while on the course, you can order a limited menu of burgers, pizza and sandwiches from The Pub and it will be brought out to wherever you are on the course.

At Irish Hills you will not find a ranger telling you to play faster or an ornery front-desk person at checkout scowling because you're taking too long. If you're a beer-and-brat kind of golfer, you'll be right at home here. When you're done, remember to keep your scorecard for a drink special at the bar. If you're looking for fancy northern Minnesota summer golf, this is not the course for you. If you've got a tight budget and don't care about the frills, Irish Hills Golf Course will be easy on your wallet and your golf ego.

ID: 5647409MN

ISLAND PINE

Region: WestCentral

1601 Wyoming Avenue West
Atwater, MN 56209
Clubhouse: 320-974-8600
Golf Shop: 320-974-8600
Type: Public   Par: 72
www.islandpinegolf.com

H

Course Rating

HOSPITALITY   9.08
PLAYABILITY   6.63
USABILITY   7.99
FACILITY   7.84
VALUE   5.16

OVERALL SCORE
755

Green Fee: $24 (weekend)
1/2 Cart Fee: $14 (weekend)

Tees	Men's	Women's	Yards
Red		70.3/123	5194
Gold	68.2/125		5772
White	70.8/130		6336
Blue	72.9/135		6799

When we called to set up a tee time at Island Pine Golf Club in Atwater, Minnesota, we told them that we wanted to start before 6:00 a.m. The person on the other end of the phone admitted that no one was there until after eight, but since we were willing to walk the first nine, they gave us the okay to get on the course and sign in before the 10th tee. We finished the first nine, picked up a cart and continued playing. You've got to like small-town golf.

Our first impression of the course, located in central Minnesota, was that it is flat, open and uninteresting. But that view quickly changed. Almost every hole has an interesting angle associated with it. The 1st hole is hidden behind a pond with four-feet-high reeds surrounding it. The 2nd hole's fairway (a par 5) is U-shaped (250 yards east, then 250 yards north, then 100 yards west). The 11th hole has an S-shaped fairway, with the green almost completely surrounded by water (and swamp). The 18th hole is on an island (we lost three balls to the pond surrounding it).

This is a most enjoyable course! The greens are in good shape, the fairways are well mowed, and the roughs are really deep. The carts are gas-powered, but the course is easily walkable, so carts aren't a necessity. There are a few cart paths, but for the most part people drive everywhere except on the greens. The clubhouse is small, but it has a fair collection of clubs, balls, etc. It's typically outfitted for this type of course. The small snack bar has four tables and a limited supply of food and drinks. (The hamburgers are quite good and reasonably priced, by the way.) The course has a small putting green but no driving range. There was no water on the course and only a few portable bathrooms. The staff is quite friendly and makes up for what the course might have lacked. While on the 10th fairway the owner drove up and we talked for 15 minutes about how he had farmed the land before turning it into a golf course in 1995. This is the kind of course that makes you want to visit again.

ISLAND VIEW

7795 Laketown Parkway
Waconia, MN 55387
Clubhouse: 952-442-6116
Golf Shop: 952-442-6116 x2
Type: Semi-Private Par: 72
www.islandviewgolfclub.com

Tees	Men's	Women's	Yards
Red		71.2/125	5385
Gold	67.6/125	72.9/129	5710
White	75.9/135	70.0/130	6252
Blue	71.4/133		6552

Region: WestCentral

Course Rating

HOSPITALITY	8.19
PLAYABILITY	7.77
USABILITY	7.76
FACILITY	7.67
VALUE	6.30

OVERALL SCORE
771

Green Fee: $52 (weekend)
1/2 Cart Fee: $17 (weekend)

Island View Golf Club is a beautiful golf course located off of Lake Waconia in Waconia, Minnesota. Although it is not an overly long course, it has many challenges and hazards that make it an interesting and fun course to play. Many of the holes have that postcard feel that one looks for when playing golf.

This 1960-built course is a very mature course with lots of large trees lining the fairways, which surprisingly do not overly punish those who stray off course. It has a number of holes where water comes into play and appropriately placed bunkers, yet it plays very fair, and one can still score well without too much trouble. The staff at Island View takes great pride in their course and it shows. The fairways, greens and tee boxes are in very good shape, being well-watered and nicely manicured. They are also very proud of their pace-of-play. In fact, the golf pro mentioned that a four-hour round is their claim to fame. The ranger does a good job of keeping everybody on pace without being bossy or pushy.

Island View is a semi-private course that is open to the public. It has full and associate memberships available but does limit the amount of total memberships allowed to prevent the course from being overplayed. This course has an attractive and extensive clubhouse that features a pro shop, men's and women's locker rooms, a restaurant with a full bar and banquet facilities for weddings and receptions. The restaurant has a nice happy hour with reduced pricing on a number of items as well as a good selection on beers on tap.

The pro shop, although somewhat small, is well-stocked with all the necessities (balls, gloves, shoes, clubs and apparel), with prices that that are pretty average for most pro shops. The course also has a driving range, putting green and chipping area that are all in close proximity to the clubhouse, which makes them very convenient and easy to use before your round.

ID: 5538709MN

IZATY'S BLACK BROOK

Region: NorthEast

40005 85th Avenue
Onamia, MN 56359
Clubhouse: 320-532-4574
Golf Shop: 320-532-4574
Type: Public   Par: 72
www.izatys.com

P
V

Course Rating

HOSPITALITY	8.34
PLAYABILITY	8.80
USABILITY	8.13
FACILITY	8.45
VALUE	7.70

OVERALL SCORE
839

Tees	Men's	Women's	Yards
Forward		71.8/131	5119
Resort	70.0/133	75.7/139	5821
Championship	72.6/139		6391
Tournament	74.3/140		6792

Green Fee: $39 (weekend)
1/2 Cart Fee: included in fee

Black Brook is back. After some downtime the course has reopened and re-hired former employees to get it back in shape. The resort is located between Onamia and Isle, Minnesota, on the shores of Lake Mille Lacs, and boasts a hotel, condos, marina, full-service restaurants, a pool and the formidable 18 holes of golf. The Sanctuary course, which always seemed to be underwater, is now closed and the staff can concentrate on Black Brook, the tougher and more scenic of the two.

Don't think for a moment that this is a walk in the park. Black Brook is a nature refuge with bogs, ponds, trees, creeks and Mille Lacs Lake at one edge. In the middle of all of that, course designer John Harbottle managed to drop 18 fairways, tees and greens. It is beautiful to look at and a real test to play. Hackers need to refer to the guide on the scorecard to select the proper set of tees for their ability. Once you have done that, you will experience a very good test of golf on a beautiful track. Just make sure you have a dozen golf balls because the hazards at Black Brook are always hungry.

The course is in excellent condition. The greens are contoured but true and the fairways are plush and well maintained. Cart paths are blacktopped so it is nearly impossible to get lost. Signage and the scorecard take the mystery out of the course. What you see is what you get, and what you see is a beautiful piece of central Minnesota lake country. The signature 14th hole borders Lake Mille Lacs and is worth the very reasonable $29 green fee to play.

The clubhouse is well stocked and the employees are well dressed, courteous and helpful. A beverage cart stops by on a regular basis, and your after-golf needs are well served by a full-service bar/restaurant with a deck that overlooks the pool. Black Brook is not the most hacker friendly course we have played, but it is so well maintained and is such a value that it has to be on your list of places to seriously consider when you are in the Mille Lacs area.

ID: 5635909MN

KELLER

Region: Twin Cities

2166 Maplewood Drive
St. Paul, MN 55109
Clubhouse: 651-766-4176
Golf Shop: 651-766-4170
Type: Public   Par: 72

www.ramseycountygolf.com

Tees	Men's	Women's	Yards
Red	66.4/119	71.5/129	5373
White	69.4/125	75.2/136	6041
White/Blue	69.8/129		6160
Blue	71.5/132		6566

Course Rating

HOSPITALITY	6.70
PLAYABILITY	7.49
USABILITY	6.91
FACILITY	6.48
VALUE	5.84

OVERALL SCORE
686

Greens Fee: $34.00 (weekend)
1/2 Cart Fee: $13.00 (weekend)

Stepping onto Keller Golf Course is like stepping back into time when the course was a regular on the PGA Tour and golf luminaries like Ken Venturi and Sam Snead were winning the annual St. Paul Open. No longer a stop on the PGA Tour because at 6566 yards it has become obsolete, it still is a stiff test for regular golfers.

Although it's been forty years since a professional golf event has been played here, Keller still has the feel of a private course with walls lined with awards, photos and tournament history. Golfers check in at the small pro shop and pick up their golf cart from a very friendly "cartman." Like in decades past, your name is called when your group is scheduled to tee off on #1, just steps away.

As soon as you hit your first drive, you will know you are on a course that is different than any other in the area, with tight doglegs, narrow fairways, elevated greens and par 3s that will test your nerve. This reviewer played the course from the blue tees, but most hackers should really consider playing from the 6041-yard white tees because it plays much longer than on paper and course knowledge will really help your score.

The course is well tended, the greens are fast and the cart service is frequent. What isn't up to par, especially for those playing the course for the first time, is the signage, yardage markers and the scorecard. As you step onto each tee box, a sign does show the distances, but finding yardage markers in the fairways is often a challenge. Also, the hole flags don't specify pin placement. Some holes only show one yardage marker thus making club selection more of a guess than should be necessary.

Keller is an Audubon-certified course with bluebird houses and restoration areas acting as out-of-bounds hazards. If you like to walk, you might want to think twice because it is quite hilly, especially the back nine. Another thing that holds this course back is its reputation for slow play, so playing during off times is a safer bet to avoiding those long rounds.

ID: 5510908MN

KIMBALL

11823 County Road 150
Kimball, MN 55353
Clubhouse: 320-398-2285
Golf Shop: 320-398-2285
Type: Semi-Private   Par: 72
www.kimballgolf.com

Region: WestCentral

Course Rating

HOSPITALITY	6.69
PLAYABILITY	5.88
USABILITY	7.14
FACILITY	5.88
VALUE	6.22

OVERALL SCORE
637

Tees	Men's	Women's	Yards
Red		71.0/116	5323
Gold	67.3/116	72.8/120	5658
White	70.6/123		6389
Blue	71.7/125		6652

Green Fee: $31 (weekend)
1/2 Cart Fee: $14 (weekend)

Kimball Golf Club in Kimball, Minnesota, is located about 30 minutes west of St. Cloud on Highway 15. The directions on their website are easy to follow, and there are obvious signs on the highway. The signs on the course are well laid out and easy to follow, even though you will overlap going from some of the greens to the next tee box.

The clubhouse is small and the amenities are limited. The snack bar, check-in desk and pro shop are all located together. The merchandise for the pro shop is on display at one end of the snack area and seems to be fairly cluttered, but you'll find all the items you'd see in any golf course's pro shop. There is ample parking and the golf carts are parked right in front of the clubhouse for easy access. The snack bar is limited on selections, including chips, pretzels and precooked hot dogs and hamburgers.

There is a driving range across from the clubhouse, and the putting green is on the other side of clubhouse. This is not a course that you would want to walk, simply due to a fairly heavy slope to the course, but if you do choose to walk it, there is a small tram from the 2nd green to the 3rd tee to get you and your clubs to the top. While the slope may make walking an adventure, it also adds excitement when playing the different holes. Mature trees also define the landscape. The course would have been tougher had there been enough rain to bring the water hazards into play, but the lack of water made our game better simply because water is like a magnet for golf balls. Typically, though, water comes into play on 11 of the 18 holes. The 15th hole, their signature hole, is a 297-yard par 4, but don't let the size tease you. This hole takes a hard dogleg left to an island green. You will want to lay up and use a short iron to get on the green. This is a fun hole. For the price, Kimball Golf Club is worth driving a little farther to find a round. The staff is friendly and knowledgeable, and the patrons are courteous and polite.

ID: 5535309MN

KORONIS HILLS

Region: WestCentral

29757 State Highway
Paynesville, MN 56362
Clubhouse: 320-243-4111
Golf Shop: 320-243-4111
Type: Semi-Private Par: 71
www.koronishillsgolf.com

V

Course Rating

HOSPITALITY	8.37
PLAYABILITY	8.10
USABILITY	8.68
FACILITY	8.37
VALUE	7.80

OVERALL SCORE
830

Tees	Men's	Women's	Yards
Green	64.7/115	69.6/118	5054
White	69.0/124	75.0/129	6005
Blue	70.1/127	76.2/132	6218

Green Fee: $30 (weekend)
1/2 Cart Fee: $14 (weekend)

Koronis Hills Golf Course in Paynesville, Minnesota, is very impressive on arrival. The beautiful flowers at the entrance are so high that you can barely make out the sign (on giant rocks) for the club. The landscaping around the clubhouse is great, and many well-cared-for plants and flowers make it very inviting. Koronis Hills is a semi-private course that is open to the public. The staff is very accommodating and helpful. The clubhouse has a good supply of merchandise that is reasonably priced. Range balls are inexpensive for a good-sized bucket, and the driving range is convenient and well marked. The carts are clean and in good condition. The course itself is very scenic. There are many huge trees and the views from everywhere are great. There are some narrow fairways because of the many trees, but it's very pretty and isn't too much of a problem. We hackers didn't lose very many balls.

The tee boxes could use some work—they seem to have a lot of divots. It appeared that either the course had a tournament recently or it just gets a lot of play. The tees are blue, white and green, but some are not facing in the direction to hit. There are a lot of yardage markers—not just sprinkler heads—in addition to the 200, 150 and 100. We didn't figure out until we finished that pin placements are marked with caps on the 150 markers.

All of the tee boxes are marked with large granite stones showing the layout, even on the forward tees. The forward tees also have ball washers and benches. The whole course is in great shape (except for the divots at the tees). They had punched the greens, but they were pretty good considering that.

The only real disappointment of our day was that there was nothing to eat. They had chips and candy but said they were completely out of sandwiches, which seems strange for a Sunday. Also, there was no sign of a beverage cart, but there was plenty of pop and beer in the clubhouse. Staff and other golfers are very pleasant. Overall it's a very pretty and fun course to play!

ID: 5636209MN

LAKE CITY

33587 Lakeview Drive
Lake City, MN 55041
Clubhouse: 651-345-3221
Golf Shop: 651-345-3221
Type: Public   Par: 71
www.lakecitygolf.com

Region: SouthEast

Course Rating

HOSPITALITY	7.49
PLAYABILITY	8.05
USABILITY	8.60
FACILITY	8.12
VALUE	6.58

OVERALL SCORE
788

Green Fee: $31 (weekend)
1/2 Cart Fee: $13 (weekend)

Tees	Men's	Women's	Yards
Red		69.1/119	5028
White	68.6/124	74.0/130	5903
Blue	70.9/128		6410

When we arrived at Lake City Country Club, we could see that we were in for a treat. Upon arriving we saw a sand beach on one of the holes and a small water fountain spouting from a pond on another. The clubhouse attendants are very friendly and helpful. The course is easy to find by following signs on Highway 61.

This course plays 6410 yards from the championship tees, which is great for the hacker; however, the trees and bunkers could definitely play a few tricks on the unfortunate soul who hits loose tee shots. Hole #1 greets you with two beautiful water hazards. Number 16 is one of the challenging holes—you have to lay up with an iron as opposed to trying to drive the green and placing the ball in a favorable spot. You have to strategically place your balls to be successful here. Using a cart is advised, as there are some steep hills on the course, but if you like to climb mountains, then go for the walk.

Hole signs show the distance needed to carry the hazards, making club selection easier for the everyday hacker. The tee boxes are nicely taken care of and the fairways are watered—both have only a few slight glitches of grass. The bunkers are hard as a rock, so they're more difficult to hit out of. The pro shop has golf equipment and apparel for sale, as well as beer, snacks and pop. A dining room and a bar and grill in the clubhouse offers meals from steak to chicken and everything in between. The deck on the clubhouse oversees the beautiful 18th green. The average golfer has a good chance of scoring well here, but trees, bunkers and water hazards try to slow you down. Some fairways are extremely thin and are surrounded by out-of-bounds, making for more of a challenge. The driving range is wide but short—it's for the golfer working on strategically placed shots, not for someone working on distance. Holes are easily marked. You'll never have trouble finding your way around the course. We recommend this course to the average golfer; it's definitely worth the trip to play here.

ID: 5504109MN

LAKE MILTONA

3868 County Road 5 NE
Alexandria, MN 56308
Clubhouse: 320-852-7078
Golf Shop: 320-852-7078
Type: Public   Par: 72

www.lakemiltonagolfclub.com

Tees	Men's	Women's	Yards
Red		70.7/121	5379
White	69.1/121	74.6/129	6096
Blue	70.8/124		6470

Region: WestCentral

Course Rating

HOSPITALITY   8.70
PLAYABILITY   8.28
USABILITY   8.52
FACILITY   7.82
VALUE   7.11

OVERALL SCORE
825

Green Fee: $31 (weekend)
1/2 Cart Fee: $13.25 (weekend)

If you haven't played Lake Miltona Golf Club recently, you'll be pleasantly surprised by the major improvements in the past years. Voted the #2 course to play in the Alexandria area by locals, the course is set to see more improvements over the coming years to increase its competitive presence with the other well-known courses in the Alexandria area. While the 6470-yard par-72 course isn't all that long, there are plenty of doglegs to keep the average golfer engaged. Electric carts are available but the course is walkable, with only a few spots requiring a bit of a jaunt between holes.

Lake Miltona Golf Club is conveniently located about ten minutes north of downtown Alexandria. The overall layout of the clubhouse, practice green and driving range is practical. The clubhouse has a smaller than usual selection of golf equipment and apparel, but it's fairly priced. There is a nice grill for a burger, chicken sandwich or appetizer sampler to enjoy after your round.

Several of the course's aspects are aesthetically pleasing—the layout, the lushness and the large greens, to name a few. But don't let appearances deceive. The greens, albeit large, are rather hard (largely due to the lack of rain), and we found it challenging to keep the ball on when hitting approach shots. The greens also proved a challenge for putting, but that's probably the karma one gets for the overall yardage being slightly shorter for a par-72.

We wish there was a bit more in the way of signage at the tees (i.e., hole diagrams), but the tee boxes are all in good condition, as are the fairways. The rough is of average length, with only a few places where the length could totally swallow your ball. The few places that water comes into play don't cause you to over think shots, and the sand is well groomed and forgiving. Overall, Lake Miltona Golf Club is a great Minnesota golf course. While the length is a tad shorter than other area par-72 courses, the greens more than make up for that and will provide ample challenge to most golfers.

ID: 5630809MN

LAKE PEPIN

70895 260th Avenue
Lake City, MN 55041
Clubhouse: 651-345-5768
Golf Shop: 651-345-5768
Type: Public   Par: 72
www.lakepepingolf.com

Region: SouthEast

Course Rating

HOSPITALITY	6.73
PLAYABILITY	5.86
USABILITY	5.86
FACILITY	6.03
VALUE	6.11

OVERALL SCORE
613

Green Fee: $25 (weekend)
1/2 Cart Fee: $13 (weekend)

Tees	Men's	Women's	Yards
Red		70.4/117	5281
White	70.0/124	75.7/128	6231
Blue	72.4/129		6752

The Schmidt family owns this relatively new golf course. It was their five-generation family farm until quite recently. Getting there takes a bit of planning, though. To find Lake Pepin Golf Course, you will drive through fields onto a gravel road. But it is worth the drive if you like to try new and challenging courses with a little adventure thrown in. Before we played, we called to ask if there was anything we should know before we started. Karen Schmidt, who picked up the phone, laughingly said we would play better if we attended church first and brought a lot of balls.

The front and back nines were designed by two different parties, but all in all, this course is all about beautiful, panoramic views. It sits atop the Lake Pepin River Valley, and everywhere you look there is unbelievable beauty. Views of the river can be found from 12 holes. Another factor that comes into play is the wind; a windy day makes this a very challenging course. Narrow fairways with a very healthy rough line each hole and are just a few feet wide at the green on most of the holes. If you appreciate links courses you will love this one.

The greens and tees are very well maintained. There are three tee boxes, but the yardage distance is only available at the back tees, which can be a little irritating if you don't play from there. Finding the back nine is a little difficult, so get directions and keep in mind you will have to go through the parking lot and across a road to get there. Better signage would make the journey a lot easier. The course pricing is extremely reasonable, and they have even better deals on Wednesdays. The gas golf carts are newer and clean, and the course has a very basic driving range. Once you have completed your round, the clubhouse has a great deck with those fabulous panoramic views we mentioned. Take time to look at the family photos and memorabilia that is dispersed throughout the interior. You can appreciate what the Schmidt family has done with their golf course.

ID: 5504109MN

LAKEVIEW Exec. 18

24692 County Highway 22
Detroit Lakes, MN 56501
Clubhouse: 218-847-8942
Golf Shop: 218-847-8942
Type: Public Par: 64
www.detroitcountryclub.com

Tees	Men's	Women's	Yards
Red		62.9/103	3986
White	60.8/101	64.6/107	4307

Region: NorthWest

Course Rating

HOSPITALITY	7.52
PLAYABILITY	6.95
USABILITY	8.08
FACILITY	7.18
VALUE	6.30

OVERALL SCORE
729

Green Fee: $25 (weekend)
1/2 Cart Fee: $11 (weekend)

Located just south of Detroit Lakes, Minnesota, the Lakeview Golf Course is a 4307-yard par-64 executive course. Next door to the Detroit Lakes Country Club, Lakeview is a hidden gem that most people pass by to play the big course up the hill, but think twice before you pass it by. It is equal to any traditional course, just shorter. Lakeview is a fully mature layout with modestly rolling hills; numerous cottonwoods, oaks and pines; and very little water. The course's strong suit is the design of the course itself. The layout does as much as it can with its limited distance by rarely having a flat green.

Where the course seems to fall down a bit is on maintenance and on-course reinvestment. While the greens and tee boxes are in good condition, bunkers are ragged around the edges with pebbly sand. Fortunately there aren't too many to worry about. Distance markers are sunken disks and appear only at 200 and 100 yards. Cart paths are almost nonexistent, but because of the compact layout, carts are not really needed. This really is a walker's course.

The difference between the white tees and the reds is only 300 yards, so men and women are basically playing the same course. Although tee boxes are in good condition, the benches, signage, colored markers and trash cans could be upgraded because they've seen better days. The course does have a putting area and a driving range, but be careful of errant drives because the driving range runs parallel to both hole #1 and #15, and it doesn't have netting.

The clubhouse is small with limited merchandise. It also appears to only serve food out of machines. There is a very small outdoor sitting area, but this isn't the place to loiter. A better option would be the restaurant and bar at the Detroit Lakes Country Club, which is open to the public. For golfers in the Detroit Lakes area hoping to get a round completed in about three hours, this is the place. It is very hacker friendly without major obstacles to prevent a good score. Also, paying $25 for 18 holes can't be bad, either.

ID: 5650109MN

LAKEVIEW

405 North Arm Drive
Mound, MN 55364
Clubhouse: 952-472-3459
Golf Shop: 952-472-3459
Type: Public Par: 69

www.lakeviewgolfoforono.com

Tees	Men's	Women's	Yards
Red		68.6/113	4907
White	65.9/111	70.9/118	5322
Blue	66.8/112		5517

Course Rating

HOSPITALITY   7.16
PLAYABILITY   6.67
USABILITY   7.76
FACILITY   6.99
VALUE   5.17

OVERALL SCORE
691

Greens Fee: $29.00 (weekend)
1/2 Cart Fee: $14.00 (weekend)

Before Pioneer Creek, Timber Creek, Bluff Creek, Deer Run and Chaska Town Course, there was Lakeview Golf Course in Orono, Minnesota. Built in 1952, it is one of the oldest courses on the westside of the Twin Cities and was built before the age of titanium, graphite and space-age golf balls.

The course has no driving range, has a very small practice green and parking area, a cramped waiting area to tee off and a simple clubhouse. It was built before golf carts were common and before the Twin Cities grew out to meet the course. It doesn't have much by way of the 19th hole except a charming little patio with a few tables. Yet, you don't visit Lakeview for the clubhouse, you come for the car trip around Lake Minnetonka, charming horse farms, and most certainly the golf.

Lakeview is a compact course at 5517 yards, and has many mature trees and a beautiful pond that makes for a wonderful approach shot on the par-4 #13. Don't let the course's lack of length fool you. It isn't as easy as it sounds. The course does all it can to make life difficult with contoured greens and blind approach shots. Although you only really need to pull out your driver on three holes, it will punish you if you land your ball in the wrong place. Overall, it is a very walkable course with a smart layout and short distances between green and tee box.

The course is well maintained and it looks like it puts most of its money there because on-course amenities are few with only one bathroom witnessed when we were there and no water coolers, so bring your own. A typical round can be completed in 3 ½ hours, but one thing to be aware of is if you plan on playing during a busy summer weekend, expect it to back up.

This course is one of those that doesn't get the attention it deserves and has quietly stood the test of time for more than 55 years. When you decide to play Lakeview, you are also getting a great value at only $29 for a weekend round, well worth the price of admission and one of the best deals in the Twin Cities.

LAKEVIEW NATIONAL

Region: NorthWest

1349 Highway 61
Two Harbors, MN 55616
Clubhouse: 218-834-2664
Golf Shop: 218-834-2664
Type: Public   Par: 72

www.lakeviewnational.com

Tees	Men's	Women's	Yards
Red	70.7/120		5251
White	70.4/126	76.7/132	6330
Blue	72.5/130		6773

Course Rating

HOSPITALITY   8.45
PLAYABILITY   5.67
USABILITY   8.00
FACILITY   5.31
VALUE   5.69

OVERALL SCORE
678

Green Fee: $25 (weekend)
1/2 Cart Fee: $14 (weekend)

Lakeview National is located in Two Harbors, Minnesota, approximately four hours northeast of the Twin Cities and about thirty minutes north of Duluth. The course is 18 holes with 4 sets of tees. The full yardage is 6,773 from the blues. The golf course is mostly flat with some small hills. There were goose droppings on the course, particularly the first fairway that made your stomach turn. On some holes, it was difficult to determine the fairways from the roughs as the fairways were not well maintained and were left with weeds that resembled the rough. Our group determined that the course was in need of major reinvestment, perhaps as much as $300,000, to bring it up to quality golf standards.

The pro shop is located adjacent to the golf course. It appeared that there was some sort of restaurant/bar but neither were open possibly due to being near the end of the season or the weather. The clubhouse was warm and had a large flat screen HD TV where the person on duty and other patrons were watching the Minnesota/Wisconsin football game. We played in light rain throughout the round.

The course has good signage. However, the cart paths were mostly rock or gravel. The greens had just been aerated a few days before but the sand had been recklessly applied to the greens making them difficult to putt on. The manager was very cordial on the phone. The person working in the pro shop was very nice. He made sure the carts were ready, made coffee and made sure we knew where the first tee was. He was inquisitive as to why we came to play and what we thought of the golf course during and after the round. The golf course is probably acceptable to Two Harbors residents because it is a course that is not terribly difficult or expensive. For those of us who are looking for a quality golf experience, we would seek out other courses that have established themselves as quality courses in the northeastern Minnesota area.

162

ID: 5561609MN

LE SUEUR

36195 311th Avenue
Le Sueur, MN 56058
Clubhouse: 507-665-2291
Golf Shop: 507-665-6292
Type: Semi-Private Par: 72

www.lesueurcountryclub.com

Tees	Men's	Women's	Yards
Red	65.1/117	69.5/120	5030
White	66.4/121	71.2/123	5329
Blue	70.0/128	75.5/133	6117
Black	71.1/130	76.9/135	6365

Region: SouthWest

Course Rating

HOSPITALITY	8.69
PLAYABILITY	8.74
USABILITY	6.63
FACILITY	8.89
VALUE	5.93

P
F

OVERALL SCORE
805

Green Fee: $49 (weekend)
1/2 Cart Fee: $22 (weekend)

After you golf a few rounds on a few courses for a few years, sometimes cours-es start to feel the same, and it is a struggle to find traits that differentiate a good golf experience from the average. But the golf course at the LeSueur Country Club pleasantly surprised us. From the minute we arrived until we left, our experience was top rate. When we arrived in the parking lot, the pro met us with our carts and gave us a short verbal tour of the course; pointed out the driving range, putting green and chipping area; then directed us to the 1st tee and showed us where the 10th tee is after the turn. The attention to detail was clear in his approach, which we would guess is his normal guest interaction and philosophy.

The course itself is located about an hour southwest of the Metro area, a couple miles outside of LeSueur. The course is semi private and does have memberships available—options are detailed on their website. In existence since 1926, this is a well-established traditional course. Mature trees, great views and interesting holes add to its appeal. It is a country club in the sense that it seems to have a longstanding tradition and philosophy to provide a wonderful, quality golf experience. There is a clubhouse, full bar and restau-rant, nice patio, swimming pool, driving range with complimentary unlimited balls, chipping green and practice bunker. It really does have it all.

From a hacker's perspective, this course is fair and not overly long. The course offers varied holes, great views and fair scoring chances. The 14th hole has to be one of the prettiest in the southern half of Minnesota. The greens are exceptionally well-kept and rolled very true. Kudos to the grounds crew—and ultimately the golfers—who take time to repair ball marks and divots. There are a few blind driving holes and some hills (carts are recommended) that may give you an up- or downhill lie, but we struggle to find any criticism of the course. Rest assured you will enjoy your day here, and we're certain it will become one of your favorites.

ID: 5605809MN

LEGACY

1515 Shumway Avenue
Faribault, MN 55021
Clubhouse: 507-332-7177
Golf Shop: 507-332-7177
Type: Public   Par: 72
www.legacygolf.net

Tees	Men's	Women's	Yards
Yellow	65.1/121	69.5/120	5031
White	69.5/129	74.9/133	6002
Black	71.4/134		6416

Region: SouthEast

Course Rating

HOSPITALITY   6.80
PLAYABILITY   7.23
USABILITY   6.94
FACILITY   6.51
VALUE   5.39

OVERALL SCORE
677

Green Fee: $35 (weekend)
1/2 Cart Fee: $16 (weekend)

About 30 minutes south of the Metro in Faribault, Minnesota, is Legacy Golf Course. The course opened in 1998 and it evolved into a full 18-hole championship course. Previously, the Shattuck-St. Mary's School utilized part of the land as a 9-hole course, which dates to the 1920s. The end result is a course that offers a sampling of different styles and terrain, all in one round. Some holes feature a traditional layout with rolling hills and tree-lined fairways and then transition to a links-style course.

This course was well kept and the greens were in excellent condition when we played in August. The clubhouse, while not large or extravagant, does nevertheless provide the basic necessities. Amenities include a driving range and a large putting green that's immaculate. The course does offer matinee pricing, for those who don't mind playing during midday and a special promo MVP card with some nice discounts attached. Four sets of tees, one for juniors, make this course accessible for all players.

The average player will likely find this course to be challenging, yet playable. While it is always easier to play from the fairway, we found that an errant drive doesn't automatic result in a bogey or worse. There are opportunities to recover. At 6000 yards from the whites tees, there are chances to make par and an occasional birdie. We especially enjoyed the large greens. Make no mistake—they are not flat or easy to putt, but they did roll true. There are water hazards and numerous sand traps on the course, but most are easily avoided. Golfers will likely want to rent a cart for their round.

For those who live in the area, the course offers an affordable single membership. We enjoyed our round at The Legacy. It's not as far from the Twin Cities as you think and we would certainly recommend it.

ID: 5502109MN

LEGENDS

8670 Credit River Boulevard
Prior Lake, MN 55372
Clubhouse: 952-226-4777
Golf Shop: 952-226-4777
Type: Public   Par: 72
www.legendsgc.com

F

Course Rating

HOSPITALITY	7.86
PLAYABILITY	8.04
USABILITY	8.44
FACILITY	8.69
VALUE	5.73

OVERALL SCORE
794

Greens Fee: $79.00 (weekend)
1/2 Cart Fee: $15.00 (weekend)

Tees	Men's	Women's	Yards
Gold		71.3/127	5297
White	69.6/133	75.5/136	6046
Blue	71.3/136		6418
Black	72.6/139		6702
Silver	74.2/142		7058

Prior Lake, Minnesota, is at the center of some of the best golf courses in the Twin Cities. With The Wilds, The Meadows at Mystic Lake and Legends all located in the city, there should be no complaints from area golfers.

Legends, perhaps a bit lesser known than the others, is a formidable competitor. It is a country club experience at a reasonable price point. The grounds are nicely laid out with a large parking lot, a club drop-off site, putting and pitching areas, a nicely appointed clubhouse with an excellent bar/restaurant area that is a must for the 19th hole and an expansive outdoor grill/patio. The course itself was in excellent condition, even later in the season. The signage is very good and the cart paths are paved and always nearby. Each cart has GPS and for a course as challenging as Legends, a godsend for certain shots.

Approaching the first tee doesn't begin to tell you the experience you will have. In fact, the front nine is considered easier to play than the back, but that is only because the fairways might be a bit wider. What awaits the unsuspecting golfer is a course that will challenge you with shots over water, across scrub areas, blind approaches, sand trap city and big doglegs. The course has it all and it isn't for the faint of heart.

This is not a course that a hacker should play if he/she expects to shoot low. It isn't going to happen. You might think you've solved the course on one hole by making a par, but it is only a temporary condition and it will bite you back. The course has been designed to require every club in your bag and smart course management. Just to make things worse, it will force you to hit terrifying shots over water requiring carries of at least 150 yards. If you are aquaphobic, you'll be sorry.

This is a course that you should treat yourself to at least once a season because it is worth the extra cost. It might not be the place you have your best round, but it will be a highlight of your summer and give you a sense of how the other half lives.

ID: 5537208MN

LES BOLSTAD

University of Minnesota
2275 West Larpenteur Avenue
St. Paul, MN 55113
Clubhouse: 612-627-4004
Golf Shop: 612-627-4000
Type: Public   Par: 71
www.uofmgolf.com

Course Rating

HOSPITALITY	7.13
PLAYABILITY	6.99
USABILITY	7.69
FACILITY	5.97
VALUE	6.68

Tees	Men's	Women's	Yards
Gold	66.6/115	71.8/122	5478
White	69.5/121	75.3/129	6117
Maroon	70.2/123	76.2/131	6278

OVERALL SCORE
698

Greens Fee: $35.00 (weekend)
1/2 Cart Fee: $16.00 (weekend)

The Les Bolstad Golf Course, located in St. Paul, Minnesota, is couched in history. This is where local Minnesota golf luminaries like John Harris and Tom Lehman learned their craft and is the site of a dozen men's and women's Big Ten Championships.

The clubhouse feels very much like a fraternity. Old trophies, wall plaques, and signed prints line the walls. The furniture is old and worn out. The kitchen area and bathrooms are in need of a renovation. Maintenance has been deferred and unfortunately, it can been seen on the course as well.

The course when this reviewer visited in the fall appeared to be in tough shape and the holes were very spotty with some being nicely groomed and others not so well. The fairways seemed very hard with large areas of poor grass. Some greens had dead areas while most were very hard as well. Strangely, almost all of the greens slope uphill so a player can hit similar approach shots to most greens. The cart paths were also very inconsistent going from asphalt to gravel to nothing in places.

One oddity of the course is that #10 & #11 actually are the only two holes that are located on the the south side of Larpenteur Avenue. You reach these holes by taking a tunnel under the road. Near and around the clubhouse there are nice plantings, but the layout of the facility seems a bit inefficient with the parking lot in between #9 and #18, but the driving range and #1 located at opposite ends of the course. A bit of walking will be necessary if you are going to hit the driving range first, but the remainder of the course is reasonably compact so a cart isn't necessary.

For golfers affiliated with the University of Minnesota, the pricing is quite reasonable, but for the rest of us, the fees are a bit expensive for what you are getting. It might be exciting to play the same course as some of the greats that graduated from the University of Minnesota, but the course itself isn't that outstanding and only provides limited challenge.

ID: 5511308MN

LESTER PARK

1860 Lester River Road
Duluth, MN 55804
Clubhouse: 218-525-0828
Golf Shop: 218-525-0828
Type: Public Par: 36/36/36

www.golfinduluth.com

Tees	Men's	Women's	Yards
Front/Back - Gold	67.1/112	72.5/121	5640
Front/Back - White	69.1/117	74.8/126	6062
Back/Lake - Gold	68.0/122	73.4/126	5708
Back/Lake - White	70.2/128	76.0/131	6169
Lake/Front - Gold	68.0/124	73.7/128	5722
Lake/Front - White	70.4/130	76.5/134	6229

Course Rating

HOSPITALITY	8.38
PLAYABILITY	7.81
USABILITY	8.08
FACILITY	6.47
VALUE	7.29

OVERALL SCORE
775

Green Fee: $29 (weekend)
1/2 Cart Fee: $14.50 (weekend)

Lester Park Golf Course is one of two 27-hole courses owned by the city of Duluth. The course is located just one mile from Highway 61 and has good signage and plenty of parking. The clubhouse has a food counter that offers sandwiches, beverages, snacks and breakfast. The pro shop carries a limited supply of both men's and women's apparel and a selection of golf equipment and accessories. The staff is friendly and helpful, and the 1st tee is right out the door from the pro shop. The course has nice gas carts (though no GPS), and while there are a few cart trails that lead from green to tee, in general there are no cart paths along the length of the holes.

We played the front and back nine (the Lake Nine is also available). Most holes feel open and inviting, but a few have some tight landing areas or fairway bunkers. Many holes play right next to each other, so a stray ball could easily find itself on an adjacent hole, and we heard "Fore!" several times during our round. A mix of mature and new trees are scattered throughout the rough, but you usually have a decent shot if you find yourself in the rough. Be sure to look at the signs on the tees, as the scorecards don't currently include hole layouts.

The greens are fast, which took us a few holes to get used to, but overall they're nice to putt on. Most greens have at least one bunker, but all holes give you the opportunity to run a shot onto the green. The fairways are generally green, but we did notice a few hard patches and some ground under repair. Several holes give you great views of Lake Superior (and we heard the Lake Nine has even better views), and overall the course has a natural feel. A few of the par 4s feel a little long for women, but overall, golfers of all abilities have the opportunity to score on this course. The assistant golf pro told us the Lake Nine is the most difficult of the 3 nines only because all holes are tree lined with less room for error. Lester Park would be a great stop on your trip to Minnesota's North Shore.

167

ID: 5580409MN

LITCHFIELD

West Pleasure Drive
Litchfield, MN 55355
Clubhouse: 320-693-6425
Golf Shop: 320-693-6059
Type: Public Par: 70
www.litchfieldgolfclub.com

Course Rating

HOSPITALITY	8.14
PLAYABILITY	6.74
USABILITY	7.36
FACILITY	8.19
VALUE	4.78

Tees	Men's	Women's	Yards
Red		68.5/117	5010
Gold	65.1/114	69.8/120	5233
White	69.0/122	74.5/130	6086
Blue	70.4/124		6398

OVERALL SCORE
724

Green Fee: $32 (weekend)
1/2 Cart Fee: $11.50 (weekend)

The Litchfield Golf Club, in the southern part of Litchfield, is about 50 miles west of Minneapolis. The course is easy to find—just head straight west from the city, and when you hit Litchfield, turn south. Litchfield is a par-70, 6398-yard course. We got to the course just after noon and had no reservations, but we were able to get right out and start on the front nine as the senior league finished up on the back.

When we got in our cart and found the 1st tee, four gentlemen were already there ready to tee off, but they pleasantly offered to let us go ahead of them. We had a problem finding the 2nd tee box, but four ladies playing the 11th pointed us to the right place. After that we had no trouble finding the other tee boxes because the rest are visible from the green. But we were pleased by how friendly the locals were that day.

The course is in wonderful shape. The fairways are wide and tree lined, and the roughs are cut almost like fairways. There aren't too many bunkers, and the water hazards that appear around several holes didn't cause any problems. The greens are flat and smooth. We never felt rushed because the course wasn't crowded and the pace was good. The course is easily walkable; the distance between a green and the next tee is short and the course is quite level. Lake Ripley is a beautiful scenic backdrop for the course.

Litchfield Golf Club has a putting green, but the driving range consists of just a net, so you won't get a chance to practice your long-distance drives before your round. Cold water is available at several places on the course and there are several restrooms. The carts are gas-powered, but cart paths are minimal. The on-site restaurant, Peter's on Lake Ripley, offers "world-class ribs." The restaurant also has a dining room for private parties up to 300. Overall, Litchfield Golf Club is a pleasant experience and the facilities are first rate.

ID: 5535509MN

LITTLE CROW

15980 Highway 23 NE
Spicer, MN 56288
Clubhouse: 320-354-2296
Golf Shop: 320-354-2296
Type: Public   Par: 36/36/36

www.littlecrowgolf.com

Tees	Men's	Women's	Yards
Willows/Pines - Gold	68.1/128	73.3/130	5695
Willows/Pines - White	70.6/133	76.2/136	6228
Pines/Oaks - Gold	67.3/121	72.3/124	5535
Pines/Oaks - White	71.3/129	77.1/134	6411
Oaks/Willows - Gold	67.8/118	72.6/127	5560
Oaks/Willows - White	71.3/125	76.9/136	6337

Region: WestCentral

Course Rating

HOSPITALITY	8.89
PLAYABILITY	8.72
USABILITY	8.93
FACILITY	8.37
VALUE	7.92

H
U
V

OVERALL SCORE
867

Green Fee: $32 (weekend)
1/2 Cart Fee: $14 (weekend)

Little Crow Country Club, just west of Paynesville, Minnesota, is easy to find. Set in the heart of New London-Spicer's beautiful lake region, the golf course is one of west central Minnesota's premier public courses. It has 27 holes and a big pro shop and restaurant. The pro greeted us and was extremely friendly and pleasant.

The pro shop has a big selection of not only men's merchandise, but also a lot of women's, and a lot of it was on sale the day we were there. The club has normal snack stuff (hot dogs, chips, etc.), but the restaurant was closed for a private party, though the menu looked good and prices are reasonable. Fortunately there are water coolers and pop machines on the course.

The cart paths are paved and well marked, but we were confused at times because some of the 27 holes cross each other. The paved paths end in wide Ts after the tee boxes, so there are not the usual bare spots of dead grass at the end of them. The tee boxes are very nice looking. There are ball washers, benches, trash cans, etc., on all tees including the forward tees. Also, the yardage markers (250, 200, 150 and 100) are very visible stakes on both sides of the fairways. Some of the sprinkler heads are also marked with yardage.

The sand is not the usual sand: it is fine and quite nice to get out of on the first try. (It's hacker friendly!) One of the bunkers was full of animal tracks—maybe deer. We couldn't quite figure out whether or not to rake that one. Everything at Little Crow appears to be very "green." The trash cans are marked for recyclables, both plastic and cans. There is a lot of league information on the bulletin boards, and even though it was not busy on the day we were there due to the late season, it looked like the course was usually pretty busy with leagues and other golfers. Overall we couldn't find anything wrong with Little Crow. The greens are very nice, fairways are plush, the course seems walkable, and it's scenic. It has a very friendly, relaxed atmosphere.

169

ID: 5628809MN

LITTLE FALLS

Region: WestCentral

1 Edgewater Drive
Little Falls, MN 56345
Clubhouse: 320-616-5520
Golf Shop: 320-616-5520
Type: Public Par: 72
www.littlefallsgolf.com

F

Course Rating

HOSPITALITY	8.55
PLAYABILITY	7.28
USABILITY	8.69
FACILITY	8.67
VALUE	7.50

Tees	Men's	Women's	Yards
Red		72.1/122	5451
White	69.7/124	75.8/130	6118

OVERALL SCORE
811

Green Fee: $22 (weekend)
1/2 Cart Fee: $11 (weekend)

The beautiful golf course at Little Falls Country Club is located just northwest of the Metro area, and it is a hacker's delight. It is a well-laid-out course with tree-lined fairways and not many changes in elevation. There is sand guarding many of the greens, but the trees are the biggest hazard here. Fortunately for the hacker, if you end up in the trees, you usually have a reasonable chance of getting your next shot back onto the fairway and even advance it.

At 6118 yards this is not a long course which, again, makes it attractive to those with higher handicaps. The best holes are the final three on the back nine. Number 16 is a beautiful par 3 from an elevated tee over a couple of nicely landscaped ponds. Number 17 is a long and difficult par 5 with the Mississippi River bordering the left side. Number 18 also runs along the river and provides a nice finish to the round. The course is well maintained and is in excellent playing condition. The greens are in beautiful shape and provide adequate challenge for any level of golfer.

The course has four sets of tees and the layout is easy to follow, with the tee for each hole clearly marked. Do be careful, however, when going from the 13th green to the 14th tee, or you may end up at the 16th tee and miss the 14th and 15th holes altogether. There is a driving range and putting green conveniently located just off the parking lot and clubhouse and adjacent to the 1st tee. The clubhouse has a small pro shop with limited supplies, and the bar and restaurant has an outside deck that overlooks the 18th green and the river beyond. The restaurant hosts receptions and banquets. The only restroom facilities on the course are located between holes 3 and 13. This is a very reasonably priced course, particularly if you walk, since the cart fee is a bit high. Season passes are a good buy if you plan to play here often. Little Falls Country Club should be on the list of must-play courses for all hackers in the Little Falls-St. Cloud area.

LOGGER'S TRAIL

11950 80th Street
Stillwater, MN 55082
Clubhouse: 651-439-7862
Golf Shop: 651-439-7862
Type: Semi-Private   Par: 72

www.sawmillgc.com

Tees	Men's	Women's	Yards
Red		70.7/122	5348
White	68.8/123		6023
Blue	71.7/129		6383
Black	74.5/133		7235

Region: Twin Cities

Course Rating

HOSPITALITY	6.71
PLAYABILITY	6.47
USABILITY	7.45
FACILITY	7.10
VALUE	6.24

OVERALL SCORE
680

Greens Fee: $44.00 (weekend)
1/2 Cart Fee: $15.00 (weekend)

A visit to Logger's Trail is like a step into the country. Only thirty minutes from downtown St. Paul, it is surrounded by hobby and horse farms and feels more like a course that might be a few hours north. Upon arrival, seeing the links style layout may fool you because it has tight fairways and narrow greens, making this course harder than it looks.

You might think that 6383 yards is a short course , but spend a little time on it and you'll know that if you can't control your ball, it will feel 500 yards longer. The lack of trees may also fool a golfer into thinking that they can spray their tee shots with impunity, but they would be sorely mistaken. Compensating for a lack of natural hazards, the course designers have added numerous strategic bunkers and berms to thwart off-target drives.

The berms are a unique feature, but hitting into them leaves your ball in dry and weedy areas, making recovery shots quite a challenge. Also, hitting out of them makes for blind shots and difficulty assessing distance. The on-course signage is very limited with yardage markers just large discs embedded in the course so expect some searching to determine what club to pull out next.

Playability and challenge are this facility's strengths, but as any hacker knows, there is more to an enjoyable golfing experience than just the course itself and that is where Logger's Trail seems to fall down. The facility's layout is very compact and tightly organized, with only a short walk from the parking lot to the first tee, yet the practice facilities are small and the clubhouse is just a converted trailer.

If you choose to play cart golf, the paths are excellent and nicely integrated into the course. If you are a walker, this course is compact enough that you won't be exhausted by the end of your round. Before your round, though, be warned that the practice putting green is only postage-stamp sized and the driving range requires most golfers to hit over water (we know what hitting over water does for our nerves).   Also, food offerings and the pro shop are very limited so stock up before you head out to the first tee.

ID: 5508208MN

LONG PRAIRIE

406 6th Street SE
Long Prairie, MN 56347
Clubhouse: 320-732-3312
Golf Shop: 320-732-3312
Type: Semi-Private Par: 72

www.longprairiecountryclub.com

Tees	Men's	Women's	Yards
Red		70.5/118	5209
Gold	68.2/117	73.0/124	5703
White	69.6/121		6024
Blue	70.8/124		6302

Region: WestCentral

Course Rating

HOSPITALITY 8.53
PLAYABILITY 8.52
USABILITY 8.15
FACILITY 8.59
VALUE 6.07

OVERALL SCORE
821

Green Fee: $34 (weekend)
1/2 Cart Fee: $15 (weekend)

Long Prairie Country Club is located in Long Prairie, Minnesota. When we arrived at the course in the early afternoon, we had no trouble getting on the course even though we didn't have reservations. We rented a cart and headed to the 1st tee. Each tee has a ball washer, a garbage can and a bench, and there are four different tee placements. The tee boxes are well kept up, as is the rest of the course. The fairways are tree lined with well-kept grass. The first rough is a bit long (the ball disappears), and the second rough is mostly large trees with open areas underneath.

The fairways are hilly, following the natural contours of the land. The greens are fairly large and smooth with well-mown grass. They are a bit slow (probably due to the recent rain) and a bit deceptive—it's hard to predict the path of the ball. In general, the course is in excellent shape. The first nine starts out as a fairly straightforward course with a few minor challenges to make it interesting. The 9th has a 90-degree dogleg up a hill, with the second shot over the trees. Number 10 is only 270 yards from the whites, with water along the left side.

Number 11 is a par 5, and we deemed it a great hole! The drive is over a hill with larger hills on either side of the fairway, so there is no hint of what's to come. The second shot is a dogleg right over wasteland (next to the driving range) and a deep gulley. Then there's an approach shot to the left to a raised green. Hole #13 is a treacherous, longer par 4. The drive is either over a swamp or along a barbed-wire fence. A slice here is a lost ball. Watch out for the lake to the left. Number 14 is a short par 3 with water in front of, on the left side and behind the green. Sixteen and 17 are also fun holes! The course is not long, but there are many interesting holes to make the day enjoyable. The manager and members we talked with were very friendly. In fact, we were invited to join a group for a fish-fry supper. This course is certainly worth a visit!

ID: 5634709MN

LONG BOW

Highway 371 N & Long Bow Trail
Walker, MN 56484
Clubhouse: 218-547-4121
Golf Shop: 218-547-4121
Type: Public Par: 72

www.longbowgolfclub.com

Tees	Men's	Women's	Yards
Red		69.1/119	5181
White	67.9/117		5817
Blue	69.8/121		6224
Black	71.2/123		6536

Region: NorthWest

Course Rating

HOSPITALITY	7.44
PLAYABILITY	7.32
USABILITY	7.60
FACILITY	6.69
VALUE	6.50

OVERALL SCORE
723

Green Fee: $40 (weekend)
1/2 Cart Fee: $15 (weekend)

Long Bow Golf Course is nestled in aspen, birch, oak and pine trees 6 miles north of Walker, Minnesota, on State Highway 371. Its setting is very picturesque and provides a fair, but challenging, test for "hackers". The par 72, championship course has narrow fairways and large undulating greens. The recommendation for "hackers" is to play the white tee-boxes which play at 5817 yards.

The course seems to play longer than its measured distance as the first cut of rough is lush and thick, and captures wayward tee shots. Fairway tee shots will get a nice roll, but errant shots get very little roll making the course play longer than its 5817 yards. One unique feature of Long Bow is that it has five par fives, five par threes and only eight par fours. The longest par five is hole number 13 and is the number one rated hole. It is particularly difficult because it has a narrow, tree-lined fairway with water/swamp guarding the entire left side of a three-tiered green.

The first par three hole, number 2, is only 134 yards, but you need to carry over 100 yards of marsh/swamp. Topped tee shots will come to rest in the reeds and are irretrievable except with waist-high waders. The remaining, lightly trapped, par threes play from 133 to 170 yards. Most all of the par fours are relatively short, 286 yards to 354 yards, but require two good shots to reach the greens in regulation. Plan to "make hay" on the par fours!

The course is in very good condition as the fairways are lush and very playable. The greens are of average size and had recently been aerated which, coupled with the undulations, made putting a little difficult. The course's many sand traps do not seem to play a big part in a "hackers" game. If you want to play a fair, but challenging course with great fall colors try Longbow. It definitely makes for a fun afternoon of golf and gives you a chance to be great/good/okay/tolerable/bad/horrible (your choice)!

ID: 5648409MN

LYNX NATIONAL

Region: WestCentral

40204 Primrose Lane
Sauk Centre, MN 56378
Clubhouse: 320-351-5969
Golf Shop: 320-352-0242
Type: Public   Par: 72

www.lynxnationalgolf.com

H

Course Rating

HOSPITALITY	8.97
PLAYABILITY	7.31
USABILITY	7.57
FACILITY	8.19
VALUE	6.45

Tees	Men's	Women's	Yards
Red		70.5/120	5244
Gold	67.6/126	73.0/126	5704
White	69.9/125		6208
Blue	72.2/129		6700

OVERALL SCORE
782

Green Fee: $25 (weekend)
1/2 Cart Fee: $10 (weekend)

Lynx National Golf Course in Sauk Centre, Minnesota, is easy to get to. Just shoot out of the Cities on I-94 west and you'll find it about an equal distance between St. Cloud and Alexandria. As you approach the course, you'll get a good view of it and the driving range on the way to the clubhouse. It's a links-style course with a Scottish feel, and it has rolling hills, prairie plants, wetlands, ponds and wild flowers, but not many trees.

The par-72 course plays 6700 yards from the blue tees, and it's all in great shape. The greens were refurbished over the summer, and the new greens are smooth, quick and fairly level. There are four separate tee boxes at every hole, each with ball washers and garbage cans. The fairways are bent grass, fairly wide and closely cut. The 2nd rough is about two inches deep. The heavy rough consists of prairie grass, wetlands and even a cornfield. A ball in the rough is really lost!

At Lynx National, the front nine is referred to as the Prairie and the back nine is the Marsh. Our favorite holes, on the Marsh, are #9 and #18. Both are dog-legs with shots over water and wetlands. The course boasts 53 sand bunkers, some of which are mid-hole bunkers that run adjacent to the fairways. They are strategically located for the golfers who try to take shortcuts.

The clubhouse has a small pro shop and a nice snack bar with tables and a patio overlooking the course. We arrived early in the morning—before the manager—so we chose to walk the course. Unfortunately we started in a heavy fog, so on the first couple of holes we had no idea where the greens were until our second shot. On the 3rd tee, though, the fog lifted a bit and we headed into the morning sun. Putting was slow until the greens dried off. After that the course played more reasonably. We found the course to be challenging, but it is possible to do well. It is walkable but long. The staff and other golfers are friendly and welcoming. It was a pleasure to play Lynx National!

ID: 5637809MN

MADDEN'S
(The Classic)
11266 Pine Beach Peninsula
Brainerd, MN 56401
Clubhouse: 800-642-5363
Golf Shop: 218-829-2811
Type: Public Par: 72
www.maddens.com

Course Rating

HOSPITALITY	8.40
PLAYABILITY	8.63
USABILITY	8.65
FACILITY	9.13
VALUE	6.26

F

OVERALL SCORE
841

Green Fee: $119 (weekend)
1/2 Cart Fee: included in fee

Tees	Men's	Women's	Yards
Red		70.0/126	4859
Gold	67.5/129	73.1/137	5438
White	70.3/134	76.6/145	6062
Blue	72.0/138		6438
Black	73.3/140		6717

First of all, let us say that The Classic at Madden's near Brainerd, Minnesota, is a beautiful golf course. Everything is in tiptop shape.

Maddens' website will tell you that The Classic opened in 1997 and is rated 33rd on the Golf Digest list of best public courses in America. But let's face it—the people at Golf Digest aren't really hackers, so here's our view.

Everything at The Classic is top-notch, but really, we'd expect nothing less from Madden's—that's the way they do things. Of course the $119 green fee raises our expectations, too. For that fee you get unlimited range balls, cart rental, complimentary rolls and coffee and a well-trained and courteous staff. Carts are new but are surprisingly without GPS. Instead, first-timers are given a yardage book. All tee boxes, fairways and greens are bent grass. Fairway widths are generous for the most part. Rough is thick but not too long. Greens are fast but not horrific; they do have a lot of slope and nuance.

There is water or marsh around most holes, usually on the sides, but several do have forced carries. Bunkers are deep and look to be in great condition. No one in our group managed to land in one, however. From the tips the course is over 7000 yards, but the whites play at just over 6000. There are a total of six sets of tees. The course requires good course management; there are blind approaches, but the staff encourages taking the cart to look before you hit.

The clubhouse has an excellent bar and grill with high-end selections of both food and drink. For lighter fare, there is a kiosk at the turn. Clearly, The Classic is a top course. Is it hacker friendly? We're not so sure; if your game is on or if you have the opportunity to play it a number of times and become more familiar, then perhaps. Or you can check your ego at the door and play from the gold tees. Regardless, if you have a chance to play here, go out and enjoy it for what it is: a beautiful course and good company.

ID: 56401A09MN

MADDEN'S
(Pine Beach West)
11266 Pine Beach Peninsula
Brainerd, MN 56401
Clubhouse: 800-642-5363
Golf Shop: 218-829-2811
Type: Public Par: 67
www.maddens.com

U

Course Rating
HOSPITALITY	8.60
PLAYABILITY	7.00
USABILITY	8.90
FACILITY	8.59
VALUE	6.23

Tees	Men's	Women's	Yards
Red		65.4/108	4382
White	64.6/113	69.2/116	5070

OVERALL SCORE
794

Green Fee: $34 (weekend)
1/2 Cart Fee: $17 (weekend)

Madden's Pine Beach West is one of four golf courses at the Madden's Resort in Brainerd, Minnesota. Besides their three 18-hole courses, they have a 9-hole "social" course. Pine Beach West is the shortest of the 18-hole courses. It has only two tee choices. Even though the course is short and doesn't have any bunkers, it has plenty of trees and water to make it challenging. We really enjoyed the scenery of the thick birch and pine woods.

The clubhouse is a nice-looking structure that is attached to some resort housing. They don't offer any food at this site, other than candy bars. They do have golf equipment and apparel for sale, and they'll loan you a cooler to put your beer in that you purchase at the course. There is no beverage cart, but water coolers are frequent. The people at the clubhouse and on the course are very friendly and helpful.

The course is well taken care of. The tee boxes aren't overly large but are well maintained, and the greens are cut well and also in great shape. They are a good challenge without being difficult to the point of being unfair. The course has some good undulation, but you probably could walk it.

Pine Beach West has only two par 5s (one on each side) and a couple par 4s that are under 300 yards. The course is very scenic and very fair. Water and trees are the major hazards. Everything is in great shape here. There are a couple of areas that are a little open, but for the most part you have a course that is carved out of the woods. That is what many people look forward to when golfing in the Brainerd area.

We think the course is hacker friendly—it offers a challenge without being overly difficult. It is in great shape and has good scenery and friendly people. Some might be disappointed in the length and that it's only a par 67, but we found it to be an enjoyable experience and feel it's a resort course you can play with the family.

176

ID: 56401B09MN

MADDEN'S
(Pine Beach East)
11266 Pine Beach Peninsula
Brainerd, MN 56401
Clubhouse: 800-642-5363
Golf Shop: 218-829-2811
Type: Public Par: 72
www.maddens.com

Tees	Men's	Women's	Yards
Red		71.2/121	5328
White	69.9/122	75.5/130	6101

Region: NorthWest

Course Rating

HOSPITALITY	8.83
PLAYABILITY	8.42
USABILITY	8.29
FACILITY	7.77
VALUE	5.93

OVERALL SCORE
815

Green Fee: $45 (weekend)
1/2 Cart Fee: $17 (weekend)

The sprawling Madden's Resort complex in Brainerd, Minnesota, has something for everyone. The complex boasts 54 holes of golf, with The Classic considered the granddaddy and Pine Beach East and West having their own charms. Pine Beach East is a traditional resort course at 6101 yards. First built in the late 1920s, it is a hacker-friendly course with open fairways, limited bunkering and only a few holes where water becomes an issue. It's generally walkable for those who prefer to hoof it—there are only a few hilly spots. With only two sets of tees, Pine Beach East isn't a very long course, but it doesn't need to be. Like the resort, the course is going to pamper you because it isn't overly hard or challenging; it's perfect for golfers who don't possess the skills needed for the 7102-yard Classic.

The clubhouse is nicely appointed with a pro shop, a lounge area, a small bar and a sit-down restaurant. While playing, you can order ahead and pick up your food when you make the turn. Probably the hardest hole is actually the 1st—a par 3—not because it is unnecessarily long, but because it's impossible to putt on. There isn't a flat spot anywhere and you'll watch your ball roll right off one side of the green if you're not careful. Another interesting hole is #6, the resort's former landing strip. At 618 yards, you'll wish you could use your driver on your second and third shot, too.

One thing you'll notice right away is the hospitality—from the front desk to the starters to the Peruvian drink attendant who will mix up a mean Bloody Mary. All are friendly and very accommodating. We even evidenced a group eating freshly caught Gull Lake fish that was prepared for them by the kitchen. Madden's has a nice practice facility with the Chris Foley Golf School, but you'll want to take a cart because it is a bit of a walk. At $45 plus cart, it isn't cheap to play Pine Beach East, and you could probably find similar courses in the Brainerd Lakes area for less, but you wouldn't get the full resort experience like you would at this outstanding course.

177

MAJESTIC OAKS
(Crossroads Course)

701 Bunker Lake Boulevard
Ham Lake, MN 55304
Clubhouse: 763-755-2140
Golf Shop: 763-755-2142
Type: Public   Par: 72

www.majesticoaksgolfclub.com

Tees	Men's	Women's	Yards
Silver		68.9/122	4849
Black	69.4/126		5879
Gold	71.8/131		6396

Region: Twin Cities

Course Rating

HOSPITALITY	7.42
PLAYABILITY	7.32
USABILITY	6.63
FACILITY	6.89
VALUE	6.58

OVERALL SCORE
707

Greens Fee: $32.00 (weekend)
1/2 Cart Fee: $15.00 (weekend)

Majestic Oaks, located just off of Highway 65 in Ham Lake, offers two 18-hole courses, Crossroads and Signature, and an additional executive 9-hole course. The pro shop is a short walk from the parking lot. A large putting green is situated just outside the clubhouse, and another putting green adjoins the driving range where you can hit a bucket of balls for $7. You'll need to head to the clubhouse to use the restroom, since the pro shop doesn't have any facilities. At the clubhouse you'll find a relaxing atmosphere with areas for sitting, a bar, spacious restaurant with an extensive menu and cheerful, friendly staff.

The Crossroads course is fairly level and the distances between holes is such that one can easily walk 18 holes without a problem. Reservations may be made four days in advance, but can't be made through the course's website.

Signs leading to the first Crossroads tee and driving range are lacking, so your best bet is to follow the cart paths in the general direction of the course. The tee boxes' conditions indicate much use; the fairways are in good shape; and the greens look fantastic. On a few holes, golfers may want to lay up in front of a hazard to insure an easier second shot. Houses surround nearly the entire course, but golfers are permitted to retrieve errant shots from the lawns. For the most part, the houses do not come into play for the average golfer.

Consider this fair warning—there are no porta-potties on Crossroads until the end of the 9th hole, and golfers don't come near the clubhouse until the 18th hole has been completed. Golfers may want to carry their own beverages since the beverage cart service was scarce when this writer was there. Majestic Oaks hosts many tournaments and events, so staff may have been busy elsewhere on the courses on this particular day.

All in all, Majestic Oaks Crossroads provides a walkable, challenging golf experience that the average duffer would find enjoyable. The clubhouse offers a comfortable spot to discuss one's great shots over appetizers or a meal and a wide choice of beverages.

ID: 55304A08MN

MAJESTIC OAKS
(Signature Course)

701 Bunker Lake Boulevard
Ham Lake, MN 55304
Clubhouse: 763-755-2140
Golf Shop: 763-755-2142
Type: Public   Par: 72

www.majesticoaksgolfclub.com

Course Rating

HOSPITALITY	8.18
PLAYABILITY	8.83
USABILITY	7.85
FACILITY	8.11
VALUE	6.25

OVERALL SCORE
811

Greens Fee: $36.00 (weekend)
1/2 Cart Fee: $15.00 (weekend)

Tees	Men's	Women's	Yards
Silver		71.6/124	5268
Black	70.8/127	76.0/133	6060
Gold	72.5/131		6442
Green	74.1/134		6792
Blue	75.5/137		7107

Majestic Oaks is quite easy to get to. It is located about one mile west of Highway 65 on Bunker Lake Boulevard in Ham Lake. It is home to an executive course and two 18-hole courses. It also consists of a large complex able to host corporate outings, weddings, and banquets. The food service available was in the bar and grill. There was a good variety of food at a reasonable cost and good service.

We found it strange that the pro shop was detached from the main complex and was small and minimally stocked. The staff was polite but exhibited a somber mood. Another oddity was the golf carts were without tops/roofs and no GPS. When it is hot and humid it would be rather uncomfortable riding in the open carts. The putting green is in close proximity to the pro shop, carts and the first and tenth tees of the course. The driving range is also close by and was well maintained.

We were impressed by the whole experience. Hole routing was excellent with cart paths that easily routed you around the course. The cart paths were somewhat weathered, but acceptable. Signage at the tees and getting you from greens to the next tee was very good. The greens were large and fair with few ball marks, but a little on the slow side. They probably need to be aerated. The fairways were in very good shape and generous widths, and the rough consistent at a minimal height. A beverage cart came by three times during our round.

The web site is mostly geared to event bookings and food service. They do have an area to book tee times online, but it was very cumbersome the few times we tried to use it so we ended up calling for a tee time. The greens fee structure is an excellent value for the quality of the course and the overall experience.

The Signature course has been around a long time and we believe it is a hidden gem in the Twin Cities.

ID: 55304B08MN

MANITOU RIDGE

3200 McKnight Road
White Bear Lake, MN 55110
Clubhouse: 651-777-2987
Golf Shop: 651-777-2987 x2
Type: Public   Par: 68

www.manitouridge.com

Region: Twin Cities

Course Rating

HOSPITALITY	7.48
PLAYABILITY	7.28
USABILITY	7.74
FACILITY	6.35
VALUE	6.77

OVERALL SCORE
723

Tees	Men's	Women's	Yards
Red		71.9/125	5468
White	69.6/123		6034
Blue	71.2/127		6401

Greens Fee: $31.00 (weekend)
1/2 Cart Fee: $13.00 (weekend)

Manitou is an Algonquian Indian word meaning a supernatural power that controls nature. Fortunately, for those of us golfers classified as hackers, Manitou Ridge Golf Course does not require supernatural intervention to post a respectable score. To the contrary, this rolling wooded course offers a number of challenging holes that allow a hacker to feel good about his game, without the sense of being patronized by straight and mundane fairways.

The most striking aspect of this course, located in White Bear Lake at the intersection of Highway 694 and McKnight Road, is its contoured topography. With rolling fairways, elevated greens and sloped putting surfaces, Manitou Ridge is as beautiful as it is interesting to play. This course uncharacteristically finds the compromise between challenge and playability. The mature tree lines, sharp ridges and other conveniently placed natural hazards enhance the beauty of the course without causing excessive hardship, allowing a player to believe he conquered traps that, in truth, posed no real danger.

In keeping with its non-championship-course designation, Manitou Ridge's predominant downfall is its lack of championship course maintenance.   Although the fairways are adequately maintained, its tee boxes, cart paths, roughs and (some) greens leave much to be desired. The roughs are frequently hard and dry, which, for hackers, is bad news, given our propensity to swing from these areas. Unfortunately, these tough spots will account for a few more strokes in your round because the terrain is so unforgiving. The greens are fairly consistent in terms of size and speed, but the imperfect maintenance yields a few frustrating dead spots. To quell your frustrations, Manitou Ridge offers wonderful on-course service, replete with a host of non-alcoholic and alcoholic beverages (including mixed drinks) and a variety of snacks. Likewise, the clubhouse offers a nice selection of potables and edibles at the turn. Overall, Manitou Ridge is a great course for the value. At $31 per round (with senior discounts, patron cards, and twilight rates available) this course should be included on your summer golf itinerary.

ID: 5511008MN

MARSHALL

Region: SouthWest

800 Country Club Drive
Marshall, MN 56258
Clubhouse: 507-532-2278
Golf Shop: 507-537-1622
Type: Semi-Private   Par: 72

www.marshallgolfclub.com

Tees	Men's	Women's	Yards
Red		69.8/126	5136
Yellow	68.5/129	73.5/134	5795
White	70.7/133	76.1/139	6266
Blue	72.2/136		6601

Course Rating

HOSPITALITY	8.57
PLAYABILITY	8.28
USABILITY	7.92
FACILITY	8.40
VALUE	7.02

OVERALL SCORE
817

Green Fee: $45 (weekend)
1/2 Cart Fee: $15 (weekend)

The Marshall Golf Club in southwest Minnesota is a wonderfully manicured course. Pulling into the parking lot and seeing the course for the first time is great. It has lush green grass and beautiful fountains in the water hazards.

The friendly clubhouse starter described the course to us and helped us find our way to the driving range. The driving range area has two chipping areas for warming up, and coupled with the two practice greens for putting, this course has one of the best practice areas that we saw all summer. When we checked in with the clubhouse, we were told that the local girl's college golf team was going to be following us—probably all of them could have beaten us.

Stepping onto the 1st tee box, you see a straight and long par 5. The 1st hole has a wide-open fairway with a fairway bunker that didn't come into play for us. The course is so well maintained and well manicured. We had our fair share of bogeys and double bogeys, but we also managed a couple birdies and a few pars. The Redwood River snakes its way through the course but really only comes into play on one or two holes. The sand bunkers are in good shape as are the greens and tee boxes.

Our favorite holes had to be #1 and #2—they're back-to-back par 5s with a great water hazard that has fountains in it and circles the 2nd green. What a picturesque scene. We had a pretty good pace-of-play, finishing in just under four hours. The other golfers were friendly and the course has signs to help you easily find all of the holes. There wasn't any beverage cart service that day, but the course layout gets you near enough to the clubhouse to make use of the fully stocked bar. The high green fee surprised us, but this course is totally worth the $60 we paid for 18 holes and a cart. The Marshall Golf Club is a beautiful setting and has a very friendly and helpful staff. This course is a must-play if you're anywhere near Marshall, Minnesota.

ID: 5625809MN

MEADOW GREENS

25238 540th Avenue
Austin, MN 55912
Clubhouse: 507-433-4878
Golf Shop: 507-433-4878
Type: Public   Par: 69

www.meadowgreensgc.com

V

Region: SouthEast

Course Rating

HOSPITALITY	8.64
PLAYABILITY	8.43
USABILITY	8.49
FACILITY	8.36
VALUE	7.97

OVERALL SCORE
844

Green Fee: $20 (weekend)
1/2 Cart Fee: $10 (weekend)

Tees	Men's	Women's	Yards
Red		65.9/110	4478
Yellow	63.7/104	67.6/114	4790
White	66.6/110	71.1/121	5420
Blue	69.3/116		5950

Who says the Spam museum is the only recreational highlight associated with Austin, Minnesota? This multi-faceted country course is located just three miles north of I-90 in Austin and definitely gives the Hormel folks a strong rival for the local entertainment dollar. This course has two distinct personalities from front nine to back. The front has an executive nine feel, coming in at just over 2000 yards. Unfortunately, the current length, number and location of the tee boxes restrict creative options related to altering distance. There are four par 3s (all very short—135, 95, 145 and 130 from the back tees), with only one par 5, which explains at least part of the distance shortfall. Despite this distance advantage, multiple out-of-bounds, thick woods and marshy bogs are looming threats, as are the small, elevated and oftentimes sloping greens that can present a stiff test for the average player.

The back nine, added later to the original nine, offers a noticeably different look and presents a completely different set of challenges. Each hole is lined on both sides by acres of oftentimes knee-high meadow grass. An errant shot into the meadow can usually be found and played, which is an added benefit. There are only a few actual bunkers to be found. Grass gullies, bunkers and elevated meadow grass dunes are their replacement. The fairways and one-cut roughs are wide and provide excellent roll, with favorable lies a common occurrence throughout. Still, despite a few instances of out-of-bounds, thick brush and water, the typical hacker need only connect solidly while making smart risk/reward decisions to score well here.

Another feature of this facility is the beautifully constructed driving range. Though it is remotely located from the clubhouse parallel to the 10th hole, it is an attractive sight, flanked by meadow grass on all sides. From check-in to the 18th green, the designers and management of the aptly named Meadow Greens have addressed every detail of golf course usability. All things considered, this track is one of the best-kept golf options in out-state Minnesota.

182

ID: 5591209MN

MEADOW LAKES

70 45th Avenue SW
Rochester, MN 55902
Clubhouse: 507-285-1190
Golf Shop: 507-285-1190
Type: Public   Par: 71
www.meadowlakesgolfclub.com

Tees	Men's	Women's	Yards
Burgundy		67.9/105	4870
Forest		70.4/110	5322
Black	68.2/118		5945
Gold	69.8/122		6304

Region: SouthEast

Course Rating

HOSPITALITY	7.48
PLAYABILITY	5.98
USABILITY	7.29
FACILITY	4.58
VALUE	6.80

OVERALL SCORE
649

Green Fee: $24 (weekend)
1/2 Cart Fee: $15 (weekend)

Located just west of downtown Rochester and its renowned Mayo Clinic is Meadow Lakes Golf Club. "Rochester's Newest Golf Course" is located just across the street from the Rochester Country Club. The website for the course has excellent directions along with a map that will lead you right to the clubhouse, so familiarity with the area is a nonissue.

The gravel parking lot gives a good idea of what's to come—an open municipal-type course with a small clubhouse and older golf carts. The clubhouse consists of a main desk area doubling as pro shop and restaurant. The restaurant has hamburgers, hot dogs and fried appetizers while the pro shop sells monogrammed balls and sweaters. As value chasers, we did notice that the twilight rate is 6 p.m. no matter what part of the season it is. This means that in early spring or late fall—when a full round can't possibly be played with a 6-p.m. tee time—we'd still be stuck paying the full rate.

The 1st hole winds almost all the way around the driving range which, along with a sizable putting green, is available for polishing your slice before the round. It is somewhat frustrating to wander from ball to ball on the 1st hole, trying to figure out which was your drive and which came from the range. The rest of the course is pretty straight and manageable.

Conditions of the course are less than impressive. The fairways look stressed and the cuts of the fairway and rough are virtually the same. It should be noted that while most of the holes are mundane, there are a few challenging ones that creatively make use of the two streams running through the property. The course is entirely flat and forgiving with a considerable amount of blind shots or water danger that, strangely, never seem to come into play. Meadow Lakes should not be considered a destination course, but if you are able to hit it at the right time of year nature you won't be disappointed with a low scoring round at a course that looks harder than it really is.

ID: 5590209MN

MEADOWBROOK

201 Meadowbrook Road
Hopkins, MN 55343
Clubhouse: 952-929-2077
Golf Shop: 952-929-2077
Type: Public   Par: 72

www.minneapolisparks.org

Tees	Men's	Women's	Yards
Red		69.5/121	4934
Yellow	68.2/124	73.4/129	5640
White	71.0/130		6252
Blue	72.3/132		6529

Course Rating

HOSPITALITY	6.94
PLAYABILITY	6.18
USABILITY	6.85
FACILITY	5.76
VALUE	5.32

OVERALL SCORE
635

Greens Fee: $32.00 (weekend)
1/2 Cart Fee: $14.00 (weekend)

Located right off Excelsior Boulevard in Hopkins, Minnesota, Meadowbrook is run and operated by the Minneapolis Parks and Recreation Board. As part of the park system, it is a course built very much to the same dynamics as Theodore Wirth, Columbia, or Hiawatha. These park courses are designed towards the playing abilities of the average golfer and are meant to cater towards the needs of that type of player. Meadowbrook slides perfectly into this category.

There is no fancy clubhouse or any "collared shirts only" signs waiting for you at Meadowbrook, and it has a very down-to-earth feel about it right away. It does lack a driving range to get warmed up, but the course will be very manageable when you get going.

Starting out with two par 5s in the first four holes means you want to get your swing going early because the 5th, 3rd, and 1st handicapped holes are coming up next. The back nine plays just a tad longer, but most of the yardage comes on the par 4s and par 5s, as the two par 3s on the back play a very modest 126 and 135 yards. We've never been big fans of wedge par 3s, it gives a rinky-dink feel to a course, but if you're struggling on the back side, the two par 3s offer a nice break.

For the most part, Meadowbrook is very straightforward. There's trouble to be found, but you have to go well out of your way to look for it most of the time, and even if you do find it there's usually a manageable way to get around it. If you're going to throw up a big number here, it's not going to be because the course is asking you to make a shot you're not capable of making. As part of the park system, the greens fees are very affordable and at $32 on the weekend, the price is tough to beat. Overall, Meadowbrook is a good dollar-for-dollar value, especially for twilight rates.

The couch-surrounded big screen TV in the clubhouse showing the Packers losing when we walked in didn't hurt either.

ID: 5534308MN

MESABA

415 East 51st Street
Hibbing, MN 55746
Clubhouse: 218-262-2851
Golf Shop: 218-263-4826
Type: Semi-Private   Par: 72

www.mesabacc.com

H

Course Rating

HOSPITALITY	9.07
PLAYABILITY	8.39
USABILITY	7.92
FACILITY	7.60
VALUE	7.17

OVERALL SCORE
822

Tees	Men's	Women's	Yards
Red		71.1/120	5406
Gold	69.3/122	74.7/128	6054
White	71.6/126	77.5/135	6573
Blue	72.6/129		6792

Green Fee: $50 (weekend)
1/2 Cart Fee: $12 (weekend)

Mesaba Country Club in Hibbing, Minnesota, is a private club that is open to the public. Some of the facilities and amenities are not as user friendly to a newcomer as they are to a member familiar with the club. You may find yourself wondering where to go next—both in the clubhouse and on the course.

The pro shop is too small for the ample stock of clothing and clubs on display. There is a good selection of both and they are quite competitive prices. The long-tenured pro is available for lessons and equipment fittings. The practice facilities are conveniently located near the pro shop and the 1st tee. There is a practice green, a chipping green, a practice bunker and a driving range. The driving range goes to about 260 yards. The conditioning of this area is very good.

Mesaba is hacker friendly on most holes. There are no long carries over water, and most of the rough can be easily played out of. There are four sets of tee boxes that bring the yardage from 6792 to 5406. If you play from the tee box that suits your game, you'll enjoy this course. General course conditioning is fairly good. Several fairways have areas of heaving from the low ground and winter conditions. Most of the bunkers are well conditioned, but some fairway bunkers need better sand and care. The condition of the greens is superb. They play fairly fast but roll very true. The slope and undulation on some greens is deceptive and makes you question your green-reading ability. A fun and pleasant golf experience is easily found here.

The restaurant and bar is a full-service facility with a complete menu. You can order anything from a light snack to a top-notch steak. The entrée pricing is comparable to the area. Quality food, great service and reasonable prices are a good way to complete your day. The staff at the course, as well as the members we talked with and the people of the area are all courteous and accommodating. Hibbing is a great place to plan a golf outing.

ID: 5574609MN

MINNESOTA NATIONAL

23247 480th Street
McGregor, MN 55760
Clubhouse: 218-426-4444
Golf Shop: 218-426-4444
Type: Public   Par: 72

www.minnesotanationalgolfcourse.com

F

Course Rating

HOSPITALITY	8.33
PLAYABILITY	8.70
USABILITY	7.89
FACILITY	8.71
VALUE	5.61

OVERALL SCORE
814

Green Fee: $64 (weekend)
1/2 Cart Fee: $16 (weekend)

Tees	Men's	Women's	Yards
Green	66.1/126	70.8/124	5157
Yellow	69.4/132	74.8/133	5874
White	71.7/137	77.6/139	6383
Blue	73.7/141		6831
Black	75.6/144		7230

Minnesota National Golf Course in McGregor, Minnesota, is truly a north-woods experience. Developed within the dense covering of towering red and white pines and abundant wildlife, nothing but nature will greet you here.

The course originally opened with a nine-hole executive course, but in 2008 an 18-hole championship course was added. The championship course is built alongside the nine-hole "33 Course," the latter of which has special junior tees to accommodate kids or for those just learning the game. Along with the new golf course came a new building for the pro shop and banquet space, plus some redoing of the cart paths. The new building is quite impressive, as is the course itself. The fairways are first-rate, with five tee boxes per hole and cart paths over most of the course.

The fairways follow the natural contours of the land (which makes them quite hilly) and are surrounded by forest. Water comes into play on ten of the holes, and there are eight dogleg fairways. Hole #1 is a par-5 dogleg with water on both sides of the fairway. Hole #5 has a right-angle dogleg with water and marsh at the turn and woods all around. Number 12 is also a right angle, where the player has to gamble on getting over a marsh or shoot around a large tree in the middle of the fairway.

All four of the par-3 holes are long and over water and marsh, with woods surrounding the green. In fact, hole 15 has a large pine tree centered directly in front of the green!

The course is 7230 yards and is attempting to appeal to the championship level of golfer. However, five tee boxes allow any hacker to enjoy playing the course! Minnesota National is certainly a first-class course! It is probably not walkable because the land is quite hilly and there are some long distances between holes. Playing here is a very enjoyable experience. The scenery is great and the golf is good!

ID: 5576009MN

MINNEWASKA

Highway 28/29 W Golf Course Road
Glenwood, MN 56334
Clubhouse: 320-634-3680
Golf Shop: 320-634-3680
Type: Semi-Private Par: 72

www.minnewaskagolfclub.com

Tees	Men's	Women's	Yards
Red		71.1/128	5221
White	70.7/133	76.6/140	6212
Blue	71.9/136		6483

Region: WestCentral

Course Rating

HOSPITALITY	8.45
PLAYABILITY	8.43
USABILITY	8.28
FACILITY	8.36
VALUE	7.33

OVERALL SCORE
828

Green Fee: $35 (weekend)
1/2 Cart Fee: $16 (weekend)

As you drive down into the city of Glenwood, Minnesota, Lake Minnewaska dominates the view. Soon, a steady breeze from this regal body of water begins to play with your mind. As you climb back up the hill to the Minnewaska Country Club, the breeze seems to intensify and visions of long drives fill your thoughts.

You take the complimentary bucket of balls you received from the friendly staff in the clubhouse and head to the driving range. After assuring yourself that the wind will both aid and hinder your tee shots—depending on the direction you are facing—move to the chipping green and the bunker practice area. Follow this up with a few minutes on the practice greens—you'll roll a number of putts because the greens have been double cut and are very fast, smooth and true. Moving to the 1st tee, you again see the beautiful views of Lake Minnewaska and experience that now familiar breeze. As you move around the course, you will certainly get to use all of your clubs. There are four par 5s and four par 3s. Fairways are well defined and in great shape, boasting fairly spacious and slightly contoured greens. Minnewaska is an older, well-established club, with many beautiful trees, yet the rough is fairly short and you can recover from most miss-hits. Bunkers are found on the majority of holes, and while they are strategically placed to "protect" the green or discourage a fairway shortcut, they often serve to save hackers from a worse disaster.

Wildlife abounds at the Minnewaska Country Club: deer, wild turkeys and fox tour the course with you. Cattle from a nearby farm appear interested in your tee shot on the 16th green. Hawks and turkey vultures fly in the distance, and varied species of birds sing you through the course. At the end of the round, gather with your foursome in the modest and welcoming clubhouse for a hot dog, brat, beer or mixed drink to share memories of great shots and missed opportunities, and to dream about "what if."

ID: 5633409MN

MISSISSIPPI DUNES

10351 Grey Cloud Trail
Cottage Grove, MN 55016
Clubhouse: 651-768-7611
Golf Shop: 651-768-7611
Type: Semi-Private   Par: 72

www.mississippidunes.com

Course Rating

HOSPITALITY	7.56
PLAYABILITY	8.87
USABILITY	8.27
FACILITY	9.15
VALUE	6.60

OVERALL SCORE
824

Tees	Men's	Women's	Yards
Gold		69.2/121	5348
White	70.2/138	75.4/135	6009
Member	71.8/141		6343
Blue	72.6/143		6509

Greens Fee: $44.00 (weekend)
1/2 Cart Fee: $16.00 (weekend)

We have all seen the British Open, watched the knee-length prairie grass whipping in the breeze and wondered what it feels like to peer over the edge of a six-foot deep pothole bunker in search of the pin. Alas, links golf is a rare thing in Minnesota. But it is available in Cottage Grove at Mississippi Dunes Golf Course.

This course is not for the faint of heart nor is it for the novice golfer. Links golf is as difficult as it appears. The bunkers are deep. The rough grass is long. And the fairways are narrow. The course is punishing for those who have difficulty maintaining a straight drive. With its sharp doglegged fairways and blind tee boxes, this course can give anxious fits to even those who can hit it "long and strong" from the tee. For those who can handle the difficult landscape, the humbling hazards at every turn and the inevitable frustrations, this beautiful course is worth the somewhat costly greens fees.

Like most championship courses, the on-course challenges are not the only frustrations. Although the service is impeccable and the snack-and-beverage cart comes around often, the only available beverages on the course are those you pay for. The course is bereft of water stations. Thus, if you are going to invest in a spectacular round of golf, factor in the cost of beverages in addition to the greens fees.

Mississippi Dunes is a well managed golf course. The fairways are immaculate, with multiple cuts of grass and smooth, quick greens. The course is nicely contoured with subtle rolling hills and pitched greens. The many sand hazards are well kept with soft sand and steep edges. Like most links courses, water does not pose much of a hazard, but the sprawling Mississippi River provides scenic views along a number of holes.

This is not the place for a new golfer, nor is it the place for a relaxing round for a hacker. However, for the hacker who seeks adventure and longs to test his game against a rare and difficult golf experience, Mississippi Dunes is worth the while … knickers and kilts are optional.

ID: 5501608MN

MISSISSIPPI NATIONAL
(The Highlands)
409 Golf Links Drive
Red Wing, MN 55066
Clubhouse: 651.388.1874
Golf Shop: 651.388.1874
Type: Public   Par: 71

www.wpgolf.com/mississippi

Tees	Men's	Women's	Yards
Red		69.3/115	5002
White	68.7/117		5877
Blue	70.5/121		6282

Region: SouthEast

Course Rating

HOSPITALITY   8.57
PLAYABILITY   7.86
USABILITY   6.89
FACILITY   7.70
VALUE   6.88

OVERALL SCORE
772

Green Fee: $38 (weekend)
1/2 Cart Fee: $16 (weekend)

Mississippi National in Red Wing, Minnesota, is a huge 36-hole facility consisting of The Lowlands and The Highlands. They offer everything a private club would have at a non-private price. The Highlands at Mississippi National is situated above the Mississippi River Valley and has some great views of Red Wing and the valley. Mississippi National does a pretty good job of maintaining their courses. Tee boxes, fairways and greens are in very playable condition. But there are areas that could use a little attention—most greens have numerous unrepaired pitch marks. But overall, the course is fairly nice.

The Highlands is an interesting course. It's not a terribly difficult as evidenced by the 117-slope rating, even though we believe it plays a little harder than that. It has a good mix of holes but maybe too many gimmick holes, like #13. It's a seemingly simple 84-yard par 3 with an elevated tee box and severe trouble long and right. The view above Red Wing and the river valley is fantastic. Other than that, what's the point of an 84-yard hole on a regulation-size golf course?

The Highlands also has too many tricky holes, such as #15—a 308-yard par 4 with a severe dogleg right. One would think that the proper play would be to set up to the 100-yard marker—until you get to your ball at exactly the 100-yard marker and find yourself blocked from the green by fairly tall trees. And when your wedge does go over the initial blockade, look out for the hidden tree right next to the green; it catches and throws your perfect approach shot into the bunker. Mississippi National would do itself—and us hackers—a favor if it got some detailed GPS on their carts. Based on the amount of hills and the great distances between some holes, The Highlands pretty much demands you take a cart. Based on observations, Mississippi National is the locals' favorite. But if you're just interested in quality golf, there are better choices nearby at a cheaper price.

ID: 55066A09MN

MISSISSIPPI NATIONAL
(The Lowlands)
409 Golf Links Drive
Red Wing, MN 55066
Clubhouse: 651.388.1874
Golf Shop: 651.388.1874
Type: Public   Par: 71

www.wpgolf.com/mississippi

Tees	Men's	Women's	Yards
Red		71.0/121	5450
White	69.7/123		6195
Blue	71.0/126		6484

Region: SouthEast

Course Rating

HOSPITALITY	8.15
PLAYABILITY	7.26
USABILITY	7.56
FACILITY	6.67
VALUE	6.22

OVERALL SCORE
735

Green Fee: $31 (weekend)
1/2 Cart Fee: $16 (weekend)

Mississippi National Golf Links Lowlands Course, located in Red Wing, Minnesota, and is about an hour from the Metro area. The course is a full-service facility with a PGA pro, a clubhouse with banquet facilities, a bar and pro shop. There are carts, a putting/chipping green and a practice bunker and driving range. The Lowlands meanders through the Hiawatha River Valley and has a good variety of holes is and quite scenic overall. The course has played host to several qualifying Senior Tours and U.S. Amateur qualifying tournaments.

The Lowlands has a good variety of holes in a traditional setting. This course has five par 5s and six par 3s from the white tees (6195 yards). There are four sets of tees available. There is plenty of trouble on the course and, although we did not consider the course overly tight, accuracy on this course is desirable. Trees, out-of-bounds and the lack of a good drive can add up to an increased score. The greens are in great condition and have subtle but prevalent breaks to challenge you. The tee boxes, however, are in inferior condition and need attention by the grounds staff. We rented carts and were glad to have them. A word of caution: There are some steep areas of the course, and the cart paths here are in need of repair, so be careful! The pace-of-play is great; the course was not very busy for a nice Saturday morning. After our round we stopped in the bar to have a couple beers. The staff was friendly and informative. On the course we were surprised that there was no beverage cart, and we did not encounter a ranger or any course personnel on our round.

Overall, we liked the course. The mix of par 5s and par 3s make this course a little different. The scenery and hole variety is great. An average golfer can expect to be challenged, but we did not find the course exceedingly difficult. The #10 hole, a par 4 at 447 yards, seems to play overly long, and the #2 par 5 is tough, hence the 2 and 1, respectively, handicap holes on the course. We would return, but probably only if the course offers better specials and deals.

ID: 55566B09MN

MONTGOMERY

900 Rogers Drive
Montgomery, MN 56069
Clubhouse: 507-364-5602
Golf Shop: 507-364-5602
Type: Semi-Private   Par: 72

www.montgomerygolfclub.com

Tees	Men's	Women's	Yards
Red		68.8/117	4977
Gold	66.4/116		5457
White	69.7/123		6193
Blue	71.3/126		6540

Region: SouthEast

Course Rating

HOSPITALITY	7.93
PLAYABILITY	6.63
USABILITY	8.31
FACILITY	7.34
VALUE	7.13

OVERALL SCORE
745

Green Fee: $30 (weekend)
1/2 Cart Fee: $18 (weekend)

Montgomery Golf Club was the very first golf course designed by Minnesota golf architect Joel Goldstrand. It opened in 1970 as a nine-hole course and was redesigned in 1993 by Goldstrand, who added a second nine and a driving range. For those who have golfed Metro courses only, this is one to add to your outings. Located in the city of Montgomery, Minnesota, and less than an hour's drive from the Metro area.

We started out our morning on the putting green and moved to a pitch, chip and putt area nearby. That, combined with a driving range, an all-grass tee and a practice bunker, gives ample practice and warm-up opportunities. As you approach the 1st tee, you realize that while the fairway landing areas appear generous, mature trees line the fairway, and accuracy is rewarded. The course includes water hazards and elevation changes—including an uphill closing hole that is a 540-yard par 5. The greens roll fairly fast, and all of them have a variety of contour to them.

Hole #8 is the #1 handicap hole on the course. It is a 513-yard par-5 dogleg right with a small, bunkered green. As you approach #9 you'll see a call box where you can place an order for refreshments at the turn. The modest clubhouse includes a snack shop and a full-service bar and has the ability to host dining for tournaments and special events. The back nine incorporates some of the original holes with the newest holes, and finishes with the longest hole on the course. We really liked the hacker-friendly par 4s here. The 6540-yard length could suggest a long course, but all of the par 4s are under 400 yards. The water hazards and the wetlands on a number of holes give the average golfer plenty to think about. The golf course is challenging and it's possible you'll use every club in your bag. Montgomery Golf Club has leagues for men and women of various ages including day leagues and evening leagues. We finished our day at the full-service golf shop where the staff thanked us and encouraged us to play again.

ID: 5606909MN

MONTICELLO

Region: Twin Cities

1209 Golf Course Road
Monticello, MN 55362
Clubhouse: 763-295-4653
Golf Shop: 763-295-4653
Type: Semi-Private   Par: 71

www.montigolf.com

Course Rating

HOSPITALITY	7.51
PLAYABILITY	7.79
USABILITY	7.39
FACILITY	6.64
VALUE	6.66

OVERALL SCORE
735

Tees	Men's	Women's	Yards
Red		70.3/119	5085
Green		71.9/123	5385
Yellow	68.6/120	74.2/128	5793
White	70.3/123		6157
Blue	71.6/126		6453

Greens Fee: $39.00 (weekend)
1/2 Cart Fee: $15.00 (weekend)

We were definitely skeptical of the Monticello Country Club's website promise that our round of golf would be "worth the drive," but the hour-long gas guzzler northwest to this semi-private course definitely proved worthwhile. Monticello is a reasonably priced course for players at all levels.

With mature trees and a nice combination of obstacles, including ponds, well-maintained sand traps, even a bubbling brook that tangles through two holes, Monticello does present its challenges. However, you do not have to be a thinker or a precision specialist here.

The greens were large and ready for the occasional three putt. Many had multiple levels and all played extremely fast. This may have been partly attributable to the colder, dryer weather at the time.

The course has a very nice practice area including a large putting green, a coin-operated driving range close to the first tee box and a practice area complete with sand bunker. This provided a great opportunity to warm up before the round.

Inside, the clubhouse is quite nice with plenty of space to sit, a gas fireplace and a full concession area. We almost needed a hammer to flush the urinal in the men's room but that was a minor issue in the overall clubhouse impression. Staff said good morning and were friendly.

There were a few negatives to our round. At least four holes on the front nine were accompanied by the sounds of Interstate 94. You might not care and it might not affect your game, but the cars and trucks will be whizzing by. We also found that the tee boxes were solid, as if the grounds crew had prepped to lay a brick patio and instead chose to put grass down.

Overall, if you're looking to have fun and hack away at a nice course, on a nice pace without the expense found at other courses, you might find the drive to Monticello to be worth it.

192

ID: 5636208MN

MOUNT FRONTENAC

Region: SouthEast

32420 Ski Road
Red Wing, MN 55066
Clubhouse: 651-388-5826
Golf Shop: 651-388-5826
Type: Public Par: 71

www.mountfrontenac.com

H
V

Course Rating

HOSPITALITY	9.08
PLAYABILITY	8.38
USABILITY	7.58
FACILITY	7.37
VALUE	8.00

OVERALL SCORE
821

Green Fee: $28 (weekend)
1/2 Cart Fee: $15 (weekend)

Tees	Men's	Women's	Yards
Red		68.0/114	4882
Gold	66.5/117	71.4/121	5494
White	68.8/121	74.2/127	6003
Blue	69.9/124		6226

We hope the people of Red Wing and the surrounding areas realize how lucky they are to have the Mount Frontenac golf course available to them. They must, because they sure have been holding on to the secret. Playing at beautiful Mount Frontenac is one heck of a deal. This may well be the undiscovered sleeper course of Minnesota.

Mount Frontenac offers you a very playable course at a very budget-conscious price. No, you won't get high-end country-club fairways and greens, but it's close. And you won't get a steak like you can get at Manny's in downtown Minneapolis. But the food is good, the selection is decent and the price is cheap.

Tee boxes are decent with the usual tee litter and typical divots on certain holes. But they're mostly level with good grass coverage and nary a bare spot. Fairways are lush with a punishing 2nd-cut rough. It's not that it's long or scraggly; it's just dense and hard to get good contact. But the fairways have mostly generous landing areas and quite a few bailout areas.

Greens are varying in size from large to small with some sloping and some minor undulations. They're soft and accept approach shots easily. While the greens are generally slow, they do putt nice. They may have a little too many unrepaired pitch marks on some greens, but overall they're pretty good.

General playability and layout of the course is very good, though we did get lost on a couple of holes due to lack of signage. There's a nice mix of long and short holes with quite a few risk/reward holes. Big hitters can go for it on many holes, and hackers can get some easy pars. The clubhouse is large with a sit-down restaurant and an outdoor patio so you can watch others play up to the 18th hole while you enjoy your meal. The clubhouse can handle large groups and they offer catering. Read the tips given on the scorecard and you will have an enjoyable round.

ID: 55066C09MN

NEW PRAGUE

400 Lexington Ave South
New Prague, MN 56071
Clubhouse: 952-758-5326
Golf Shop: 952-758-5326
Type: Public   Par: 71

www.newpraguegolf.com

Tees	Men's	Women's	Yards
Red		69.3/122	5033
Gold	67.9/127	73.2/131	5716
White	69.6/130	75.2/135	6096
Blue	71.0/133		6401

Region: WestCentral

Course Rating

HOSPITALITY	9.05
PLAYABILITY	8.76
USABILITY	7.76
FACILITY	7.97
VALUE	5.86

OVERALL SCORE
822

Green Fee: $36 (weekend)
1/2 Cart Fee: $15 (weekend)

This municipal course, built in 1931, is located right in the town of New Prague, Minnesota. The course has a country club atmosphere, with a new clubhouse, pro shop and restaurant. The interior is extremely well kept and there's a locker room with showers and lockers available for members. The upper level of the clubhouse has a great view of the course and a patio for relaxing.

We played the course on a beautiful late September morning and thoroughly enjoyed our round. The course was in excellent condition and the greens were quite fast, cut short and rolled very true. The greens have just enough breaks to be challenging, but are not overwhelming. On the weekday we played, we found the pin placements to be very challenging. Even on this Thursday morning, the course was quite busy—a testament to its apparent popularity.

This course has a traditional layout and is 6096 yards from the white tees. There are four sets of tee boxes to accommodate all skill levels. From *Team Hacker*'s perspective, an average drive is usually enough to give golfers an excellent chance to score well. The ball will roll, so concentrate your efforts on control vs. length to hit the fairways. The course is relatively flat and certainly walkable, but there are carts available. More than 40 sand traps line the course, but don't let that scare you away. While they're a bit rocky, they seemed to be fairly placed and avoidable for the most part. Water is not a real issue on the course, but the hazards the course does have are nicely incorporated in the layout. Because it's right in the town of New Prague, we found the course to be tightly compacted. Some greens and tee boxes are quite close together and it's necessary to watch for errant balls. The cart paths are sometimes reminiscent of spaghetti junction and will take a little bit of patience to navigate. A little new paint would help lead golfers to the next hole. They do some yardage markings on the paths, which are helpful.

ID: 5607109MN

NEW ULM

Region: SouthWest

1 Golf Drive
New Ulm, MN 56073
Clubhouse: 507-354-8896
Golf Shop: 507-359-4410
Type: Semi-Private   Par: 71
www.golfnewulm.com

Tees	Men's	Women's	Yards
Red		69.0/119	4892
White	72.4/128	67.7/124	5514
Yellow	69.5/128	74.5/133	5926
Blue	71.0/130		6242

Course Rating

HOSPITALITY	8.34
PLAYABILITY	8.28
USABILITY	7.74
FACILITY	8.47
VALUE	7.37

OVERALL SCORE
812

Green Fee: $38 (weekend)
1/2 Cart Fee: $16 (weekend)

New Ulm Country Club was established in 1929 and is located in New Ulm, Minnesota, right next to Flandreau State Park. Residents of New Ulm who aren't members are allowed to golf once per month. The course is medium length and plays 6242 yards from the back tees, although there are four sets of tees to choose from. The course has a chipping and putting green, but the driving range is only 150 yards.

The course was in excellent shape from tee to green. Every fairway on the course was well maintained. There was some kind of hazard that came into play on almost every hole. The dominant hazard is the sand with was at least one bunker on each hole except #15. The greens were in great shape and very easy to putt on. A couple holes feature water hazards, such as the par-5 9th hole, which has water guarding the green in front. The most impressive hole was probably #16, a short par 4 that's listed as 272 yards from the front tee box. It has a slight dogleg right, which actually makes the hole only 257 yards as the crow flies, so it's tempting to go for the green on your tee shot. If do though, you could end up paying for it. There are front and right bunkers guarding the green and many mature trees help protect the green as well.

New Ulm Country Club has a very nice clubhouse and is able to seat more than 300 people. It's great for groom's dinners, wedding receptions and family reunions. The clubhouse staff was very friendly. Our service and food was excellent with reasonable pricing. An outdoor patio area allows patrons to enjoy watching other golfers putt out on #18. The pro shop had a good selection of bags, balls, hats, clothing and clubs, as well. New Ulm Country Club is well maintained and the kind of course a hacker could score well on. The only blight we found was that the short driving range, but otherwise everything else has the feel of a championship course. If you want to golf at a great and scenic course, New Ulm Country Club is definitely worth a look.

ID: 5607309MN

NORTH LINKS

41553 520th Street
North Mankato, MN 56003
Clubhouse: 507-947-3355
Golf Shop: 507-947-3355
Type: Public   Par: 72
www.northlinksgolf.com

Tees	Men's	Women's	Yards
Red		66.9/114	4682
Yellow	64.7/108		5101
White	67.4/113		5690
Blue	69.4/117		6133

Region: SouthWest

Course Rating

HOSPITALITY	8.38
PLAYABILITY	6.88
USABILITY	7.93
FACILITY	7.18
VALUE	7.40

OVERALL SCORE
756

Green Fee: $29 (weekend)
1/2 Cart Fee: $13 (weekend)

North Links Golf Course is located about 60 miles from the southern Metro area in North Mankato, Minnesota. A short, flat course with a fair amount of water in play, North Links will not leave you disappointed after the drive. Located adjacent to farmland off Highway 14, it is easy to find and a ton of fun to play.

Practice facilities include a driving range just across the road that has well-marked distances to fine tune those irons. There's also a large putting green directly in between the clubhouse and the 1st tee. The clubhouse is large as well, with a pro shop for any golf necessities that might not have made the journey. There's a large bar and restaurant area with LCD TVs. Service was quick and friendly across the board. Especially notable was the beverage cart, which seemed to show up almost every other hole.

The course itself is very straight forward, with plenty of bail-out area for the errant hook or slice. Water hazards are the main adversary, with some holes demanding a 50- to 100-yard carry. A unique steel bridge between #3 and #4 is probably the longest we've seen on a golf course and traverses a small gorge with forest on either side. This course deserves high marks for upkeep, with distinct differences in long and short rough length, defined fairways and quick greens. Distance markers are always available and easy to locate without searching. North Links is favorable for golfers who play the forward tees, since they offer a shorter distance, but still are relatively close to the rest of the tee boxes—meaning everyone gets the same challenge for each hole.

Regular green fees and carts are not expensive, but twilight rates offer the most bang for your buck. If you're driving on Highway 169 or simply looking for a chance to get out of town with your buddies for an afternoon, North Links Golf Course offers an excellent golf experience within a reasonable distance at a great price.

ID: 5600309MN

NORTHERN HILLS

4721 West Circle Drive NW
Rochester, MN 55901
Clubhouse: 507-281-6170
Golf Shop: 507-281-6170
Type: Public   Par: 72

www.rochestermn.gov

Tees	Men's	Women's	Yards
Gold	66.7/122	71.6/128	5398
White	69.2/126	74.6/134	5931
Champ	70.7/130		6271

Region: SouthEast

Course Rating

HOSPITALITY	7.78
PLAYABILITY	6.71
USABILITY	6.43
FACILITY	4.94
VALUE	6.30

OVERALL SCORE
661

Green Fee: $24 (weekend)
1/2 Cart Fee: $14 (weekend)

Northern Hills Golf Course is located in Rochester, Minnesota, a city with many tall buildings, but none near this municipal course. There aren't any mile-high protective nets either. Playing this course doesn't feel like golfing in the city, which is definitely a plus.

Municipal courses often have a reputation for being bare-boned and in rough shape. Unfortunately, Northern Hills has indeed seen better days. The locals playing in the foursome ahead of us said the course was in the worst condition they had ever seen. However, this course isn't without character and charm. Elevation changes, rivers, ponds, trees . . . all would make for a beautiful round if the course weren't so beat up. The fairways are brown and hard as a rock in many places. Additionally, several of the greens have been severely spiked, chipped and chunked.

Hole #1 tests you immediately (don't go left). It pays to have local knowledge on hole #5. (You see that green right in front of you? The one you just hit at? That's not yours.) Thirteen has "double-digit score" written all over it. And #18 tries to kick you on your way out the door.

The service is friendly and the course is truly hacker friendly. We met many beginners in the clubhouse; not one of them broke 100. Some had triple-digit scores just on nine holes. But they couldn't wait to play Northern Hills again. Yes, anyone and everyone can and does play this course. If you're not critical of the color of grass you're playing on, don't mind mini-potholes on the greens and just love a simple round of golf inside city limits—this is the perfect course for you.

ID: 5590109MN

NORTHFIELD

707 Prairie Street
Northfield, MN 55057
Clubhouse: 507-645-4026
Golf Shop: 507-645-4026
Type: Semi-Private   Par: 72
www.northfieldgolfclub.com

Tees	Men's	Women's	Yards
Gold		71.0/129	5204
White	69.0/134	74.1/136	5760
Blue	71.4/139	79.3/147	6270
Black	73.3/143		6703

Region: SouthEast

Course Rating

HOSPITALITY   7.84
PLAYABILITY   8.12
USABILITY   8.13
FACILITY   8.13
VALUE   5.93

OVERALL SCORE
783

Green Fee: $50 (weekend)
1/2 Cart Fee: $16 (weekend)

Northfield, Minnesota, was was where one of America's most notorious gun-slinging outlaws, Jesse James, stopped by in an attempted robbery of the First National Bank. His courage, strategic acumen and discipline as a roving bandit are legendary. You'll need these qualities when playing Northfield Golf Club.

The course is located 40 minutes south of the Twin Cities, just off Interstate 35 in Northfield. It has a unique and demanding layout that requires precision and accuracy to overcome the course's many bunkers. Although there are many challenges for golfers of all skill levels, the course is not to be feared by hackers.

The course design, with its calming surroundings, might lull golfers into a false sense of security. One must remain diligent, as the course is often misleading. What at first appears to be a well-positioned shot may prove imprudent, especially from the tee. A number of tee boxes are elevated above dogleg fairways with deceptively narrow openings. On such holes, golfers should leave their drivers in the bag. Likewise, many of the greens are smaller than they seem and the strategically placed sand traps can easily add strokes to your score.

This is one of the most beautiful and fascinating golf courses in southern Minnesota. Its clever design requires a thoughtful approach to the game that heightens the enjoyment of play. Unfortunately, most golfers will need to play a few rounds at Northfield in order to navigate the course. Poor signage and unmarked trails can cause confusion between holes. There is a chipping green and a putting green, although the nearest driving range is more than a mile from the course. In addition, the notable absence of golf course personnel and on-course amenities detracts from an otherwise enjoyable golf experience.

ID: 5505709MN

198

OAK GLEN

1599 McKusick Road
Stillwater, MN 55082
Clubhouse: 651-439-6981
Golf Shop: 651-439-6963
Type: Public   Par: 72
www.oakglengolf.com

Tees	Men's	Women's	Yards
Red		73.2/134	5626
Gold	69.0/126	74.4/137	5839
White	71.2/131		6320
Blue	72.4/132		6574

Region: Twin Cities

Course Rating

HOSPITALITY	7.14
PLAYABILITY	7.81
USABILITY	8.02
FACILITY	6.84
VALUE	5.93

OVERALL SCORE
735

Greens Fee: $37.00 (weekend)
1/2 Cart Fee: $13.00 (weekend)

Oak Glen Golf Course is a nice find and a reasonable value for what you get. The fairways and greens are very well kept, with nice green grass throughout, even in the middle of a dry Minnesota summer.

The distance plays fairly and, while decent shots are required to hit the greens in regulation, it is certainly an attainable goal for a hacker or average golfer. The rough is not too punishing and the ponds, which are beautiful, are also lateral drops.

The driving range, putting green, and 9-hole par-3 executive course are all located conveniently by the clubhouse.

Our cart, for whatever reason, needed some transmission work, as it kept lurching and had no get-up-and-go. A noticeable amount of the clientele also went out of their way to let us know that this course was their turf, which was interesting. In their defense, they said that Oak Glen was their best-kept local secret and they wanted to keep it that way. Fair enough. We got the hint.

When we made the turn, the single employee behind the register had some problems, to the effect that the marshal actually made a comment to us to hurry up on #10, even though nobody waited on us during the entire back nine.

The cart girl was very friendly and helpful. She took one of our credit cards back to the clubhouse bar to start a tab and then came back to deliver a mixed drink. We saw plenty of her and she came with a decent selection of beverages. A member of our foursome also tipped her to go retrieve a baseball cap that was left two holes back, which she did with a smile.

The course is scenic and the greens are large, forgiving, soft, and consistent.

The website is very informative and helpful. It was very easy to get a tee time, even as late as Friday with a beautiful forecast. If you wanted to spend $50 to play on a Saturday, near the Metro, you should definitely consider hitting Oak Glen.

ID: 5508208MN

OAK HARBOR

2805 24th Street NW
Baudette, Minnesota 56623
Clubhouse: 218-634-9939
Golf Shop: 218-634-9939
Type: Public Par: 72

www.oakharborgolfcourse.com

Tees	Men's	Women's	Yards
Red		68.0/111	4953
White	67.4/112	72.3/120	5725
Blue	69.5/116		6191
Gold	71.1/119		6549

Region: NorthWest

Course Rating

HOSPITALITY 8.37
PLAYABILITY 7.83
USABILITY 8.54
FACILITY 7.62
VALUE 6.67

OVERALL SCORE
796

Green Fee: $33 (weekend)
1/2 Cart Fee: $15 (weekend)

Situated near the Rainy River north of Baudette, Minnesota, Oak Harbor Golf Course has an established front nine and a back nine that has been open for only two years. The front nine has a traditional woodlands feel to it while the back nine is links style. The front nine opened in 1968 and follows the contours of the wooded river valley. The back nine is Scottish links in the north-woods with open fairways, bunkers and fast contoured greens.

The course is actually nine miles north of Baudette, known as "the walleye capital of the world", and just off the southeastern edge of Lake of the Woods, well-known for its fishing. It boasts 65,000 miles of shoreline and 14,582 islands. At 90 miles long and 55 miles wide, it is the largest fresh water lake after the Great Lakes. In keeping with the area's major attraction, the course has a 73-foot walleye sand bunker. Not to be unbowed by the weather, the course stays open May 1st to October 15th. The 19th Hole Bar & Grill runs weekly specials and they have a modest pro shop with typical shop offerings Because of the lateness in the season and the cold weather in October, we played the course on the last day it was open. In fact, the clubhouse was in the process of being closed up for the season – they only had coffee and pop available, but even at that late date, the people working in the clubhouse were very friendly and helpful. In warmer months, the clubhouse has a fine array of food and drink options.

Oak Harbor is a very playable course that is easy to walk. It provides a nice alternative for fishermen on windy days who don't want to venture out on Lake of the Woods to fight the waves. At 6549 yards, it is a course that will give hackers just enough challenge and the contrast between the old and new nines is striking. If you want to stay overnight, Border View Lodge, Sportsman's Lodge or Wheelers Point Resort are all good options. It is worth the extra effort to pack your clubs if you come up for a fishing trip and stay on the south side of Lake of the Woods.

200

ID: 5662309MN

OAK HILL

8852 Indian Road NW
Rice, Minnesota 56367
Clubhouse: 320-259-8969
Golf Shop: 320-259-8969
Type: Public   Par: 72
www.oakhillgolfclub.com

Region: NorthWest

Course Rating

HOSPITALITY	8.18
PLAYABILITY	7.44
USABILITY	8.62
FACILITY	8.36
VALUE	5.42

OVERALL SCORE
780

Green Fee: $23 (weekend)
1/2 Cart Fee: $14 (weekend)

Tees	Men's	Women's	Yards
Red		69.2/118	5006
White	69.5/122		6035
Blue	71.8/130		6534

Drive approximately 12 miles north of St. Cloud on Highway 10 and you'll find Oak Hill Golf Course in Rice, Minnesota. The clubhouse is a quite comfortable, with a lounge area, small pro shop and snack bar. The patio has a scenic overlook of the course and four greens.

The course is carved out of the woods and follows the natural contours of the land, with oak trees surrounding many of the fairways. The course was in excellent shape! Each tee box (usually two per hole) had a ball washer, garbage can and bench. It is easy to get around the course; the asphalt cart paths join the green to the next tee box.

The fairways are bent grass, in great condition and well mowed. The first rough is also mowed to about one or two inches. The outer rough is in the oak trees or heavier forest, which can result in some lost balls. Bunkers are filled with soft sand. The greens are well tended (although they had just been aerated before we arrived) and show the quality of care.

While most holes look fairly straight forward, the do offer some fun challenges. Hole #7, a par 5, has an S-curve fairway over four hills and valleys. It is impossible to see the pin until the last hill and there is an invisible sand trap just in front of the green. Hole #8 is also hilly with a serious dogleg left. Reaching the green requires a shot over the trees. The tree-lined fairway of the 9th hole follows a curved path and narrows as it approaches the green. The 13th hole has the only water hazard on the course and you can't see it until it's too late—watch out if you tend to slice.

The course is not long, but the hazards on almost every hole make this a fun and interesting course to play. We were also impressed by the friendliness of the staff and members. We felt quite at home here and Oak Hill Golf Course certainly requires a return visit.

ID: 5636709MN

OAK MARSH

Region: Twin Cities

526 Inwood Avenue North
Oakdale, MN 55128
Clubhouse: 651-730-8886
Golf Shop: 651-730-8886
Type: Public   Par: 70

www.wpgolf.com/oakmarsh

Tees	Men's	Women's	Yards
Red		66.9/112	4648
Gold	65.9/112	70.4/119	5273
White	68.2/117	73.3/125	5793
Blue	70.0/121		6184

Course Rating

HOSPITALITY	7.20
PLAYABILITY	7.76
USABILITY	7.28
FACILITY	7.46
VALUE	5.73

OVERALL SCORE
728

Greens Fee: $36.00 (weekend)
1/2 Cart Fee: $16.00 (weekend)

Located in Oakdale, Minnesota, Oak Marsh Golf Course is a compact course that seems out of place surrounded by residential on one side and commercial offices and retail on the other. Like urban courses (this one is actually in a suburb), it must contend with the hubbub and noise of the city, but once you move into the course a few holes, those concerns fade away.

At only 5793 yards from the white tees, you'd think the course provides no challenge. Well, don't prejudge it. Yes, there are some long holes with little by way of hazards, but there are also a number of holes that require hitting over or alongside water. These require you to be judicious when pulling out your driver. Regardless, unless you have a water phobia, the course plays reasonably easy for a hacker.

Where the course seems to slip is the sometimes confusing signage for a first timer and the occasional long distances between holes and from the clubhouse to the first tee. It doesn't have much elevation so walking the course is a definite possibility. It also has a centrally located driving range and putting green very close to the first tee so practicing before your round is very convenient. If you choose a cart, they are equipped with new UpLink GPS, which is a nice feature, but the screen is so large that it requires looking through the windshield from the side.

The clubhouse doubles as an event center and has a full bar, a full-service Oak Marsh Grille, a deck and expansive patio. The course management really emphasizes its function space for weddings and other events and can host up to 300 people. You might get the sense that golf is secondary to events and from a profitability sense, you'd probably be right.

For folks on the east side of the Twin Cities, Oak Marsh Golf Course should be considered as a playing option, but it does tend to be a bit more spendy than similar city courses.

ID: 5512808MN

OAK SUMMIT

2751 County Road 16 SW
Rochester, MN 55902
Clubhouse: 507-252-1808
Golf Shop: 507-252-1808
Type: Public   Par: 70
www.oaksummitgolf.com

Region: SouthEast

Course Rating

HOSPITALITY	8.21
PLAYABILITY	7.92
USABILITY	8.36
FACILITY	7.84
VALUE	7.71

OVERALL SCORE
805

Green Fee: $26 (weekend)
1/2 Cart Fee: $15 (weekend)

Tees	Men's	Women's	Yards
Red		68.8/111	5080
Gold	66.3/116		5399
White	69.3/118		6055
Blue	71.0/118		6434

Oak Summit Golf Course is just across the road from the quiet Rochester airport off County Road 16 in Rochester, Minnesota. While this beautiful course isn't long (6055 yards from the white tees), it does have some reasonable challenges the average golfer will enjoy. Blind shots are bountiful throughout the course, but they do provide you with a yardage card that we found very helpful. The greens were incredibly fast and held most shots fairly well.

The fairways were in good condition. The course is about 80% irrigated and well maintained. There were a few bunkers that were in okay condition. The sand wasn't especially soft, more like the type you'd find on the playground, but it allowed for decent shots out of the hazard. The rough was not real long, so an errant shot was not tragic. Overall, we loved the open feel of the course. There were a few holes that were *very* tight with water on one side and trees on the other, but this made for a fun challenge. We moved through our round in a little over four hours, which we thought was fine. The course is well marked and we had no trouble getting from one hole to the next.

The staff was very friendly and helpful, answering our questions professionally. We saw the beverage cart four times on our round, which was quite nice! The locals were incredible as well, making our round a fun experience. The clubhouse is small, so don't expect anything fancy. There is a pavilion next to the clubhouse for groups of 30 or more. Hotdogs, cold sandwiches and pizza are served, along with beer and hard lemonade. The pro shop was even smaller, but adequate. We had no problem finding a parking spot even though there was a small tournament that day. The driving range is very close to the clubhouse and prices ($6 for 70 balls) are more than reasonable. There is a nice putting green near the 1st tee, so you can practice as you wait for your tee time. Weekend rounds aren't any more expensive at Oak Summit. They do have some excellent specials too. The yearly rates for this course are affordable with a single membership just $700.

ID: 5590209MN

OAKCREST

5th Street South
Roseau, Minnesota 56751
Clubhouse: 218-463-3016
Golf Shop: 218-463-3016
Type: Public   Par: 71

www.oakcrestgolfcourse.com

Tees	Men's	Women's	Yards
Red		68.9/117	5054
White	69.6/123		6076
Blue	70.9/124		6371

Region: NorthWest

Course Rating

U

HOSPITALITY	8.67
PLAYABILITY	8.16
USABILITY	8.85
FACILITY	8.30
VALUE	7.42

OVERALL SCORE
837

Green Fee: $24 (weekend)
1/2 Cart Fee: $12 (weekend)

A hidden gem of Minnesota golf can be found in this state's farthest northwest corner. Oakcrest Golf Club, located in Roseau, Minnesota, is a municipal course that was redesigned by Joel Goldstrand in the 1990s and displays a contrast in styles between the two nines. The front nine has a Scottish links-style feel, with a very open terrain and friendly to any hacker. A few of the holes are a bit long, but with four sets of tees, golfers should be able to find a distance and challenge suitable to their game. The summertime fairways run firm and fast, giving golfers an extra 5–10 yards off the tee. The greens are medium sized and putt quick, smooth and true.

The original back nine is a very fair test of play. It features shorter, tighter holes in oak tree-lined fairways. The Roseau River runs along the property and borders three holes. This side features three interesting par 3s and two par 5s that can be reached in two by a big swinging hacker.

The facility has a driving range and chipping green located right next to the #1 tee box for a golfers to loosen up those stiff joints after a long car ride. In addition, the course has a fairly good-sized putting green at the entrance and situated between holes #1 and #10. The on-course restroom and shelter facilities are logically located and easy to access. The clubhouse features a well-stocked bar with a new patio overlooking the 18th green. Golfers can enjoy short-order food items from the menu or try a frozen candy bar, a favorite of the local members.

Oakcrest Golf Club is very easy to access and play. Tee times are not required but encouraged and the pace of play is typically very quick. The course can be walked since it's fairly flat, but there are plenty of nice electric golf carts available for rent at reasonable prices. The clubhouse and grounds staff were very friendly and helpful. For the quality and value, Roseau's Oakcrest Golf Club is truly worth the drive to northwestern Minnesota.

ID: 5675109MN

OAKDALE

55106 County Road 38
Buffalo Lake, MN 55314
Clubhouse: 320-587-0525
Golf Shop: 320-587-0525
Type: Public   Par: 72

www.oakdalegolfclub.com

Tees	Men's	Women's	Yards
Red		70.0/120	5148
Gold	66.2/118	70.8/122	5304
White	71.2/127	76.9/134	6398
Blue	72.1/129		6609

Region: SouthWest

Course Rating

HOSPITALITY   8.44
PLAYABILITY   8.34
USABILITY   8.45
FACILITY   8.31
VALUE   6.76

OVERALL SCORE
822

Green Fee: $30 (weekend)
1/2 Cart Fee: $15 (weekend)

On County Road 38, beside Lake Allie, you will find a relatively unknown gem. Oakdale Golf Course, located in Buffalo Lake, Minnesota, is a beautiful and well-maintained golf course that's worth the drive. Nine holes were developed in 1965 and another nine were added in 1995. The original holes are lined with majestic oak trees and divided between the front and back nine, with three holes on the front and six on the back. There are a number of trees on the new holes, but they have yet to mature.

When arriving, you'll notice the attractive clubhouse, with its wonderful landscaping and flowers. The second floor patio has some great views of the course. The bar and grill area seats 125. The food was the normal fare of appetizers, salads, and sandwiches. While the pro shop is small, it's well stocked. The staff was very friendly and helpful. To the right of the 10th tee is a nice practice putting green and to the right of the 18th green is a driving range with 10–12 stalls. There is no practice sand bunker. Golfers had better have their game in order from the 1st tee. The 1st hole is a 387-yard severe dogleg right, with trees left and right and a large stone-lined pond. Our first encounter with water came on the 6th hole, a 140-yard downhill par 3 with a kidney shaped pond guarding the front and left sides of the green.

We were fortunate not to have the opportunity to test the bunkers, but they were all level, average size and well maintained, with good sand and texture. The fairways are generous in width, but if missed, the large oak trees can be an issue. The rough was well groomed at 1–2 inches. Out of bounds and hazards were well marked except on #15. The front nine is quite long at 3362 yards and the back nine is much shorter at 3036 yards for a total of 6398 yards from the white tees.

Oakdale is an old-style golf course, not like the newer upscale ones, but we believe it ranks up there with the best of them.

205

ID: 5531409MN

ONEKA RIDGE

Region: Twin Cities

5610 North 12th Street
White Bear Lake, MN 55110
Clubhouse: 651-429-2390
Golf Shop: 651-429-2390
Type: Public   Par: 72

www.onekaridgegc.com

Course Rating

HOSPITALITY	6.29
PLAYABILITY	7.07
USABILITY	6.93
FACILITY	6.13
VALUE	6.38

OVERALL SCORE
664

Tees	Men's	Women's	Yards
Red		69.6/117	5166
White	69.7/121	74.6/128	6061
Blue	71.1/126		6360

Greens Fee: $32.00 (weekend)
1/2 Cart Fee: $14.00 (weekend)

Located in White Bear Lake, Minnesota, Oneka Ridge Golf Course plays to 6061 yards. The website claims a practice green with a practice bunker, but this reviewer did not see the bunker anywhere. The one practice green that was found near the first hole was a decent size with no holes cut in it, just the little stick-in flags.

The range was a little bit away from the clubhouse and you had to pass by #10 and #14 to get to it. It's on the small size with only about 7 stalls. There were 3 target "greens" on the range that were actually just sand hills.

Tee boxes are in fine shape. One nice feature is that each hole has an aerial photo showing the entire hole with landing areas marked out with distances. Fairways are in pretty good condition, not overly wide or too small either.

Greens are in fine shape with your typical 4–5 pitch marks per green but they rolled decently once they dried up from the morning dew. Greens were mostly sized medium-large and fairly flat with some character.

Overall flow of the course was decent and you could easily find your next hole. Signage wasn't that necessary since the green you just played and the next box are a very short distance apart. One major complaint is that the course "feels" tight. It's not the individual holes themselves that are tight, quite the contrary. It's the way they have this course laid out that makes you feel you are on top of other holes around you. If you are having a bad day with the sticks, you could easily be hitting into other tee boxes or other greens.

The clubhouse is on the smallish side but has inside and outside seating areas to rest after the round. Food selection is inexpensive, but is very typical microwaveable fare. One nice feature for those who like to forget things like scorecards is that you can get one from the pro shop which you pass a million times, or on #2 and #11.

This is a scoreable course with few trouble spots so your score shouldn't suffer, but don't expect much in the way of amenities.

ID: 5511008MN

ORTONVILLE

145 Golf Club Road
Ortonville, MN 56278
Clubhouse: 320-839-3606
Golf Shop: 320-839-3606
Type: Public   Par: 72
www.ortonvillegolfcourse.com

Tees	Men's	Women's	Yards
Red		70.9/116	5419
White	68.7/118	74.2/123	6001

Region: WestCentral

Course Rating

HOSPITALITY	8.85
PLAYABILITY	6.82
USABILITY	8.38
FACILITY	7.37
VALUE	5.53

OVERALL SCORE
759

Green Fee: $29 (weekend)
1/2 Cart Fee: $14 (weekend)

Ortonville Golf Course has a beautiful atmosphere by a gorgeous lake. Located in Ortonville, Minnesota, this small-town municipal course is extremely well maintained. There aren't any practice areas or driving range, unfortunately.

The golf course is beautifully cut with some great holes overlooking the water. It is suitable for golfers with a 20+ handicap since it's so short and straight; there aren't any true doglegs. This course offers a mix of beauty and playability. The holes are picturesque, the rough is easy to hit out of, and the hazards aren't too much of a threat. The hazards were clearly defined and easy to see. We didn't have too much difficulty finding the holes. There was one instance when we had to look closely at the scorecard to figure out where to go, so some signage would be nice.

The clubhouse boasts a bar and grill with quite a selection of items and fast service. It's possible to order food at the turn without holding up play. The costs are very appropriate in most cases, with beverages being the only possible exception. The restaurant food seems appropriate for a clubhouse restaurant and should fit any hackers' budget without a problem. Caps are $12 and Ortonville shirts, pullovers and visors are available for fair prices, as well. The pro shop also offers a decent selection of golf balls.

Overall, we would recommend this course to any hacker wishing for a chance to score well without fearing some awful hazard. It's an affordable way to spend an afternoon out on the course in western Minnesota.

ID: 5627809MN

PARKVIEW Exec. 18

1310 Cliff Road
Eagan, MN 55123
Clubhouse: 651-452-5098
Golf Shop: 651-452-5098
Type: Public   Par: 63

www.parkviewgolfclub.com

Tees	Men's	Women's	Yards
Blue		62.8/99	4064
Gold	61.5/98	65.1/104	4479

Region: Twin Cities

Course Rating

HOSPITALITY   6.89
PLAYABILITY   6.30
USABILITY   7.85
FACILITY   5.90
VALUE   6.01

OVERALL SCORE
667

Greens Fee: $27.25 (weekend)
1/2 Cart Fee: $11.75 (weekend)

Known for its "first to open, last to close" policy, Parkview Golf Club is a beginner's course and makes an effort to reach out to juniors and less skilled players. At only 4479 yards from the gold tees, it presents little challenge to accomplished players, but is a good place to learn the ropes.

The course is well used and shows it. When visited, the tee boxes showed a lot of divots and the greens had a number of areas that needed seeding or better maintenance. The course itself is very unimaginative—a lot of flat, straight fairways. Only a few holes present any challenge and you'll find those at the end of your round. For golfers just starting out, be warned that many greens are elevated so even if an approach shot lands on the green, it is likely to roll off the other side, adding to your score.

This is a walker's course and a cart is superfluous and an unnecessary expense. The signage around the course tends to be spotty. Most holes are easy to figure out, but for first timers, the course needs more directional signage and distance markers to make playing easier.

The practice facilities are small, need better maintenance and are not in great shape. The putting green is small and the coin-operated driving range is narrow with odd target hills complete with fake sand traps. A second putting area actually has a couple of practice sand traps that you rarely find at courses around town. They take pace-of-play seriously so watch for the electric chair near the entrance for those who are found to have been convicted of "slow play."

Parkview is a basic, no-frills course. It does try to reach out to the beginner with individual and group lessons as well as golf camps throughout the summer and is a nice place for seniors looking to finish eighteen holes in under 3 ½ hours.

For more accomplished players, this is not the course for you, but for those wanting to work on their game in a relaxed, no-pressure environment, Parkview might be a stop on your itinerary.

ID: 5512308MN

PEBBLE CREEK

14000 Clubhouse Lane
Becker, MN 55308
Clubhouse: 763-263-4653
Golf Shop: 763-263-4653
Type: Public   Par: 36/36/36

www.pebblecreekgolf.com

Tees	Men's	Women's	Yards
Red/White (middle)	68.3/119	73.7/126	5756
Red/White (champ)	73.3/140		6872
White/Blue (middle)	67.9/119	73.1/128	5639
White/Blue (champ)	72.6/136		6696
Blue/Red (middle)	68.7/122	73.7/129	5803
Blue/Red (champ)	73.0/139		6818

Region: Twin Cities

Course Rating

HOSPITALITY	6.79
PLAYABILITY	7.97
USABILITY	7.37
FACILITY	6.85
VALUE	6.41

OVERALL SCORE
723

Greens Fee: $42.00 (weekend)
1/2 Cart Fee: $14.00 (weekend)

If you are planning a trip to St. Cloud, Pebble Creek in Becker, Minnesota, might be a stop you'd want to make on your way.   One of the highlights is the creek that flows throughout many of the holes, hence the name. Pebble Creek is large enough that some might call it a river, and it twists and turns to flow alongside and across many of the holes in a way that is quite beautiful. The course is also bordered by an old-growth forest of leafy trees, which is also very stunning and adds a sense of calming peace.

What does not help with that calming peace is the huge lack of signage. We were constantly guessing which way to go for the next hole, and were wrong many times. Distance to the pin was always a toss-up, and finding the correct tee box just seemed to be harder than it needed to be. Luckily, the pace of play was pretty ideal, as there was wide spacing between tee times on a rather nice Sunday afternoon.

One feature of this course is the choice to play two of three 9-hole courses. Each is really challenging, with constant hazards and somewhat narrow fairways, so hackers had better bring their A-game or be ready for some high scores.

The banquet facility and full-service bar upstairs in the clubhouse are really nice, with a few flat screen TVs and a deck for relaxing after your round. This reviewer was the only customer in the place and the girl behind the counter seemed a bit disinterested in providing service. The food selection was a little scarce as well. Admittedly, however, an establishment cannot be judged based on the service from one employee alone. In contrast, the on-course cart girl was Johnny-on-the-spot, with a very friendly disposition.

All in all, this really is a beautiful course, and will certainly flush out the most accurate golfer in your group. The biggest hang-up might be the value component. The greens and fairway conditions are average, so at $56 to ride 18 holes on the weekend, there are certainly options out there that may give a bigger bang for the buck.

209

ID: 5530808MN

PERHAM LAKESIDE

2727 450th Street
Perham, MN 56573
Clubhouse: 218-346-6070
Golf Shop: 218-346-6070
Type: Public   Par: 37/36/36

www.perhamlakeside.com

V

Course Rating

HOSPITALITY	8.64
PLAYABILITY	8.46
USABILITY	8.69
FACILITY	7.85
VALUE	7.96

OVERALL SCORE
841

Green Fee: $38 (weekend)
1/2 Cart Fee: $12 (weekend)

Tees	Men's	Women's	Yards
Maple/Oak - White	68.7/119	74.0/130	5888
Maple/Oak - Blue	71.3/125		6449
Oak/Pine - White	68.2/121	72.8/130	5787
Oak/Pine - Blue	71.0/127		6395
Pine/Maple - White	69.5/121	74.7/134	6053
Pine/Maple - Blue	72.1/126		6634

Located in Perham, Minnesota, home of Barrel O' Fun Potato Chips, a Bongards' Creameries plant and Kenny's Candy Company (better watch your weight here), Perham Lakeside Golf Club is a sprawling 27-hole facility located north of town. Established in 1946 as a 9-hole course, it was expanded in 2000 to three distinct nines: Pine, Oak and Maple.

Designed by Joel Goldstrand, this course borders Little Pine Lake and has an extensive golf learning center just across the street. One thing you'll notice is the business community support and their logos on the course are evidence of their contributions. The clubhouse has all the modern amenities and boasts an event room that will hold 275 people. We were there during a wedding and the facility could easily handle both an event as well as regular customers eating dinner at the Mulligan's Pub & Eatery.

The course boasts four sets of tees and some nice touches like granite hole signage, landscaped tee boxes and a three-hole junior course that is free to the public. The course also reaches out to young players; adding a junior under 18 to a single adult membership is only $85 annually. Another surprise is the pro shop. It is chock-full of merchandise like clothing, equipment and accessories, which is very unusual these days. Judging by the course's website, they clearly understand marketing and give golfers a lot of information about each hole as well as video footage. Although unavailable at the time we visited, tee times can be made online.

When playing the course, golfers can select their round based on the difficulty of the nines. According to the club pro, the Pine/Maple pairing is the most difficult, an opinion seconded by locals. The course also caters to the locals with twilight, junior and range specials, but don't let that stop you because the locals are happy to have you there. The rates are great, the food and service excellent, and the golf makes it a top course when you're traveling in the Detroit Lakes area.

210

ID: 5657309MN

PEZHEKEE NATIONAL

20000 South Lakeshore Drive
Glenwood, MN 56334
Clubhouse: 320-634-4501
Golf Shop: 320-634-4501
Type: Public   Par: 72
www.petersresort.com/golf.html

Region: NorthWest

Course Rating

HOSPITALITY	7.17
PLAYABILITY	6.28
USABILITY	5.73
FACILITY	5.86
VALUE	4.31

Tees	Men's	Women's	Yards
Red		71.9/126	5389
Gold	68.8/125		5842
White	72.2/132		6592
Blue	75.2/138		7263

OVERALL SCORE
613

Green Fee: $37 (weekend)
1/2 Cart Fee: $14 (weekend)

This was a tricky course to find (especially in the fog). Located in Glenwood, Minnesota, Pezheekee National Golf Course is in resort country (we saw a cart driving on the street to the course). The tiny parking lot will hold only 6–10 cars. The clubhouse is small, but has a pro shop, full bar and restaurant. There is a putting green, but no driving range. There were four tee boxes with garbage bags, ball washers and benches, although unfortunately there was no water on the course.

Standing on the first tee, Pezheekee National seems to be a very scenic course with narrow fairways, bounded by large trees on both sides. The fairways were green with a mixture of grass and weeds. The greens were in fairly good shape, but a little slow. The sand traps consisted of gravel.

There were several holes where we had to drive over a pond with surrounding cattails. Three greens still had plugs on the green and no hole to shoot at. While this was obviously temporary, it showed a lack of interest in course maintenance.

There were several interesting holes. On #10, we could not tell which way the dogleg turned. On #11, we teed off from a hilltop to a dogleg left where we had to hit to a virtual island green surrounded by cattails. Not much room for error! The course was very scenic with lake views, heavy forests, ponds and rolling hills. Each hole seemed to have a new variety of problems, which made it fun to play. It was a long course: 6595 yards from the whites and 7263 from the blues. The par 3s ranged from 161 to199 yards and the par 5s reached 546 yards.

The course is walkable, but strenuous. As we were searching for the clubhouse after the 18th hole, we passed the 19th (over a pond and hill), but decided against walking back to find the tee. Do yourself a favor and pay the $14 for a cart rental.

ID: 5633409MN

PHALEN PARK

1615 Phalen Drive
St. Paul, MN 55106
Clubhouse: 651-778-0424
Golf Shop: 651-778-0413
Type: Public   Par: 70

www.golfstpaul.org

Tees	Men's	Women's	Yards
Red		69.6/116	5311
White	67.5/116		5881
Blue	68.4/118		6092

Region: Twin Cities

Course Rating

HOSPITALITY	7.12
PLAYABILITY	6.68
USABILITY	6.98
FACILITY	6.02
VALUE	6.36

OVERALL SCORE
672

Greens Fee: $30.00 (weekend)
1/2 Cart Fee: $14.00 (weekend)

Phalen Park Golf Course is a classic Saint Paul, Minnesota, municipal course mixing a challenging collection of holes with enjoyable service. If you need a little warm-up time upon your arrival there is a decent-sized range and a basic practice green to hone your putting stroke. Their practice area is far from mesmerizing but it does the trick to get the kinks out.

The clubhouse feels more like a rec center but this is a city municipal course so a plush clubhouse should never be expected. The concession stand has all of the things you would expect at a golf course concession stand and also has some of the best hot dogs in the Metro area.

While the course is loaded with trees lining both sides of just about every hole, the holes lay out very nicely for the hacker. The front opens with an easy and relatively short par 4 that is easily parable. The front nine is considerably easier than the back as several blind tee shots come into play.

Because it is a municipal track, the greens and fairways are a bit tattered due to the sheer traffic the course endures. And a lot of that traffic is being pretty rough on the course, evidenced by deep unreplaced divots in the fairways and ball marks on the greens.

If you can get past the blemishes there really are some nice holes including a challenging par-5 on #4. We also liked the par-3 #17 that looks like you have to go over water to get there but the water is actually not in play—if you can convince yourself of that before the shot.

The service overall was welcoming as people in the pro shop, concession stand and on the beverage cart were all extremely friendly.

This course is shorter, playing only a shade over 5800 yards from the middle tees, but don't confuse short with easy. The course will challenge you and you are almost guaranteed to score better after at least one round of experience on it.

ID: 5510608MN

PHEASANT ACRES

10705 County Road 116
Rogers, MN 55374
Clubhouse: 763-428-8244
Golf Shop: 763-428-8244
Type: Public   Par: 72

www.pheasantacresgolf.com

Tees	Men's	Women's	Yards
Red		69.1/118	5082
Gold	67.3/115		5632
White	69.3/119		6099
Blue	71.2/122		6523

Region: Twin Cities

Course Rating

HOSPITALITY   7.76
PLAYABILITY   8.31
USABILITY   7.91
FACILITY   7.92
VALUE   7.23

OVERALL SCORE
793

Greens Fee: $34.00 (weekend)
1/2 Cart Fee: $14.00 (weekend)

Located in the northwest corner of Hennepin County, Pheasant Acres Golf Course in Rogers, Minnesota, is easy to locate and fun to play. Easiest access is from Highway 55, north on County Road 116 until you see the course on your left. You can also access the course by driving Highway 94 to County Road 30 (Maple Grove) west to County Road 116 and north to the course.

Driving range, chipping green and putting green are located adjacent to the clubhouse and the clubhouse itself offers a full-service restaurant and bar. While relatively small, the clubhouse makes use of all of its space. A pro shop is on-site with the typical selection of clothing and gear. PGA Professional Instructor Steve Fessler is available for private and group lessons. There are a number of various leagues one can join and always a special for greens fees.

The 18-hole course has some 30 traps and 16 ponds as well as some wooded areas. Roughs are well groomed and a ball in the rough is easily located. The course is fairly easy to walk with only a couple of uphill stretches and those are gradual in slope. A nice mixture of well-placed challenges are offered to the golfer, but strategic play should keep one out of trouble through most of the course. The course offers outhouses and toilets at well-spaced points. There are coin-operated pop machines at mid points on each nine. The beverage cart is usually circling the course as well.

When we golfed this course we found the staff always friendly and the other golfers cordial. This course offers a decent challenge to sharpen your skills at rates that are as competitive as any in the Metro area. If you are anywhere near Rogers, stop in at Pheasant Acres Golf Course.

PINE ISLAND

Region: SouthEast

920 8th Street SE
Pine Island, MN 55963
Clubhouse: 507-356-8252
Golf Shop: 507-356-8252
Type: Semi-Private   Par: 71

www.pigc.net

V

Course Rating

HOSPITALITY	8.17
PLAYABILITY	6.00
USABILITY	7.57
FACILITY	5.89
VALUE	8.33

Tees	Men's	Women's	Yards
Red		68.8/118	4946
Gold	65.4/118	69.9/120	5149
White	69.8/127	75.2/132	6114
Blue	71.8/131		6563

OVERALL SCORE
707

Green Fee: $25 (weekend)
1/2 Cart Fee: included in fee

Pine Island Golf Course is just off Highway 52, between Rochester and Cannon Falls, Minnesota. Established in 1994 as a nine-hole course, the second nine holes were added in 2001. We played Pine Island on a Monday morning in early June. The course was quite busy, but tee times were spaced adequately for relaxed play. The practice green was under repair, but we were able to visit the driving range. A small clubhouse had only basic food offerings, along with a small pro shop to peruse. There isn't a bar service, so you will have to go into town if you're looking for a drink.

The course condition was about what we expected, not impeccable, but it would be unfair to be too critical of the course. What it does offer is a decent layout with basic amenities to provide hackers with a fun day of golf at an incredible value. Average players can reasonably expect to score around par.

There are three sets of tees to choose from. Hazards are few and although there is some water on the course, we found it to be a non-factor for the most part. The course is scenic enough and provides enough variation to keep your interest. Pine Island is known for its large green and we didn't find them too challenging. One of our favorite features of the course was an aerial photo of the hole layout at the tee box. This photo was marked with distances, making it easy to gauge your expected tee shot lie.

One thing that cannot be denied is the value. Green fees during the week are just $20, including a cart rental. And the weekend rates are only $5 more! To top it off, membership packages start at just $500. Golfers would be hard-pressed to find a better deal. For the value alone, we would play here again. Expect Pine Island to be a busy, well-attended course in the future.

ID: 5596309MN

PINE RIDGE

34500 Hillcrest Road
Motley, MN 56466
Clubhouse: 218-575-3300
Golf Shop: 218-575-3300
Type: Public   Par: 73

www.brainerd.net/~prgolfcl

Tees	Men's	Women's	Yards
Bronze	63.3/115	67.8/120	4778
Silver	68.7/126	74.0/134	5744
Pearl	70.5/130	76.3/138	6145
Gold	71.9/133		6449

Region: WestCentral

Course Rating

HOSPITALITY	8.25
PLAYABILITY	7.39
USABILITY	7.24
FACILITY	7.84
VALUE	7.43

OVERALL SCORE
765

Green Fee: $39 (weekend)
1/2 Cart Fee: included in fee

Pine Ridge Golf Club, south of Motley, Minnesota, is a rare treat in early September. Early spring can be harsh, with hard fairways and greens, but by late summer Pine Ridge is in its prime. It is one of the prettiest courses in central Minnesota, without the high costs of a resort course. The rolling hills make the course quite scenic, but it's not easily walked. Greens are large and in good shape; they are well sloped but putt true. Most fairways are reasonably wide, but there are a few tight ones. Virtually every hole has trees on both sides. In the summer, the woods are cleared of leaves and branches, so finding a ball is pretty easy. Bunkers are fairly shallow with good sand. Only one hole truly has water in play, with a forced carry on the right side of the fairway.

The course's restaurant, The Ridge Rib and Steak House, has a good menu and reasonable prices. They also offer banquet services for both golfing and non-golfing events. The pro shop offers snacks and a variety of beverages. And the staff is really friendly.

What we liked best about Pine Ridge is the scenery. The holes are picturesque and golfers can see a variety of wildlife, such as birds, deer, rabbits and even the occasional fox or beaver while playing their round. Also the course layout makes sense. You never have to stop and wonder, where do I go now? There is almost no need for signage. While hackers will find this course friendly overall, make no mistake: course management is key.

Pine Ridge caters to area golfers. Be sure to visit the course's website for Internet specials. With an affordable green fee and single memberships only $375, Pine Ridge Golf Club is a great value for your golf dollar. We would encourage any hacker to give it a shot.

PIONEER CREEK

705 Copeland Road
Maple Plain, MN 55359
Clubhouse: 952-955-3982
Golf Shop: 952-955-3982
Type: Public   Par: 72

www.pioneercreek.com

Course Rating

HOSPITALITY	6.35
PLAYABILITY	5.80
USABILITY	6.25
FACILITY	5.76
VALUE	4.83

OVERALL SCORE
592

Tees	Men's	Women's	Yards
Red		69.7/121	5147
Gold	68.4/123	73.5/129	5840
White	70.4/128	76.0/134	6291
Blue	72.0/130		6618
Black	73.5/133		6953

Greens Fee: $39.00 (weekend)
1/2 Cart Fee: $14.00 (weekend)

If you are looking for golf on the westside of the Twin Cities, Pioneer Creek Golf Course in Maple Plain, Minnesota, can be approached on County Road 6 from either direction and you will see the clubhouse on the north side of the road. At the time of this writing we found the area a little dusty as there was new construction going on across the road from the clubhouse so roll up your windows.

This is a typical farm-country golf course with a nice layout. The tee boxes, rough and greens were in good shape but the fairways were hard and dry. There is a nice mixture of hazards (woods, water, sand and swamp) but only two holes really challenge accuracy. The greens are relatively small and the cups all seem to be elevated, making putts a challenge. There is little in the way of signage but the asphalt cart paths take the golfer from one hole to the next without the need for signs. There is not a level fairway on the course and the golf course's rolling contours makes for a good workout for the walker.

The course has many on-course Satellite toilets so a pit stop is just a few holes away. One sour note was the cleanliness and condition of the golf carts. Most carts could use a cleaning and the one we drove emitted a piercing whine from the rear axle that gave us a headache by the end of the round.

The log cabin clubhouse is pretty bare bones but was clean and the staff cordial and helpful. It offers the traditional golf course grub (snack bar) and a decent collection of gear and clothing. No great deals but some nice looking stuff. Fees for golf, driving range and carts are typical of this type of country course so you should be able to find a rate that will fit your budget.

There are enough challenges to make the course interesting but the wide fairways should keep you out of trouble most of the time with an opportunity for par on most holes and a birdie shot every now and then. For a little refreshment after the game, try the Ox Yoke Inn in Lyndale just a couple blocks east of Copeland on 92 heading towards St. Boni.

ID: 5535908MN

POKEGAMA

3910 Golf Course Road
Grand Rapids, MN 55744
Clubhouse: 218-326-3444
Golf Shop: 888-307-3444
Type: Public   Par: 71
www.pokegamagolf.com

Course Rating

HOSPITALITY	8.28
PLAYABILITY	8.09
USABILITY	8.47
FACILITY	7.80
VALUE	6.88

Tees	Men's	Women's	Yards
Red		67.7/116	5046
Red/Yellow		70.9/121	5284
Yellow	66.6/116	71.6/125	5585
White	68.5/117	73.8/129	6105
Blue	70.3/121	76.0/134	6481

OVERALL SCORE
805

Green Fee: $35 (weekend)
1/2 Cart Fee: $16 (weekend)

Pokegama Golf Course is a Grand Rapids, Minnesota municipal facility on the shores of Pokegama Lake. Given the beautiful setting, it's not surprising the Minnesota PGA has chosen this course to host many state golf events. It is well manicured and very hacker-friendly, but challenging to golfers of all levels. The tees offer course lengths from 6481 yards down to 5046 yards. If golfers play from the tees appropriate to their skill level, they should enjoy playing this course.

The clubhouse is currently being renovated and is scheduled to open in the spring of 2010. The new facility will have paths to the park and beach. The pro shop space is understandably limited, but has a moderate selection of clubs, clothing and golf gear. They have the equipment and knowledge to do club fitting. The golf pro gives group and private lessons and has a premier practice facility at his disposal. There are two driving ranges, a putting green, a chipping green with a practice bunker, and a short game green. Like the course, these areas are well maintained.

The electric carts are equipped with a GPS system that gives the yardage to the center of the green. This is not as effective as a full screen picture and information system, but it helps when not familiar with the course.

Water can come into play on a few holes, but only one requires a carry. There is out of bounds on several holes, although it's usually on the left so a right-handed golfer with a tendency to slice should be in the clear. All the woods are free of brush, making it easier to find errant shots.

The restaurant has a limited menu, but the service was very friendly and efficient. Eat and drink on the deck and enjoy the views of Pokegama Lake. Take a break and then go play another round for just the price of the cart.

ID: 5574409MN

POMME DE TERRE

24860 State Highway 9
Morris, MN 56267
Clubhouse: 320-589-1009
Golf Shop: 320-589-1009
Type: Semi-Private   Par: 72
www.pdtgolfclub.com

Tees	Men's	Women's	Yards
Red	64.3/115	68.3/117	4914
Combo	67.1/120		5528
White	68.9/124	74.0/129	5940
Blue	70.8/128		6371

Region: WestCentral

Course Rating

HOSPITALITY	8.87
PLAYABILITY	8.46
USABILITY	7.77
FACILITY	8.61
VALUE	7.21

OVERALL SCORE
832

Green Fee: $26.50 (weekend)
1/2 Cart Fee: $13 (weekend)

If you're in the Morris, Minnesota area and up for a good golf outing, don't miss Pomme de Terre Golf Course. The 6371-yard, par-72 course is a bit challenging in areas, but ultimately a very pleasurable golfing experience. With an upgrade in 2007 to 18 holes, this Joel Goldstrand-designed course has both a traditional and links-style look and feel. Given the layout of the newer holes, we highly recommend using a cart unless you desire a workout.

The brand-new 3500 square foot clubhouse is very pleasing to the eye and fits very well with the course environment. Inside, there is a very nice pro shop, with a wide variety of golf equipment and apparel. While there is no full-service restaurant, there is a wide variety of snacks (hot or cold) and beverages available that can be enjoyed on the huge deck overlooking the 18th green. On the course, tee box signage was more than adequate. We also appreciated the well-marked cart paths; there were only a few spots where we had to stop and determine which way to go.

Aside from a few tee boxes in need of repair (which shouldn't normally affect one's game), the course was in wonderful shape. Although considered a bit narrow, the bluegrass fairways were very well kept and will reward straight drivers. On the original nine, there are some older trees, which can affect play if golfers find the rough. On the new nine, the links-style holes had fescue and other long native grasses as punishment for the errant shot, usually resulting in a lost ball. Although two were a bit small, the greens were definitely one of the high points of this course and were extremely well manicured. They rolled true and pin placement was forgiving the day we played.

"Pomme de Terre" literally translated means "apple of the earth"—in other words, a potato and the people in this area are definitely down to earth. We found both the locals and staff very friendly and we look forward to playing Pomme de Terre Golf Course again.

218

ID: 5626709MN

PRAIRIE VIEW

Region: SouthWest

Highway 266 North
Worthington, MN 56187
Clubhouse: 507-372-8670
Golf Shop: 507-372-8670
Type: Public   Par: 71

www.ci.worthington.mn.us/Prairie View 2.htm

Tees	Men's	Women's	Yards
Red		69.7/119	5105
White	69.1/120	74.6/130	5989
Blue	70.8/124		6368

Course Rating

HOSPITALITY	7.52
PLAYABILITY	8.43
USABILITY	7.11
FACILITY	8.00
VALUE	6.58

OVERALL SCORE
769

Green Fee: $21 (weekend)
1/2 Cart Fee: $13.50 (weekend)

The spirit of the links course is alive at Prairie View Golf Links in Worthington, Minnesota. Though Worthington isn't seaside or lakeside, the gentle hills, wildflower areas, tall grass and pothole bunkers are reminiscent of the old courses in Scotland. This course is difficult in some areas, but with wide fairways and minimal rough, it's nothing a hacker can't handle.

The signage was great on the course. Wildflowers areas are treated like ground under repair, which means a free drop with no penalty—except the loss of your ball. We hit into those areas a few times and couldn't find our ball or anyone else's, so bring a few extra sleeves. Although we didn't personally test the few pothole bunkers, the certainly looked impressive—some were 2 to 3 feet deep.

Without many shady trees, the sun can get quite hot. Thankfully, their beverage cart service was great. Most of the holes are average in length, maybe even a bit short. However, there is a longer par 3 that's about 200 yards. Golfers will have a few blind shots to make. It's hard to pick a favorite hole, but it's obvious #18 is a great finishing hole, with water looming in front of the green. Like the 18th, there are a couple holes where golfers will have to decide between the aggressive or safe play.

This municipal course has all the amenities (driving range, practice area, putting green) that golfers expect. Overall, the friendliness of the staff (particularly the clubhouse manager), great course layout and inexpensive prices make the trip to Worthington a worthwhile venture. We would gladly return a few times a year just to enjoy this great links-style course.

ID: 5618709MN

PRESTWICK

9555 Wedgewood Drive
Woodbury, MN 55125
Clubhouse: 651-731-4779
Golf Shop: 651-731-4779
Type: Public   Par: 72

www.prestwick.com

P

Course Rating

HOSPITALITY	6.97
PLAYABILITY	8.80
USABILITY	7.96
FACILITY	7.72
VALUE	5.06

OVERALL SCORE
764

Tees	Men's	Women's	Yards
Red		71.2/121	5228
Gold	68.7/120	74.0/127	5740
White	71.3/125	77.2/134	6319
Blue	73.2/130		6750

Greens Fee: $69.00 (weekend)
1/2 Cart Fee: $17.00 (weekend)

Getting to Prestwick Golf Course, located in Woodbury, Minnesota, was a challenge because the street signage is a bit confusing with Wedgewood on one side of the street and Edgewood on the other. Checking in was a bit off-putting. The person behind the desk seemed like she was having a phone texting emergency and was preoccupied with what was on her cell phone instead of helping us pay and get started. After a few direct questions, she finally realized we had never played there before and then directed her full attention to helping us get going.

We had to wait a bit at the first tee so we chatted up the starter. He was friendly, gave a lot of info about the course, but seemed a bit guarded. When we started to get caught up with the group ahead, they seemed a bit standoffish and paid us no notice. In contrast, the best person of the day was a single golfer. He had a home nearby and Prestwick was his home course. He was warm and welcoming.

The carts are one of the best things about the round. Very nice, clean, newer electric carts with GPS. Second best thing about the round is that you are able to order your turn meal from the cart. Which we did. We even got a confirmation that the order was received. Pretty tasty chicken salad wrap with good kettle chips.

The course itself was in good condition with your usual divots on the par 3s. The fairways were also in good condition and of decent width with an out-of-bounds on almost every hole. When we played the course, if we found ourselves in the sand, it seemed to be of poorer quality and still had not dried up from rain two days previous. The greens were fast and did not hold approach shots as well as anticipated.

The 19th hole, called Axel's at Prestwick, is a full bar and restaurant and does a good business catering to non-golfing customers in the evenings. It has a fireplace, a wall of windows and live music. If our perceptions were only based on the single that joined us, we would think differently about Prestwick. But all other things considered, Prestwick seemed like a semi-private course trying to be private and only put up with non-members because they needed the income.

ID: 5512508MN

PRINCETON

301 Golf Club Road
Princeton, MN 55371
Clubhouse: 763-389-2006
Golf Shop: 763-389-5109
Type: Public   Par: 71

www.princetongc.com

H

Course Rating

HOSPITALITY	8.91
PLAYABILITY	6.81
USABILITY	8.42
FACILITY	8.35
VALUE	7.35

OVERALL SCORE

794

Green Fee: $32 (weekend)
1/2 Cart Fee: $14 (weekend)

Tees	Men's	Women's	Yards
Red		69.8/119	4967
Gold	68.8/120	74.4/130	5770
White	70.5/127	76.5/135	6150
Blue	71.5/129		6381

Princeton Golf Course is situated by the Rum River, just 45 minutes north of the Twin Cities. We viewed the website for this course, located in Princeton, Minnesota, prior to our visit. Princeton's pictures were uninspiring and we expected a flat, boring, typical city course. We were wrong.

While the course is fairly flat—making it easy to walk—that's okay. Princeton has a pretty good layout with some interesting holes and the course was in excellent condition when we visited. Tee boxes were topnotch and the fairways were plush, the kind where you can take a divot and not worry about breaking a wrist on hardpan.

Parts of the course were wide open, but some holes required a little target golf. There is a good mix of water and sand to give you grief. Still, golfers aren't punished too badly for errant shots. Hackers can score well even if they are not hitting well.

The greens have a lot of character, with gently rolling undulations and some sloping. They rolled nice and true. Do not concede any putt: there is just enough trickery in these greens to give your opponent fits and a two-footer is easily missed.

There is a driving range and a practice area on site, as well as a full-service restaurant that's open year-round. The restaurant offers a decent menu with reasonable prices and a full bar for your post-round refreshments. We recommend the sweet potato french fries.

Princeton Golf Course is primarily frequented by the local members who are very loyal to their course, but also very friendly and helpful. The green fees are very reasonable and be sure to check out their new multi-round cards: 5 rounds for $50 or 10 rounds for $100. We would gladly go back and play this course again.

ID: 5537109MN

PURPLE HAWK

36000 Highway 65 NE
Cambridge, MN 55008
Clubhouse: 763-689-3800
Golf Shop: 763-689-3800
Type: Semi-Private   Par: 72

www.purplehawk.com

Course Rating

HOSPITALITY	8.70
PLAYABILITY	8.60
USABILITY	8.93
FACILITY	8.06
VALUE	7.44

U

OVERALL SCORE
849

Green Fee: $27 (weekend)
1/2 Cart Fee: $12 (weekend)

Tees	Men's	Women's	Yards
Red		72.8/125	5627
White	70.8/130	77.1/134	6385
Blue	72.4/132		6711

Purple Hawk Country Club has been called one of the best kept secrets in the north Metro. Located just three miles north of Cambridge, Minnesota, this exceptional semi-private course welcomes the public. There are four tee boxes to choose from, measuring from 5627 to 6711 yards.

The course is easy to walk, with low rolling hills and greens relatively close to the next tee box. There are a substantial amount of trees, but the grounds crew does such an excellent job keeping them trimmed that even if golfers do miss the fairway, they still have a fair chance to advance their next shot without fear of declaring a lost ball. The fairways, as well as the rough, are trimmed to a nice height. The greens are fair to the hacker in us; they have some well-defined slopes and run quite true, providing good speed and ball roll. The sand traps are well placed, well maintained and contain a fine grade of sand, which makes it easier to escape these hazards. Several holes on the course follow the rolling hills, creating some slight blind shots from the tee box, but these holes are straight, eliminating any questions on which way to go. Each tee box has a ball washer, trash can and bench for a quick rest while waiting to tee off. The fairways are equipped with distance markers at 250, 200,150 and 100 yards. Some holes also have well-placed markings in the middle of the fairway, indicating the yardage to the hazards. The flags on the greens show front, middle or back pin positions.

The pro shop offers a wide variety of equipment for standard golf-course prices. The course has individual and family memberships available, as well as a junior golf program. The club pros provide single or group lessons. A full bar and restaurant offer great food at a reasonable price and the entire staff was very helpful, as well as exceptionally personable. Purple Hawk Country Club has hosted many qualifying tournaments, such as MGA junior events, the Minnesota State Women's Open and the State Senior Publinks. Our advice: take the drive north and enjoy this course while it's still a secret.

ID: 5500809MN

RED WING

1311 West 6th Street
Red Wing, MN 55066
Clubhouse: 651-388-9524
Golf Shop: 651-388-9524 ext. 4
Type: Semi-Private   Par: 71
www.redwinggolfclub.com

Region: SouthEast

Course Rating

HOSPITALITY	7.80
PLAYABILITY	6.81
USABILITY	5.85
FACILITY	5.50
VALUE	4.05

OVERALL SCORE

639

Green Fee: $39 (weekend)
1/2 Cart Fee: $17 (weekend)

Tees	Men's	Women's	Yards
Red		68.7/118	4771
Gold	68.2/123	73.4/128	5614
White	69.6/126	75.1/131	5914
Blue	70.8/129		6190

The Red Wing Golf Club in Red Wing, Minnesota, is hidden, literally. The entrance to this semi-private course, founded in 1915, looks like a driveway. Located along the rolling hillsides and bluffs of the Mississippi River, this course has many elevation changes, making it difficult to walk. In addition to the hills and valleys, the greens and tees are not close together. We liked the interesting layout, but some of the holes don't follow in a logical order—golfers should pay attention to the signs.

The fairways were in good condition and the tee boxes were fair (grass a little long). The greens had experienced a lot of winterkill when we visited; there was some on almost every hole, although most of the greens still played true. The only other drawbacks were some blind shots and a couple quirky holes (par 5s that take the driver out of your hand because of a sharp dogleg).

There is no driving range, just a net to hit into. The clubhouse was adequate size, with hotdogs, brats, sandwiches, a full bar and adequate seating. They do have a banquet room upstairs for events.

The course is somewhat short (5914 from the whites, 6190 from the blues), but the undulation creates plenty of challenges. We liked the scenery (wild deer and views of the Mississippi valley) and the small-town friendliness. The green fee is slightly more expensive than average ($39) and we thought the $17 fee for a cart rental (pretty much a necessity on this course) was high.

This course should suit most hackers just fine, especially those that like some elevation changes.

ID: 55066D09MN

REDWOOD FALLS

Region: SouthWest

101 East Oak Street
Redwood Falls, MN 56283
Clubhouse: 507-627-8901
Golf Shop: 507-627-8901
Type: Public   Par: 70
www.redwoodfallsgolf.com

Course Rating

HOSPITALITY	6.57
PLAYABILITY	6.48
USABILITY	6.88
FACILITY	7.84
VALUE	5.31

Tees	Men's	Women's	Yards
Front		69.4/112	4958
Middle	68.1/118	73.6/121	5698
Back	69.9/122		6087

OVERALL SCORE
665

Green Fee: $31 (weekend)
1/2 Cart Fee: $15 (weekend)

The Redwood Falls Golf Club is located in the beautiful Redwood River Valley. The water fountains, trees and the lush green color of the whole course make this Redwood Falls, Minnesota, course a pleasure to play. The course requires accuracy, although it's okay to miss some fairways and it's not necessary to drive the ball 300 yards to score well.

Overall this course is in immaculate shape from tee to green. The rough was a little long in some spots and posed a challenge for missed shots. The bunkers were in great shape and well maintained, but it had just rained when we played the course, so the sand was a little heavy. They have a nice practice putting green, but no driving range. We noticed only one spot on the course with standing water; otherwise the course was in great condition and looked well maintained.

There are also plenty of water hazards that come into play, although no holes require a forced carry from the tee. For example, hole #3 has an island green like the 17th at the TPC Sawgrass, except this hole is a par 4 instead of a par 3. Golfers are forced to lay up on their tee shots because the green is surrounded by water on three sides, with just a walkway on the left. We were very impressed with the professional design.

This course has a nice building with a clubhouse and pro shop. However, their pro shop had little inventory, with only a small selection of putters, clothes and some golf balls. Their restaurant had a limited menu, which included sub sandwiches and pizzas that were priced a little higher than average. They did have a good selection of alcoholic beverages, ranging from mixed drinks to bottled beer and wine. Overall, we found Redwood Falls enjoyable yet challenging to play. The staff and the other patrons were really friendly. The course does have a few drawbacks, but hackers looking for a pleasant golf experience are sure to find it here.

ID: 5628309MN

RICH SPRING

17467 Fairway Circle
Cold Spring, MN 56320
Clubhouse: 320-685-8810
Golf Shop: 320-685-8810
Type: Semi-Private   Par: 72

www.richspringgolf.com

H
V

Course Rating

HOSPITALITY	8.98
PLAYABILITY	8.10
USABILITY	8.40
FACILITY	8.47
VALUE	7.82

OVERALL SCORE
841

Tees	Men's	Women's	Yards
Red	65.4/125	70.1/122	5228
Gold	67.6/130		5546
White	70.5/136		6251
Blue	72.4/137		6564

Green Fee: $32 (weekend)
1/2 Cart Fee: $13.50 (weekend)

A short drive southwest of St. Cloud is all that's necessary to find Rich Spring Golf Course, located in Cold Spring, Minnesota. This par-72 course plays 6564 yards from the blue tees, although like most players, we choose the whites. Parking was sufficient even on a beautiful busy weekend. For any forgotten equipment, the clubhouse was full of merchandise and the staff was very pleasant. Also within the clubhouse is the Lakeview Bar and Grill. It has grill food, a soup and salad bar, as well as full entrees with nightly specials., complete with indoor and outdoor seating. Both the driving range and putting green are conveniently located. Even though there were two different events going on, the staff was friendly and organized. On-course service was attentive without being annoying.

The course is situated on a chain of lakes and some holes have nice views of the neighboring waterways. It is a very forgiving course off most tee boxes. However, tree-lined fairways demand more accuracy from approach shots. Don't be fooled—there are plenty of challenges. Water comes into play on several holes, as do bunkers. The course was nicely manicured and the greens played true, despite heavy traffic. The par 3s were challenging, averaging around 170 yards in length. Number 6 was a favorite hole, requiring a carry over water and past bunkers guarding the front of the green.

It was obvious how much pride the owners have for their course. Tee boxes were nicely landscaped with beautiful flowers and attractive signage. _Team Hacker_ would recommend a cart because some tee-to-green distances are sizeable. At $32 for a weekend green fee, Rich Springs is a nice value. Setting a tee time by phone or online is easy. The website is very informative and has pictures of each hole, although the photos don't always do them justice. This course has something to offer for everyone. If you are in the Cold Spring area, give this course a try—you won't regret it. We had fun and hope to play it again.

ID: 5632009MN

RICH VALLEY

3855 145th Street East
Rosemount, MN 55068
Clubhouse: 651-437-4653
Golf Shop: 651-437-4653
Type: Public   Par: 64
www.rich-valley-golf-course.com

Tees	Men's	Women's	Yards
Red/White	63.7/95	65.1/99	4924
Red/Blue	64.1/100	64.4/101	5058
White/Blue	63.0/98	63.7/98	5289

Region: Twin Cities

Course Rating

HOSPITALITY   6.97
PLAYABILITY   6.15
USABILITY   6.92
FACILITY   6.06
VALUE   6.85

OVERALL SCORE
657

Greens Fee: $25.00 (weekend)
1/2 Cart Fee: $12.00 (weekend)

On your way south on Highway 52 to Rochester, Red Wing and environs, you may find yourself yearning for a little golf as you pass through Rosemount, Minnesota. There you may want to stop in at Rich Valley Golf Club. This 27-hole course is carved out of a former farm field and is still surrounded by corn and soybeans.

Unlike other courses in the area, it does things differently. It is very short with each set of nine holes only about 2500 yards. You can select any two of the nines if you are playing 18 holes and then stop back into the clubhouse to play the remaining nine.

The facility has a cozy clubhouse that looks a lot like a large residential house, complete with the owner's catalogs for scrapbooking. The parking lot is a short distance from the front door and the driving range is just around the corner. Inside is a basic layout and food offerings are what you'd typically find.

Although you are really in the country, you can see the skyline of the Rosemount oil refinery in the distance and hear a continual din of highway noise because the course's layout is so open. The course itself is very basic and flat—numerous short par 4s punctuated with an occasional par 5. This is not a course with natural hazards like water or swampy areas so you will be hard-pressed to lose your ball. If you can hit your drives straight, you will feel like a big-time player because you'll be able to drive the green in two.

Getting around the course is easy, but keep checking the map because signage is very poor and hard to see from a distance. Course conditions are average, with an apparent lack of ongoing maintenance. Hole positions seem to not have changed over the summer, sand traps were quite gravelly and hard, and the women's tees look like they were just an afterthought.

As a playing challenge, this is not a very difficult course. If you are there for an interesting round you'll be disappointed. If you want to play a quick round at a local, small-town, inexpensive track that is a good place for beginners, then Rich Valley will work for you.

226

ID: 5506808MN

RIDGES AT SAND CREEK

Region: Twin Cities

21775 Ridges Drive
Jordan, MN 55352
Clubhouse: 952-492-2644
Golf Shop: 952-492-2644
Type: Public   Par: 72

www.ridgesatsandcreek.com

Tees	Men's	Women's	Yards
Red		70.2/123	5136
Gold	68.1/126	73.5/131	5739
White	69.8/130	75.6/135	6115
Blue	71.8/134		6547
Black	73.6/137		6936

Course Rating

HOSPITALITY	8.63
PLAYABILITY	8.00
USABILITY	7.11
FACILITY	7.98
VALUE	7.03

OVERALL SCORE
788

Greens Fee: $43.00 (weekend)
1/2 Cart Fee: $15.00 (weekend)

Ridges at Sand Creek is a beautiful course in Jordan, Minnesota, that combines everything a hacker needs to be successful—short rough, short par 3s and a detailed scorecard outlining each hole.

Located just off Highway 21, the Ridges clubhouse is two stories and combines a pro shop, banquet center and restaurant offering a full menu (our post-round quesadillas were better than we've had at several chain restaurants). The staff are warm and welcoming and ready to assist and seem to do it all with a smile. Mike Malone, the owner, is especially nice and willing to "talk golf" with the visitors.

A large practice green gives golfers a chance to get a feel for the greens without feeling crowded. The nearby driving range is not very impressive but suffices for getting a few swings in before stepping to the first tee.

The course feels like it is really two courses in one. About six of the holes are wide open where an errant drive won't hurt you very much. But the remaining twelve are cut out of the forest like a hot ice cream scoop through a pint of Rocky Road. Trees line the fairways and make a towering backdrop behind the greens. Creeks run across the fairways in conspicuous places but they were incredibly dry for the midsummer. The par 3s on the course are quite short, including an incredibly dainty 90-yarder on the back nine. The rough is not long so a pushed or pulled drive, while not ideal, won't kill you.

The biggest complaint would have to be the condition of some of the tee boxes. A rubber mallet was literally needed to pound a tee into the box and that tee was then snapped like a twig upon impact with the driver. A little more water would seem to be the obvious cure. The greens had a good pace to them and pin placement was generally favorable to the golfer. Finding Ridges is quite easy with just one exit off of Highway 169 putting you right at the course. Make sure to bring a few extra balls for those tree-lined holes.

ID: 5535208MN

RIDGEWOOD

2159 County Road 7 NE
Longville, MN 56655
Clubhouse: 218-363-2444
Golf Shop: 218-363-2444
Type: Public   Par: 72

www.ridgewoodgolf.com

Tees	Men's	Women's	Yards
Red		69.9/119	5103
White	70.7/126	76.5/134	6317
Blue	71.7/129		6556

Region: NorthEast

Course Rating

HOSPITALITY	7.87
PLAYABILITY	7.61
USABILITY	8.17
FACILITY	7.34
VALUE	7.17

OVERALL SCORE
770

Green Fee: $35 (weekend)
1/2 Cart Fee: $10 (weekend)

Ridgewood Country Club in Longville, Minnesota, is a top-notch public course with 18 holes and a short executive 9-hole course. The new clubhouse has a pro shop and a restaurant. Although the pro shop prices were average, it had very little merchandise. Be aware that, except for Friday and Saturday nights, the kitchen usually closes at 2:00 pm. The staff, however, was pleasant and courteous.

The putting green is a little out of the way, but in top condition. The driving range is next to the first tee box and well maintained, as was the practice bunker.

The course was in great shape; the bentgrass greens rolled true and plenty fast. The fairways, rough, tee boxes and bunkers were all well maintained. We did find ourselves wondering where the next tee box was a few times, without any signs to point us in the right direction. There weren't many cart paths, but they are working on upgrading them.

The course is fairly hacker-friendly. The rough is forgiving, although trees in the middle of the fairway can test your mettle. There are several bunkers, but many didn't seem to come into play. The par 4s on the back nine are quite long for the average hacker. On most holes, there wasn't much of a difference between the blue and white tees. We noticed forward gold tees on some holes, but they aren't listed on the scorecard.

The executive course is 920 yards with holes from 53 to 145 yards. The conditioning of this course was spectacular. We recommend it as a great way to have some fun and practice your short game.

Overall, Ridgewood is a great facility at a very competitive price. If you are in the area put it on your playlist.

ID: 5665509MN

RIVER OAKS

11099 South Highway 61
Cottage Grove, MN 55016
Clubhouse: 651-438-2121
Golf Shop: 651-438-2121
Type: Public   Par: 71

www.riveroaksmunigolf.com

Tees	Men's	Women's	Yards
Red		69.9/120	5165
White	69.2/123		5956
Blue	71.4/127		6418

P
U

Course Rating

HOSPITALITY	8.39
PLAYABILITY	8.91
USABILITY	9.06
FACILITY	8.24
VALUE	6.99

OVERALL SCORE
852

Greens Fee: $32.50 (weekend)
1/2 Cart Fee: $15.50 (weekend)

Even a novice golfer can appreciate the distinctions that make a well-managed golf course stand out from the rest. The grass seems greener there, the staff friendlier, the greens smoother, the pace of play steadier and the sense of contentment reflected by the patrons is unmistakable. If these subtleties elude you, defer to the judgment of other golfers by gauging how far in advance you need to book your tee time. Many very nice courses do go unnoticed, but word spreads quickly about the really good courses, which can make booking a tee time your first challenge.

Located off of Highway 61 just south of Cottage Grove, Minnesota, River Oaks is a sprawling 6400-yard course located in the beautiful Mississippi River Valley. Its varied holes present breathtaking, panoramic views of the Mississippi River, mature tree lines and cleverly placed hazards, which can frustrate the ambitious golfer who would prefer to "go for the green" rather than lay up with a more prudent shot. However, that is not to say that River Oaks is designed exclusively for the "scratch" golfer. One of the more enjoyable aspects of this course is that it provides avenues for a variety of shots, forcing the golfer to think through a strategy for attacking the pin.

With its numerous amenities, it is no small wonder why River Oaks is often fully booked with weekend tournaments and events. The inviting clubhouse and veranda provide a relaxing venue to rehash your round or to host an event. More often than not the head golf pro, Bruce Anderson, will welcome you to River Oaks and the starter or ranger will wish you well or stop to ask how you are enjoying your round. Along the course, you will find plenty of water stations and restrooms to make your round more comfortable. In addition, your beer, soda or sports drink will barely be empty by the time the refreshment cart makes its way back to your group. Although you may need to plan ahead to book a tee time, River Oaks is a great place to play one or more rounds over the course of the summer. Even at full price, $32.50 for a weekend round, the value is unmistakable.

ID: 5501608MN

RIVER OAKS

54384 244th Street
Austin, MN 55912
Clubhouse: 507-433-9098
Golf Shop: 507-433-9098
Type: Public   Par: 71
no website

Region: SouthEast

Course Rating

HOSPITALITY	8.11
PLAYABILITY	6.29
USABILITY	6.28
FACILITY	7.16
VALUE	6.58

OVERALL SCORE
690

Green Fee: $25 (weekend)
1/2 Cart Fee: $12.50 (weekend)

Tees	Men's	Women's	Yards
Red		70.5/121	5261
Gold	66.2/118	71.3/123	5426
White	69.0/123	74.7/130	6026

Judging by the brisk activity we saw outside the clubhouse, this Austin, Minnesota, course has developed a loyal following. Founded in 1938, the original owners of River Oaks Golf Club must have seen the aesthetic potential in the Cedar River and its scenic, wooded, natural surroundings. As the name indicates, the riverside has plenty of mature trees and countless majestic oaks to provide character and beauty.

Though the clubhouse is currently nothing more than a small, steel building, sharing accommodations with the cart maintenance facility, new ownership has broken ground on several much-needed improvements, such as a new clubhouse and driving range. Amenities of any kind are in short supply; players who frequent River Oaks do so largely for the golf facilities.

The front nine is fairly straightforward with limited out-of-bounds or water issues to impede play. The one-cut rough is green and rolls well. The fairways are plush, resulting in plenty of good lies. The greens are in great shape and putt well, though some are a little on the small side. Overall, the front side is a fair test of a hacker's skill. While the front nine is accented by oak-lined fairways, the back is much tighter. Thicker wooded areas, drop-offs into trouble spots, more out-of-bounds areas and water, in the form of the broad Cedar River, all come into play. Despite this trouble, the length (2728 yards) makes the back nine an opportunity for conservative golfers to score well. This side offers several reasonable chances to make birdie, with par 4s of 297, 347, 315 and 288 yards. Overall, the benefits outweigh the drawbacks at River Oaks. In it's current state, there are few amenities, but the true attraction is the on-course experience. Despite the number of golfers we encountered, the course seems well designed without any frustrating bottlenecks—we played our round in just over three hours. Once construction is completed, River Oaks seems destined to be a much-improved option for hackers and intermediate players alike.

ID: 5591209MN

RIVER OAKS

23742 County Road 2
Cold Spring, MN 56320
Clubhouse: 320-685-4138
Golf Shop: 320-685-4138
Type: Public   Par: 70
www.riveroaksgc.net

Region: WestCentral

Course Rating

HOSPITALITY	7.38
PLAYABILITY	7.82
USABILITY	7.76
FACILITY	7.02
VALUE	6.84

OVERALL SCORE
748

Green Fee: $24 (weekend)
1/2 Cart Fee: $12 (weekend)

Tees	Men's	Women's	Yards
Red		68.7/114	4910
Gold	65.7/113	70.7/117	5207
White	69.8/121		6055

Set on the outskirts of a lovely little town in central Minnesota, River Oaks Golf Course in Cold Spring, Minnesota, proved to be worth the drive. There is a lack of signage and we nearly drove past the entrance. But once we found the course, we were pleasantly surprised by the ponds, fountains and the overall beauty. After checking in at the bar, which also serves as the pro shop, we saw a limited variety of cold sandwiches for purchase. Some clothing and hats were reasonably priced, however, there were very few clubs for sale.

Since this was our first time at River Oaks, we depended on signs to lead us through the course. Unfortunately, this is the course's biggest downfall. Signs are small or difficult to read. The scorecard wasn't that helpful, but we eventually we were able to find our way around. Pace-of-play was almost perfect and we finished 18 holes in under four hours.

Greens are large and very well maintained. The front nine has more water hazards than the back and it certainly would behoove golfers to check out the scorecard maps prior to teeing off. The rough was nicely kept, so the course was very forgiving on those errant shots. Since the fairways are lined with mature trees, we never ran into other golfers playing from our fairway to their own.

There were four tee boxes on each hole and while nearly all the blue and white tees were equipped with wastebaskets and ball washers, very few forward tees were. It would be nice if all tee boxes had the same amenities to accommodate golfers of every skill level. Yard markers were basically non-existent throughout the course. Although there were water stations on the course, we never saw the beverage cart.

All in all, the course is beautiful, fun and well maintained. The pricing makes it worth the drive and the hazards give it just the right amount of challenge for all hackers.

ID: 5632009MN

RIVERS' BEND

24461 Heron Road
Preston, MN 55965
Clubhouse: 800-552-2512
Golf Shop: 507-467-2512
Type: Public   Par: 70

www.barnresort.com/golf.htm

Course Rating

HOSPITALITY   8.85
PLAYABILITY   6.64
USABILITY   6.94
FACILITY   5.79
VALUE   5.55

Tees	Men's	Women's	Yards
Red		68.1/113	4923
White	66.9/112	71.9/121	5606
Blue	68.4/116		5953

OVERALL SCORE
702

Green Fee: $28 (weekend)
1/2 Cart Fee: $12 (weekend)

Far removed from the glitz and glamour of the no-expense-spared resort courses lies Rivers' Bend. This is a relatively new, country-style golf course at the Old Barn Resort, nestled in southeastern Minnesota's bluff country. This quaint, quiet place also has a trout stream, bike trail, tubing and full-service restaurant. The entire family will love it here. There's so much more to Rivers' Bend than just golf and more people should come here to enjoy this beautiful course.

It's important to remember this is a very new course: the back nine opened in 2005. It still has some maturing to do, but what it has become in the past five years alone is amazing. Less than an hour drive south of Rochester, this course is well deserving of your time and money. As fun and scenic as this course is, it does still need a lot of work. Cart paths around tees and greens, consistent mowing, additional signage and a better practice area would be a good start. Distance markers at 200, 150 and 100 yards on *both* sides of the fairway would also be helpful. Fortunately, the owners and staff are not content with the status quo, but committed to making this course a place people will want to come back to. They know this means a lot more work and money.

This course aesthetically has it all: a river, streams, trees, plains, bluffs, bridges and wildlife galore. The design deserves a lot of praise as well (maybe with the exception of hole #16). The front nine is simple and open, a great scoring nine. The back nine is dramatically different from the front. While the front almost seems like a warm up, holes 9–18 require calculation and precision.

The golf experience and the staff exceeds expectations, but the course still needs additional work to bring it up to the same level. This is a nice place to golf and get away from the city in southeast Minnesota and will only get better over time.

ID: 5596509MN

RIVERWOOD NATIONAL

Region: Twin Cities

10444 95th Street NE
Otsego, MN 55362
Clubhouse: 763-271-5000
Golf Shop: 763-271-5000
Type: Public   Par: 72

www.riverwoodnational.com

Tees	Men's	Women's	Yards
Red		67.8/115	4722
White	69.4/131	75.3/131	6064
Blue	70.8/135		6376
Black	73.7/140		7012

Course Rating

HOSPITALITY	6.89
PLAYABILITY	6.98
USABILITY	6.55
FACILITY	6.02
VALUE	6.14

OVERALL SCORE
664

Greens Fee: $35.00 (weekend)
1/2 Cart Fee: $13.00 (weekend)

Just shy of an hour northwest of the cities on Interstate 94 brings you to the growing extended suburban community of Otsego, Minnesota, and the Riverwood National Golf Course. Before you even step on the course, Riverwood does a great job of making you feel like your drive was worthwhile. A great clubhouse, nice facilities and awesome golf carts provide a buffer for any frustration that might get built up while hacking away on the course. Digital scorecard, GPS system and menu hooked into the clubhouse restaurant are just some of the features found within the dashboard of your golf cart, which can be rented for 18 holes on a weekend for a very reasonable $13.

A championship course by title, Riverwood seems to do its best to offer a fair experience to golfers of all skill levels. Though the challenge is there, the course is not overbearingly difficult for golfers with lesser skill sets. The majority of holes offer a safe out for those not willing to roll the dice on a perfect swing, and the room for error is pretty even across the board. There is, however, trouble that can be found, and a couple holes are potential snowmen waiting to happen. Despite this, the course maintains its level of fairness by tending to surround these tougher holes with less demanding ones. This means that even though a couple scores might jump up and bite you, if you can keep your composure and move on to the next tee box with a clear conscience, you have a chance to make up for it on the following hole.

Overall, Riverwood is an enjoyable course. Stepping onto the first tee box you know that the course is not going to roll over for you, but it is also not difficult to the point where you're going to want to bury your seven-iron in a pond after your third straight triple bogey. A welcoming atmosphere and a fair challenge come to mind, and for a little jaunt up Interstate 94 it's not a bad pick for a golfer of any skill level. Plus, a happy hour pit stop at the sports bar conveniently located between the course and Interstate 94 will help turn the story about that cut-slice-tree-green shot you hit on #11 into a reason to come back again.

ID: 5536208MN

ROSE LAKE

2456 104th Street
Fairmont, MN 56031
Clubhouse: 507-235-5274
Golf Shop: 507-235-5274
Type: Semi-Private   Par: 71

www.roselakegolfclub.com

Course Rating

HOSPITALITY	8.83
PLAYABILITY	8.55
USABILITY	8.45
FACILITY	8.64
VALUE	7.13

F

OVERALL SCORE
847

Tees	Men's	Women's	Yards
Red		70.3/118	5222
White	69.1/125	74.6/128	6001
Blue	69.9/127		6177

Green Fee: $30 (weekend)
1/2 Cart Fee: $15 (weekend)

Rose Lake Golf Club is located just east of Fairmont, Minnesota, on a quiet country road. The course opened with nine holes in 1957 and additional nine were added in 1987 by Joel Goldstrand. The course uses three sets of tees, ranging from 5222 to 6177 yards. The course is walkable, but there is only one restroom on the course. Beverage carts are used only on special occasions.

The clubhouse looks like an old farmhouse and we were greeted by a friendly person at the register. The pro shop was well equipped and reasonably priced. The putting and chipping greens are next to the parking lot. The driving range is a quarter-mile away—but the coin-operated machine to get range balls is next to the clubhouse. For golfers who would like to hit more than one bucket, this is a little inconvenient.

Only the 150-yard markers are visible from the tee box. The fairways are lined with mature trees. The well-positioned greens are nestled in among the trees and lakes, which make for a picturesque and natural beauty. A few deer and ducks complete the view. The country road the course borders does come into play on holes 1, 5, 10 and 11 and could result in some penalty strokes if you stray out of bounds. Water comes into play on #5. Number 6 is a beautiful par 4 that narrows to a small green below a tree-covered hill and a lake on the right. Following is an uphill par 3 that can play longer or shorter, depending on the wind. Number 11 is the hardest hole with water on the left and middle and out of bounds on the right. On this hole, the back tees are actually easier to play than the middle tees. The 13th hole is a par 3 over water with an easy drop zone. The 18th is elevated with a two-tier green.

The restaurant has everything from hot dogs to steaks, pizza to desserts. There is also a full-service bar. Prices are very reasonable and the food was great. The course was fun and a challenge to play. The weekly green fee is a little steep for the area, but we would play this course again.

234

RUM RIVER HILLS

Region: Twin Cities

16659 St. Francis Boulevard
Ramsey, MN 55303
Clubhouse: 763-753-3339
Golf Shop: 763-753-3339
Type: Public   Par: 71

www.rumriverhills.com

Tees	Men's	Women's	Yards
Red		70.4/123	5024
White	68.8/124	74.2/132	5738
Blue	70.4/127	76.3/136	6091
Black	71.4/129		6308

Course Rating

HOSPITALITY	6.03
PLAYABILITY	6.76
USABILITY	7.21
FACILITY	6.97
VALUE	7.52

OVERALL SCORE
677

Greens Fee: $32.00 (weekend)
1/2 Cart Fee: $15.00 (weekend)

For those of us located in the Twin Cities, Rum River Hills Golf Club in Ramsey, Minnesota, seems way out there in the country. It is a bit of a drive tucked away on Highway 47, but what really makes it different is that it is a contrast in two parts: the clubhouse and the course.

The clubhouse has the feel of an Elk's Lodge complete with a tiny stage, wood paneling and pull tabs. The course, on the other hand, is picturesque and challenging with more than half the holes having water hazards to contend with. The clubhouse was built when the course opened in 1983 and appears to not have changed since Day One. Designed by noted golf course architect Joel Goldstrand, Rum River Hills is not a flat blue-collar track, but a tree-lined course with lots of water, bunkers and other ways to lose your golf balls. It is much tougher than meets the eye.

The course itself a tale of two nines with the front nine being much tighter than the back. Course management and shot accuracy should be required for the front, and "grip it and rip it" should be called for on the back. The course is nicely manicured and the greens are pristine. The course length at the white tees is only 5738 yards, so if you are a long hitter, you might want to take a step back to the blues. The ladies are taken into consideration here with their own ball washers, granite signage and garbage cans. Touches not often seen at most courses.

In contrast, the off-course amenities seemed a bit lacking. The parking lot needed a paving, the putting green seemed a bit sparse and the driving range was very basic. The golf carts were older and appeared to not have been cleaned since spring. Although we were part of a small group of golfers that played the course late in the year, the service was weak and we got a cold shoulder in the bar from the locals like we were invading their private club.

Rum River Hills Golf Club's course is really a hidden gem that it worth a visit, but the rest of the golfing experience did little to make us want to return again.

ID: 5530308MN

RUSH CREEK

7801 Troy Lane
Maple Grove, MN 55311
Clubhouse: 763-494-0400
Golf Shop: 763-494-8844
Type: Public   Par: 72

www.rushcreek.com

Region: Twin Cities

Course Rating

HOSPITALITY	8.15
PLAYABILITY	8.58
USABILITY	8.09
FACILITY	8.54
VALUE	6.01

OVERALL SCORE
811

Greens Fee: $105.00 (weekend)
1/2 Cart Fee: $19.00 (weekend)

Tees	Men's	Women's	Yards
Green		72.0/131	5317
Silver	71.3/137	77.2/141	6204
Blue	73.2/140	79.4/146	6747
Gold	74.8/144		7117

We are tempted to write a one sentence review about Rush Creek Golf Club in Maple Grove, Minnesota. The place is simply exquisite. Ok, we'll write more but be warned, typed words won't do this course justice.

We rolled into the parking lot early one Friday morning and were immediately greeted by a very nice gentleman who took our bags and set them up for us on a cart. We got there early before the round to work some kinks out. The course has an expansive area to warm up, from an enormous practice green to a driving range with a full set of slots. (Side note: if we had to come up with a complaint about Rush Creek it would be that the driving range faces dead towards the rising sun in the morning so it is hard at times to track your ball.

The course itself is lush. Fairways almost seem to be divot-free and the rough is not incredibly difficult to get out from. The greens were large and in perfect shape. This could be due to the fact that the starter gave us each a tool to replace ball marks in the greens.

Water does come into play on a good number of holes as the entire course seems to be intertwined with a creek-like area (perhaps that is why they call it Rush Creek) but don't let it get in your head. On most holes you can clear it with little trouble.

The par 3s are a reasonable distance, all around 150–160 yards, and the par 5s provide a good chance to score well. Hole #13 is a classic, forcing you to go over water twice. The shots you need to hit are not very hard but that water looms in your head like a bad dream.

Service at Rush Creek is phenomenal. Everywhere you turn the staff is there and willing to help to make your time on the golf course the best time of your day. When you're done with your round, take an opportunity to enjoy the beautiful porch of the clubhouse decked out with comfortable furniture and fire pits. Drinks and a full menu are served on the patio so eat up.

ID: 5531108MN

RUTTGER'S
(Sugarbrooke)

37584 Otis Lane
Cohasset, MN 55721
Clubhouse: 218-327-1462
Golf Shop: 218-327-1462
Type: Public   Par: 71

www.sugarlakelodge.com/golf/

Region: NorthEast

Course Rating

HOSPITALITY	8.82
PLAYABILITY	7.39
USABILITY	7.97
FACILITY	7.86
VALUE	6.13

Tees	Men's	Women's	Yards
Red		69.0/119	5032
Yellow	68.8/119	74.0/130	5929
White	69.9/122		6195
Blue	71.7/125		6548

OVERALL SCORE
781

Green Fee: $35 (weekend)
1/2 Cart Fee: $15 (weekend)

Sugarbrooke Golf Course is part of the Ruttger's Sugar Lake Lodge resort in Cohasset, Minnesota. Just a few miles from Grand Rapids, this is an 18-hole, hacker-friendly, resort-style course. The pro shop, as expected, has plenty of golf clothing with resort insignia, but there are no clubs or other golf gear and there isn't a pro available for lessons either. The golf rates and merchandise are reasonable for a resort.

The practice facilities are conveniently located near the first tees. The driving range is well marked for distance and in superb condition. Strangely, the practice green is shaped like a donut and very sloped. This isn't indicative of the greens on the course, but it does give golfers a feel for the speed of them.

There are three sets of tees to choose from and the course yardage ranges from 6548 for the back tees to 5032 for the forward tees. Distance markers were easy to locate on the tee boxes and in the fairways. There aren't any long carries over water or deep rough. Water does comes into play on six holes, but except for #18 it's easily avoidable. The front nine is certainly more open and hacker-friendly than the back, but the course is fairly forgiving overall and can be played without bruising a hacker's ego.

The course was in excellent shape. The tee boxes were flat and well manicured. The fairways were in pristine condition. Nearly perfect, the greens putted fast, but true. Bunkers are not in short supply at Sugarbrooke. They can come into play off the tee and also protect more than a few greens. While the maintenance crew does ensure they're properly raked, the bunkers are filled with coarse sand and have a few rocks in them. At the clubhouse, Jack's Grill serves a good selection of lunch items and full entrees. The prices were a little high, but the quality of the food was very good. Otis' Restaurant in the main lodge offers breakfast and fine evening dining. This is a very scenic and serene resort where hackers can come to get away from it all.

ID: 5572109MN

RUTTGER'S
(The Lakes)

25039 Tame Fish Lake Road
Deerwood, MN 56444
Clubhouse: 218-678-4646
Golf Shop: 218-678-4646
Type: Public   Par: 72

www.ruttgers.com/activities/thelakes.htm

Region: NorthEast

Course Rating

H
V

HOSPITALITY	9.02
PLAYABILITY	8.68
USABILITY	8.69
FACILITY	8.46
VALUE	7.69

Tees	Men's	Women's	Yards
Red		70.5/121	4945
White	68.8/130	74.7/130	5699
Blue	71.4/136		6280
Black	74.0/138		6800

OVERALL SCORE
864

Green Fee: $75 (weekend)
1/2 Cart Fee: included in fee

The Ruttger's Bay Lake Lodge in Deerwood, Minnesota, has two courses. Alec's Nine is a short 9-hole course for golfers who like to walk, younger players and those working on their short game. The Lakes has a moderately challenging 18-hole resort layout. It first opened in 1992 and is 6626 yards spread out over 100+ acres of rolling terrain. The Lakes is extremely playable.

In today's market for extremely long holes, we are happy to say Ruttger's hasn't sold out to the idea that longer is better. Using trees, slopes and many doglegs, along with some interesting sand bunkers, the course is challenging yet still fun. We bought the yardage book sold at the pro shop since the carts don't have GPS. This well-designed notebook only costs $3 and can be used to track shots and score your game.

Hackers might need that yardage book and some quality shots to score well on holes 3–5. The front nine starts off friendly enough, with a par 4 that's 350 yards from the white tees. Hole #5, however, was the most unhackable on the course. A blind approach shot and a narrow, sloped fairway make this hole really tough. Scout ahead if you haven't played this hole before. Luckily holes #7 and #9 are both easy par 3s. The back nine is more open and golfers can use their drivers on the wider fairways. The back par 5s didn't seem as long or hard as those on the front nine. We really liked #13, a par 4 with three sand bunkers guarding the front of the green.

The Ruttger's staff prides itself on value and service. With over 111 years of business and four generations, they know how to please. Alec's Nine was the first resort course in the state when it opened in 1921. They've outlasted many other golf courses, so they must be doing something right. Providing outstanding service and value—especially during hard times—is a winning idea that's hard to beat. Extra amenities, like a free bottle of water and complimentary range balls, make it easy to enjoy a round at Ruttger's.

ID: 5644409MN

SANBROOK

2181 NE County Road 5
Isanti, MN 55040
Clubhouse: 763-444-9904
Golf Shop: 763-444-9904
Type: Public   Par: 72

www.sanbrook.com

Tees	Men's	Women's	Yards
Red		68.2/114	4994
White	68.8/118	74.1/127	6060
Blue	70.4/121		6407

Region: NorthEast

Course Rating

HOSPITALITY	6.19
PLAYABILITY	5.17
USABILITY	7.14
FACILITY	4.31
VALUE	5.48

OVERALL SCORE
572

Green Fee: $27 (weekend)
1/2 Cart Fee: $13 (weekend)

Sanbrook Golf Course is a low-budget course in Isanti, Minnesota. Basically, the owner and a few high school kids run the day-to-day operations. This course will not win any awards for design or maintenance and it seems like the owner doesn't care one way or another.

There is a combination garage, storage shed, maintenance shack and clubhouse on site. The "clubhouse" part of the building is very small. Tucked in the corner was a hot dog warming machine with a couple of crusty hotdogs that should have been thrown away long before we arrived. The golf product selection is slim and the bathrooms are dirty and dimly lit.

Even though the weekend green fee is only $27, we still think it's overpriced. The tee boxes were very small and not level. At approximately 8 feet across, they were just long enough to contain the white and blue markers. Finding a level place to tee from became an adventure. These "elevated" tee boxes are basically mounded dirt piles that were seeded for grass. The fairways were okay, but had too many weeds to be considered a satisfactory playing surface. They were cut to approximately one to one and a half inches in height and provided a surface that tended to raise the ball up. Don't bother looking at sprinkler heads for distance markers; they are not there. Instead, the sides of the fairways are staked at 200, 150 and 100 yards. The rough was adequate.

The greens were the only shining part of the course. Generally large in size (with a couple of small ones mixed in), they had different shapes and undulations, which made them interesting. The greens were in very nice condition, with no evidence of pitch marks whatsoever. The surface was plush and spongy which helped to heel them from any wear and tear. Unfortunately, they were also *extremely* slow. Through all 18 holes, we had trouble getting used to them. The management at Sanbrook has invested little effort—and it shows. It's a cheap option if you're near the area, but do not make this a destination.

239

ID: 5504009MN

SAWMILL

11177 North McKusick Road
Stillwater, MN 55082
Clubhouse: 651-439-7862 x2
Golf Shop: 651-439-7862 x2
Type: Semi-Private   Par: 70

www.sawmillgc.com

Tees	Men's	Women's	Yards
Red		68.5/124	4891
White	67.3/118	71.8/131	5470
Blue	68.6/121	73.5/134	5766
Black	71.2/123		6238

Region: Twin Cities

Course Rating

HOSPITALITY	7.81
PLAYABILITY	7.43
USABILITY	8.16
FACILITY	6.28
VALUE	7.24

OVERALL SCORE
748

Greens Fee: $28.00 (weekend)
1/2 Cart Fee: $15.00 (weekend)

Sawmill Golf Course is tucked away in the woods about 5 miles off of Highway 36 in Stillwater, Minnesota, and if you have any desire to score well, you may want to tuck away that driver on about seven of the holes.

At their current rates, $28 for 18 holes, this course has to be the best hole-for-hole deal in the Metro area. The beauty and challenge of the 150-yard par-3 fifth hole is worth four bucks alone. You tee off straight over a monster pond that has to eat golf balls like Kobayashi eats Nathan's hot dogs, but it's not that tough a hole if you can put the water out of your head.

Several of the longer holes that require a driver are tree lined and picturesque but don't try to kill that drive or you may just need a chainsaw to find it in the wood. The opening par 5 is a pretty simple hole and can be a confidence booster if you par it. The course has great terrain as several of the holes go up and down hill. The only complaint is that the fairways were rather wet—likely attributable to the previous night's rain and not overwatering by the grounds crew.

Get to the course early and there are several areas to help you warm up. Plenty of room in the parking lot allows for a quick stretch before you reach the clubhouse where you'll find three chipping and putting areas. Buy a bucket of balls and you can hit the driver off the range about 30 yards from the first tee.

Staff on the course are fantastic and we even had a chance to shoot the breeze with course designer Dan Pohl after the round. The clubhouse, while situated perfectly, is nothing to write home about but it does suffice for a place to grab a quick bite and pay for your round.

Lastly, you may hear rumors swirling that this course is set for demolition so that a condo community can be built. That is not the case—at least not for another five years. So, get to the course, grab those twenties out of your wallet and get out on this short, yet challenging track. And leave the money you save with the staff— they deserve it.

ID: 5508208MN

SHADOWBROOKE

3192 State Highway 7
Lester Prairie, MN 55354
Clubhouse: 320-395-4250
Golf Shop: 320-395-4250
Type: Public   Par: 71
www.shadowbrooke.com

Region: WestCentral

Course Rating

HOSPITALITY	7.58
PLAYABILITY	6.45
USABILITY	8.07
FACILITY	7.31
VALUE	6.74

Tees	Men's	Women's	Yards
Red		68.3/115	4906
Gold	64.5/114	69.1/116	5033
White	69.1/123	74.6/128	6040
Blue	70.5/125		6349

OVERALL SCORE
721

Green Fee: $29 (weekend)
1/2 Cart Fee: $12 (weekend)

There's both good news and bad news about Shadowbrooke Golf Course. Luckily, the good outweighs the bad at this course in Lester Prairie, Minnesota. We happened to arrive before our tee time, so were able to start early.

The clubhouse made us a little nervous. It was a very, very old house. It seemed like someone was living there, since the women's restroom doubled as a laundry room. There was little merchandise (maybe a few hats) and a sign stated there would be no pro shop merchandise in 2009. There were, however, a few grandfather clocks for sale. The only food available was hot dogs. The clubhouse staff did tell us to plan ahead because there would be no beverage cart. Apparently, they usually do have a cart out, but four staff members were attending a funeral. The golf carts were very old and in poor condition. Many were dirty and some were wet.

In spite of all this, we had fun. The entire course was very scenic. The holes were unique and quite hacker-friendly. The fairways were in great condition and played nicely, as did the greens (some were spongy but good). There were distance markers at 200, 150 and 100 yards and pin placements were marked by red, white and blue flags.

There were many cart paths. They could use a few more arrows in certain spots, but we didn't get lost. The woods were thick enough to obscure other players and holes. (Mosquitoes could be a problem at some times.) Many other golfers chose to walk and there appeared to be nice shortcuts for them from green to next tee. We had to forgive the clubhouse and carts because the course was so beautiful. Many holes were very unique and even though they were challenging, there was room to keep the ball in play. The forward tees avoided much of the trouble. Shadowbrooke was very busy and the affordable twilight rates make it easy to see why. Overall, it was a very interesting and enjoyable experience.

ID: 5535409MN

SHAMROCK

19625 Larkin Road
Corcoran, MN 55340
Clubhouse: 763-478-9977
Golf Shop: 763-478-9977
Type: Public   Par: 72

www.shamrockgolfcourse.com

Tees	Men's	Women's	Yards
Red		72.7/117	5793
White	69.1/113	74.8/121	6171
Blue	70.3/115		6423

Region: Twin Cities

Course Rating

HOSPITALITY	7.52
PLAYABILITY	6.14
USABILITY	8.40
FACILITY	7.12
VALUE	6.08

OVERALL SCORE
708

Greens Fee: $28.00 (weekend)
1/2 Cart Fee: $16.00 (weekend)

Easily accessible from the northwest side of town, Shamrock Golf Course is located just off County Road 116 (Highway 55) and Country Road 10 (Interstate 494) in Hamel, Minnesota. Course terrain is gently rolling with generous fairways and short rough.

This is an excellent course to work on your game and build a little confidence. Sand comes into play on four holes and water on six holes. An easy course for the walkers, it plays at 6171 yards from the whites and it's hard to lose balls on this course. There is only one Satellite toilet on the course so it can get a little touch-and-go for those with a sensitive bladder.

There isn't much for signage but the asphalt cart paths make getting from one hole to the next easy. The average hacker should feel good about his/her score by the end of the round.

A family of Trumpeter Swans make their home on the pond just outside the clubhouse. The clubhouse is rather spartan with the average grill fare and beer. The clubhouse staff are friendly and helpful. The clubhouse does have a sheltered deck for relaxing after the round. It also offers some good deals on clubs and grips through a local clubmaker. There is no driving range and a rather small putting area. The course offers senior and junior rates, twilight and midday rates. There is no pro at the course and no lessons offered. Overall it offers competitive fees and an excellent opportunity to hone your shots without the fear of getting into trouble on every shot.

Minnesota was ranked by the National Golf Association in 2005 as the nation's number one golf state based based on per capita participation. Wisconsin ranked a close second.

ID: 5534008MN

SHORELAND

43781 Golf Course Road
St Peter, MN 56082
Clubhouse: 507-931-4400
Golf Shop: 507-931-3470
Type: Semi-Private   Par: 69
www.shorelandcc.com

Tees	Men's	Women's	Yards
Red		67.6/116	4637
Gold	63.8/115	68.0/117	4699
White	67.7/123		5592

Region: SouthWest

Course Rating

HOSPITALITY   8.62
PLAYABILITY   8.10
USABILITY   8.60
FACILITY   7.67
VALUE   7.23

OVERALL SCORE
818

Green Fee: $34 (weekend)
1/2 Cart Fee: $15 (weekend)

Shoreland Country Club is located just east of St. Peter, Minnesota in the beautiful Minnesota River Valley. The course is short and plays well for those who don't hit the ball a long way. However, with trees lining almost every fairway , accuracy is key.

The course itself is in good shape with the exception of a few spots of crabgrass in the fairways. The rough was fairly easy to hit from in most places. Bunkers are few and far between, but those the course does have are in pretty good shape and they do come into play. Most are greenside, but there are a couple that line the fairways and can affect tee shots. There's also some tall rough that's almost links-style. Water doesn't come into play on this course except for hole 16, which is located on the shore of Lake Emily. The signature hole is the 18th, a 167-yard par 3. Do not let the short yardage fool you—this hole is ranked one of the hardest for a reason. The green can cause problems for even the best golfers. It's very small and a putt from above the hole can easily run off the green, especially if it's dry. There's also a bunker that guards the front and right of the green. Taking a bogey is a great score if golfers end up in this tricky hazard.

Shoreland Country Club has nice practice facilities and the putting green has room to practice chipping, as well. The driving range is located across the road from the pro shop. The clubhouse is nice with a bar and restaurant that has a great menu and wide selection of drinks. The course also has a swimming pool, so you can bring your whole family along and enjoy a day at the course. The pro shop has a decent selection of merchandise. Those in need of lessons or club repair can rely on the club pro. Our overall impression of Shoreland is a well-maintained course, with the exception of a few spots of crabgrass and the lack of varied hazards. The staff was very helpful, both in the clubhouse and in the pro shop. If you are looking for an enjoyable golf experience both on and off the course, this would be a good place to go.

ID: 5608209MN

SOLDIERS MEMORIAL

244 East Soldiers Field Drive
Rochester, MN 55902
Clubhouse: 507-281-6176
Golf Shop: 507-281-6176
Type: Public   Par: 70

www.rochestermn.gov/departments/park/golf

H

Course Rating

HOSPITALITY	8.89
PLAYABILITY	8.21
USABILITY	8.19
FACILITY	8.09
VALUE	7.07

OVERALL SCORE
824

Tees	Men's	Women's	Yards
Gold	65.6/117	70.3/120	5345
Blue	67.3/120	72.4/124	5714
The Tips	67.8/121		5823

Green Fee: $24 (weekend)
1/2 Cart Fee: $13 (weekend)

"Short and sweet" is an accurate description for this mature municipal golf course located in Rochester, Minnesota. City streets define the outer limits of Soldiers Memorial Field Golf Course and the holes run parallel to one another, which is a typical layout when land is at a premium. The course was certainly busy on the Monday morning we visited.

The course itself is part of Soldiers Memorial Park and upon arrival players are greeted with adequate directional signage and flowering planters. The clubhouse has a pro shop, a restaurant with seating areas and locker rooms. The pro shop is well lit and well stocked. We were greeted and recognized immediately by the friendly staff.

The front nine is straightforward with only a few hazards to negotiate. The holes are straight and the fairways are lined with massive mature trees. Water comes come into play on holes 5, 6 and 9 and there are out-of-bounds areas on holes 1 and 3. While most are not long, these holes are certainly not easy and require accuracy. There is, however, a 212-yard par 3, which is a bit challenging for the average player. With the fall rain, the fairways and rough were very green and lush, without much roll. The greens were in great shape, not too fast and rolled true. They are medium to large in size and seemed to hold approach shots quite well.

The back nine is nearly a carbon copy of the front, with short straight holes and many mature trees to penalize errant plays. There are water hazards on #10 and #18 and out-of-bounds stakes line the 12th, 13th and 14th holes. The par 3s are short and there are two par 4s that big swingers may be able to reach on their drives, making birdie a realistic possibility. Overall, this golf course provides a typical city layout with some challenges, but more opportunities for the average hacker to score well. Given the great food and friendly customer service, we'll be returning to this well-managed course soon.

244

SOUTHBROOK

511 Morrison Avenue South
Annandale, MN 55302
Clubhouse: 877-292-9630
Golf Shop: 320-274-2341
Type: Public   Par: 72
www.southbrookgolf.com

Course Rating

HOSPITALITY	8.61
PLAYABILITY	8.32
USABILITY	8.50
FACILITY	8.01
VALUE	7.18

OVERALL SCORE
827

Green Fee: $30 (weekend)
1/2 Cart Fee: $12 (weekend)

Tees	Men's	Women's	Yards
Red		68.7/113	5067
Yellow	66.9/113	72.0/120	5664
White	68.9/117	74.6/126	6120
Blue	70.8/121		6525

Southbrook Golf Club lies on the outskirts of Annandale, Minnesota, and about 40 miles west of the Twin Cities. It's close to the intersection of Highways 24 and 55 and while there isn't enough signage on the highways, the directions on the website are very good.

The course is fairly flat, so walking the course is easy enough, although they have plenty of golf carts and pull carts for rent, as well. There is good signage at each tee box. Golfers can find tees to accommodate their skill level, with four different sets to choose from and ranging from 5067 to 6525 yards. There are distance markers in the fairways, including birdhouses that function as the 150-yard marker. The fairways themselves are wide and well maintained and the roughs are kept up nicely, as well. The greens were in good shape for the most part, but some showed evidence of past pin placements. There were enough cart paths to cover the whole course and they were well marked.

The front nine is in a residential area and golfers must cross the street several times. The back nine is more rural, with a cornfield as the backdrop for part of the course. One challenging hole was #10, a blind dogleg to the left with an opening of only 15 yards to the green. The fellow players on the course were aware of proper golf etiquette and were very amiable.

The clubhouse has two levels, with the restaurant on the upper level and the pro shop on the lower. The restaurant offers a full menu and overlooks the golf course. The personnel at the restaurant and clubhouse were friendly and knowledgeable about the course and the area. They have ample parking for just about any size group. There is a driving range available, although it's across the street and does not belong to the golf course. Golf lessons are available upon request.

We had a very enjoyable time at Southbrook and would recommend it to anyone in the area.

ID: 5530209MN

SOUTHERN HILLS

18950 Chippendale Avenue West
Farmington, MN 55024
Clubhouse: 651-463-4653
Golf Shop: 651-463-4653
Type: Public   Par: 71
www.southernhillsgolfcourse.com

Tees	Men's	Women's	Yards
Red		68.1/118	4970
White	69.1/125	74.2/131	6073
Blue	70.1/128		6314

Region: Twin Cities

Course Rating

HOSPITALITY	7.57
PLAYABILITY	7.18
USABILITY	8.05
FACILITY	7.05
VALUE	7.46

OVERALL SCORE
746

Greens Fee: $36.25 (weekend)
1/2 Cart Fee: $14.75 (weekend)

Southern Hills Golf Course in Farmington, Minnesota, provides a good balance of playability, interesting hole layouts, and good course conditions.

The clubhouse is a very unique structure with a porch that wraps around all four sides and a dining hall. It would make for a great place to have a cocktail on a warm summer evening.

The practice area is a long narrow green that was groomed very well. The green allowed any practice putt you could imagine from big breakers to straight tap-ins. The driving range was rather small and located down the left side of the first hole creating a close out-of-bounds area.

Staff was very friendly upon arrival, but on-course staff seemed to be lacking for a Sunday morning. There was no starter or even a call to let you know you were up. Also with the start times being only 8 minutes apart, there is a need for a ranger to be "laying down the law" on the course to keep the pace of play to a reasonable rate.

The course provides enough challenge for the hacker but not too much as to make the experience unenjoyable. While there are not many trees which come into play, it does yield a vast amount of other hazards which are located quite well in landing zones. Many of these hazards could be avoided with a little course knowledge. There is a variety of holes from short par 4s to long par 3s many of which offer some good risk/reward opportunities. The par 5s are all very reach-able but are very strategically protected so "going for it" does not come without some risk.

The overall shape of the course was very good. Fairways were nice and green, but a little shaggy. Greens rolled true and had a good pace but were very puttable. The rough was a little dry, but was all cut to a manageable length except in the hazard areas where it was allowed to grow wild. Navigating the course seemed quite easy except for a couple of adjacent tee boxes and small tee signs.

ID: 5502408MN

SPRING BROOK

2276 200th Avenue
Mora, MN 55051
Clubhouse: 320-679-2317
Golf Shop: 320-679-2317
Type: Semi-Private   Par: 70
www.springbrookgc.com

Region: NorthEast

Course Rating

HOSPITALITY	8.42
PLAYABILITY	8.23
USABILITY	7.96
FACILITY	8.64
VALUE	6.43

Tees	Men's	Women's	Yards
Red	63.6/119	68.9/117	4794
Gold	66.9/126	73.0/126	5532
White	68.5/129	74.9/130	5871
Black	70.0/132		6202

OVERALL SCORE
811

Green Fee: $32 (weekend)
1/2 Cart Fee: $18 (weekend)

Spring Brook Golf Course is north of the Twin Cities on Highway 65. Just outside of Mora, Minnesota, we had no problem finding the course. Like a lot of small-town golf courses (Mora's population is roughly 3300), the people are very friendly. We played in the morning and when we asked about breakfast, the server in the restaurant area couldn't find a frozen egg sandwich. Instead, she prepared two of them for us in a matter of minutes. Needless to say, we were impressed with that kind of service.

The course was in great shape. The tee boxes, fairways, rough and greens were all very green and plush. The tee boxes could have been cut a little shorter, but the greens were perfect. They were cut long enough to hold approach shots, but not so long as to slow down putts. The fairways had just been aerated, so we played lift, clean and replace. From some greens, it was difficult to locate the next tee box and we had to do a little searching. They could use a few more directional signs.

The course is a mix of woods, water, wetlands and slight undulation. There are three holes across the road that are wide open except for sand traps. There are some nice elevation changes on the course, with some raised tees and greens. We found #12 to be interesting. It is a short 283-yard par 4. To shorten the hole considerably requires a 200-yard carry over the wetlands. Otherwise, the safe route is to lay up on the left at about 160 yards. The par-5 17th hole, playing 476 yards, is a very sharp dogleg left. The landing area is a blind shot and there could be better signage to indicate the distance to the opening.

Overall, we really enjoyed the course. The people were great and the course was picturesque and in excellent condition. Spring Brook Golf Course is also very affordable: The $32 green fee is a great deal and worth the drive.

ID: 5505109MN

ST. CHARLES

1920 Gladiola Drive
St. Charles, MN 55972
Clubhouse: 507-932-5444
Golf Shop: 507-932-5444
Type: Public   Par: 72

www.stcharlesgolfclub.com

Tees	Men's	Women's	Yards
Red		68.4/112	5340
White	68.1/114		6149
Blue	69.6/117		6439

Region: SouthEast

Course Rating

HOSPITALITY   8.62
PLAYABILITY   6.66
USABILITY   8.26
FACILITY   6.65
VALUE   7.05

OVERALL SCORE
751

Green Fee: $15 (weekend)
1/2 Cart Fee: $10 (weekend)

Whoever said "golf is a good walk spoiled" clearly never walked St. Charles Golf Course in St. Charles, Minnesota. You could shoot 200 on this rolling well-manicured course and still enjoy the walk. The course is close to Interstate 90 and yet you can really hear the freeway on only two holes. Wayne, the course owner, manager and architect, still mows the fairways daily and greets every guest who walks in the door with a kind smile and plenty of "Minnesota Nice." You simply could not ask for friendlier service.

The first six holes of the front nine are wide open and it's relatively easy to score par or even birdie. Then comes the signature hole #7—a beautiful uphill par-3. The beauty can be so distracting that even single-digit handicappers can incur a few penalty strokes. On #8, it's best to play directly over the big tree, but no doubt the resident squirrels have quite a golf ball collection. The front nine ends with a challenging and long par 5.

The back nine has a few difficult greens (especially on #10 and #12). Watch out for #14. This par 3 is both long and difficult.

There isn't a bunker on the course and only one large body of water to carry. The greens are gently sloped, pristine and unscarred. The fairways are wide and welcoming and the cows grazing nearby seldom laugh at you. The rough, though rock-hard and dry in some areas, is not tough to play from. With a fun and imaginative layout, golfers can expect to score true to their handicap.

St. Charles is simply a fantastic value for the cost. Golfers of virtually any age and skill level will have a great time playing this course.

ID: 5597209MN

ST. JAMES

77818 Old Highway 60 SE
St. James, Minnesota 56081
Clubhouse: 507-375-7484
Golf Shop: 507-375-7484
Type: Public   Par: 72
www.stjamesgc.com

V

Region: SouthWest

Course Rating

HOSPITALITY	8.56
PLAYABILITY	7.16
USABILITY	8.60
FACILITY	8.00
VALUE	7.68

Tees	Men's	Women's	Yards
Red		69.5/126	4959
Gold	67.0/128	71.5/130	5321
White	71.9/138	77.5/142	6402
Black	73.9/142		6832

OVERALL SCORE
797

Green Fee: $28 (weekend)
1/2 Cart Fee: $10 (weekend)

The St. James Golf Course is located about 40 miles southwest of Mankato on Highway 60 in St. James, Minnesota. The meandering Watonwan River borders many holes and well-established trees, as well as natural vegetation frame the course. The clubhouse has a banquet room and pro shop, which has plenty of golf items on display. A golf professional is available for private lessons. The putting and chipping greens are near the clubhouse. The driving range is located behind the cart sheds, which is a little inconvenient if golfers want to hit more than one bucket of balls.

Players may choose from four sets of tees at St. James, although distances for the gold tees are not given on the scorecard. The course is a bit longer than average, with the white tees listed at 6402 yards. Unfortunately, the only visible distance marker from the tee is the 150-yard stake. The greens are relatively close to the next tee box, so golfers who prefer to walk shouldn't have any problems.

The front nine is wide open and fairly straightforward, although there are plenty of water hazards. The first par-3 hole is #4 with a lake in between the tee and the green. The par-3 7th hole's claim to fame is the only square green in southern Minnesota. Number 10 is a narrow 200-yard par 3 with trees on both sides and the Watonwan River on the left. To make this hole even more challenging, the green is very small and hard to hit. The par-5 12th hole is the second hardest on the course, with a pond protecting a little green that's well hidden by trees. Water comes into play on #13 and #14, as well. The 15th tee box is on top of a hill and offers a great view of the course.

Hackers looking for an interesting and challenging game of golf should come to St. James Golf Course. At $38 per round, it's very affordable and worth the drive. Come after 4 pm and take advantage of the great twilight rates, as well as the beautiful sunset.

ID: 5608109MN

STONEBROOKE

2693 County Road 79
Shakopee, MN 55379
Clubhouse: 952-496-3171
Golf Shop: 952-496-3171
Type: Public   Par: 71

www.stonebrooke.com

Region: Twin Cities

U
F

Course Rating

HOSPITALITY	7.85
PLAYABILITY	7.34
USABILITY	8.92
FACILITY	8.68
VALUE	6.24

OVERALL SCORE
787

Tees	Men's	Women's	Yards
Red		69.4/124	4830
White	68.5/131	74.4/134	5728
Blue	70.2/135	76.5/139	6104
Black	71.9/138		6475

Greens Fee: $55.50 (weekend)
1/2 Cart Fee: $16.00 (weekend)

Stonebrooke Golf Club, located in Shakopee, Minnesota, was developed in 1989 by Laurent Companies which builds homes and master-planned communities. Stonebrooke reflects this in the clubhouse design, the wonderful landscaping and maintenance of the course.

The driving range is located across the road near the Waters Edge executive course, which is also part of the Stonebrooke golf complex. This requires taking a golf cart to get to the range. The practice putting green is on a slope and we couldn't find any area on the putting green where there was a flat, straight putt. The course plays to a par 71.

The course has gently rolling fairways with generous fairway widths, trees, a number of environmentally sensitive areas, swamps, small ponds and little streams. Some of the bridges over the creek are miniature covered bridges. For the men there are four forced carries over water or swamps, of about 165–185 yards from the white tees. The greens provide a formidable challenge as they are quite large, faster than the average and have many undulations.

The signature hole is #8. The hole is only 320 yards, but from the white tee you need a drive to carry from 165–185 yards across the bay of the lake. Once teeing off you will load your clubs and cart on a pontoon boat which will ferry you across the bay to the fairway.

All the cart paths are blacktopped and it's easy to navigate the course. There is good signage throughout. The gas-powered carts all have GPS.

Stonebrooke has a wide variety of rates. If you book your tee time online you will receive a free golf cart. They have a wonderful website which has a variety of information and some neat course pictures, too.

Stonebrooke is a well-maintained, well-run golf course that is a good test of golf and strives to provide a country club experience at a cost between an average and an upscale golf course.

ID: 5537908MN

STONERIDGE

13600 North Hudson Boulevard
Stillwater, MN 55082
Clubhouse: 651-436-4653
Golf Shop: 651-436-4653 x4
Type: Semi-Private   Par: 72
www.stoneridgegc.com

Tees	Men's	Women's	Yards
Green		70.7/126	5247
White	70.2/134	75.6/136	6131
Blue	72.8/139		6702
Black	74.2/142		6992

Region: Twin Cities

Course Rating

HOSPITALITY   7.35
PLAYABILITY   7.63
USABILITY   6.69
FACILITY   7.68
VALUE   6.07

OVERALL SCORE
722

Greens Fee: $79.00 (weekend)
1/2 Cart Fee: $26.00 (weekend)

Stoneridge Golf Club in Stillwater, Minnesota, is located adjacent to Interstate 94 and very close to the Minnesota/Wisconsin border. It is a links style course, reminiscent of the courses of Scotland and Ireland. This course mimics a golf purist's vision of a "real golf course." It has been regarded in some venues as being "one of the best public courses in Minnesota."

Upon our arrival we were met in the parking lot by attendants on carts who asked to take our clubs and have them ready for us after check-in. We walked into the large clubhouse to check in and were greeted by name. They gave us information about the course, and a free ball repair tool to use with their repair system. We were offered bottled water gratis, and also a bucket of balls to hit before our round. There is a driving range and practice green close to the first hole. Our clubs were ready and waiting for us as we boarded our cart and started our round.

This is a very difficult course, with undulating fairways and greens and peppered with expansive and/or deep bunkers on nearly every hole. Playing to about 6150 yards from the white tees, it is imperative that you are in the fairway on your drives or on the greens in regulation to have any chance at a par.

If you are a very low handicap player and feel the need to find new challenges, this course is for you. For the mid-teen on up handicap player, this most likely will not be an enjoyable experience for you. There is little landscaping on the course in keeping with the links style. One thing we found that we did not like was the fact that the cart paths often left us quite a distance from the greens. We were continually parking the cart and grabbing a couple clubs, or more, and heading off to our ball. After our round, attendants were there to greet us again, providing assistance if we needed it.

The folks at Stoneridge were very personable and accommodating—we could not have asked for more. Unfortunately, we were there for the golf, and to look for the hacker friendly aspects in our round, and we found them few and far between on this day.

ID: 5508208MN

STONES THROW

Region: NorthEast

15679 Central Avenue
Milaca, MN 56353
Clubhouse: 320-983-2110
Golf Shop: 320-983-2110
Type: Public   Par: 70

www.stonesthrowgolf.com

U

Course Rating

HOSPITALITY	8.53
PLAYABILITY	7.79
USABILITY	8.91
FACILITY	7.76
VALUE	6.70

OVERALL SCORE
808

Green Fee: $42 (weekend)
1/2 Cart Fee: included in fee

Tees	Men's	Women's	Yards
Red	69.5/120		4910
Gold	65.6/121	70.3/122	5060
White	69.6/129	75.2/132	5943
Blue	70.5/129		6103

Formerly known as Milaca Golf Course, Stones Throw Golf Course is just west of Highway 169 in Milaca, Minnesota. Established in 1955, this is a member-owned course that's open to the public and offers good golf, great food and wonderful ambiance.

The clubhouse is large and sparsely furnished. There's a full bar and dining area, but, more importantly, the course has a short-order menu at a delightful counter just like a small-town diner. The staff was very friendly and helpful, as were the members and other golfers we encountered. Those looking for a well-stocked pro shop can forget it. It isn't a priority for this course, though they do have a few items for golfers in need.

The course is quite pretty. Although only an hour's drive from the Twin Cities, it wouldn't be out of place in the Bemidji area. Ponds, trees, bridges spanning creeks and a stretch of the Rum River serving as a border for holes #10 and #11 are the beautiful surrounding golfers can enjoy.

The course itself isn't meticulously maintained. There's a weed here and there in the fairways and a lot of rocks in the traps, but it isn't enough to detract from the overall playing experience. The course is very enjoyable. The greens are well situated and run true, if a bit slow. The layout features four sets of tees and ample fairways. Even though none of the tees except the blues are over 6000 yards, don't get complacent. Creeks, ponds and trees will require your attention. The par-3 15th hole is a good example. It seems simple enough on the scorecard—135 yards from the whites, but the hole consists of a tee, a green and a marsh. Miss anywhere and golfers will be forced to tee up another ball

If you are in the Milaca area, be sure to stop by Stones Throw. You're almost guaranteed a very relaxed and enjoyable round of golf.

ID: 5635309MN

STRAIGHT RIVER Exec. 18

23442 Cates Avenue
Faribault, Minnesota 55021
Clubhouse: 507-334-5108
Golf Shop: 507-334-5108
Type: Public   Par: 59

www.straightrivergc.com

Course Rating

HOSPITALITY	8.65
PLAYABILITY	8.22
USABILITY	7.93
FACILITY	6.79
VALUE	7.21

Tees	Men's	Women's	Yards
Red			2830
Blue	70.0/113		3410

NOTE: neither the course website or the MGA website had current yardage stats available at presstime (Jan-2010).

OVERALL SCORE
795

Green Fee: $20 (weekend)
1/2 Cart Fee: $10 (weekend)

Straight River Golf Course is located in Faribault, Minnesota. Despite its name, the Straight River is anything but straight and makes for some beautiful scenery. Course amenities include a driving range and a practice green. The clubhouse was simple, but very nice. Golfers can grab a bit to eat and the prices were fairly reasonable. Currently, there isn't a pro shop. However, the course is under new management, so there could be plans to build one in the future.

This course does have carts available to rent, although we were a little surprised by the lack of cart paths (paved or unpaved)—golfers just drive on the grass. What makes Straight River unique is its layout. The front nine is an executive course, while the back nine is a par-3 course. It is a very open course and, understandably, not very long at just 3410 yards. Since there aren't many hazards, don't expect to lose many balls. However, it's a good course for golfers to work on their short game. The greens are very large with nice undulations, but the grass was long on the day we visited, so they played quite slow. Although the bunkers were all neatly raked, the sand in those traps wasn't the greatest. The tee boxes showed some wear and tear, and didn't measure up to the conditions we've seen at other courses. Tee signage was fine and helpful with the layout. There was no beverage cart the day we played the course.

Straight River's prices are very good and they had some great specials in the fall. Throughout the year, Thursdays are Ladies' Day with golf, food and drink specials. A single membership is only $275—for those that live in the area, it's not a bad deal. Hackers on a budget, this is your course. Although we would not put this on our list of must-play courses, Straight River does offer a good round of golf with some very friendly folks in a beautiful part of Minnesota.

SUNDANCE

15420 113th Avenue North
Dayton, MN 55369
Clubhouse: 763-420-4800
Golf Shop: 763-420-4700
Type: Public   Par: 72

www.sundancegolfbowl.com

Tees	Men's	Women's	Yards
Red		71.6/125	5406
White	69.9/129	75.9/134	6192
Blue	70.9/131		6415

Region: Twin Cities

Course Rating

HOSPITALITY	7.63
PLAYABILITY	8.35
USABILITY	8.05
FACILITY	7.57
VALUE	6.81

OVERALL SCORE
784

Greens Fee: $33.00 (weekend)
1/2 Cart Fee: $14.00 (weekend)

Sundance Golf and Bowl, located in Dayton, Minnesota, is a full-service facility close to the Metro area with rural rates. Located in northern Hennepin County, Sundance is easily accessible from either County Road 81 (Maple Grove) or Highway 169 (Champlin). Follow County Road 121 to 113th Avenue North (Dehn's Country Manor Restaurant is on the corner) and head west to the clubhouse.

This is a full-service facility with driving range, chipping green, putting green and pro shop. In addition, Fritzy's Sports Bar offers a full menu (Thursday is ladies night when female golfers get a free drink ticket) and there is a banquet facility that seats 275 persons. Sundance also offers a 24-lane bowling facility next door. Be sure to check the course website for online specials and rates before you go or book your tee time online.

The on-course amenities are clean and well managed. The practice areas are located adjacent to the clubhouse for easy access for walkers. The course's slope is gentle so walking is comfortable. Carts are clean and well maintained. The large clubhouse offers a congenial sports bar (Fritzy's) that offers a full menu. The clubhouse also offers a banquet facility for tournaments or private functions. The pro-shop offers the full range of services from clothing to clubs to grips. The beverage cart makes regular rounds so your thirst should be satiated.

This is a great course for hackers to hone their game. The fairways are generous in width and the hazards are well placed to reward the accurate shot but allow one to play to the opposite side of the fairways or green to avoid hazards if one doesn't trust the shot that needs to be made. We found the fairways, rough and greens to be well maintained.

Hayden Hills Executive Golf Course (also reviewed in this guide) is a couple of miles down the road. It is a short 18-hole course that can be finished in two hours and makes a good practice course to play prior to your round at Sundance. Makes for a great day of golf finished up by happy hour at Fritzy's Sports Bar.

ID: 5536908MN

SUPERIOR NATIONAL

5731 Highway 61
Lutsen, MN 55612
Clubhouse: 888-564-6543
Golf Shop: 218-663-7195
Type: Public   Par: 72

www.superiornational.com

Region: NorthEast

Course Rating

HOSPITALITY	7.67
PLAYABILITY	7.11
USABILITY	7.16
FACILITY	7.80
VALUE	5.56

Tees	Men's	Women's	Yards
Mountain/Canyon (Gold)	67.2/131	72.8/130	5412
Mountain/Canyon (Blue)	73.4/144		6768
Canyon/River (Gold)	67.1/131	72.6/131	5382
Canyon/River (Blue)	71.6/139		6369
River/Mountain (Gold)	67.2/128	72.5/130	5418
River/Mountain (Blue)	72.5/138		6575

OVERALL SCORE
721

Green Fee: $72.00 (weekend)
1/2 Cart Fee: included in fee

Superior National at Lutsen is located in Lutsen, Minnesota, approximately five hours northeast of the Twin Cities. The course is 27 holes with 5 sets of tees. We played the Mountain course as the front nine and the Canyon course as the back nine, and toured the River. This course is hilly with many trees, creeks and beautiful views of Lake Superior.

The pro shop is at the clubhouse entrance with a restaurant and bar inside. Amenities also include a driving range and putting green. The course is not walkable due to hills and distances between greens and tee boxes.

The course is user-friendly with good signage, blacktop cart paths and well marked hazards. The sand traps, however, didn't have sufficient sand to enable good shots and contained small pebbles, which didn't make getting out of the traps any easier.

Golfers with a low handicap will fare better on this course. The hills, narrow fairways and some blind shots can create some sticky situations. The ball must kept in play on the fairway or near rough—otherwise it will end up in the thick woods that line each of the holes.

Making contact with the golf course for a tee time was a little irritating. The head pro was not a friendly person. In person, he wasn't very customer-friendly either. He seemed unhappy with the weather, but maybe he was just having a bad day.

Since the golf course is located in far northeastern Minnesota with a limited golf season, the rates are high. The regular green fee for summer play is $72, which includes a cart. It does seem a bit pricey for what you get. If you happen to be in the area on vacation or for business purposes, it might be worth a stop.

ID: 5561209MN

TANNERS BROOK

5810 190th Street
Forest Lake, MN 55025
Clubhouse: 651-464-2300
Golf Shop: 651-464-2300
Type: Public   Par: 71

www.tannersbrook.com

V

Region: Twin Cities

Course Rating

HOSPITALITY	7.85
PLAYABILITY	7.19
USABILITY	6.98
FACILITY	6.91
VALUE	7.69

OVERALL SCORE
732

Greens Fee: $33.00 (weekend)
1/2 Cart Fee: $14.00 (weekend)

Tees	Men's	Women's	Yards
Red		70.9/124	5332
Gold	67.9/124	73.2/129	5753
White	70.3/127	76.3/135	6283
Blue	72.4/129		6691
Black	73.3/130		6887

Tanners Brook Golf Course in Forest Lake, Minnesota, provides what you could call a hacker's dream. Imagine tall prairie grass as far as the eye could see; a picturesque site with wide fairways and rough plenty far out of reach. This is then coupled with short fast fairways and very receptive greens that brings the distance on the scorecard down to a manageable length for the everyday hacker.

Tanners Brook's clubhouse is a subtle structure from the outside but warm and welcoming on the interior. Set in a farm landscape and nestled right next to an old barn, it creates a very interesting composition. Adjacent to the clubhouse is a practice green and a driving area. There is also a nice putting green located right behind the first tee, so you may continue to warm up while you are waiting to tee off.

The first tee is not very well marked since it is across the parking lot and the road. When we were looking for the first tee the staff was gracious to help us and even gave us a ride to the first tee, which was well appreciated.

The course offers quite a variety of total distances and even from the tips the course is quite reasonable because of the hard, fast, and wide-open fairways. Hitting from these fairways into the greens is a joy. The greens are not only receptive to iron shots, they also roll with a good pace and are very true. The par 5s are reachable with a couple of good hits, but through the use of water and bunkers there is some risk and reward involved. One complaint about the course is the par 3s—while they are nice holes, they seemed a bit long and would have been much more enjoyable a club or two shorter in length. Besides the long walk to the #1 and #10 tee boxes, the course was enjoyable to walk. The holes where well spaced without creating long walks from tee to green.

Overall this is a good course for the everyday hacker, greens fees are reasonable and the course is well maintained. What it may lack in memorable signature holes it makes up for in enjoyment and playability, which is why we play golf in the first place, right?

ID: 5502508MN

TERRITORY

Region: WestCentral

480 55th Avenue SE
St. Cloud, MN 56304
Clubhouse: 320-258-4653
Golf Shop: 320-258-4653
Type: Public   Par: 72
www.territorygc.com

**P
U**

Course Rating

HOSPITALITY	8.70
PLAYABILITY	8.97
USABILITY	9.00
FACILITY	7.60
VALUE	7.56

Tees	Men's	Women's	Yards
Gold		69.0/120	5199
Blue	69.3/116		6202
Black	71.0/121		6550
Silver	72.9/125		6921

OVERALL SCORE
856

Green Fee: $32 (weekend)
1/2 Cart Fee: $13 (weekend)

Territory Golf Club, located just south of downtown St. Cloud, Minnesota, is primarily a links-style course, featuring open vistas, wild grasses and marsh areas. Holes 11–17 are across the street in the deep woods, giving the course a completely different feel. Standing on the practice green or the patio of the Coyote Moon Grill, golfers can get a great view of the course. The holes look challenging and inspire anticipation to play and experience what the course has to offer.

Territory knows how to maintain a golf course. The tee boxes were in good shape, except for being littered with some broken tees and the par-3 boxes a lot of divots. Fairways are expansive and cut short. Wild grasses and marsh areas are primarily just for show and only truly come into play on holes 3, 6 and 18. The multiple-tiered greens are large with many undulations. Golfers should carefully consider their approach shots before striking the ball.

This course is walkable, but it is nice to have a cart. A couple of holes do have a considerable distance between the green and the next tee. We might recommend a cart just for the GPS features, which gives an overhead view of each hole and green and a description of how to best play each hole.

The pro shop area isn't large, but it's not small either. There's a nice selection of Territory-brand shirts and hats for relatively reasonable prices. The rest of the clubhouse features a banquet area for 250 guests and a restaurant able to handle 40 guests. Both areas are catered by the staff of the Coyote Moon Grill, which has a full lunch and dinner menu. Coyote Moon is a great place for an after-round lunch or dinner. It has an outdoorsy, northern feel.

Territory isn't overly long or difficult, but still has enough challenges to keep hackers interested. It's a course that will likely require you to use every club in your bag. We'll definitely be back for another round.

ID: 5630409MN

THE BRIDGES

22852 County Road 17
Winona, MN 55987
Clubhouse: 507-452-3535
Golf Shop: 507-452-3535
Type: Public   Par: 71

www.winonagolf.com

P

Course Rating

HOSPITALITY	8.67
PLAYABILITY	8.76
USABILITY	8.14
FACILITY	8.21
VALUE	6.40

Tees	Men's	Women's	Yards
Red	65.8/125	71.1/117	5091
White	69.1/132	75.2/125	5823
Blue	71.7/137		6395
Gold	73.6/141		6824

OVERALL SCORE
829

Green Fee: $31 (weekend)
1/2 Cart Fee: $17 (weekend)

Set in the Pleasant Valley area in Winona, Minnesota, The Bridges Golf Club originally opened in 1920 as the Winona Country Club. It was redesigned by Robert Trent Jones in the 1960s into an 18-hole layout. A later modification of the 18th hole made room for the driving range. Now as a public course, The Bridges has retained many of its private club features.

The course's website is very informative, with maps and directions, a photo tour, history of the course and information on fees, programs, specials and membership options. The pro shop is well supplied with equipment, apparel and accessories. The head pro offers private lessons and swing analysis, as well as assistance with club fitting and equipment. The clubhouse amenities include men's and women's locker rooms, the Signature restaurant and the Visions event center. The driving range and putting green are in excellent condition. And each hole features a well-groomed fairway, a soft green and a beautiful scenic landscape. We encountered a family of deer along the perimeter of the course on the 14th hole.

The Bridges has a number of challenges, like sand traps, water, naturalized areas, elevation changes and mature trees that define the fairways. Pleasant Creek winds through the course and comes into play on nine of the holes. Four sets of tees allow golfers to pick a course experience matched to their own level of skill. The course is walkable, but given the nature of the rolling landscape it will be much more enjoyable to a newcomer on a cart. The fairways aren't narrow, although they're often framed by hazards. Greens are moderately soft and do have some undulation. Watch out for the 11th and 12th holes—they have hidden greens.

Golfers can phone ahead for refreshments using a call box on the 9th tee. After your round, relax in the bar and dining room at Signatures while you plan your next outing at The Bridges.

ID: 5598709MN

THE CROSSINGS

1101 West Highway 212
Montevideo, MN 56265
Clubhouse: 320-269-8600
Golf Shop: 320-269-6828
Type: Semi-Private   Par: 71
www.montegolf.com

Region: WestCentral

Course Rating

HOSPITALITY	8.15
PLAYABILITY	7.81
USABILITY	8.20
FACILITY	7.60
VALUE	7.16

Tees	Men's	Women's	Yards
Red		70.0/116	4964
Gold	65.8/112	70.8/118	5110
White	68.7/118	74.3/125	5735
Blue	70.7/122		6190

OVERALL SCORE
788

Green Fee: $29 (weekend)
1/2 Cart Fee: $14 (weekend)

The Crossings Golf Club in Montevideo, Minnesota is a scenic pleasure. Positioned near the Minnesota River, it has a wide variety of mature trees. The clubhouse is fully stocked with all the goodies needed to play a round of golf; attached is a restaurant and bar with a large deck overlooking the course. The Crossings is a great setting for a nice, but sometimes challenging golf course.

Winding through the trees and listening to the nearby river makes for a pleasant experience. However, this par-72 course does have some difficult holes, but others are a little easier with opportunities to score well. For the most part, the trees just provide a pretty frame for the holes and don't often come into play.

The back tees are over 6100 yards, so we chose to play from the whites at 5735 yards. We liked the 1st hole, a par 3. The tee box is elevated roughly 50 feet above the green, often tricking golfers into coming up short on that first shot. Our favorite hole is also one of the hardest. Number 13 has two doglegs, first left then right and there's prairie grass in front of the tee box for the first 175 yards. The barber's pole in the middle of the fairway is 239 yards away, but golfers who come up a little short are still okay. It's a fun hole that will require all the concentration you can muster. The finishing hole is little tricky, too. The layout for #18 is a reflection of the 1st. The tee box is about 40 or 50 feet below the green, but this is a par 4. Although the scorecard lists the distance as only 231 yards, it's almost all uphill, making the hole play much longer.

The pace-of-play was great—we finished in about three hours. Overall the course was very scenic and fun to play. The course is semi-private and can be a little expensive during the summer, but they have some great fall specials. If you're getting tired of playing the same local courses late in the year, take a trip to Montevideo and have a great time playing a fun and rewarding course.

ID: 5626509MN

THE JEWEL

1900 Clubhouse Drive
Lake City, MN 55041
Clubhouse: 800-738-7714
Golf Shop: 651-345-2672
Type: Public   Par: 71

www.jewelgolfclub.com

Tees	Men's	Women's	Yards
Red		67.9/115	4907
Copper	66.8/118	71.4/123	5526
White	69.0/122	74.5/129	6014
Blue	72.0/128		6669
Champion	73.8/131		7050

Region: SouthEast

H
P
F

Course Rating

HOSPITALITY	9.20
PLAYABILITY	8.87
USABILITY	8.63
FACILITY	9.11
VALUE	6.04

OVERALL SCORE
866

Green Fee: $70.00 (weekend)
1/2 Cart Fee: $16.00 (weekend)

The Jewel, located in Lake City, Minnesota, is a matrimonial symbol of the bond between the bluffs and the Mississippi, between links-style golf and all-terrain play. Originally intended as a private golf club community, with no expense spared, the course is now open to the public and available for anyone who wants the sternest test in southeast Minnesota.

If you've ever played an immaculate private course by invitation and wished you could play it whenever you wanted without having to "know someone" or pay for an annual membership, this is the course for you. The service should be the best and it is. If this course were in the Brainerd area, the green fee would be double.

Golfers are permitted to play the course without cart, but for those who aren't also marathon runners, it's not the brightest idea. And the championship tees should be considered for show by anyone with a 10+ handicap—don't even think about it. Also, if you haven't heard the term before, you'll know it after a round here: fescue grass. It eats golf balls. *Seriously.*

The Jewel is groomed daily like a PGA Tour course. The bunkers are strategically placed to make you calculate every single shot and regret those you didn't. Hole #3 is the signature hole of the front, a true test of 2nd shot accuracy. The course gets easier on holes 5–7. Hole #10 is the Jewel's jewel. Water really only comes into play twice on the course. Some holes will tempt you to quit early, but hang in there. Every hole is different, catering to every level of golfer in a different way. You'll use every club in your bag and maybe even buy another putter at the turn. To enjoy the full experience, play the tees that are an accurate description of your game. This is not the course to think you're better than you actually are. Final words of advice. If you decide to play here, make sure someone in your group buys the $5 yardage book. It will likely save you at least that in golf balls.

ID: 5504109MN

THE LINKS AT NORTHFORK

Region: Twin Cities

9333 Alpine Drive NW
Ramsey, MN 55303
Clubhouse: 763-241-0506
Golf Shop: 763-241-0506
Type: Public   Par: 72
www.golfthelinks.com

U

Course Rating

HOSPITALITY	8.15
PLAYABILITY	8.68
USABILITY	8.98
FACILITY	8.36
VALUE	7.30

OVERALL SCORE
842

Tees	Men's	Women's	Yards
Forward	67.0/121	71.9/126	5242
Middle	72.0/131	78.0/138	6344
Back	73.4/133	79.8/142	6653
Champion	74.9/139	81.6/146	6989

Greens Fee: $42.00 (weekend)
1/2 Cart Fee: $14.08 (weekend)

Golf provides a unique opportunity to gather with old friends and to meet new ones, especially when playing with a mixed foursome. The experience is heightened when one is fortunate enough to be paired with a clubhouse member who is intimately familiar with the intricacies of the course. As we learned, such a round-mate is invaluable when playing a course as difficult as The Links at Northfork in Ramsey, Minnesota.

The Links at Northfork is a friendly place for a very challenging round of golf. The course is designed as a traditional links course, long and open with contentious hazards throughout. The rough is long and punishing, leaving little room for errant drives. Water is a predominant risk on 10 of the 18 holes. The Links does not have the deep pothole bunkers you will find at St. Andrew's, but sand is a constant threat regardless of your position on the tee box or in the fairway. Even course veterans respect and fear the strategically placed hazards.

Most top-tier golf courses have a signature aspect that makes them memorable. Aside from its uncommon links design, the signature element at The Links at Northfork is its premier practice facilities. The driving range is conveniently located just steps from the clubhouse with some of the most reasonable rates in the Twin Cities. The Links offers two putting greens and a practice sand trap. However, the most notable component of the practice facilities is the 3-hole primer course. Access to this 3-hole loop is complimentary with any round, adding value to the $42 greens fees and allowing the golfer to walk to the first tee box with full confidence. In addition, the on-course amenities make an otherwise challenging round more comfortable, with water stations every four holes, four sets of tee boxes, ball washers at every hole and an omnipresent beverage cart.

The Links at Northfork is a beautiful golf course with an uncommon design. Its amenities and service are second to none. Although the course is quite difficult, it is "hackable" for the average golfer with the temperament to withstand frustrating hazards and a high score. For a taste of challenging links golf in the Twin Cities, The Links at Northfork is the place to go.

261

ID: 5530308MN

THE MEADOWS

401 34th Street South
Moorhead, MN 56560
Clubhouse: 218-299-7888
Golf Shop: 218-299-7888
Type: Public   Par: 72
www.moorheadgolf.com/meadows

Tees	Men's	Women's	Yards
Red		696/117	5150
White	69.6/119	75.2/128	6162
Blue	71.1/122		6490
Black	72.8/126		6862

Region: NorthWest

Course Rating

HOSPITALITY   7.65
PLAYABILITY   8.23
USABILITY   8.54
FACILITY   8.45
VALUE   7.62

OVERALL SCORE
812

Green Fee: $29 (weekend)
1/2 Cart Fee: $14.75 (weekend)

The Meadows is a links-style course in Moorhead, Minnesota. It's owned by the City of Moorhead and operated by the Parks & Recreation department. Just a few miles off Interstate 94, it's located on the north side of Moorhead.

First open in 1992, this course was designed by the renowned Midwestern golf architect Joel Goldstrand. In the Scottish tradition of links golf, there is not a single tree on the course. Instead, tall prairie grasses, wildflowers, scrub areas, sand and a creek all make for challenging golf. Yet, what really makes this course demanding is the wind that blows in from North Dakota. The Meadow's motto is, "If you're not playing in the wind, you're not playing golf."

Like its sister course in Moorhead, Village Green, The Meadows is a 6862-yard par-72 course that's deceptively difficult, especially on a blustery day. With four tee boxes, it can accommodate all types of players. Tee box signage is very good and fairway distance markers can be found at 200, 150 and 100 yards. Those new to the course will certainly appreciate the golf carts with colored GPS monitors and a yardage card with numerous distances. Golfers can also order food straight from the cart and pick it up at the turn. There is a driving range for practice, but estimating distances is a bit dicey because they only use a few colored flags for reference.

The modern clubhouse has a small pro shop, sitting areas and a grill called Lockwood's that serves burgers, brats and chicken. On the lower level is a banquet facility that can accommodate up to 144 people for events. The bar upstairs has tap beers and mixed drinks with happy-hour specials every day of the week. These specials also apply on the course when ordering from the beverage cart. The staff is friendly and efficient, making this course the go-to place for corporate or charity golf events. At only $29 for a round, The Meadows is a great value. If spending a weekend in the area, consider playing both Moorhead courses while there. Just watch out for that North Dakota wind.

ID: 5656009MN

THE MEADOWS AT MYSTIC

Region: Twin Cities

2400 Mystic Lake Drive
Prior Lake, MN 55372
Clubhouse: 952-233-5533
Golf Shop: 952-233-5533
Type: Public   Par: 72
www.mysticlakegolf.com

Course Rating

HOSPITALITY	7.38
PLAYABILITY	8.62
USABILITY	7.79
FACILITY	7.01
VALUE	5.36

OVERALL SCORE
758

Greens Fee: $85.00 (weekend)
1/2 Cart Fee: included in fee

Tees	Men's	Women's	Yards
Gold		71.2/131	5293
Green	68.5/134	74.1/137	5823
White	70.8/139	76.9/143	6318
Blue	72.3/142		6668
Black	74.6/146		7144

The Meadows at Mystic Lake is located behind Mystic Lake Casino in Prior Lake, Minnesota. This is a championship course and it plays that way.

This is a very nice layout with many picturesque features like waterfalls, wildlife statues, streams, lakes and some very nice architecture. We suppose that all those features are there to take your mind off the fact that for some reason, you can't figure out why you can't get a par to save your life. This is not a very hacker-friendly course. If you know the layout and play some good course management, you might be able to get in the low 90s, but it's unlikely.

Most fairways are set in a semivalley with raised borders framing the hole. Those borders are filled with high, dense, native prairie grasses, which makes finding your ball nearly impossible and playing from there downright wicked.

In general, throughout the regular playing season, this course is in top condition with tee boxes, fairways and greens in great shape. It better be for the price they are asking. However, this review was done near the end of October and although they had a reduced rate, the conditions were quite poor.

Tee boxes were in need of repair due to divots and a couple were not even flat and level. Fairways were a mixed bag with some being fine and in good condition and others punched and sanded. Greens were okay except there seemed to be an inconsistency in speed and amount of break from one green to another. Carts were nice, newer electric models with GPS.

At the turn, there is grill service and a patio area where we were greeted by a very nice and polite server willing to help except he had almost no items available from the menu at 12:30 p.m. The 19th hole is a nice restaurant with good reasonably-priced food, but remember this facility is dry and does not serve alcohol.

Final thought. This is a challenging picturesque course that you play once, maybe twice a year. Just think that you are on vacation at a resort course and are there to enjoy yourself and not worry about what will be your final score.

263

ID: 5537208MN

THE OAKS

73671 170th Avenue
Hayfield, MN 55940
Clubhouse: 507-477-3233
Golf Shop: 507-477-3233
Type: Public   Par: 72

www.oaksinhayfield.com

Tees	Men's	Women's	Yards
Red		72.1/125	5585
Gold	67.8/121	73.1/128	5883
White	69.0/123	74.7/131	6055
Blue	71.0/127		6478

Region: SouthEast

Course Rating

HOSPITALITY	8.17
PLAYABILITY	8.05
USABILITY	8.23
FACILITY	7.71
VALUE	6.29

OVERALL SCORE
789

Green Fee: $31.50 (weekend)
1/2 Cart Fee: $16.75 (weekend)

The Oaks is a picturesque course in Hayfield, Minnesota, about 25 miles from Rochester. Inside the clubhouse at this course is the Primetime Bar & Grille, which serves lunch and dinner, as well as breakfast on the weekends. There's also a pool table, for those who've had enough golf for one day. The pro shop carries a wide variety of equipment and the golf pro on site is available for private lessons (with special rates for juniors) and club fitting.

It's a well-maintained course. The course layout is easy to follow as well and there's excellent signage. While this course is flat (which should favor the hacker), there are obstacles in the form of water hazards and mature oaks and pines. In fact, there's water on the first three out of four holes. The par-3 14th hole is interesting, with a horseshoe-shaped creek that surrounds most of the green, which is further protected by a sand trap. Bunkers, while less prevalent than the water hazards, do come into play on some holes and are mostly greenside.

This course isn't overly long (6478 yards from the back tees), but there are enough challenges to make for an interesting round. The fairways and the rough were in excellent condition; the ground felt nice and soft and we enjoyed playing on the bluegrass. The scenery is beautiful and the water fountains in the middle of the ponds are a nice touch.

The staff was friendly and helpful and we enjoyed our round here. The weekend green fee is certainly reasonable and the annual memberships are more than affordable. Daily specials are another reason The Oaks draws quite a few golfers from the Rochester area.

ID: 5594009MN

THE PONDS

2881 229th Avenue NW
St. Francis, MN 55070
Clubhouse: 763-753-1100
Golf Shop: 763-753-1100
Type: Public   Par: 36/36/36
www.thepondsgolf.com

Region: Twin Cities

Course Rating

HOSPITALITY	7.40
PLAYABILITY	7.36
USABILITY	8.16
FACILITY	7.39
VALUE	7.54

Tees	Men's	Women's	Yards
Red/White (white)	68.5/127	73.6/129	5744
Red/White (blue)	71.9/134	77.8/137	6493
White/Blue (white)	67.1/128	72.2/129	5532
White/Blue (blue)	72.0/137	78.1/142	6599
Blue/Red (white)	67.9/129	73.1/128	5594
Blue/Red (blue)	72.3/138	78.4/139	6550

OVERALL SCORE
755

Greens Fee: $32.00 (weekend)
1/2 Cart Fee: $14.00 (weekend)

On the northern edge of the Twin Cities is a course that will have you telling everyone what a great golfer you are. It's called The Ponds Golf Course and is located about 40 minutes north in St. Francis, Minnesota. Its 27 holes are intertwined within a relatively new housing development and the layout is very hacker friendly.

The course gets its name from the many "ponds" that line the course. Calling them ponds might be a bit generous, but swampy areas do abound and you'll find yourself hitting over them more times than you can count. If you have an aversion to hitting over water, this course might cure you of it. The three different nines (red, white, blue) are all relatively the same, but locals claim that the blue and white nines seem to be the most popular.

The course is also very walkable and it has extremely wide fairways, few trees and little elevation changes. It is a links style course wrapped through swamps and meadow and without nasty pocket bunkers. Although walkable, the signage doesn't help matters for the first timer. The tee boxes have small colored markers, but they are painted two different colors so you never know which set of nine you are on. Also, when you play the blue and white nines, they run near each other so you could easily find yourself on the wrong hole. It might be recommended to take a cart the first time just for that reason.

Other than the signage, the course is well maintained, the greens are in great condition, the sand traps well-tended and the asphalt paths, when they are present, are easy to follow. The driving range, found by carting under the highway, is quite average and surprisingly runs alongside one of the holes and could be a potential safety issue with a wicked hook. If you want to start on the red nine, you'll have to cross back through the tunnel to play it. The clubhouse is very small by today's standards, but they pack in a pro shop, a full bar, a sit-down restaurant area, an event room for parties and a back patio. The space has a nice intimate feel to it like you've just entered the local bar.

ID: 5507008MN

THE REFUGE

21250 Yellow Pine Street
Oak Grove, MN 55011
Clubhouse: 763-753-8383
Golf Shop: 763-753-8383
Type: Public   Par: 71

www.refugegolfclub.com

Course Rating

HOSPITALITY	8.18
PLAYABILITY	9.00
USABILITY	9.15
FACILITY	9.16
VALUE	6.73

P
U
F

OVERALL SCORE
862

Tees	Men's	Women's	Yards
Purple		69.4/131	4819
Gold		72.4/139	5372
White	69.7/143	74.9/144	5819
Green	71.4/146		6188
Black	73.0/149		6534

Greens Fee: $41.00 (weekend)
1/2 Cart Fee: $15.00 (weekend)

Reflecting on a summer of golf, most golfers have one course that stands out in his or her mind as the premier golf experience of the season. The course seems to sparkle. The greens are soft and smooth, the fairways perfectly manicured, the sand is fine, the rough is luscious yet playable and the clubhouse is inviting. If this sounds like an ideal golf destination, visit The Refuge Golf Club in Oak Grove, Minnesota.

Oak Grove? Yes, pull out your map. It is worth the drive. Oak Grove is located on Highway 65, approximately 25 miles north of Minneapolis. This sleepy country suburb is home to one of the finest golf courses in the state. This course is carved out of a beautiful, wooded expanse with natural water hazards and boundaries that are as pleasing to the eye as they are challenging to navigate. Although narrow and winding, the fairways call to and guide you through the banks of trees, winding rivers and vast ponds. The sand traps, which pose a threat on nearly half of the holes, are soft like a Caribbean beach. It is truly a remarkable place to golf.

In addition, The Refuge is one of the friendliest courses around. Maybe it is the serene landscape or the relaxed nature of a rural suburb, but everyone is warm, endearing and helpful. The clubhouse attendants and other staff have one purpose in their work: to ensure that each golfer has the most enjoyable golf experience possible. Even one's fellow patrons are patient and eager to offer suggestions about navigating the course. Likewise, the accommodations and amenities are first class. The beautiful clubhouse has a vast banquet facility that is perfect for any event from a wedding to a corporate reception. For golfers, the food is hot and ready on the barbecue for a quick bite at the turn, and the snack and beverage cart appears often to satiate nearly any craving.

Although the course is well managed, its one flaw is in the spacing of golf parties, which leads to congestion on the back nine. Nevertheless, The Refuge is an amazing golf experience that is worth the drive and the slightly higher than average greens fees. Treat yourself, at least once a summer, and find refuge from the panic of city life at The Refuge Golf Club in Oak Grove.

ID: 5501108MN

THE SUMMIT

31286 Highway 19 Boulevard
Cannon Falls, MN 55009
Clubhouse: 877-582-4653
Golf Shop: 507-263-4648
Type: Public   Par: 72

www.summitgolfclub.com

Tees	Men's	Women's	Yards
Red		7.09/122	5165
Gold	69.9/129		5986
White	72.1/132		6471
Blue	74.6/138		7022

Course Rating

HOSPITALITY	6.35
PLAYABILITY	8.02
USABILITY	7.51
FACILITY	6.14
VALUE	6.58

OVERALL SCORE
708

Green Fee: $38 (weekend)
1/2 Cart Fee: $14 (weekend)

The Summit, located in Cannon Falls, Minnesota, starts out slow and easy, like a casual Sunday afternoon walk and ends with a roller coaster thrill ride. The front nine is fairly flat and open with small sapling trees mixed in with some mature trees. Errant drives are easily located and usually playable. By the 3rd hole, we were beginning to wonder why this course had a 139 slope rating. Holes 4 and 5 had narrow tree-lined fairways, but the landing areas were forgiving.

While the front was nice, the fun starts on the back and it seems like the course designers used all the tricks up their sleeves. Many holes feature an elevated tee box with a slim chute that give way to a very generous landing area and finish with an approach to an elevated green. Don't lose steam before the 18th—it's not an easy finish and golfers will need their skills to finish strong. This par 4 has a landing area 200 yards out and ends with a 150–160 yard approach shot over a large pond.

The tee boxes were okay with some needing repair. For the most part they were flat, playable and recently cut. Although a little dry and in need of water, the fairways were cut short and in good shape. There aren't any distances marked on the sprinkler heads, but there are 200-, 150- and 100-yard stakes down the fairways. The 150-yard stake also denotes the pin placement. The rough wasn't too long, but it was dense. Green sizes are mixed from medium to large and all have some undulation. Players should be careful when reading their putts.

The Summit does have a driving range, as well as a decent-sized putting green that can be used to practice chipping. The clubhouse is small with a limited selection of clothing and golf attire. There isn't much for food options. During the summer, The Summit offers junior lessons and sponsors a junior league at their par-3 course. It's a great way to get younger players interested in the game.

ID: 5500909MN

THE VINTAGE

27923 McGivern Drive
Staples, MN 56479
Clubhouse: 218-894-9907
Golf Shop: 218-894-9907
Type: Public   Par: 72
www.vintagegolfclub.com

Tees	Men's	Women's	Yards
Red		69.5/122	5042
Gold	66.6/123	71.6/126	5420
White	70.2/130	76.0/135	6219
Blue	71.9/136		6571

Region: NorthWest

Course Rating

HOSPITALITY	8.20
PLAYABILITY	7.73
USABILITY	8.22
FACILITY	7.70
VALUE	7.68

OVERALL SCORE
793

Green Fee: $29 (weekend)
1/2 Cart Fee: $12 (weekend)

Cut out of the woods along the scenic Crow Wing River, The Vintage is a hidden gem for golfers. Located in Staples, Minnesota, it originally opened in 1929 as a 9-hole course called Terrace Golf Course and was shareholder-owned. It was redesigned into an 18-hole layout by Joel Goldstrand in 1996. Today, it's a very scenic course with lots of wildlife. It's not uncommon to see deer, fox and a wide variety of birds.

Even though it rained for part of our visit, we still had a great round of golf on a beautiful course. It was in excellent condition with the fairways and greens in great shape. While the course isn't overly long, there are certainly some obstacles that can inspire intimidation in a golfer. A number of holes have water or wetlands running along the fairway and there are forced carries on four holes (two are par 3s). There are also shallow bunkers around most greens, but the landing areas are generously wide on many holes. The greens were true with consistent speed and the rough was cut to a reasonable length. The golf course superintendent and staff have done an excellent job of cutting away underbrush in various areas, making it easier to find those errant balls and making the course more playable. The clubhouse, though small, has a quaint, northern feel to it. They offer simple, good food at very fair prices, as well as a variety of adult beverages. Other amenities include a driving range and a practice bunker. There are also two practice greens: one for putting only, the other for both putting and chipping.

Under new ownership since 2006, The Vintage has become a community-oriented operation, hosting a number of fund raising events for the local schools, hospital and other causes. The management and staff are very courteous and helpful. Rates are quite reasonable; the weekend green fee is only $29 in the summer and this is a walkable course (perhaps excluding the trek from the 18th green back to clubhouse). The Vintage is a very hacker-friendly course and a gem.

ID: 5647909MN

THE WILDERNESS

Region: NorthEast

1450 Bois Forte Road
Tower, MN 55790
Clubhouse: 800-992-4680
Golf Shop: 218-753-8917
Type: Public   Par: 72
www.golfthewilderness.com

H
P
F

Course Rating

HOSPITALITY	9.07
PLAYABILITY	8.90
USABILITY	8.36
FACILITY	8.67
VALUE	5.48

OVERALL SCORE
846

Green Fee: $94.00 (weekend)
1/2 Cart Fee: included in fee

Tees	Men's	Women's	Yards
Red		71.7/129	5324
White	70.4/131		6147
Black	71.8/134		6460
Blue	73.2/137		6772
Gold	75.3/142		7207

The Wilderness at Fortune Bay in Tower, Minnesota, is owned by the Bois Forte Band of Chippewa and operated by Kemper Sports. Both know how to take care of their guests.

The rates are at the high end of the scale and there are very few deals to be found. The pro shop has the normal assortment of clothing a resort course has. An electric GPS-equipped cart and unlimited range balls are included in the green fee. The practice green, practice sand bunker and driving range are all well-maintained amenities and conveniently located between the clubhouse and the first tee.

We found the course to be quite friendly to golfers of all levels. There are five tee boxes that range in length from 5324 to 7207 yards. There are very few times you have to carry the ball any distance over a hazard. Obvious trouble can be found if your shots go astray and a few fairways are split by a rock ledge outcropping and rough. The greens were in near perfect condition and not too severely sloped. The course in general was well groomed. There were a few winterkill spots, but that is inevitable in northern Minnesota.

The restaurant at the clubhouse is top-notch and offers a wide variety of menu options, from a burger grilled and served outside on the large patio, to fine dining inside. The wait staff was very friendly and efficient. Prices are a little on the upside, but the quality and service justifies that.

The Wilderness is an Audubon Cooperative Sanctuary. The environment seems to be carefully considered, while maintaining near ideal course conditions. The surrounding scenery and views of Lake Vermillion are impressive. We did see a large black bear near the sixth green but he let us play through.

We would recommend a trip to The Wilderness at Fortune Bay since the course and customer service is excellent all around.

ID: 5579009MN

THE WILDS

3151 Wilds Ridge
Prior Lake, MN 55372
Clubhouse: 952-445-3500
Golf Shop: 952-445-3500 x4
Type: Public   Par: 72
www.golfthewilds.com

Tees	Men's	Women's	Yards
Forward	65.9/134	71.1/132	5118
Wilds	71.0/145	77.3/145	6241
Champion	72.1/147		6489
Weiskopf	74.5/152		7025

Region: Twin Cities

Course Rating

HOSPITALITY	8.05
PLAYABILITY	8.06
USABILITY	8.29
FACILITY	7.50
VALUE	6.36

OVERALL SCORE
785

Greens Fee: $80.00 (weekend)
1/2 Cart Fee: $16.00 (weekend)

If you think that The Wilds in Prior Lake, Minnesota, considered the Twin Cities first upscale public course when it opened in 1996, is too rich for your blood, think again. Times have changed and with a patronage card, you can snag tee time as low as $55 a round (includes cart and free range balls). It may surprise you how golfing luxury can fit into your budget.

The Tom Weiskopf-designed course has everything you'd expect from a quality track: imaginative course layout, well-kept fairways and challenging greens. With tee boxes from 5118 to 7025 yards, it is able to accommodate players of various skill levels. This reviewer played with a three-handicapper and the course challenged us all. The key to success here is keeping your ego in check and choosing the right tee box for your game.

If you are a straight ball hitter you should have nothing to worry about here. If you are not, don't think of the long carries you will be required to hit or the deep rough if your shot goes off line. Also don't think of the 152 slope or the 74.2 par rating from the Weiskopf tees either. Those things will play with your head.

Like any quality course, The Wilds clubhouse is right out of a country club. Well appointed, there is a large pro shop, a reasonably priced restaurant and banquet facilities that can accommodate 350 people. Staying for the 19th hole is an easy decision in the great bar with a friendly barkeep.

Very popular for corporate events (they do over 110 events annually), the course gets a lot of use and can be busy. The course is a bit thin on distance markers and you'll see a lot of rooftops in the fully developed neighborhood surrounding the course, but try to remember to ask at the pro shop for the purple yardage book that will tell you everything you need to know about playing the course.

If you want to treat yourself to a country club experience on a hacker's budget, The Wilds is one of the top courses in the South Metro, especially towards the end of the season when you can take advantage of their "pay the temperature" special.

ID: 5537208MN

THEODORE WIRTH

1301 Theordore Wirth Parkway
Golden Valley, MN 55422
Clubhouse: 763-522-4584
Golf Shop: 763-522-4584
Type: Public   Par: 72
www.minneapolisparks.org

Region: Twin Cities

Course Rating

HOSPITALITY	7.00
PLAYABILITY	6.58
USABILITY	7.67
FACILITY	6.26
VALUE	6.85

OVERALL SCORE
688

Tees	Men's	Women's	Yards
Red		71.2/117	5285
Gold	68.1/124	73.4/121	5666
White	70.9/130	76.9/128	6295
Blue	72.2/132		6575

Greens Fee: $30.00 (weekend)
1/2 Cart Fee: $14.00 (weekend)

If you are a short straight hitter, this is the course you can win on! But if you like to hit the 250–300 yard bombs that don't always go straight, don't bet the farm when you are playing Theodore Wirth Golf Course in Golden Valley, Minnesota. For a Minneapolis Park's run golf course, Theodore Wirth will give you a challenge at a reasonable price. Located just off of Highway 55, it is easy to get to. Also the area has a lot to offer the rest of the non-golfers while you enjoy this 18-hole course that was established in 1916.

The Minneapolis Parks board does its best to keep the tees, fairways, greens, and first cut of rough in good playing condition. For the extras, cart paths, sand traps, course ranger, food service, the park could use some more funding to improve these services. The 18-hole par 72 course plays 6295 yards from the white tees—which is not long, but you better hit it straight! The fairways are well groomed, and in the rough you can usually find your ball. But leave the clubs that you slice with in the bag. Past the first cut of rough are heavy woods or water areas. Also, there are a number of tee-offs where you are faced with blind shots.

The layout of the front nine holes is very friendly for the walker. The back nine holes will challenge that same walker's stamina. Every hole on the back, except the par-5 #12, has an incline and/or decline that you have to contend with. Each hole has the 100, 150, and 200 yardage markers, along with some sprinkler head markers. Tee-off signage is adequate. The first hole is the only one to provide extra information on distance to the water. Benches, garbage cans and ball washers are at each tee-off, and there is a beverage cart. Porta-potties are conveniently located on the course but only one rain shelter was observed. Overall the whole course setting with mature trees, natural water hazards and the occassional deer running through at dusk cannot be beat.

After our first experience with Theodore Wirth Golf Course would we play it again? Yes, and we would leave our driver in the bag!

ID: 5542208MN

THIEF RIVER

Region: NorthWest

13697 188th Street NE
Thief River Falls, MN 56701
Clubhouse: 218-681-2955
Golf Shop: 218-681-2955
Type: Public   Par: 72
www.thiefrivergolfclub.com

V

Course Rating

HOSPITALITY	8.38
PLAYABILITY	7.41
USABILITY	8.61
FACILITY	8.14
VALUE	7.77

Tees	Men's	Women's	Yards
Yelllow	67.3/118	72.7/126	5671
White	69.3/122		6114
Blue	70.3/124		6334

OVERALL SCORE
804

Green Fee: $27 (weekend)
1/2 Cart Fee: $11.50 (weekend)

Thief River Golf Club is about 1 mile north of Thief River Falls, Minnesota. This par-72 golf course measures just over 6100 yards from the white tees. With holes meandering along and across the Thief River and opportunities to view wildlife and waterfowl, this course is a great way to spend an afternoon.

Holes 1 and 2 are straightforward par 4s and give golfers an opportunity to score well if they keep the ball in play. It gets more interesting on hole 5, a 414-yard par 5 with a severe dogleg left that borders the Thief River. A solid tee shot followed by a good approach can lead to a birdie, but the green features some major undulation and can test your short game. The 6th hole is a straightaway 254-yard par 4 that seems easy, although there are bunkers left, right and behind the green.

The newer back nine (completed in 1993) is a fun set of holes that are also challenging. The manager's favorite hole is #12, a par 4 with a soft dogleg left and a difficult green to hit and hold, even from a short range. The 14th hole is a par 5 that's particularly long (it plays as a par 6 from the forward tees). We enjoyed #16, a par 5, dogleg right that features a split fairway with oak trees in the middle. It plays 532 yards if played the conventional way, around the trees. However, a tee shot placed down the narrow right-side fairway provides a direct shortcut to the green and an opportunity to score low.

The greens are firm and fast. The course can be walked since it's fairly flat, but the course has a nice selection gas golf carts available for rent at reasonable prices. There's a nice-sized putting green and chipping area near the clubhouse and a driving range just a short distance from #1 tee. The clubhouse has a good selection of golf equipment and apparel for sale. Thief River Golf Club is accessible and very easy to play. Tee times are encouraged and the pace-of-play is typically quick. The staff was very friendly and helpful and made for an enjoyable outing.

THUMPER POND

300 Thumper Lodge Road
Ottertail, MN 56571
Clubhouse: 218-367-2000
Golf Shop: 218-367-6501
Type: Public   Par: 72

www.thumperpond.com

Tees	Men's	Women's	Yards
Gray		72.7/128	5342
Black	70.1/124		6043
White	71.2/126		6281
Gold	72.5/132		6606

Region: WestCentral

Course Rating

HOSPITALITY	8.44
PLAYABILITY	8.25
USABILITY	8.38
FACILITY	7.51
VALUE	6.74

OVERALL SCORE
806

Green Fee: $43 (weekend)
1/2 Cart Fee: $13 (weekend)

Thumper Pond Golf Course in Ottertail is a fairly new course in west-central Minnesota. If you're in Battle Lake, Perham, Frazee, Wadena, or Detroit Lakes, it's certainly worth a visit. The Thumper Pond resort offers hotel accommodations and includes a restaurant, banquet and meeting facilities, a spa, plus an indoor water park for year-round enjoyment.

From the back tees, the course is over 6600 yards; the 6281 yards from the whites are much more manageable. With a total of five tees for most holes, the course should accommodate most golfers. The course conditions were good overall. We found the tee boxes to be a little hard, but the fairways and greens were in very good shape. The rough was reasonably long and thick. There weren't any multi-tiered greens; they were generally straightforward. We did repair several ball marks, but that's more indicative of the other patrons' poor etiquette, rather than any lapse in maintenance.

The front nine is relatively flat and a bit narrow in places, since many holes are lined with pine trees on both sides. The back nine is more contoured and generally a little wider, as well as more scenic. Golfers who are able to hit well will be rewarded, but bad shots will typically result in penalties. There are quite a few greenside bunkers, but they are in good shape, not overly deep and it's not difficult to get out of them. Water comes into play on only five holes and there aren't many areas that are out of bounds. In fact even if a few shots are errant, odds are you'll find the ball. And pace-of-play was excellent.

Thumper's staff is friendly and efficient. The beverage cart comes around frequently. The clubhouse offers a small snack bar where you can get a hot dog, chips or a drink at the turn. There's also a full-service restaurant with reasonable prices. To be sure, Thumper is not a golf destination resort like those in Brainerd. But it is a very hacker-friendly course, so bring your clubs if you're going to be in the area.

273

ID: 5657109MN

TIANNA

7470 State Highway 34 NW
Walker, MN 56484
Clubhouse: 218-547-1712
Golf Shop: 218-547-1712
Type: Semi-Private   Par: 72

www.tianna.com

Tees	Men's	Women's	Yards
Red		72.0/124	5430
Gold	68.0/119		5615
White	71.0/125		6323
Blue	72.0/127		6550

Region: NorthWest

Course Rating

HOSPITALITY	8.81
PLAYABILITY	8.06
USABILITY	8.79
FACILITY	7.38
VALUE	6.92

OVERALL SCORE
818

Green Fee: $55 (weekend)
1/2 Cart Fee: included in fee

Two miles south of Walker, Minnesota, on Highway 34 is the Tianna Country Club. Check out their very informative website for a tour of the course, the daily event calendar, a course history and complete information on rates, specials, tournaments, leagues and instruction. Inside the clubhouse, you'll find the pro shop, locker rooms and the bar and restaurant area with a roomy deck overlooking the course. The clubhouse staff was both friendly and welcoming.

Tianna plays 6550 yards from the blues and the forward tees shorten that distance by more than 1000 yards. Each tee box sign has a clear picture of the hole layout. Golfers will want to check the scorecard or the tee sign for orientation on the five or six holes that don't offer a clear view of the green. Four distinct tee boxes allow players to tailor the course to their own skill level. Some of the challenges include tree-lined fairways and soft greens frequently guarded by a pair of front-edge sand traps. Water is an added distraction on the 2nd, 5th, 17th and 18th holes and there's the occasional fairway trap, as well. Be especially aware of the out-of-bounds markers on the 12 holes that border the driving range and the property's perimeter.

Our favorite hole was #2, featuring a series of tiered tees high above a circular green 140–180 yards in the distance. Fly the ball high off the tee to carry the tall sedge, a water hazard and the trap in front of the left side in order to hit and hold the green. Once on the green, look back to see the full beauty of this hole. Our only disappointments were a surprising amount of litter on the tee boxes (broken tees and cigarette butts) and some overgrown boundaries in the mulched areas. Back at the clubhouse, relax and enjoy a sandwich, salad or full meal with appetizers, while enjoying the views out on the deck. Besides beer and soda, wine and full bar service are available. After a bite, you may want to stick around and take advantage of twilight rates.

ID: 5648409MN

TIMBER CREEK

9750 County Road 24
Watertown, MN 55388
Clubhouse: 952-955-3600
Golf Shop: 952-955-3600
Type: Semi-Private   Par: 72
www.timbercreekgolf.com

Course Rating

HOSPITALITY	7.00
PLAYABILITY	7.18
USABILITY	6.50
FACILITY	6.69
VALUE	6.50

Tees	Men's	Women's	Yards
Red		71.8/129	5331
Gold	67.4/126	72.4/131	5436
White	70.6/133	76.3/139	6137
Blue	71.7/136	77.7/142	6390
Black	72.8/137		6621

OVERALL SCORE
686

Greens Fee: $34.00 (weekend)
1/2 Cart Fee: $14.00 (weekend)

On the westside of the Twin Cities is a gem of a course. Nestled next to horse and hobby farms, Timber Creek is a quiet example of rural golf. With tight tree-lined fairways and a few intimidating gimmick holes, the course is 6621 yards from the tips and without local knowledge, it plays a lot longer than advertised.

When checking in, the guy at the front desk asked if we wanted a tip sheet so we'd have a better idea of how to play the course (they called it their virtual caddy). We declined. Big mistake. This is not a wide-open urban track where you can spray your ball in all directions. Course management, always hard for a hacker, is a very good idea.

Approaching the course from the highway you might miss Timber Creek's unas-suming signage (if you see horses, you've gone too far). Once there, the rut-filled gravel entrance road might make you think this is a neglected and under main-tained course. Not so. The course was lush, tree-lined and in great shape. The only knock on maintenance was that the greens had a lot of small dead spots and a few tee boxes were completely denuded of turf which seemed very out-of-character to the rest of the course.

The staff was quite friendly in a small town sort of way. Upon arriving, you felt that this was your local golf club and you had been playing here for years. The clubhouse is casual, the food reasonable but unremarkable, and the facility layout compact. One unusual course rule was that you can't drive the golf carts onto the parking lot so try to park close to the clubhouse when you arrive.

The pricing does have a bias toward locals, but there are also a lot of off-time and senior specials available. Timber Creek is the kind of course you must play more than once before you see it reflected in your score. It is not really a good walking course and you have numerous opportunities to find yourself in trouble spots (the reviewer hit six trees incidentally), but it will surely grow on you the more you play it. If you live on the west side of the Twin Cities and haven't ever played this course, it's worth the extra few miles for a visit.

ID: 5538808MN

TIPSINAH MOUNDS

15185 Golf Course Road
Elbow Lake, MN 56531
Clubhouse: 218-685-4271
Golf Shop: 218-685-4271
Type: Semi-Private   Par: 70

www.tmoundsgolf.com

Tees	Men's	Women's	Yards
Red	63.5/107	68.2/111	4909
Gold	67.1/114	72.5/120	5688
White	68.8/117	74.6/125	6066
Blue	69.5/119		6219

Region: WestCentral

Course Rating

HOSPITALITY	8.38
PLAYABILITY	6.71
USABILITY	8.16
FACILITY	7.93
VALUE	7.64

OVERALL SCORE
769

Green Fee: $28 (weekend)
1/2 Cart Fee: $11.50 (weekend)

Just five minutes off Interstate 94 between Alexandria and Fergus Falls, Tipsinah Mounds Golf Course is a fun course worth playing if you're in the Elbow Lake area. The par-70 course overlooking Pomme de Terre Lake is modeled and named after the nearby Indian burial mounds. Designed by Joel Goldstrand, the course utilizes snake-like mounds as hazards and buffers between some holes. The starter reassured us the mounds on the course contained no remains and only our own spirits would haunt our game.

The driving range and practice green are conveniently located close to the clubhouse. Built in 1982, the clubhouse does show some signs of wear and tear. It's a bit small with a basic layout and scattered seating to enjoy a burger or brat off the gas grill on the deck. A smattering of golf apparel and equipment were on display for sale. The staff was extremely friendly and accommodating, which is always pleasant.

Standing on the 1st tee, the various mounds that separate the 1st hole and the 9th are in clear view. The tee box signs were very helpful with accurate distances and picture of the hole layouts. We found the bluegrass fairways to be well watered, well manicured and soft (save for a few hard areas that were mainly due to statewide drought). The one-cut rough was not too challenging. The hazards were appropriate for those with a 20 handicap, with water coming into play on only two holes. The greens at Tipsinah Mounds were definitely the course's showcase. Some might think them a bit spongy, but we found them large, consistent in speed and interesting to read. On several of the greens, we noted that different pin locations could easily make the course more challenging. Golfers shouldn't have a problem walking this course, though electric golf carts are available. Overall, we found Tipsinah Mounds to be a very fun outing and well worth the price of admission. The friendly staff, courteous players and pace-of-play are enough to convince us to take another swing at this course.

ID: 5653109MN

TYLER COMMUNITY

Region: SouthWest

420 County Road 7
Tyler, MN 56178
Clubhouse: 507-247-3242
Golf Shop: 507-247-3242
Type: Semi-Private   Par: 71
www.frontiernet.net/~tribute/tylergolfclub.htm

Course Rating

HOSPITALITY	8.16
PLAYABILITY	7.04
USABILITY	7.70
FACILITY	7.83
VALUE	6.45

Tees	Men's	Women's	Yards
Red		70.7/117	5355
White	68.5/117	73.8/124	5924
Blue	69.9/121		6244

OVERALL SCORE
751

Green Fee: $27 (weekend)
1/2 Cart Fee: $11 (weekend)

Golfers may wish they had their pilot's license because there's a grass runway and hangers right on the property of the Tyler Community Golf Club. It sure would be a fun way to get to this picturesque course. The driving range is right next to the runway, but no planes were taking off or landing the day we played.

The clubhouse staff was very friendly, but there weren't many golf-related products (such as clubs or shoes) for sale. They did have a variety of balls, spikes, tees and logo clothes. The course itself is very well maintained and very scenic. Stepping on the 1st tee box, the rolling hills and trees seemed like a picture on a postcard. The wide fairways were a welcoming site. The cart paths were concrete and had arrows to the next hole, especially helpful for the first-time visitor.

Although many of the holes do have water and a sand trap or two, most don't come into play. The greens seemed to be smaller than average, but it's a nice change of pace and offers a different kind of challenge. Quite a few of the holes have elevation changes of some sort. Number 10 is a straight and long par 5 that is uphill all the way from the tee to green. The 11th hole has a waterfall behind the green and the 12th has water on either side. Of course, this makes for some scenic views. There were some tough spots, but there were also some easier holes where hackers have a chance at par.

There was no beverage-cart service, but the staff did offer us the use of a cooler, which we thought was nice. Additionally, after watching us look for a lost ball, the ranger stopped by and gave us some of the balls he'd found while out on the course. And if you're lucky enough to score a hole-in-one, be sure to let the clubhouse know; your feat will be posted on the course's website. Overall the course was fun and challenging, the staff friendly and helpful. If you're ever near Tyler, make the trip to this golf course—you'll be happy you did.

ID: 5617809MN

VALLEY HIGH

9203 Mound Prairie Drive
Houston, MN 55943
Clubhouse: 507-894-4444
Golf Shop: 507-894-4444
Type: Public Par: 71

www.valleyhighgolfclub.net

Region: SouthEast

H
V

Course Rating

HOSPITALITY	9.14
PLAYABILITY	7.69
USABILITY	8.47
FACILITY	7.41
VALUE	7.78

OVERALL SCORE
818

Green Fee: $22 (weekend)
1/2 Cart Fee: $10 (weekend)

Tees	Men's	Women's	Yards
Red		69.3/113	5014
Gold	65.1/110	69.8/116	5308
White	68.2/116	73.6/124	5916
Blue	69.2/118		6127

Houston, Texas may have a problem, but not Houston, Minnesota. If it does, it's not golf related. Home to family owned and operated Valley High, Houston sits as pretty as the course itself. Which is pretty pretty. Nestled into the bluffs and coulees (yes, that's a real word) near the Mississippi this track is tattooed with pride of ownership. They have work to do (they know it) but they have the plans and are actually implementing them. Ask for the owner (he's always there) and he'll reveal the many upgrades coming in 2010-11. And when you're done golfing, give him your ideas for what else he could do. He'll listen… He values the experience of "his" golfers.

Play this course before the leaves fall, or you'll lose balls in the middle of the fairway. Effective leaf-blowers here (and cart paths) would be valuable additions. That should tell you there are lots of trees. They add to the beauty of the course, but also to the difficulty. Take advantage of Hole #1 if you can, the next eleven are quite challenging. If you were ever going to warm up on a driving range, this is the place to do it (an alternative warm up would be the most beautiful 9-hole course in Minnesota, Pine Creek, in nearby La Crescent). Either way…warm up first!

This course is tough, we won't sugarcoat that. The greens pose few problems themselves… but getting on them can be a royal pain. There are half a dozen decent birdie opportunities if you're a long straight hitter or Tiger. Otherwise, buckle up. It's a bumpy ride until 12, where you can catch your breath on the anomaly of a "short and simple" Par 3. If you remove the driver from your bag on 15 it should only be to smack yourself with it. Put it back. 15 is a "hate-able" hole, and #16 is a crazy "signature hole" desperately in need of the removal of one tree on the left. (The one in the middle of the green is fine, yes, middle of the green). There's a test in every iron or driver shot at this course. Every. Single. One. If you're up for the challenge, Valley High awaits. Do yourself a favor… do the "Hokey Pokey." Play yourself a round. This is what it's all about!

ID: 5594309MN

VALLEY VIEW

23795 Laredo Avenue
Belle Plaine, MN 56011
Clubhouse: 952-873-4653
Golf Shop: 952-873-4653
Type: Public   Par: 71
www.vvgolf.com

Region: Twin Cities

Course Rating

HOSPITALITY	5.99
PLAYABILITY	6.56
USABILITY	7.21
FACILITY	5.78
VALUE	6.36

Tees	Men's	Women's	Yards
Red		69.8/120	4921
Gold	68.5/123	74.0/128	5667
White	69.9/125	75.6/132	5962
Blue	71.0/128		6208

OVERALL SCORE
641

Greens Fee: $35.00 (weekend)
1/2 Cart Fee: $16.00 (weekend)

Located in Belle Plaine, Minnesota, Valley View Golf Course is reasonably priced and moderately challenging but it feels cramped as though they squeezed 18 holes of golf into an area with enough acres for 16 holes. Combine that with some ugly customer service and the course left us with a lot to be desired.

Valley View was very easy to find and the clubhouse had a very welcoming appeal as we checked in for our round. The woman in the pro shop checked us in, gave us cart keys and pointed us in the direction of the carts. Things were off to a great start. They started to slide as we got outside. Our cart was drenched in dew and we ended up having to use our golf towel to wipe down the whole cart.

The practice area includes a nice putting green, a chipping area and a driving range. While not immaculate (the putting green was incredibly sandy), they do the trick to help iron out the kinks before the first tee.

The course starts with a relatively easy hole, par-4 dogleg right. Just don't slice it or you'll be hunting amongst range balls to find it and hitting three as it is out-of-bounds. The holes continued to be moderately challenging with shots over water and around trees which was fun but every hole seemed cramped.

After our initial encounter in the pro shop, the service was paltry the rest of the way. The call box on #8 for food didn't work after three attempts to call for a hot dog. The cart girl we stopped on #9 (a ridiculously long 230-yard par 3) had no input on it and said "I just drive the cart." No brats were ready in the clubhouse and the kid behind the counter swore the intercom system worked. All he could offer was the "hot dogs I just put out in the crock pot over there." We already felt like we were risking our lives on some of the holes on the course; we weren't about to risk food poisoning from the clubhouse.

Overall the golf was pretty good, the service was pretty bad and the whole experience was just okay. We hope if we're ever back it leaves us with a better impression.

ID: 5601108MN

VALLEYWOOD

4851 125th Street West
Apple Valley, MN 55124
Clubhouse: 952-953-2324
Golf Shop: 952-953-2324
Type: Public   Par: 71
www.cityofapplevalley.org

Tees	Men's	Women's	Yards
Red	65.2/109	69.4/117	4960
Blue	70.0/119	75.3/129	6030
Gold	71.8/122		6407

Region: Twin Cities

Course Rating

HOSPITALITY   6.20
PLAYABILITY   6.36
USABILITY   7.60
FACILITY   6.86
VALUE   5.99

OVERALL SCORE
661

Greens Fee: $53.00 (weekend)
1/2 Cart Fee: $15.00 (weekend)

While there are tougher tests out there than Valleywood Golf Course in Apple Valley, Minnesota, it combines just enough length with the demand for precise shot-making in such a way to make it better suited for separating a flight of low-handicap golfers in a white-knuckle tournament format than for a casual round with the guys on a Sunday afternoon.

The course was in terrific shape. The fairways were green and trimmed and dotted by only the expected number of healing divots, and the rough was nice and green yet short enough to play from with a fairway wood most of the time. The greens were a little firmer than expected given recent rain, but most still held an iron shot even if it wasn't perfectly struck. Many of them were domed or undulating, however, making chips and long putts a bit of an adventure. Pace of play was on the slow side but that might have been because it was Father's Day and there were a couple of families taking Dad out for a round that weren't familiar with the etiquette of the game. The rangers did a nice job of minimizing the impact on the rest of the players.

The on-course amenities were merely adequate. The beverage cart stopped by every four or five holes and the staff was friendly and accommodating. The selections were the usual golf course fare—beer and soft drinks on the cart, hot dogs and brats at the concessions stand in the clubhouse—and the prices were reasonable. There were no bathrooms on the course, so we had to either use the porta-potties or wait until we reached the clubhouse, which itself was pretty utilitarian (there was, however, a complimentary bottle of sunscreen in the men's room for anyone who'd forgotten theirs, which was a pleasant surprise).

All told, Valleywood is a good choice for the golfer who's looking for an enjoyable yet challenging on-course experience and doesn't much care about anything else, but if you're a 20+ handicap looking for a relaxing round with your buddies followed by dinner and drinks at the 19th hole, you might want to spend your weekend elsewhere.

ID: 5512408MN

VICTORY LINKS

1700 105th Avenue NE
Blaine, MN 55449
Clubhouse: 763-717-3240
Golf Shop: 763-717-3240
Type: Public   Par: 71
www.golfnygc.org

Region: Twin Cities

Course Rating

HOSPITALITY	6.21
PLAYABILITY	6.25
USABILITY	7.14
FACILITY	6.93
VALUE	5.74

OVERALL SCORE
647

Tees	Men's	Women's	Yards
Flagstone	62.8/115	66.1/113	4475
Bronze	63.9/118	68.1/118	4848
Silver	67.2/124	72.1/126	5560
Gold	70.5/131	76.1/134	6282
Iron	74.7/135		7092

Greens Fee: $42.00 (weekend)
1/2 Cart Fee: $14.00 (weekend)

The full name of the course is Victory Links at the National Youth Golf Center and is part of the National Sports Center in Blaine, Minnesota. It is a very pleasant and well thought out course. Golf course staff are friendly and helpful. Several holes offer very aesthetically appealing views. It is a relatively level course that is easy to walk and when visited, the fairways and greens were in tournament condition. With the exception of the noise from planes taking off at the Anoka County Airport (next door) which is surprisingly busy, the holes are well screened from the road and traffic noise and sight lines, which gives the golfer the feeling of a rural golf course in the heart of a major metro area.

This course is fundamentally designed to develop the young golfer. There are multiple tee boxes on each hole to relate to the golfer's ability. The course ranges from 2834 yards (for juniors) to 7100 yards depending on the golfer's tee box selection. Several lesson plans are available through the pro shop targeted towards youth development.

A unique concept of this course is the 18-hole putting course. Time permitting, you may want to avail yourself of this amenity before your round of golf. A keen putting eye is important on this course as the greens are tricky and the cups unforgiving. Fellow hackers will find that hitting the center of the cup is necessary to ensure a drop.

Facilities are lacking in some regards. There are no restaurant facilities but there is a hot dog stand and beverage cart. Women golfers might want to bring along some extra Kleenex as the only restrooms are at the clubhouse and Satelite potties are few and far between.

While Victory Links is not the cheapest course around it is a very pretty course that offers as much challenge as you may desire. Be warned though, it has the longest walk to the first tee of any course in the Twin Cities, but once you get there, the starter is quite a friendly fellow.

ID: 5544908MN

VIKING MEADOWS

Region: Twin Cities

1788 Viking Boulevard
Cedar, MN 55011
Clubhouse: 763-434-4205
Golf Shop: 763-434-4205
Type: Public   Par: 72

www.vikingmeadows.com

Course Rating

HOSPITALITY	8.26
PLAYABILITY	8.15
USABILITY	7.78
FACILITY	7.73
VALUE	6.49

Tees	Men's	Women's	Yards
Red		71.2/120	5598
Gold	67.8/117	73.0/124	5745
White	69.9/122		6207
Blue	70.9/124		6428

OVERALL SCORE
787

Greens Fee: $28.00 (weekend)
1/2 Cart Fee: $15.00 (weekend)

Very easy to find, Viking Meadows is located only a seven iron east of Highway 65 on Viking Boulevard in East Bethel, Minnesota. The course, marked by ample signage and a long tree-lined drive, brings you to the generous parking lot and clubhouse. Carts are not allowed in the parking lot, so drop your gear in the club drop area or lug it with you. The clubhouse is modest but carries the usual trappings in a compact setting. Fast food, pizza, beverages and a small selection of golf equipment and clothing are there. The front desk is right inside the door and the staff is friendly and accommodating.

The woods may be the first thing you notice once you are on the course. The course has a "Brainerd-like" look with a lot of pines, maples, poplars and birch trees. Outside, between the clubhouse and the first tee, a large display gives you diagrams of all the holes along with 4 sets of yardages. You have a feel for the course before you ever tee it up.

Viking Meadows is a dream course for seniors, juniors, ladies and hackers. There is no stigma for seniors or juniors playing gold tees and the ladies are given ample but fair compensation from the reds. The fairways are generally wide but there are enough hazards to test golfers and to get all of your clubs in play. The course is well maintained and the fairways and greens are in very good condition.

The hazards include sand traps (not a stone to be found in them), water on several holes and a few forest carries over the marshland and creeks that dot the course. The cart paths do not cover the entire course or even continue from tee to green in most cases. However, they are strategically placed and it would be difficult to get lost on this layout. A first-time golfer at Viking Meadows would not have a problem navigating the 18 holes. All in all, intelligent and thoughtful signage and design make this an easy trek for newbies.

Viking Meadows may be lacking in clubhouse amenities but it more than makes up for it in the playability and attractive appearance of the course.

ID: 5501108MN

VILLAGE GREEN

Region: NorthWest

401 34th Street South
Moorhead, MN 56560
Clubhouse: 218-299-7888
Golf Shop: 218-299-7888
Type: Public   Par: 72

www.moorheadgolf.com/villagegreen

V

Course Rating

HOSPITALITY	8.46
PLAYABILITY	8.72
USABILITY	8.61
FACILITY	8.20
VALUE	7.87

OVERALL SCORE
847

Green Fee: $30 (weekend)
1/2 Cart Fee: $13 (weekend)

Tees	Men's	Women's	Yards
Red		70.0/117	5304
White	70.4/121		5652
Blue	72.2/124		6728

Village Green Golf Course, located just off Interstate 94 in Moorhead, Minnesota, is owned by the City of Moorhead and is a 6728-yard par-72 municipal course. Once you find the course, you'll see it's a very nice facility.

The clubhouse is a nice building with a traditional layout. It has a small grill called Scobey's that serves sandwiches, chicken and other standard course fare. There's also has a nice patio area overlooking the putting green and a small sitting area. A topnotch practice area, including a driving range with numerous distance markers, a very large putting green and a sand and pitching area, is just across the street.

The first nine holes (currently the back nine) were built in 1981 and the second nine was added in 1994 (now the front nine). They are distinctly different, as the new nine is far more compact than the old. The course has three sets of tees and there's excellent tee box signage with distances and colored maps of each hole. Ball washers and benches are on the blue and white tees, as well as the forward tees. There's a new permanent bathroom near hole #6 and portable bathrooms about every five holes. Vertical fairway distance markers are easy to find at 200, 150 and 100 yards.

The ample water and sand hazards are sure to be a challenge for lesser-skilled players. The fairways appear to be wide, with few trees to block your way and you'll think the course looks easy. It's not. Golfers will have to contend with strategically placed hazards and contoured greens, and the course plays true to its 6728-yard length. Village Green is a favorite of locals and the staff should be proud of its course. The maintenance crew is outstanding. Even though the course experienced 3 inches of rain the day before we visited, the greens and tee boxes looked well tended and the fairways looked great. At only $29 for a weekend round, the course is also an excellent value. Hackers visiting the Fargo/Moorhead area should check it out.

ID: 5656009MN

VINTAGE Exec. 18

10444 95th Street NE
Otsego, MN 55362
Clubhouse: 763-271-5000
Golf Shop: 763-271-5000
Type: Public   Par: 58

www.riverwoodnational.com

Tees	Men's	Women's	Yards
Blue	57.2/87	57.7/93	3177

Region: Twin Cities

Course Rating

HOSPITALITY	7.36
PLAYABILITY	6.96
USABILITY	7.45
FACILITY	5.62
VALUE	6.97

OVERALL SCORE
696

Greens Fee: $21.00 (weekend)
1/2 Cart Fee: $ 9.50 (weekend)

Vintage Golf Course, located in Otsego, Minnesota, is an 18-hole executive style golf course located just across the street from its big sister Riverwood National. When you pull into the parking lot just in front of the very small clubhouse, the facilities do not look very impressive. Looks can be deceiving. They definitely are deceiving in this case. Yes, the clubhouse is small but inside you are greeted by warm and friendly staff ready to get you out on the course for your lightning-quick round. The clubhouse has a small bar area, well stocked with drinks, snacks and hot dogs. The pro shop is somewhat limited at Vintage with a few shirts, hats and golf balls but you can stop across the street into the bigger pro shop if you need more apparel.

The course is almost links style with low rolling hills, open fairways and very few if any trees. It is a nice mix of par 3s and 4s with most of the par 3s reachable by a wedge or 9-iron. The par 4s are spaced nicely throughout the course to provide a good test and a needed change of pace during your round. The course is well maintained with very few sand traps and short fairway grass. If you keep the ball in play around the greens you can stay close to par. Vintage is comparable to a links style course in another respect. If you hit your ball into the long grass you will have a difficult time finding it. If you are fortunate enough to locate it in the ankle-high rough you may break your wrists trying to hit it back into play. In combination, the longer grass and well-placed water hazards will steal a couple golf balls and a few strokes from your score. The greens are big enough to provide a good target from the tee box but are soft with very little slope to make for relatively easy putting.

Vintage is a fun course to get out and work on your short iron golf game, which is a weak link for most hackers. Also, finishing your round of golf under the 2 1/2 hour mark for approximately $20 is refreshing. However, as is the case with most executive style courses, you are left wanting just a little more.

ID: 5536208MN

VIRGINIA

1308 18th Street North
Virginia, MN 55792
Clubhouse: 218-748-7530
Golf Shop: 218-748-7530
Type: Public   Par: 71

www.virginiamn.us/golf course.htm

Region: NorthEast

Course Rating

HOSPITALITY	8.97
PLAYABILITY	7.74
USABILITY	8.85
FACILITY	6.69
VALUE	7.25

OVERALL SCORE
806

Green Fee: $25 (weekend)
1/2 Cart Fee: $14 (weekend)

Tees	Men's	Women's	Yards
Red		68.7/114	5089
Blue	69.7/123		6256

The Virginia Golf Course in Virginia, Minnesota, is a municipal course that is a little constrained by the neighboring houses and businesses. The facilities, however, are new. Michael's On the Course is a year-round restaurant that serves full meals and lunches at a competitive price. The pro shop has a modest supply of clubs and golf gear at average prices. The golf pro and his staff were courteous and helpful.

A round at Virginia is a good value. The weekend green fee is just $25. A cart is $14, but it's not really necessary since this is an easy course to walk. It's not very hilly and the next tee box is usually close. The practice green is conveniently located next to the clubhouse and 1st tee. It's speed and condition seemed to be comparable to the greens on the course. The driving range, however, is a cart or car ride away from the clubhouse. Unfortunately, it's also dry, hard and short, as well.

The course has a fairly forgiving layout. with no heavy woods to lose a ball in. There are some trees, but no heavy woods that would result in a lost ball. Water comes into play on nine holes, although there aren't any forced carries from the tee or approach shots over water. There are some out-of-bounds areas to contend with on five holes.

The course condition is average for a municipal course. The greens were in good shape, but there were some winterkill spots left. Generally, the fairways looked good, although a couple had evidence of frost heaving. Some of the tee boxes were rather uneven and in poor condition. Several times we were confused about the yardage of a hole because of a discrepancy between the scorecard yardages and the yardage listed on the signs. This was especially noticeable on the par 3s. Overall, hackers can expect to play a decent round of golf at Virginia for a very cheap price. It's perfect for the golfer on a budget.

WAPICADA

4498 15th Street NE
Sauk Rapids, MN 56379
Clubhouse: 320-251-7804
Golf Shop: 320-251-7804
Type: Semi-Private   Par: 72

www.wapicada.com

Tees	Men's	Women's	Yards
Red		71.5/122	5491
Gold	66.8/116	72.3/123	5629
White	69.7/122		6269
Blue	71.4/125		6610

Region: WestCentral

Course Rating

HOSPITALITY	8.90
PLAYABILITY	8.86
USABILITY	8.84
FACILITY	8.98
VALUE	5.73

H
P
U
F

OVERALL SCORE
857

Green Fee: $31 (weekend)
1/2 Cart Fee: $13 (weekend)

Wapicada Golf Club, located in Sauk Rapids, Minnesota, isn't far from St. Cloud. The clubhouse has a lovely banquet area (with seating for up to 250 people), as well as a bar and grill. Practice facilities include a two-tiered driving range, two putting greens, a 70-yard chipping green, 150-yard practice green and two practice bunkers.

The course was in excellent shape. The tee boxes had ball washers, garbage cans and benches. Cart paths lead you from the green to the next tee. The fairways were like plush lawns and the rough was cut short. There are large trees on both sides of the fairways and it's hard to lose a ball on the course. While there is some water on the course, it only comes into play on a few holes and is mainly for aesthetic value. Greenside bunkers will keep golfers on their toes, however; 14 of the 18 holes have them. Overall, the whole course was in first-class shape.

The first three holes are fairly straightforward. The 4th is the first of several interesting holes. Drives must be carried over a creek and wetland area and curve around a 90-degree dogleg. The 9th hole is an exciting par 4 (one of the hardest on the course) with water hazards and bunkers to complicate approach shots. The par-5 14th is reachable in two, but players should be careful not overshoot the green; it slopes away, making for a difficult chip.

This course is walkable, enjoyable to play and well worth the price. It's easy to see why it's been chosen to host high school state golf tournaments in the past. Wapicada is a beautiful, scenic course in exceptional condition.

WARROAD ESTATES

37293 Elm Drive
Warroad, MN 56763
Clubhouse: 218-386-2025
Golf Shop: 218-386-2025
Type: Public   Par: 72
www.warroadestates.com

Course Rating

HOSPITALITY	8.27
PLAYABILITY	7.61
USABILITY	8.66
FACILITY	8.24
VALUE	6.93

Tees	Men's	Women's	Yards
Red		71.1/119	5360
White	70.0/121	75.8/129	6207
Blue	71.7/125		6578
Gold	73.3/128		6942

OVERALL SCORE
801

Green Fee: $32 (weekend)
1/2 Cart Fee: $14 (weekend)

Touted as the "jewel of the north," Warroad Estates Golf Course is a scenic 18-hole course that was established in 1977. It's just north of Warroad, Minnesota, along Lake of the Woods and draws Canadian, as well as Minnesotan players.

The facility has a nice-size putting and chipping area. The clubhouse features a well-stocked bar with a patio overlooking the course's 9th green. Golfers can enjoy a number of items from the menu including pizza, appetizers and sandwiches from the grill, as well as the house special, the Big Bertha Burger.

The course begins with a par 3, but the front nine ends with a couple great golf holes. Number 8 is a par 5 with a dogleg left that's reachable in two for the big-swinging hacker. But this hole requires accuracy as well as length; it has lateral hazards to the left, right and even behind the green. The 9th hole is a dogleg right that's a par 4, measuring over 400 yards from all tees except the forward set. What's unique about this hole is the Minnesota-shaped green. Those who miss the pin placement will have a tough two-putt on their hands.

The back nine will test your mettle. It features water hazards bordering or crossing every hole. The fairways are plenty wide, but we would advise bringing an extra sleeve of balls if the wind is blowing. The greens are smooth with some nice undulation to make those lag putts interesting.

Tee times are not required, although they are encouraged and the pace-of-play seems fairly quick. Since the course is fairly flat, it can be walked, but it's also long and some holes have a sizeable green-to-tee distance. There is a nice selection of electric golf carts available for rent at reasonable prices. The clubhouse and grounds staff was very friendly and helpful. If you're looking for an enjoyable day out on the course in Minnesota's north woods, check out Warroad Estates Golf Course.

ID: 5676309MN

WASECA LAKESIDE

37160 Clear Lake Drive
Waseca, MN 56093
Clubhouse: 507-835-2574
Golf Shop: 507-835-2574
Type: Semi-Private   Par: 71

www.wasecagolf.com

Tees	Men's	Women's	Yards
Red		68.9/120	4966
White	68.3/123	73.6/131	5823
Blue	69.3/125		6053

Region: SouthEast

Course Rating

HOSPITALITY	7.11
PLAYABILITY	6.65
USABILITY	7.44
FACILITY	6.83
VALUE	6.63

OVERALL SCORE
695

Green Fee: $32 (weekend)
1/2 Cart Fee: $15 (weekend)

If you feel the expanded need for a mini golf vacation, head to Waseca Lakeside Club in Waseca, Minnesota. There are beautiful views, a cool breeze off the lake, blue skies, boats, plenty of bird watching and a plethora of trees. We even spotted an eagle when we visited. You could play these same 18 holes day after day. As a Waseca member said to us, "It's the prettiest course you've ever played."

The clubhouse was a moderate size and accommodating. There are locker rooms and while the pro shop was nothing fancy, it was adequate, carrying a small amount golf equipment. There is a driving range on site and a practice green directly outside the pro shop. Golfers can rent gas golf carts, although they were a bit dirty on the day we played. A golf professional is on staff and available for lessons. The entire clubhouse staff was especially friendly and helpful.

This course is quite walkable and there are numerous water stations. Players won't lose many golf balls at Waseca Lakeside, making it very hacker friendly. Although there are quite a few sand traps (we counted 31), most are well placed. Undulating fairways lined with numerous trees will test your accuracy. The tee boxes were decent, with three sets to choose from and the greens were fair and challenging. There didn't seem to be a big difference between the cut of the fairways and rough. Some par 3s are quite long and challenging.

The course was under construction when we visited. They were creating a new 9th hole and had a temporary par 3 in the meantime. They were also in the process of paving their cart paths. Still, all the construction did not detract from the beauty and our enjoyment of the course. The $30 weekend green fee isn't a bad value.

ID: 5609309MN

WEDGEWOOD COVE

2200 West 9th Street
Albert Lea, MN 56007
Clubhouse: 507-373-2007
Golf Shop: 507-373-2007
Type: Public   Par: 72
www.wedgewoodcove.com

Region: SouthEast

Course Rating

HOSPITALITY	8.72
PLAYABILITY	8.61
USABILITY	7.51
FACILITY	8.27
VALUE	6.33

Tees	Men's	Women's	Yards
Red		69.7/117	5136
Gold	68.0/122	73.5/125	5806
White	70.1/127	76.0/130	6261
Blue	71.6/129		6594
Black	73.4/133		6993

OVERALL SCORE
814

Green Fee: $55 (weekend)
1/2 Cart Fee: included in fee

Some courses offer you more than you expect. Wedgewood Cove Golf Club is one such course. This new 18-hole experience in Albert Lea, Minnesota is just a few hundred yards west the water tower and Pickerel Lake.

New courses typically increase their rates as they mature. If Wedgewood Cove decides to buck this trend, this course could be hacker heaven! The 2010 weekend green fee of $55 includes range balls and a cart rental. The carts are equipped with GPS and while the course layout doesn't make this feature necessary, it does make the experience much more fun. The screen even displays the score for the latest Twins game and shows how far away other carts on the hole are.

It's sometimes hard to believe Wedgewood Cove isn't a private club, but perhaps that's due to the economy. Golfers should keep in mind, however, this course was planned as part of an overall golf community. Houses line the fairways, which is intruding and tends to take away from the experience.

The clubhouse is quite large, but the snack prices are actually humane. There are a few improvements that could be made, however. There really should be a fence or net separating the driving range and the right side of hole #1. The complete lack of bathrooms on the course was also surprising.

The course was in fantastic condition. The links-style layout seems to use the natural terrain. Holes 1, 9 and 10–18 can safely be played by any hacker— until the fescue grass matures. The real fun is on holes 2–8, which are more challenging, but also more beautiful. The 2nd hole in particular, with more than one dogleg, is quite entertaining.

It's possible that some day this course will be a private amenity, available only to residents of Wedgewood Cove Estates. But it's open to the public today and *Team Hacker* suggests you take advantage of that fact.

ID: 5600709MN

WENDIGO

20108 Golf Crest Road
Grand Rapids, MN 55744
Clubhouse: 218-327-2211
Golf Shop: 218-327-2211
Type: Public   Par: 71/72

www.wendigolodge.com

F

Course Rating

HOSPITALITY	8.69
PLAYABILITY	8.53
USABILITY	7.01
FACILITY	8.68
VALUE	5.01

OVERALL SCORE
794

Green Fee: $60 (weekend)
1/2 Cart Fee: included in fee

Tees	Men's	Women's	Yards
Red		70.2/122	5130
White	69.7/130	75.7/134	6113
Blue	71.3/133		6474
Gold	72.7/137		6784

Located just south of Grand Rapids, Minnesota, on Highway 169, Wendigo Golf Club is the perfect place to go to get rid of all of the stress of city life. The first glimpse of this course almost takes your breath away with its lush beauty. The long fairways and perfectly groomed greens are quite a sight and plain to see even from the parking lot. This course is impeccably maintained and has the look of an exclusive country club with all of the friendliness and charm of a small-town course.

It's evident the course designers thought carefully about the layout and wisely took advantage of the natural landscape. The wide fairways, huge greens and cart paths that wind through the pristine wilderness are picturesque, to say the least. A rare feature of this course is its 4th hole; it can be played either as a par 3 or a par 4. The choice is completely up to the individual golfer. Players are almost guaranteed to see wildlife during their round. Within the first nine holes, we were able to spot about a dozen deer, bald eagles, geese and even a turtle plodding along one of the fairways. And, living up to the state motto of "Land of 10,000 Lakes," there is plenty of water. The 9th hole demands a carry over water to the green from all tee boxes.

The scorecard is very detailed. The hazards are also clearly defined and there are distance markers on almost every hole. With a good mix of par 3s, 4s and 5s, the course is a fun experience even for the average player. The pace-of-play was a bit off the mark; we finished our round in about 4.5 hours, but just in time to watch a spectacular Minnesota sunset from the deck of Fairways Restaurant and Lounge.

The $60 is a bit spendy for a hacker, but carts are included. Be sure to check out the website for unlimited golf specials. Wendigo was definitely worth the drive and we can't wait to return!

ID: 5574409MN

WHISPERING PINES

Region: WestCentral

8713 70th Street NW
Annandale, MN 55302
Clubhouse: 320-274-8721
Golf Shop: 320-274-8721
Type: Public   Par: 71
www.whisperingpinesgolf.com

Course Rating

HOSPITALITY	7.83
PLAYABILITY	6.45
USABILITY	7.91
FACILITY	6.68
VALUE	6.86

OVERALL SCORE
716

Green Fee: $29 (weekend)
1/2 Cart Fee: $12 (weekend)

Tees	Men's	Women's	Yards
Red		69.8/122	5003
White	70.7/131	76.1/135	6134
Blue	72.0/134		6421

Whispering Pines Golf Course in Annandale, Minnesota, is kind of hidden, due to road construction. (According to the clubhouse staff, there's been road construction here each summer for three years.) The course wasn't busy, especially for a Saturday morning.

Whispering Pines is definitely a no frills course. The clubhouse was small and empty. There wasn't much for merchandise in the pro shop and there weren't any sale items. Along with some candy bars, only hot dogs were available for food; there is no bar or restaurant. Unfortunately, the TV was broken (we visited during the 2009 PGA Championship and were hoping for an update on the scores). There is a nice patio area with a grill, but no sign of use. We also didn't see a beverage cart during our round, even though signs insisted only products purchased on site were allowed.

The golf holes, however, are unusually pretty. The course is quite thick with trees, making it very scenic, even somewhat secluded. Distance markers at 200, 150 and 100 yards lined the fairways. The greens used red, white and blue flags to denote pin placements. The forward tees were very hacker friendly, but some of the white tees were confusing. Some of the hazards aren't noted on the scorecard. Also, some of the holes had drop areas, but they also weren't depicted. One local rule that was noted was a free drop from all flower beds.

The cart paths were not paved and were in poor condition. They were quite rough and confusing in some places. There were a few signs indicating the direction to the next tee, but arrows on the cart path in certain spots were faded. Although we did see a few golfers walking, renting a cart seems like a more enjoyable option. Be sure to check out their website for weekday and weekend specials. Whispering Pines also accepts all coupons from competitors in a 45-mile radius.

ID: 5530209MN

WHITEFISH

7883 County Road 16
Pequot Lakes, MN 56472
Clubhouse: 218-543-4900
Golf Shop: 218-543-4900
Type: Public   Par: 72
www.whitefishgolf.com

Course Rating

HOSPITALITY	7.86
PLAYABILITY	8.03
USABILITY	7.90
FACILITY	7.90
VALUE	6.75

Tees	Men's	Women's	Yards
Red		71.7/127	5500
White	69.9/129		6166
Blue	71.2/131		6462

OVERALL SCORE
781

Green Fee: $47 (weekend)
1/2 Cart Fee: $15 (weekend)

Whitefish Golf Club in Pequot Lakes, Minnesota, is another beautiful course carved out of the woods in the Brainerd area. It's part of the Brainerd Golf Trail, which includes the Cragun's and the Grand View resort courses, in addition to several other courses within a 20 or so mile radius of Brainerd. It isn't nearly as expensive as the resort courses, but it's still very nice. First open in 1968 as a 9-hole course, the second nine holes were added in 1983.

With beautiful tree-lined fairways that were in great condition and greens that putt true, Whitefish is a great course. There are water hazards, but only one forced carry. The bunkers are reasonably deep (no pothole bunkers here) and looked like they were in excellent condition.

t's a straightforward course, though a little shorter than some, playing under 6166 from the whites and only 6462 from the blues. While this certainly makes it hacker friendly, there are a few spots where it gets a little tight and, as expected, an errant shot into the woods will cost you. In fact, those who have trouble keeping the ball straight and in play will likely score several double-bogeys. Although there are a few hills, it is still a walkable course.

The clubhouse staff was friendly and as professional as can be. Unfortunately the groups ahead of us were playing a bit slow, although it was a gorgeous day and the scenery at Whitefish made it hard to care. At the 9th tee we phoned in a lunch order for the turn. The selection includes hot dogs, burgers and a number of deli sandwiches. All were reasonably priced and tasted pretty good, too.

Whitefish is a little bit off the beaten path, but it is certainly worth playing and a great alternative to some of the pricier Brainerd courses.

WHITETAIL RUN

Region: NorthWest

11394 Leaf River Road
Wadena, MN 56482
Clubhouse: 218-631-7718
Golf Shop: 218-631-7718
Type: Public   Par: 72
www.whitetailrungolfcourse.com

Course Rating

HOSPITALITY	8.10
PLAYABILITY	7.82
USABILITY	8.14
FACILITY	7.11
VALUE	7.59

OVERALL SCORE
782

Tees	Men's	Women's	Yards
Red		70.0/118	5266
Green	65.2/113		5266
White	70.1/123	76.0/131	6339
Blue	71.6/125		6654

Green Fee: $28 (weekend)
1/2 Cart Fee: $13 (weekend)

Just north of Wadena, Minnesota is Whitetail Run Golf Course. Originally a 9-hole course built in 1926, it was redesigned into an 18-hole layout 70 years later. The two sides are as different as night and day. The original course is shorter and the fairways are lined with mature trees. It's a bit narrow and the greens are also a little smaller. But the smooth fairways, soft greens and few real hazards make it hacker friendly.

The back nine is a completely different course. Though not necessarily harder, it is a links-style course, open and windswept. The fairways are harder than those on the front, but they're also wider and longer. Greens were also larger with more contours, but fortunately just as consistent as those on the front in terms of speed, firmness and roll. And while there is more room for error on the back, truly errant shots are more costly because of water and wetland. We enjoyed one par 3 that had a green protected not only by a pair of bunkers and deep rough, but by an old concrete silo, as well. Since the front and back nine play so differently, two golfers are likely to have differing experiences.

The clubhouse was recently renovated in 2002 and is both neat and clean. A driving range is just behind the clubhouse, but the practice bunker is near #5 tee box. The pro shop carries an assortment of balls, clothes and hats with some clubs for sale, too. There's a nice patio area that overlooks the 9th and 18th greens, as well as a dining area downstairs to accommodate special events. The staff was friendly, as were the members we met.

Whitetail Run offers a variety of membership plans and player discounts. It's an enjoyable course that's a good golfing value and well worth playing.

WILD MARSH

1710 Montrose Boulevard South
Buffalo, MN 55313
Clubhouse: 763-682-4476
Golf Shop: 763-682-4476 x2
Type: Public   Par: 71
www.wildmarsh.com

U

Course Rating

HOSPITALITY	8.16
PLAYABILITY	8.71
USABILITY	9.07
FACILITY	7.97
VALUE	6.80

OVERALL SCORE
834

Tees	Men's	Women's	Yards
Red		67.3/117	4551
White	67.7/130	72.8/130	5559
Blue	69.8/134	75.5/135	6032
Black	72.0/139		6505

Greens Fee: $39.00 (weekend)
1/2 Cart Fee: $16.00 (weekend)

Wild Marsh Golf Course located in Buffalo, Minnesota, is true to its name. It's an "up north" style course with all the "big city" amenities. A great golf experience is enhanced by the course being very well maintained and a management and staff that take pride in their work.

Located just 25 miles from the intersection of Interstate 494 and Highway 55, Wild Marsh has 18 unique holes. All of the holes are cut through marshes, around lakes and trees, and tries to take advantage of the natural rolling terrain. The front nine is more secluded compared to the back nine and snake through residential homes.

With four tee boxes, red – 4551 yards, white – 5559 yards, blue – 6032 yards, and black – 6505 yards) the distance factor off the tee is not a major concern. The course also tries to reach out to the hacker. One advantage that was very helpful was the use of yardage markers. If you are faced with a tee shot that needed to clear a marshy area, a distance marker was embedded at the tee-off. If you do spray off the tee the first cut of rough is cleaned out making it easy to find your ball, but go further into the rough and you'll just have to admit it is a lost ball instead of looking for it in "the bush." The pin placement uses the red (front), white (middle), and blue (back) flags to indicate hole placement on the greens. The greens are nicely sized with some slight dips and slopes.

The course has a great web site which will give you all the information you'll need, from seasonal rates to memberships, league play, pro shop deals and the restaurant menu. Also the advantage of booking tee times online is provided though the website.

If you are looking for a peaceful golf experience in a relaxed atmosphere, at the same time being challenged to use every club in your bag, visit Wild Marsh Golf Course in Buffalo, Minnesota.

ID: 5531308MN

WILDFLOWER

19790 County Highway 20
Detroit Lakes, MN 56501
Clubhouse: 218-439-3357
Golf Shop: 218-439-3357
Type: Public   Par: 72
www.wildflowergolfcourse.com

Course Rating

HOSPITALITY	7.05
PLAYABILITY	6.89
USABILITY	7.42
FACILITY	7.67
VALUE	6.39

Tees	Men's	Women's	Yards
Green		71.8/118	5301
Burgundy	69.3/122	74.7/124	5824
Gold	71.0/125		6191
Blue	72.6/128		6551
Black	74.4/133		7000

OVERALL SCORE
710

Green Fee: $49 (weekend)
1/2 Cart Fee: $16 (weekend)

Southwest of Detroit Lakes, Minnesota, is Wildflower Golf Course, a sprawling links-style course that was carved from farmlands by Joel Goldstrand. It's meant to be a championship golf course and first opened in 1983. Inside the small clubhouse is a small pro shop and standard food offerings with a deck outside. The putting green is around the corner and a huge driving range is a short walk away. The staff was friendly and the golf pro is one of the few that will provide video lessons.

The course lives up to its name with large fields of wildflowers. The holes twist between woods and treeless fields. This is not a course for walkers and the t-shirt in the clubhouse that reads "I walked Wildflower and survived" is evidence of that. Take a cart; it's worth the extra money. Although beautiful with some nice vistas and wide fairways, Wildflower seems a bit out of place. It was built during the trend for championship courses, but the surrounding area, including a more opulent clubhouse, wasn't developed. There are five tee boxes to choose from, but most players decide to use the burgundy or gold at roughly 6000 yards.

The on-course experience was a bit disappointing. For those new to the course, it's tough to navigate and the signage is limited. The tee box signs, benches and ball washers are very basic. The distance markers are hard to see, but the course is working on a yardage book they hope to make available in 2010. The carts, although in nice condition, could help matters if equipped with GPS. A $49 green fee is a bit spendy for what you get, but they do offer a lot of deals and specials throughout the year.

Wildflower is probably the most difficult and unusual course you'll play in the area. It is not for the faint of heart, especially the first time and it's easy to see why the course has been host to numerous MGA qualifying tournaments. Fans of links-style courses should schedule a visit, but it's best to come with some course knowledge.

ID: 5650109MN

WILLINGERS

6900 Canby Trail
Northfield, MN 55057
Clubhouse: 952-652-2500
Golf Shop: 952-652-2500
Type: Public   Par: 72
www.willingersgc.com

Tees	Men's	Women's	Yards
Red		71.6/133	5166
White	70.5/142	76.0/142	5936
Blue	72.3/144	78.0/146	6310
Black	74.6/149		6809

Region: SouthEast

Course Rating

HOSPITALITY	7.37
PLAYABILITY	7.95
USABILITY	8.82
FACILITY	8.39
VALUE	6.01

OVERALL SCORE
785

Green Fee: $48 (weekend)
1/2 Cart Fee: $15 (weekend)

Willingers Golf Club is in Northfield, Minnesota and opened in 1991. It has received many national and local awards and has held a number of USGA and MGA events. It's definitely an upscale golf course, but costs less than those closer to the Twin Cities.

The two-level clubhouse has a well-stocked pro shop and men's and women's locker rooms on the lower level. On the upper level is a full bar and dinning area, an outside deck and a banquet facility that can hold 150 people. Willingers Grille serves lunch and dinner and is open for dinner service Fridays and Saturdays during the off-season. A very large putting green, as well as a chipping and bunker practice area is located between the 1st tee and 9th green. The driving range is behind the 9th green. The electric golf carts do have GPS.

Most players chose the white tees, which are 5936 yards. Those looking for a challenge can certainly find it; the tournament tees are 6809 yards in length and have a slope rating of 150. Regardless of which tees you choose, the course will keep you on your toes, starting with the 1st hole. It's a dogleg right with wetlands down the right side and three bunkers guard the green. The front nine overall is relatively flat and wanders through wetlands that come into play on six holes. There is a nice mixture of long and short holes, as well as doglegs both left and right, so the wind has an impact.

The back nine is a completely different course with many hills, trees and hazards on only three holes. Hole #11 is a short 334-yard par 4 that has a 90-degree dogleg. A tee shot on the right side of the fairway can mean trouble in the form of large oak trees between you and the green. The 12th hole is one of the most photographed at Willingers—and also one of the hardest. It's a long par 4 that plays 405 yards from an elevated tee. The long, narrow green is very difficult to read.

ID: 5505709MN

WILLOW CREEK

Region: SouthEast

1700 48th Street SW
Rochester, MN 55902
Clubhouse: 507-285-0305
Golf Shop: 507-285-0305
Type: Public   Par: 70
www.wpgolf.com/willowcreek

Course Rating

HOSPITALITY	8.54
PLAYABILITY	7.94
USABILITY	8.62
FACILITY	7.16
VALUE	7.48

Tees	Men's	Women's	Yards
Red		70.3/119	5145
White	68.2/119	73.0/125	5648
Blue	69.8/121		5996

OVERALL SCORE
806

Green Fee: $28 (weekend)
1/2 Cart Fee: $13 (weekend)

There are quite a few golf courses in the Rochester, Minnesota area. Most residents have played Eastwood, Northern Hills and Soldier's Field. But many haven't played Willow Creek Golf Course. That needs to change.

Perhaps it's little known because of the lack of advertising and signs on Highway 63. In any case, it has something for everyone. It even has an additional par-29 executive course called Little Willow, which is perfect for beginners or youth. It is a reasonable course to walk, even on a hot summer day. But those that do should bring plenty of water. There is limited beverage cart service and there are no water stations on the course—one of very few drawbacks.

There are plenty of minor elevation changes as you meander through the forest-like setting, but few steep climbs and none of great length. Many holes, however, require accuracy off the tee. There are plenty of woods to swallow up errant shots.

And true to its name, the Willow Creek is prevalent on this course. There are many other ponds and lakes scattered across the course, which are defined as hazards, but golfers aren't likely to lose any balls since they don't really come into play. The fairways are well kept and the greens are carpet-like. Beware on downhill putts though, as some greens have relatively steep slopes. The signature hole, without a doubt, is the 9th and it plays 20 yards longer than the distance marked.

The course caters to leagues, tournaments and group outings on a regular basis. The food is phenomenal and the clubhouse service is extremely professional. They take every measure possible to accommodate your every need with grace and a smile. Overall, Willow Creek is extremely enjoyable and worth every dollar and minute.

ID: 5590209MN

WORTHINGTON

851 West Oxford Street
Worthington, MN 56187
Clubhouse: 507-376-5142
Golf Shop: 507-376-4281
Type: Semi-Private   Par: 71
no website

Course Rating

HOSPITALITY	7.91
PLAYABILITY	7.74
USABILITY	6.83
FACILITY	7.38
VALUE	6.07

OVERALL SCORE
738

Green Fee: $30 (weekend)
1/2 Cart Fee: $15 (weekend)

Tees	Men's	Women's	Yards
Red		70.8/124	5202
White	69.2/129	75.1/133	5982
Blue	70.4/131		6250

The Worthington Country Club is a mature, lush golf course with lots of challenges. On the edge of Worthington, Minnesota, it has a swimming pool, a bar and nice banquet facilities. It also has locker rooms available for members.

From the 1st tee box, it's hard to miss all the trees lining the fairway. The fairway is fairly wide, but those big trees make hitting a straight shot paramount for scoring well. Most of the holes are set up this way, which makes the course more challenging. The greens were very fast on the day we visited, even though it had rained the day before. That sure made chipping and putting difficult, but not impossible. The sand traps were nicely manicured with well-defined edges and weren't very deep.

We enjoyed playing hole #10. It's a 110-yard par 3 that, at first glance, looks easy. The elevated tee box down to an island green, however, makes club selection tricky. The hole is further complicated by a sloped green. Since all the greens were speedy, a simple lag putt could turn into a very hard shot.

The course has yardage disks in the middle of the fairways and yardage stakes at the edges. Most of the sprinklers were marked with distances, as well, so we didn't really miss the carts with GPS that most courses have. Although there are water stations throughout the course, there didn't appear to be any beverage cart service. The snack shack out on the course has cold sandwiches, pop and beer available.

Overall, the course is beautiful with lots of different trees, nice water features and birds chirping. The course is well maintained and although the green fee at Worthington Country Club is a little pricey, we feel like we got our money's worth.

ID: 5618709MN

ZUMBROTA

80 Golf Links Avenue
Zumbrota, MN 55992
Clubhouse: 507-732-5817
Golf Shop: 507-732-5817
Type: Semi-Private   Par: 69
www.zumbrotagolfclub.com

Region: SouthEast

Course Rating

HOSPITALITY	5.10
PLAYABILITY	5.41
USABILITY	6.17
FACILITY	5.77
VALUE	6.16

OVERALL SCORE
561

Green Fee: $26 (weekend)
1/2 Cart Fee: $14 (weekend)

Tees	Men's	Women's	Yards
Red		67.5/122	4590
Gold	63.8/123	68.7/125	4812
White	66.5/129	71.9/132	5410
Blue	68.8/133		5907

Just an hour south of the Metro area off Highway 52 is the Zumbrota Golf Club. The course does have carts available, which are recommended for the terrain of this course. Four sets of tees are available and the course is a little shorter than average at just under 6000 yards from the blue tees. There is a clubhouse with a full-service bar and grill and a good selection of menu items at better than average pricing. Amenities include a small practice green, but there is no driving range at this course. We didn't see a beverage cart when we played and there isn't any water on the course, so plan accordingly.

The front nine dates back to 1927 and has a traditional, scenic look with mature trees lining the fairways. While distance isn't important, accuracy is, or else golfers will find themselves in the woods. Like many older courses that have since been redesigned into an 18-hole layout, the back nine at Zumbrota is quite different from the front and has a more links-style look. It's been cut out of rolling farmland and is wide open with very few trees. Long, native grasses and bunkers are the hazards on these nine holes.

We played this course using an incredible online coupon. Their weekday "Early Bird Special" was an outstanding $16 including a cart! Our round started off nicely and the course was well kept. It became clear early on the pin placements were extremely difficult. Ultimately, this led to a long round (more than five hours) and a wait on nearly every hole. At the turn, we walked in on the conversation the group ahead of us was having with Will Lancaster, the general manager and PGA professional. They, too, were commenting on the difficult pin locations and we agreed. The GM quite arrogantly stated we all "needed to have a PGA pro give us a putting lesson," as he considered all the pins to be fairly placed. We wish we could say he was only joking. The lack of customer service exhibited by this person was inexcusable. Although this course can be a great value with the online specials, we would never return, based on the interaction with the general manager and PGA pro.

ID: 5599209MN

Wisconsin Bonus Pack!!

35 Additional Courses

Minnesotans and Wisconsinites both like to cross the border and play courses on both sides of the Mississippi River. As a bonus, we've rated additional golf courses in Wisconsin from Amery to Viroqua. You'll find great golf in Hudson, Hayward, LaCrosse, Superior, Prescott, River Falls and at other courses up and down the river. Check the website for additional courses not found in this book.

www.HackersCentralOnline.com

AMERY

601 Deronda Street
Amery, WI 54001
Clubhouse: 715-268-7213
Golf Shop: 715-268-7213
Type: Public   Par: 72
www.amerygolfclub.com

Tees	Men's	Women's	Yards
Red		71.2/117	5289
White	69.9/119	74.4/131	5958
Blue	70.6/123		6286

Region: Wisconsin

Course Rating

HOSPITALITY	8.01
PLAYABILITY	7.87
USABILITY	8.22
FACILITY	8.09
VALUE	6.85

OVERALL SCORE

790

Green Fee: $35 (weekend)
1/2 Cart Fee: $14.50 (weekend)

Racing to get our round in before the Minnesota golf season ended, we ventured out with temps in the low 60's. A calm sunny day made for a great round of golf. The late season special of the day was 18 holes with cart for $20, which is a great price. Regular summer greens fees were a little higher than the average we have seen in Wisconsin, but not overly costly.

Located less than an hour northeast of the East Metro, Amery Golf Club was an easy drive. The course dates back to 1922 and is a well established, mature course. Full clubhouse facilities, bar, driving range, and putting green, pro shop, it's all here. There are carts for rental, but you could easily walk this beautiful, scenic course.

Our group played this day from the white tees, and at 5958 yards, was a good length for the average golfer. The course is wide open enough to be hacker friendly, but you still have the feeling of being in the woods, and far from the city on most holes. Be ready to play though as you start your round, because the first hole is a very challenging Par 5, and the number 1 handicap hole on the course. The course meanders nicely over the topography and in our opinion was just great. Large bodies of water, mature trees, some rolling hills, great scenery. Kudos to the designer for melding the layout with the existing geography, and coming up with a real gem. No two holes seem the same, and we particularly liked 10,11 and 12. Hole number 10, in our opinion was one of the most scenic and well laid out, that we have seen all year. The greens were, for the most part, large, and in great shape. There is plenty of "trouble" on the course, but is avoidable, depending on your style of play. Risk/reward is definitely a factor on several holes and shots as you play your round.

Overall, we had a great time at a great course, and unlike some of the courses we have played and reviewed this year, this one is definitely on the list of favorites, and one we look forward to returning to play again next year.

ID: 5400109WI

BADLANDS

1018 80th Avenue
Roberts, WI 54023
Clubhouse: 715-749-4150
Golf Shop: 715-749-4150
Type: Par: 72
www.badlandsgolfwi.org

Region: Wisconsin

Course Rating

HOSPITALITY	9.02
PLAYABILITY	7.55
USABILITY	7.74
FACILITY	8.09
VALUE	7.94

OVERALL SCORE
808

Green Fee: $22 (weekend)
1/2 Cart Fee: $11 (weekend)

Tees	Men's	Women's	Yards
Red		67.5/112	4835
Gold	66.2/107	70.6/120	5604
White	68.3/119		6042
Black	69.3/121		6280

Run, don't walk, to Badlands Golf Course in Roberts, Wisconsin, for a great day of golf. The family-owned course, just across the St. Croix River, is a short drive from the east Metro. With a driving range, a putting green and rental carts, this course caters to and encourages all levels of players.

We were very pleased as we played our round. The fairways are mostly open, and while there are some tree-lined areas, we found them very forgiving and large enough to accommodate the wayward tee shot. The length of the course— 6042 yards from the white tees—seemed a little short to us. With a decent tee shot, we found ourselves time and again with a mid-iron shot to the green. The greens are well kept and fairly large, and the shorter height of the rough made finding our ball easier. Some hills and a few blind tee shots required us to ride ahead on a couple holes to get a better idea of where to aim. The hills are just enough to add interest and variation but are not overly obtrusive. Hazards, both sand and water, are present on the course but are not overly dominating. We found them to be fairly placed and relatively avoidable. On the #3 par 4, the green is nearly entirely surrounded by water— sort of a mini 17th hole at Sawgrass.

A clubhouse at the turn offers hot dogs, sandwiches and drinks. In addition, they have a larger menu for a sit-down meal before or after your round. In 2009 the golf course offered a season-long special of $24 for 18 holes, including cart. The special was every day during the week and Saturday and Sunday after noon. The rate was only slightly higher before noon on weekends at $30.

The very hands-on owner was a great host. He drove out to meet us on the course, and he checked in once or twice to see if we had any questions. Our opinion was unanimous: This is a near perfect course. From *Team Hacker's* perspective, Badlands Golf Course is unassuming, unpretentious and friendly, all at a great price.

ID: 5402309WI

BIG FISH

14122W True North Lane
Hayward, WI 54843
Clubhouse: 715-934-4770
Golf Shop: 715-934-4770
Type: Public   Par: 72
www.bigfishgolf.com

Region: Wisconsin

Course Rating

HOSPITALITY	8.53
PLAYABILITY	7.93
USABILITY	8.35
FACILITY	7.71
VALUE	5.66

OVERALL SCORE
790

Green Fee: $75 (weekend)
1/2 Cart Fee: included in fee

Tees	Men's	Women's	Yards
Forward		68.6/116	4938
Club	67.5/115	72.2/126	5638
Member	69.5/126		6058
Championship	71.9/131		6608
Tournament	73.9/135		7190

Big Fish Golf Club in Hayward, Wisconsin, was designed by legendary golf course architect Pete Dye, whose better-known designs include TPC Sawgrass and Whistling Straits. If those are his A courses, this is his C. Big Fish is not an entirely bad course; it is half beautiful and a whole lot of fun. However, our expectations when driving five hours to get there were not met. Big Fish's clever advertising and glossy marketing took us hook, line and sinker.

We feel that Big Fish is overpriced. They tout their price as the best of Dye's courses, but that doesn't say much. You don't get what you pay for here. The golf carts should have GPS; they don't. The course charges for range balls; they shouldn't. The fairways are beat up and the greens need some work, as well. They tell you there are distance markers in the fairways, but it's not true. (They don't even have yardage books for sale, as similarly-built premier courses do.) Overall, this is a second-rate course with a first-rate name.

But enough of the bad; there's a lot of good here, too. The front nine is a links-style course with several bunkers and pot bunkers. It's relatively wide open and tree free, but the road and casino views on a couple holes are unfortunate. There is fescue, but on the front it's not tall or thick or even a half-hazard. Holes 3 and 7 try to bait your ball into joining the fish, and #9 is a great finisher, but it can blow up your whole scorecard. Yet the greatness of Big Fish awaits you on the back nine. (Snag a mid-round restroom break and a quick nibble at the comfortable and cute building overlooking the 9th green.)

There's tons of beauty on the back nine. Number 10 was the first hole that met our expectations of the course. Hole 12 is a great downhill par 3 (crazy long but picturesque from the tips), and 13 is unbelievable—a downhill par 5 that, if reversed, would have to be a par 9. We consider either #13 or #16 to be the signature hole, and #18 superbly reels you back into the clubhouse.

ID: 5484309WI

BRISTOL RIDGE

1970 County Road C
Somerset, WI 54025
Clubhouse: 888-872-5596
Golf Shop: 715-247-3673
Type: Public   Par: 72

www.bristolridgegolfcourse.com

Tees	Men's	Women's	Yards
Red		69.9/123	5132
White	71.2/130	76.8/139	6366
Blue	72.2/133		6582

Region: Wisconsin

Course Rating

HOSPITALITY	8.53
PLAYABILITY	8.78
USABILITY	8.43
FACILITY	8.10
VALUE	6.06

OVERALL SCORE
827

Green Fee: $35 (weekend)
1/2 Cart Fee: $12 (weekend)

Bristol Ridge Golf Course in Somerset, Wisconsin, is an 18-hole, par-72 championship course with a full-service clubhouse, pro shop, bar and complete dining facility. We arrived at the course early (well before opening at 7 am), and we decided to walk (since no one was there that early to give us a cart). The groundskeeper joined us after we teed off at the first hole and informed us we were too early. We assured him that we would wait for the mowers to finish, and we were okay to go. The mowers at the first hole got out of our way and let us know that getting ahead of them would work out. Everyone went out of their way let us play!

The tree-lined fairways follow the natural contours of the land and are well-kept. There are several water hazards and sand traps, and the rough is reasonable (except for the heavy woods lining most fairways). The tee boxes are in good shape, and most if not all have ball washers and benches. The greens are smooth, fast and rolling. Water and portable bathrooms are conveniently available.

There are several interesting (tricky) holes at Bristol Ridge. The 1st hole, a par 5, requires a drive over water, up a hill, around a corner and down to the green. The 2nd hole requires a drive over a hill and between trees on both sides of the fairway, then up a hill to the green. The 4th hole, a par 3, is 170 yards over water and swamp. The 11th hole is short, but water surrounds the green on three sides. In short, most of the holes are hardly straightforward.

After the rounds we talked with the manager and one of the members, who are proud of their course and were happy that we enjoyed playing it. This is an interesting, tough and challenging course. The quality of the experience was high and the reasonable price makes it a good value. It is a walkable course, even though it is hilly—a cart might improve the experience. We will surely play it again!

ID: 5402509WI

CLIFTON HIGHLANDS

N6890 1230th Street
Prescott, WI 54021
Clubhouse: 715-262-5141
Golf Shop: 715-262-5141
Type: Semi-Private   Par: 72
www.cliftonhighlands.com

Course Rating

HOSPITALITY	7.57
PLAYABILITY	7.73
USABILITY	8.60
FACILITY	8.81
VALUE	6.52

Tees	Men's	Women's	Yards
Red		70.1/120	5235
Gold	66.9/111	71.6/121	5741
White	69.9/125		6236
Blue	71.9/129		6660

OVERALL SCORE
790

Green Fee: $30 (weekend)
1/2 Cart Fee: $14 (weekend)

Nestled in the rolling farm country of western Wisconsin, Clifton Highlands Golf Club in Prescott is a well-designed course with interesting holes to challenge all levels of golfers. It is also beautifully maintained with well-groomed fairways, greens and tee boxes, and the blacktop cart paths make navigating the course very easy. Although Clifton Highlands is not a long course, it does require good course management and well-placed shots. The biggest challenges of this course are the greens—although the locals say they enjoy them, we found them to be brutal. Almost every green has a very pronounced back-to-front slope. When asked for advice on playing this course, the gentleman in the pro shop said, "Keep it below the hole," and he couldn't have been more right. Barely-stroked putts that missed from above the hole would roll until they hit the fringe or beyond. Three-putt greens were all too common on this round. The friendly pro-shop staff provided us with a printed cheat sheet on how to play the course, which was helpful.

The pro shop has the usual supply of clothing and equipment, and the clubhouse has a full bar and grill. Food during the daytime seems to be basically brats and hot dogs, and there did not seem to be a beverage cart during our round, but the course was not being heavily played that day. The course has a driving range located off the 1st fairway and a large putting green just off the 1st tee. The level practice green doesn't hint at things to come. In addition to the regulation 18-hole course, Clifton Highlands has a very nice 1081-yard par-3 course, which is perched atop a large hill, the base of which is surrounded by the last five holes of the regular course.

Although this is a highly rated course, it's not particularly hacker-friendly. The fairways are lined with strategically placed pine trees that eat errant tee shots; deep woods and cornfields border some fairways; and the greens will give fits to someone playing the course for the first time. However, it is a pretty and interesting course to play and the prices are reasonable.

305

ID: 5402109WI

CLIFTON HOLLOW

Region: Wisconsin

W12166 820th Avenue
River Falls, WI 54022
Clubhouse: 715-425-9781
Golf Shop: 715-425-9781
Type: Public   Par: 72

www.cliftonhollow.com

Tees	Men's	Women's	Yards
Red		69.2/118	5074
White	69.1/122	74.5/127	6015
Blue	70.6/127		6429

Course Rating

HOSPITALITY	8.86
PLAYABILITY	8.59
USABILITY	9.08
FACILITY	7.41
VALUE	6.80

OVERALL SCORE

840

Green Fee: $32 (weekend)
1/2 Cart Fee: $13 (weekend)

Clifton Hollow Golf Club in River Falls, Wisconsin, opened in 1974 with its first nine holes. Soon after, the second nine was added along with a par-3 course, a mini golf course and a supper club. Unfortunately the mini golf and supper club did not last. But what remains is a hacker-friendly 18-hole championship golf course. Clifton Hollow is a very family-friendly course. While playing, we saw many groups of men and women enjoying the course. The course has three tee boxes to choose from—red, white and blue—ranging from 5074 yards to 6429 yards, and topping out at a manageable slope of 127. While playing, you will experience a variety of holes and challenges while you enjoy the wide tree-lined fairways.

Clifton Hollow is not a bomb-and-gouge course. It will challenge you to play all the clubs in your bag. With many doglegs and short par 4s, the smart golfer will think on the tee box before reaching for the driver and swinging away. That is not to say that a driver is not needed—it is on a few holes. But there are quite a few nice risk/reward holes that are fun and challenging.

Most holes play pretty straightforward with some risk/reward elements involved, and you may be thinking, "This isn't so bad." Until you get to the greens. The greens are this course's main defense with undulations, slopes and just darn nasty fast-breaking putts. But don't be discouraged; not all holes are like this. It's important to remember that if it's nice from the tee then the green will get you; if it's hard from the tee, the green will be welcoming.

Overall the conditions are very good. Tee boxes are clean and playable. Fairways are wide at times and narrow at others. The recently cut and weed-free fairways are a pleasure to play from. Greens are medium size and in good condition with a few unrepaired ball marks. It's a fine course for beginner and advanced players, and it offers catering services thru West Wind catering. You won't be disappointed with your experience here.

ID: 5402209WI

COLDWATER CANYON

4052 River Road
Wisconsin Dells, WI 53965
Clubhouse: 608-254-8489
Golf Shop: 608-254-8489
Type: Public Par: 69
www.chulavistaresort.com

Region: Wisconsin

Course Rating

HOSPITALITY	8.64
PLAYABILITY	8.69
USABILITY	8.43
FACILITY	8.97
VALUE	6.79

OVERALL SCORE
848

Tees	Men's	Women's	Yards
Red		65.7/107	4527
Gold	64.5/107	69.0/113	5095
White	66.0/110		5431
Black	67.2/113		5697

NOTE: Will expand to 6500 yards in 2010.

Green Fee: $82 (weekend)
1/2 Cart Fee: included in fee

Coldwater Canyon Golf Course at the Wisconsin Dells' Chula Vista Resort is a wonderful destination. The course is in great shape and is fun to play, but because it's a resort course, you will pay resort prices. However, these rates are reasonable compared to many resorts, and they offer some great prices on packages pre-Memorial Day and post-Labor Day, as well as decent twilight rates. This course has everything: not only a nice clubhouse with full-service dining and a full liquor bar, but it can handle large groups for golf outings and weddings, etc. The pro told us they had 80 golf outings this year.

One thing that many people may have a negative outlook on regarding the course is its length. At 5700 yards from the tips, 5400 yards from the white tees, 5100 yards from the gold and 4500 yards from the red tees, some might think this is not a challenging course. But trust us, you will be challenged. With the front nine cut out of the woods and lined with canyons, and the back nine dealing with rolling terrain, there are challenges. With a few of the holes particularly challenging, it was nice to score on some shorter par 4s. That will change in 2010, however, when the course will open at 6500 yards. But even at the shorter distances, this course is challenging, fair and fun. There are many yardage markers on the sprinkler heads and 150- and 100-yard stakes and markers in the fairway.

The front side is the original nine that opened in 1927. It has narrower tree-lined fairways with some hills and lush fairways and rough. The back is more of a links-style play with a number of generous fairways and plenty of waste areas, sand and water to keep you honest. If you are wild off the tee you will find trouble. The greens and bunkers are great. The greens are a nice size and run true with just a few ball marks, and the many bunkers appeared to be filled with very nice sand. All in all, this is a great destination golf getaway that will just get better next year with the longer layout. The only thing missing is GPS on the carts.

ID: 5396509WI

CUMBERLAND

Region: Wisconsin

2400 5th Street
Cumberland, WI 54829
Clubhouse: 715-822-4333
Golf Shop: 715-822-4333
Type: Public   Par: 72

www.cumberlandgolfclub.com

Tees	Men's	Women's	Yards
Gold		69.4/119	5006
White	69.8/123	74.7/134	5995
Blue	70.8/129		6271

Course Rating

HOSPITALITY   8.46
PLAYABILITY   8.01
USABILITY   8.03
FACILITY   8.38
VALUE   6.18

OVERALL SCORE
800

Green Fee: $34 (weekend)
1/2 Cart Fee: $15 (weekend)

The trip to Cumberland Golf Club from the Twin Cities Metro area is about an hour and a half trip through western Wisconsin. It's a fairly easy drive, but better signage off the highways would make the course easier to find.

Cumberland Golf Club's website does not do the course justice. From the website photo, it looks like the course is going to be flat with a few trees, but it's more challenging than that. While there are a couple of holes that are somewhat open, you quickly forget you are at a municipal course and instead feel you're playing on a course in the north woods.

The staff and people at the clubhouse are very friendly and helpful. They warmly welcomed us and helped us with any questions. The pro shop has a small selection of golfing apparel for sale, but we didn't see any equipment offered. The prices for everything are reasonable. Putters Grill & Bar has large windows that face the golf course, and it offers an extensive menu and a full bar.

We found the course fair but challenging. You have to walk or drive your cart (as we did) a good 300–400 yards to the 1st tee box. Other than starting that far away from the clubhouse, we thought the rest of the layout was well thought out. The front nine is a little more open than the back, but there are plenty of trees, bunkers and water to get you into trouble. The course isn't exceptionally long (around 6000 from the whites), but on the back nine some of the fairways are pretty tight as you aim through a tunnel of trees. The tee boxes are in good shape—they're not too short and you have three options at every hole. The forward tees are shorter by almost 1050 yards. The greens are hacker friendly: not to short, not too much slant and a good size. The fairways are in good shape, if not a little narrow in places. We really enjoyed the golf course in Cumberland, Wisconsin. With all the trees, sand and water, it is definitely a challenging course, but it is scenic and enjoyable.

ID: 5482909WI

FREDERIC

Highway 35 North
Frederic, WI 54837
Clubhouse: 715-327-8250
Golf Shop: 715-327-8250
Type: Public   Par: 72
www.fredericgolfcourse.com

Region: Wisconsin

Course Rating

HOSPITALITY	8.50
PLAYABILITY	8.28
USABILITY	8.60
FACILITY	8.40
VALUE	7.25

Tees	Men's	Women's	Yards
Red		68.3/114	5061
Gold	65.2/111	71.1/119	5549
White	69.2/121		6198
Blue	70.6/123		6462

OVERALL SCORE
831

Green Fee: $30 (weekend)
1/2 Cart Fee: $16 (weekend)

Sometimes it's fun to play a course you're not familiar with, hoping the experience will be good, and you're likely to hit satisfaction with Frederic Golf Course in Frederic, Wisconsin. The layout runs from 6462 yards at the tips to 5061 yards at the forward tees. The course mixes things up with an array of gentle doglegs both right and left, along with straightaway holes. The par 3s are set up with minimal risk to allow you to take your best shot. Once you get past the 1st hole you'll find some of the nicest rolling fairway around, which complements this course extremely well. They provide some slightly blind shots on a few holes, but not in a bad way. The fairways are mowed to a perfect height, with the rough receiving equal attention.

Separating the fairways are well-maintained tree lines, all sufficiently trimmed so you can have an out for that off-line shot. The greens and fringes are exceptionally well-maintained and groomed. They run true and fast with slopes that make you take a second look before you make your putt. The course also has well-placed bunkers throughout the fairways and around the greens. The sand is well-maintained and easy to play from. The distance markers are always in sight and well-defined, while the pins on the greens are marked with colored flags that clearly show their positions whether it's from the front, middle or back. You can tell the tee boxes get moved around so the grass doesn't get too chewed up very much.

The course is extremely walkable. Each hole has benches, and water and bathrooms are positioned around the course so you're never far from either. The tee boxes also have trash cans and ball washers. There is a nice practice green and driving range next to the clubhouse for warming up. The clubhouse also offers a small, well-supplied pro shop with expected prices and a full bar and grill. The facility is also available for events. The exceptional website allows you to set up tee times or get directions. With a course this nice, it's not surprising to find that the people here are helpful and great to talk to.

ID: 5483709WI

HAYWARD G & T

Region: Wisconsin

16005 Wittwer Street
Hayward, WI 54843
Clubhouse: 715-634-2760
Golf Shop: 715-634-2760
Type: Par:

www.haywardgolf.com

Tees	Men's	Women's	Yards
Red		69.9/117	5200
White	73.6/128	68.4/119	5909
Blue	70.7/125		6420
Black	72.0/129		6718

Course Rating

HOSPITALITY	8.75
PLAYABILITY	9.07
USABILITY	9.00
FACILITY	8.25
VALUE	7.17

OVERALL SCORE
866

Green Fee: $40 (weekend)
1/2 Cart Fee: $15 (weekend)

Hayward Golf & Tennis Club, located in Hayward, Wisconsin, is 135 miles from the Mpls/St. Paul Metro area, but after playing a round of golf here, you'll walk away feeling more than impressed.

The 6718-yard par-72 course was established in 1924 and redesigned by Ken Killian in 1998. The course has a slope of 129, four tee locations, 10 doglegs, 52 bunkers and 4 well-placed water hazards, making this layout challenging yet fair. It has been rated one of the top 100 good value courses in the United States. Hayward Golf & Tennis Club is a pace-aware course, meaning there is a clock on every tee box to let you know if you are keeping up with the 4-hour, 10-minute pace.

The lodge-type clubhouse has a complete pro shop, and The Caddyshak Bar & Grill, the full-service bar and restaurant, offers extras such as a Friday-night fish fry and a Sunday buffet. WiFi is also available indoors and on the outdoor patio. Check in at the pro shop, grab a cart and head to the practice greens or the driving range.

The staff will call your name over the loudspeaker when your tee time is up. Head to the 1st tee, which is elevated and lined with flowers and stone. The signage is a layout of the hole and the yardage from each of the three markers. The reds have signage of their own on tee boxes that are fairly compensated for distance. The blacktop cart paths lead from green to tee, the latter of which are large and well groomed. The fairways are wide and lush and the greens are manicured to perfection.

You may think it's a long drive to the Hayward area just to play golf, but this would be one drive worth the time. Hayward is officially designated the golf capital of Wisconsin, and Hayward Golf and Tennis is the #1 most played 18-hole course in northern Wisconsin. When you can play a course this nice for $37, this one cannot be missed.

ID: 54843A09WI

HAYWARD NATIONAL

Region: Wisconsin

15986 W. Fun Valley Road
Hayward, WI 54843
Clubhouse: 715-634-6727
Golf Shop: 715-634-6727
Type: Public Par: 70
www.haywardnationalgolf.com

Course Rating

HOSPITALITY	7.90
PLAYABILITY	8.10
USABILITY	8.65
FACILITY	6.89
VALUE	8.08

OVERALL SCORE
798

Green Fee: $30 (weekend)
1/2 Cart Fee: $16.50 (weekend)

Tees	Men's	Women's	Yards
Red		67.3/109	4731
Gold	65.0/110	69.6/114	5068
White	69.2/118		5855
Blue	71.2/121		6364

Hayward National Golf Club is two and a half miles south of Hayward, Wisconsin. The small sign on the corner of Fun Valley Road points you in the direction of the golf course. Hayward National was set up to be a learning center as well as a championship course. It has an established junior golf program with special junior tees on all holes, and it's the perfect course for a family outing.

The clubhouse is new; it's very spacious and has a covered carport at the front door. The facility features a pro shop, bar and grill and changing rooms for men and women. The outdoor Trellis Patio is a great place to sit and unwind.

This course has two distinct nines. The front nine is The Pines and the back nine is The Marsh. The Pines is lined with tall pines (hence the name) on both sides of every fairway. When hitting straight shots the trees don't come into play, but if you don't hit straight shots, balls are generally easy to find resting in the pine needles. The Marsh takes you on a completely different type of adventure. It is more of a target-type nine. To be on the safe side, the pro recommends hitting the ball at the 150-yard marker. Straying from this advice could land your ball in the tall grass.

The course is well-maintained with the fairways and greens in excellent condition. The signage on the tees shows both a picture of the hole plus the yardage for all four sets of tees. The cart paths are mostly gravel, and getting from the green to the tee is a guessing game on some of the holes.

Hayward National has a world-class driving range and practice facility, and the large putting green is well-maintained. They have a PGA pro on staff, who is available for group or individual lessons. Over all, Hayward National is a very enjoyable course to play. The course can be challenging, but it is not too difficult for golfers with modest skill sets. The course does offer a decent challenge to sharpen one's skills at rates that are affordable and competitive with other courses in the area.

ID: 54843B09WI

HIAWATHA

10229 Ellsworth Road
Tomah, WI 54660
Clubhouse: 608-372-5589
Golf Shop: 608-372-5589
Type: Par:

www.golfhiawatha.com

Tees	Men's	Women's	Yards
Red		69.5/119	5320
White	69.4/124	75.7/131	6199
Blue	70.9/126		6520

Region: Wisconsin

Course Rating

HOSPITALITY	7.53
PLAYABILITY	8.16
USABILITY	7.89
FACILITY	7.32
VALUE	7.85

OVERALL SCORE
779

Green Fee: $30 (weekend)
1/2 Cart Fee: $17 (weekend)

Located at the junction of I-90 and I-94 in Tomah, Wisconsin, getting to 50-year-old Hiawatha Golf Club is an easy drive. Nice signage on Highway 21 directs you to the course, which is set in a rural moraine of rolling hills.

The Hiawatha clubhouse contains both a pro shop and a bar and restaurant. Check-in was fast and informative as we were directed to the practice green and driving range. E-Z-Go gas carts are clean and located next to the ample parking lot. Flanking the lot is an eight-cup practice green and massive driving range. We played on the Friday of a holiday weekend and were surprised there was no beverage cart. They should have told us at check-in because there was also no water on the course. But we refreshed at the turn and had a good day of golf anyway. Don't let the first two holes ruin your day. They are tough. It's rare that you start a round on a 520-yard par-5 dogleg left and then onto a hilly par 4 with an elevated tee box, tilted fairway and difficult, undulating green. Take your lumps because the remainder of the golf course offers scenic views and good golf conditions.

The greens are fast yet playable with some bumps, humps and swings. They're fun because they require a good read. An interesting 15-step clock tower on #3 allows you to spot forward groups prior to tee off; it also features temperature and humidity gauges. Well-defined fairways are in great shape—they have that lush, spongy feel and are lined by two inches of rough. Beware of the tall natural grass areas, as they make ball retrieval impossible. Note that you will have to keep an eye out in front of you because the hills can obscure the forward group. Walking is an option but would be a workout. On each tee box are layout markers, beautifully carved and painted on granite with planting beds of flowers. Each tee box offers blue, white, gold and red tees. Hiawatha Golf Club has a good website and accepts online advance reservations. Plan a picnic under the beautiful covered pavilion overlooking the 18th green.

ID: 5466009WI

HUDSON

201 Carmichael Road
Hudson, WI 54016
Clubhouse: 715-386-3390
Golf Shop: 715-386-3390
Type: Semi-Private   Par:
www.hudsongolfclub.com

Region: Wisconsin

Course Rating

HOSPITALITY	8.72
PLAYABILITY	8.80
USABILITY	7.63
FACILITY	8.88
VALUE	5.92

Tees	Men's	Women's	Yards
Red		69.0/121	5021
Gold	66.9/119		5503
White	69.3/127		6049
Blue	71.0/131		6435

OVERALL SCORE
827

Green Fee: $54 (weekend)
1/2 Cart Fee: included in fee

Hudson Golf Club in Hudson, Wisconsin, is a private course that opened to the public in July of 2009. The course offers limited hours of play and a separate rate for the public. We were welcomed to a full-service facility (pro shop, full bar, restaurant, snacks, grill, banquet facilities and locker rooms) with a friendly staff. (There was not beverage cart on the course, though.)

The view from the pro shop is the 10th and 18th holes. We signed in and were advised that this is not a walking course, but we decided to walk anyway. (We were later informed by the ranger that not many golfers walk this course—and it's obvious why!) The first fairway is about a two-block walk past the driving range. The course is in wonderful shape. The tee boxes have no tees lying around and we didn't see any pockmarks. It's all well kept!

The fairways are tree-lined and the grass is short, soft and lush. The greens are fast and in pristine condition. The 1st fairway, a par 5, is a long dogleg over a hill. We could not see the green until after the second shot. This is true of many holes: The green cannot be seen from the tee box. Water comes into play on six holes.

The first nine holes are walkable, but the second nine became more interesting. On the 10th hole we had a beautiful view of a valley with another hill on the far side. We teed off from the hill into the valley (50 – 100 feet down), over a pond, up the hill and to the green at the same height as the tee box. Many tee boxes were up or down hills from the preceding green. The hill from the 12th hole to the 13th tee box is particularly steep. The 18th tee box is about 150 steps up a hill, making it the highest tee box on the course. There is a good view of the clubhouse from there. The course is in excellent shape. Even though it is a tough course, it is possible to do well. We just recommend that you use a cart. The staff is friendly and helpful, and we really enjoyed the experience. (We'll be back!)

ID: 5401609WI

KILKARNEY HILLS

Region: Wisconsin

163 Radio Road
River Falls, WI 54022
Clubhouse: 715-425-8501
Golf Shop: 715-425-8501
Type: Public   Par: 72
www.kilkarneyhills.com

Tees	Men's	Women's	Yards
Red		70.0/117	6065
Gold	67.7/111	72.7/125	5672
White	69.7/117		6091
Blue	71.7/122		6500

Course Rating

HOSPITALITY	7.40
PLAYABILITY	6.34
USABILITY	7.21
FACILITY	6.18
VALUE	6.54

OVERALL SCORE
678

Green Fee: $33 (weekend)
1/2 Cart Fee: $15 (weekend)

Western Wisconsin is known for rolling hills, mature trees and expansive scenery. Kilkarney Hills in River Falls fits this description. Less than ten miles south of I-94, it is surrounded by rural Wisconsin cornfields and comes up on you suddenly, so watch for the turnoff. The course facility is compact and tightly put together. It's a very short walk to the clubhouse, the driving range and the first tee. At only 6500 yards from the tips, it is well within the grasp of most golfers, and even being a risk-taker by cutting the corner (like on #12) may have its rewards. As short as the course might be, it still is not for walkers because some of the hills are more like mini-mountains.

The course has few hazards, thus allowing for the potential to score well, except for a couple of holes where the green is partially surrounded by water. For an average golfer, the course lends itself to safe drives and approach shots. For better players, this course probably won't provide the challenge they're looking for. One thing that is very surprising is the absolutely awful bunkers. The person responsible for their maintenance appears to need a refresher course in bunker raking, and he doesn't do a much better job with the cart paths. These oversights are in contrast to the fairways and greens, which appear to be in good condition.

Where this course shines is with its clubhouse and reasonable rates. The clubhouse has a full sit-down bar with hot food options from the kitchen, flat screen TVs, video games, a wonderful balcony that overlooks the course and a very large event center that can accommodate up to 350 guests. The facility seems to know that the golf course isn't its strongest suit, so it tries hard to make the experience enjoyable by offering low green fees, excellent customer service and some of the least expensive memberships around. For a quick and inexpensive round of golf that is likely to boost your golf ego, Kilkarney Hills is a short drive. After your day on the course, you might have enjoyed it so much that your stay at the 19th hole might be longer than planned.

ID: 5402208WI

KROOKED KREEK

2448 75th Avenue (County Rd M)
Osceola, WI 54020
Clubhouse: 715-294-3673
Golf Shop: 715-294-3673
Type: Public Par: 72
www.krookedkreek.com

Tees	Men's	Women's	Yards
Red		68.6/113	4886
White	70.1/118	75.3/134	6109
Blue	70.6/123		6401

Region: Wisconsin

Course Rating

HOSPITALITY	8.60
PLAYABILITY	8.08
USABILITY	8.99
FACILITY	8.20
VALUE	6.85

OVERALL SCORE
829

Green Fee: $30 (weekend)
1/2 Cart Fee: $13 (weekend)

Some of the best high-value golf available to Minnesota hackers is a short drive into western Wisconsin. Krooked Kreek Golf Course in Osceola, Wisconsin, is a playable course with a very welcoming attitude. Before we even stepped onto the course we were greeted by friendly staff. The warm clubhouse with its tiny pro shop, huge horseshoe-shaped bar and comfortable dining room welcomed us. Built in 1990, the course's prices are reasonable whether you are a daily-fee player or a member.

The practice facilities are small but ample and well maintained, and everything you need is close by and well identified. The course is walkable, but the distances between some greens and tees made us happy that we decided to use one of the course's electric carts.

Krooked Kreek has two very distinct nines: a short and friendly front nine and a back nine that will challenge your game and your composure. There are plenty of hazards on the front, but they are all easily avoidable. The rough is cut to a manageable length and signage at the tee boxes locates the areas to avoid. Tee boxes are level and well maintained, as are the fairways and greens. Distances are clearly marked on sprinklers. There are a couple of doglegs to tempt the big guns and some strategically placed water that will make you think about your club selection. The greens run true and are well maintained.

Once you have been lulled into a sense of security on the front nine, make sure you're loaded up with golf balls as you head to the 10th tee. The back nine is a stark contrast to the front. There is water on seven of the holes, and three of the par 4s are longer than 370 yards. The finishing hole is a par 4 that stretches 410 yards from the white tees and will determine just how tired you are as you finish. If #13 isn't your unlucky number when you tee up, it may well be after you play the Kreek's #13. Loaded with value, playability and great hospitality, Krooked Kreek is well worth the short drive.

ID: 5402009WI

LAKE WISSOTA

16108 97th Avenue
Chippewa Falls, WI 54729
Clubhouse: 715-382-5276
Golf Shop: 715-382-5276
Type: Public Par: 71

www.lakewissota.com

Tees	Men's	Women's	Yards
Red		68.0/113	4806
White	67.5/116	73.0/126	5653
Blue	69.2/120		6015

Region: Wisconsin

Course Rating

HOSPITALITY   8.73
PLAYABILITY   8.49
USABILITY   8.53
FACILITY   7.91
VALUE   7.00

OVERALL SCORE
832

Green Fee: $25 (weekend)
1/2 Cart Fee: $12.50 (weekend)

Driving into the Lake Wissota golf course in Chippewa Falls, Wisconsin, you are immediately impressed by the beauty and upkeep of the place. There is a driving range to your right and a huge practice green to your left. The clubhouse looks like a Southern plantation mansion and has great banquet facilities, a well-stocked pro shop and a lunch/bar right next to the pro shop. Everyone was very helpful and considerate and service was very good.

The course is in excellent condition except, as with all courses in this area, the rough is a little dry and thin. The sandy soil makes it difficult to keep the rough lush. This makes a few of the holes more difficult because if you are a little long or off target, it's easier for the ball to get into trouble. This is a very fun course for the average golfer to play because it is not super long, but you have to use commonsense course management and usually be fairly straight. Like most courses in this area, most holes are tree lined. Water comes into play on six holes. The hardest hole is #10. It is a par 4 around a pond, and even the scorecard's guide to playing the hole shows you taking three shots to get on. A bogey on this hole feels more like a birdie. The greens are in great shape and putt very true. You will not have very many putts without some kind of break.

The green fees are very reasonable for this quality of course, and the food and drinks in the clubhouse are average prices for the area. The drink cart on the course came around often enough even on the cool day we played. The course is only five or six miles from Lake Wissota State Park, and about the same from Chippewa Falls. This course is located on Lake Wissota, with a few of the holes playing right along the lake. The views on the course and from the clubhouse make the golf experience here even more fun. The Lake Wissota golf course is a very nice course for the money, and it's worth driving a little farther than usual for fun, affordable golf.

ID: 5472909WI

LAKEWOODS

21540 County Road M
Cable, WI 54821
Clubhouse: 715-794-2561
Golf Shop: 715-794-2561
Type: Public   Par: 71
www.lakewoodsresort.com

Tees	Men's	Women's	Yards
Red		66.9/123	4312
Gold	67.2/128		5048
White	69.2/133		5447
Blue	70.9/137		6062

Region: Wisconsin

Course Rating

HOSPITALITY	8.05
PLAYABILITY	8.20
USABILITY	8.67
FACILITY	8.29
VALUE	6.45

OVERALL SCORE
810

Green Fee: $42 (weekend)
1/2 Cart Fee: $18 (weekend)

Lakewoods Resort's Forest Ridges golf course is a Joel Goldstrand design that it is expertly cut into the shadow of the Chequamegon National Forest. Just eight miles east of Cable, Wisconsin, this championship course at Lakewoods Resort doesn't play all that long, especially from the middle tees, so a good score is achievable. It is, however, very tight with water, out-of-bounds, undulating terrain and deep woods—just to name a few of the hazards you'll have to face. Nearly every hole boasts breathtaking views from either above or below and would be absolutely stunning in September when the leaves are at their optimum fall color.

Though the front nine is tight, the back nine is even tighter. The fairways, while narrow and sloping, yield excellent lies, and the roughs are nicely trimmed. Unfortunately, the distance between the fairway and deep woods is often just a matter of a few short yards. The greens are in excellent shape and hold well, although judging distance for certain approach shots can be quite challenging. Thankfully, each golf cart is equipped with a GPS system that provides hole-by-hole tips for the best way to play each hole and avoid the unseen obstacles that lie ahead for the unsuspecting first-timer. There are four separate tee box islands for each hole, many at varying altitudes, making hole appearance multi-faceted and changeable.

Though there are amazing aesthetic views throughout, there are two back-nine holes in particular that are worth the price of the green fee. Number 13 is 169 yards from the whites and 181 yards from the blacks. It is one of the most intimidating shots you'll ever face because you must carry at least 140 yards over a lake to hit a smallish green with a wooded drop-off on both sides. Number 16 is another stunner. It's a fairly short par 4, but follow the GPS instructions to give yourself the best shot at finessing your approach shot into this cattail-guarded, pine-tree-surrounded green. The sheer visual beauty of this resort course will make it worth every minute of effort you make here.

317

ID: 5482109WI

LUCK

1520 South Shore Drive
Luck, WI 54853
Clubhouse: 715-472-2939
Golf Shop: 715-472-2939
Type: Public Par: 72

www.luckgolfcourse.com

Tees	Men's	Women's	Yards
Red		69.9/115	5130
White	68.2/114		5773
Blue	69.3/117		6102

Region: Wisconsin

Course Rating

HOSPITALITY	8.04
PLAYABILITY	7.18
USABILITY	7.50
FACILITY	7.76
VALUE	7.43

OVERALL SCORE
757

Green Fee: $34 (weekend)
1/2 Cart Fee: $15 (weekend)

We played Luck Golf Course in Luck, Wisconsin, on a crisp October morning when the fall colors were beautiful. The drive from the Twin Cities is about an hour and 15 minutes. The clubhouse's setting on Big Butternut Lake is beautiful and has great views; the interior was recently remodeled with beautiful maple woodwork. They offer delicious handmade bratwurst and hot dogs from Van Meter's Meats, the hometown butchers. Breakfast and lunch offerings include pastries, sandwiches and hamburgers along with a variety of chips, candy, beer and pop.

The 1st tee box is quite a distance from the clubhouse; you have to cross a road four times, so walking is possible but it's a little bit of a workout. The most difficult part of the course is the greens. They are average size, but some of them have a pretty good slant. They are in great shape—no dead spots—and they are cut shorter than most municipal courses. The fairways are also in great shape, but they're cut fairly long. There are a few doglegs—a couple are pretty sharp. The course is relatively short (5773 from the whites), but because of the tree-lined fairways and water on about half the holes, it is challenging enough. There is very little sand on the course, which makes it easier, but there are enough trees to keep you honest. In fact, on some of the holes you can't see any other golfers due to the privacy the trees provided. You definitely feel like you're playing an up-north course. Some of the holes remind us of the courses in the Brainerd area, which are a lot more expensive to play.

It is worth the drive to play this affordable course. They advertise themselves as the best golf value in northwest Wisconsin, and they may have a point. Their fall rates were $25 for 18 with a cart, which is a great value. Overall it is a challenging course and might even be a little beyond the average hacker. If you like playing in the woods and like the challenge of driving straight and putting on faster greens with some slope to them, this is a great test!

ID: 5485309WI

NEMADJI

Region: Wisconsin

5 North 58th Street
Superior, WI 54880
Clubhouse: 866-364-6537
Golf Shop: 715-394-0266
Type: Public   Par: 72/71
www. nemadjigolf.com

Course Rating

HOSPITALITY	8.92
PLAYABILITY	8.38
USABILITY	8.95
FACILITY	8.56
VALUE	7.70

Tees	Men's	Women's	Yards
East/West - Gold	65.5/107	69.6/123	5127
East/West - Blue	70.0/130		6261
East/West - Black	72.3/130		6760
North/South - Gold	64.1/103	68.3/116	5043
North/South - Blue	67.7/119		5879
North/South - Black	69.5/122		6299

OVERALL SCORE
859

Green Fee: $39 (weekend)
1/2 Cart Fee: $12 (weekend)

Located in Superior, Wisconsin (just across the bridge from Duluth), Nemadji Golf Club has everything you could ask for in a course. With 36 holes of golf, a driving range, a 3-hole practice course and putting and chipping greens, the possibilities are endless! Situated next to Lake Superior, this course is cool and comfortable, but a bit windy at times, so bring a jacket.

The course offers five sets of tees and challenges for golfers of every level, from beginner to professional. The North and South Nine are leisurely and laid back, while the East and West Nine are a bit more rigorous and hilly. The greens on all 36 holes are absolutely beautiful, fast and well groomed. All four courses follow the natural topography and are very woodsy and wide, providing great scenery. Everything looks so natural you'd swear it's been here forever, which it nearly has—Nemadji opened in 1931. The signage was very easy to follow on and the extensive cart paths make it nearly impossible to get lost or confused on the course.

There are so many leagues (both men's and women's), that it's hard to keep track of them all. No worries, there are so many holes to play you won't mind all the league play. Tee times can be made up to 30 days in advance. Groups are spaced seven minutes apart and the pace-of-play is comfortable. We did not feel rushed, nor did we wait too long on any of the holes. The staff and fellow golfers were all very friendly and knowledgeable, a real joy to talk to.

The course is certainly affordable and a good value. There are twilight discounts, driving range deals and a "Special Offers" section on their website, offering a free round of golf when you sign up for the e-newsletter. Nemadji Golf Club is a hacker's dream.

ID: 5488009WI

NEW RICHMOND

1226 180th Street
New Richmond, WI 54017
Clubhouse: 800-570-9302
Golf Shop: 715-246-6724
Type: Public   Par: 72
www.nrgolfclub.com

Region: Wisconsin

Course Rating

HOSPITALITY	8.69
PLAYABILITY	8.74
USABILITY	8.60
FACILITY	8.22
VALUE	5.57

Tees	Men's	Women's	Yards
Gold	66.5/119	71.6/125	5350
White	71.1/128	76.7/139	6344
Blue	72.7/133		6726

OVERALL SCORE
830

Green Fee: $37 (weekend)
1/2 Cart Fee: $15 (weekend)

Located in the city of New Richmond, Wisconsin, New Richmond Golf Course is 30 miles northeast of St. Paul. Situated along the Willow River, it features 18 championship holes (the Old Course) and a 9-hole layout (the Links Course The course has a warm and inviting clubhouse. The grill and bar offer plenty of snacks and the pro shop is fully stocked. Additional amenities include a driving range, chipping green and a putting green. There is no water on the course except a drinking fountain on the tee box of #10. There is a beverage cart, although we didn't see it on the day of our visit.

We arrived at the course early in the morning and saw many cars in the parking lot with several people on the putting green and driving range. We found out we came during a scheduled high school tournament and the manager suggested we tee off between groups! We got right on the course and had no problems with the pace-of-play. The course manager bent over backwards to help the golfers!

The tee boxes were in good shape and each had ball washers, garbage cans and benches. There three sets of tee boxes, with a 1000-yard difference between gold and white. The fairways and greens also were in excellent condition. Plenty of bunkers (39 in all) line the holes, but they're all filled with soft sand. Water hazards are less prominent, although they do come into play on five holes.

The first three holes were fairly straight forward. There is an abrupt change in the level of difficulty at the 4th hole. The opening in the trees on this dogleg is less than the width of the green. The 5th hole, a par 5, has water on both sides of the fairway near the green. The 7th hole is a 194-yard par 3 from the blue tees and features trees, water and wetlands. The course is hilly and a bit long. It's possible to score well with a little care and the course is quite scenic with many interesting holes. The people were friendly and we had a great time.

320

ID: 5401709WI

PHEASANT HILLS

Region: Wisconsin

1025 170th Street
Hammond, WI 54015
Clubhouse: 715-796-2500
Golf Shop: 715-796-2500
Type: Public   Par: 72

www.pheasanthillsgolf.com

Course Rating

HOSPITALITY	7.60
PLAYABILITY	6.72
USABILITY	8.79
FACILITY	6.60
VALUE	6.58

Tees	Men's	Women's	Yards
Red		69.5/116	5175
Gold	68.2/119	74.1/126	6000
White	71.7/124		6546
Blue	73.4/127		7093

OVERALL SCORE
732

Green Fee: $30 (weekend)
1/2 Cart Fee: $10 (weekend)

Pheasant Hills Golf Course opened in 2004 and is a much-needed 18-hole regulation course in Hammond, Wisconsin. Residents' options were previously limited to the local 9-hole course or traveling elsewhere. This course is in a residential development, but don't worry—the homes do not intrude on your play.

We visited this course in late September, when it was practically empty, but in prime condition. Medium-sized flat tee boxes, generous fairways and large semi-undulating greens—all of them very green, lush and well maintained. Pheasant Hills uses a variety of tactics to divide adjoining fairways, like rough, mounded areas, water and trees. While other golfers can intrude on your fairway on a couple of holes, it's unlikely for the majority of your round.

Water appears on 13 of the 18 holes, but most of it does not come into play and is there solely for the aesthetic value. Most of the water features are designed with native elements, creating a scenic feel. The sand traps had edges that were somewhat unkempt and contained a gray, grainy loose type of sand. They were quite playable and the lips of the traps were rarely a factor. Favorite hole: the 6th, a 163-yard par 3 with a large pond you must fly over.

Three practice greens to choose from: one for putting, one for chipping and one for sand practice. The driving range is 250 yards long, but there was at least 50 yards past that for you to bomb away.

Overall it's a playable course with some interesting design features. Average hackers should be able to score well here and have a good time for a good price.

ID: 5401509WI

RIVER FALLS

Region: Wisconsin

1011 County Road M
River Falls, WI 54022
Clubhouse: 715-425-7253
Golf Shop: 715-425-7253
Type: Semi-Private   Par: 72
www.riverfallsgolfclub.com

Course Rating

HOSPITALITY	8.68
PLAYABILITY	8.65
USABILITY	8.83
FACILITY	8.30
VALUE	6.58

Tees	Men's	Women's	Yards
Red		69.9/118	5142
White	69.2/120		5963
Blue	72.0/126		6596

OVERALL SCORE
843

Green Fee: $25 (weekend)
1/2 Cart Fee: $10 (weekend)

River Falls Golf Course is conveniently located only nine miles east of Hudson in River Falls, Wisconsin, just a short 30-minute drive from the Twin Cities. Built in the old style of the 1930s, this is one of the jewels of the St. Croix River Valley. Rolling terrain, hills and wooded areas make for a very versatile day on the course. It is always enjoyable to play among the trees without a house anywhere near the course.

The pro shop has a great assortment of men's and women's clothes, with shorts and shirts, as well as the usual hats, gloves and balls. The clothes are a step above the norm, for color and style. The prices are very reasonable and the women's clothes are unlike what we've seen at other pro shops. This 18-hole semi-private golf course features a clubhouse with a full bar and a varied menu of grilled selections. Options include hamburgers, chicken sandwiches and, since this is Wisconsin, cheese curds are also available. There is a banquet facility available for events. The course also has a driving range and a golf pro available for group or private lessons.

Some of the fairways are tight, but they are well marked for distances. The bunkers can be somewhat challenging since the sand is a little sparse in places. All the greens were in great condition; they held our shots and putted true. The tee boxes were in good shape and fair for all skill levels. The forward tees are still challenging for any hacker.

This is a very walkable course. If you like to ride, gas carts are available for a reasonable rate. There are evening leagues for both men and women on Tuesdays. Visit the course's website for special deals like Marvelous Mondays and Wonderful Wednesdays. These reasonable rates are only one of the many reasons to cross the Wisconsin border and play River Falls Golf Course.

ID: 5402209WI

RIVER RUN

1210 East Montgomery Street
Sparta, WI 54656
Clubhouse: 608-269-3022
Golf Shop: 608-269-3022
Type: Public   Par: 72
www.riverrunsparta.com

Region: Wisconsin

Course Rating

HOSPITALITY	8.63
PLAYABILITY	8.15
USABILITY	8.32
FACILITY	8.34
VALUE	8.16

Tees	Men's	Women's	Yards
Forward	Par/Slope		5473
Gold	Information		
White	Unavailable		
Champions			6622

NOTE: website did not contain complete par/slope information at presstime (Jan-2010).

OVERALL SCORE
834

Green Fee: $29 (weekend)
1/2 Cart Fee: $15 (weekend)

Municipal courses often depend on their golf course superintendents to make the most of their modest resources. Luckily, River Run Golf Course (formerly Sparta Golf Course) is in good hands. Located in an unusual government complex in the heart of Sparta, Wisconsin, the course consists of nine holes built in the 1960s and an additional nine built in the 1980s.

The front nine looks like a typical 1960s municipal course; the telephone poles and highway overpasses aren't exactly picturesque. The previous night's four inches of rain had worried us about soggy conditions, but we were pleasantly surprised to find the course in lush condition. Although they didn't break as much as we would have thought, the bentgrass greens were in good shape. The fairways were nice and the course had a very manageable cut of rough.

The back nine at River Run, however, is a real treat. It has the look and feel of a country club course and features mature pine trees, large fairways, great greens, well-placed bunkers and a terrific layout. Adding to the aesthetic appeal are the plantings beds, folk art, log steps, birdhouses of all types, bird feeders and a wonderful variety of wildlife. We saw turkeys run across our green as we putted out on #13. There are more than 50 sand traps and occasional water hazards, but they don't really come into play except on hole #2, which requires a 150-yard carry over a pond. Near the 14th green is a small cemetery, the final resting place for 150 children who were wards of the state between 1887 and 1976. The course was designed with respect to this special place. Carts are available to rent, although the course is easy to walk. A large modern clubhouse features a well-stocked pro shop, lounge area, dining room and bar area. The restaurant offers an impressive menu. Practice facilities are located next to the clubhouse. Overall, River Run is a well-run operation and a good hacker value.

ID: 5465609WI

ROLLING OAKS

440 West Division Avenue
Barron, WI 54812
Clubhouse: 715-537-3409
Golf Shop: 715-537-3409
Type: Public   Par: 71
www.rollingoaksgolf.net

Tees	Men's	Women's	Yards
Red		62.1/107	4731
White	66.5/116		5699
Blue	68.0/119		6085

Region: Wisconsin

Course Rating

HOSPITALITY	7.88
PLAYABILITY	6.92
USABILITY	7.43
FACILITY	4.68
VALUE	6.22

OVERALL SCORE
731

Green Fee: $30 (weekend)
1/2 Cart Fee: $14 (weekend)

Rolling Oaks Golf Course is a very nice course. Golfers come to this Barron, Wisconsin, course for one thing—to golf. There is no pro shop or on-site meal preparation. Snacks, pizza and deli-express sandwiches are available. The open area has a large bar and seating area, which are very well maintained and comfortable with a friendly staff. As stated earlier, you come here to play golf, have an after-round beverage and that's about it.

There is no driving range, just a net. There is a nice putting green where you can also do a little chipping. The staff seems to be quite accommodating. On the day we were there, a charity scramble on the front nine had groups of eight. It sounded like they had fun! Despite this, we were able to play quickly and were done in less than four hours.

Rolling Oaks is a well-maintained and fun course for hackers. The fairways were in very nice condition for mid July. The greens were large and well con-toured, with very few ball marks. Although a less-desirable location than the green, the bunkers were nice with fine sand.

The holes were diverse and had fairly large landing areas from most tees. However, there are plenty of trees, waste areas, water hazards and fairway bunkers to keep you on your toes. Golfers who keep the ball fairly straight can score well from the blue tees. This 6085-yard course isn't long, but very pretty and in great condition.

A $42 green fee that includes a cart makes it a nice value. If you get a chance, play Rolling Oaks. You won't be disappointed.

ID: 5481209WI

SIREN NATIONAL

Region: Wisconsin

8606 Waldora Road
Siren, WI 54872
Clubhouse: 866-747-3645
Golf Shop: 715-349-8000
Type: Public   Par: 73

www.sirennational.com

Course Rating

HOSPITALITY	8.61
PLAYABILITY	8.51
USABILITY	7.73
FACILITY	8.52
VALUE	5.81

Tees	Men's	Women's	Yards
Red		66.9/112	4662
Gold	66.3/105		5246
White	69.4/125		6088
Blue	71.6/130		6578
Black	73.1/132		6926

OVERALL SCORE
811

Green Fee: $32 (weekend)
1/2 Cart Fee: $16 (weekend)

Siren National is located near Falun in Siren, Wisconsin. The driving range is to the left and the clubhouse is straight ahead and the practice green (doughnut shaped with a pond in the middle) is behind.

We decided to use a cart, which seemed prudent since very few golfers walk the course. When we drove to the first tee box, the golf course superintendent was mowing. We talked with him for several minutes and he seemed quite proud of the course and its improvements.

The first hole is a bit intimidating. This par 5 requires a drive over a ravine and a second shot up a hill. The fairway is a dogleg right and the green is finally visible on the approach shot. The second hole, thankfully, is straightforward (except for ponds 190 yards away on both sides of the fairway). Next is a par 3, 165 yards from the white tees. This hole requires another carry over a ravine to a green on a ledge with a 20–30 foot rock wall. At least the pond that was at the bottom has been replaced by grass, but golfers still do not want to miss the green! Many of the holes have similar little quirks that keep the game interesting. Most of the par 5s are on the front nine.

The course was in great shape. The greens were fast, smooth and contoured. The bentgrass fairways were well kept and golfers had five sets of tee boxes to accommodate their skill level. There were water stations available on the course, along with several portable bathrooms. Playing the course was like walking through the forest. The scenery was beautiful and we could see for miles in places. There were wetlands, ponds, creeks and bunkers on many holes. The woods along the fairways were so dense that errant balls were really lost.

We had a very enjoyable experience. Siren National is not easy, but with course management, it is possible to do well.

ID: 5487209WI

SKYLINE

Region: Wisconsin

612 N. 11th Street
Black River Falls, WI 54615
Clubhouse: 715-284-2613
Golf Shop: 715-284-2613
Type: Public   Par: 72
www.golfskyline.com

Course Rating

HOSPITALITY	7.43
PLAYABILITY	7.53
USABILITY	7.44
FACILITY	6.55
VALUE	7.05

Tees	Men's	Women's	Yards
Red		69.5/112	
Gold	65.4/108	70.2/114	
White	68.9/114		
Blue	70.6/124		6371

NOTE: neither the course website or the WSGA website had yardage stats available at presstime (Jan-2010).

OVERALL SCORE
729

Green Fee: $30 (weekend)
1/2 Cart Fee: $16 (weekend)

Skyline Golf Course in located in the river town of Black River Falls, Wisconsin. A two-hour drive from the Metro, the course is just a few blocks off Main Street and partially cut within a residential area. This traditional-style course recently celebrated its 50th anniversary. A newer clubhouse with a full bar and menu sits at the highest point of the course and offers some nice scenic views of the course and rolling hills. There are carts available and we recommend using one, as the front nine is quite hilly. The on-site pro shop carries shoes, clothing and clubs, along with balls, tees and the like.

We visited on a Saturday afternoon in late August and we were able to play immediately, despite not having a tee time. We found the course to have an interesting variety of holes. We especially liked the back nine, with towering pine forests that feel like a remote, peaceful, forested area. We played from the white tees, which are just under 6000 yards, and found that an average drive left us in position to reach most greens in regulation with a short iron. The course seemed to play shorter than the marked distances. Many of the par 4s are around 300 yards. We were disappointed that the greens were quite beat up around the cup. The wear and tear appeared excessive, even for heavy play. It seemed as though the pins had not been moved in a few days. There are sand traps and some water hazards, but they seemed to be avoidable for the most part. The front nine is more open and the back is tighter, with some fairways cut through the woods.

We were surprised by the lack of staff, especially since we visited on the weekend. Unfortunately, there was no beverage cart service. The bar did have a nice special of five beers for $10. We enjoyed this course and would play here again. The $46 green fee was a little higher than other area courses in Wisconsin. Next time, we would likely visit the course's website, which offers daily golf specials and online tee times. Overall, a little better maintenance and more staff could turn a good golf experience at Skyline into a great one.

326

SPRING VALLEY

345 Hidden Fox Court
Spring Valley, WI 54767
Clubhouse: 715-778-5513
Golf Shop: 715-778-5513
Type: Public   Par: 72
www.playspringvalleygolf.com

Tees	Men's	Women's	Yards
Red		68.5/117	4765
Yellow	67.5/118		5485
White	68.6/123		5714
Blue	70.1/124		6053

Region: Wisconsin

Course Rating

HOSPITALITY   7.42
PLAYABILITY   6.85
USABILITY   8.04
FACILITY   8.21
VALUE   6.58

OVERALL SCORE
741

Green Fee: $27 (weekend)
1/2 Cart Fee: $12 (weekend)

Proclaiming itself "the area's most scenic," Spring Valley Golf Course is, indeed, a beautiful little course. Carved through a wooded valley in Spring Valley, Wisconsin, it offers good value for the money. Just over an hour from the Twin Cities, this par-72 course is 6053 yards from the blue tees. However, it plays more difficult than the distance might imply. While the course may seem short, the hills might mean some golfers should consider using a cart rather than walking. The course is well marked with helpful signage that is easy to follow.

The first seven holes of the front nine are quite straightforward, with open fairways and widely spaced trees. This may give hackers a false sense of security. After a bit of a walk between the 7th and 8th holes, things change. Fairways get tighter and the trees increase in number and density. The back nine features three par-5 holes and three par 3s. The par-4 10th hole is a steep downhill dogleg with a tricky narrow fairway, which then slopes up to a tough two-tiered green. Two par 5s follow—and they will challenge the best of hackers. The final par 5 is their signature hole, #16. Here golfers are faced not only with a long distance and a sharp dogleg, but with a severely sloped fairway, making a level lie almost impossible.

This family-owned and operated course has a friendly and helpful staff. They obviously take pride in their course. There are two well-kept practice greens, but there is no driving range. The traditional-style clubhouse has a pro shop, and an adjoining snack area and bar where you can relax after your round. There is a large restaurant upstairs that's available for special events. This is a beautiful well-maintained course in the Wisconsin countryside, but it may prove to be a bit frustrating for hackers. Golfers need to hit the fairway if they hope to post a decent score. Spring Valley is a quality course and well worth a try if you are less concerned about your score and more interested in playing a scenic course.

ID: 5476709WI

ST. CROIX NATIONAL

Region: Wisconsin

1603 32nd Street
Somerset, WI 54025
Clubhouse: 715-247-4200
Golf Shop: 715-247-4200
Type: Public   Par: 72

www.stcroixnationalgolf.com

Course Rating

HOSPITALITY	8.87
PLAYABILITY	8.73
USABILITY	8.57
FACILITY	8.66
VALUE	7.40

Tees	Men's	Women's	Yards
Gold		71.3/125	5251
White	70.4/129	76.3/136	6144
Blue	72.2/133		6544
Black	73.9/138		6909

OVERALL SCORE
859

Green Fee: $49 (weekend)
1/2 Cart Fee: included in fee

The St. Croix River Valley in Wisconsin features rolling hills and beautiful vistas and St. Croix National Golf Club takes great advantage of these assets. Located between Hudson and Somerset, Wisconsin, it's a beautiful course that's also fun to play. The wooded areas and sloping terrain make St. Croix National appear more like a resort course than a typical urban one. The spacious clubhouse and pro shop are staffed by friendly individuals who aim to please. Incredible views from the clubhouse deck are just part of the appeal.

There's a practice bunker, putting green and chipping area. Particularly interesting is the driving range, where golfers stand high above a valley that collects their practice shots. It's a taste of what's to come, since a number of holes will be challenging for those with vertigo. Noting the topography, we decided to use one and found it to be relatively new and clean. Golfers can also rent handheld GPS for $5, but the paved cart paths, well-designed tee signs and fairway distance markers might make that purchase unnecessary. St. Croix National offers four sets of tees, ranging from 5251 to 6909 yards. Given the length, average hackers will likely be most comfortable playing from the white tees at 6144 yards.

The course is well maintained with the tee boxes being the only exception; most were in need of maintenance, filling or grading. The course is visually daunting, but the fairways are ample and there are plenty of places to bail out, if needed. Meticulously sculpted, well-trimmed sand traps are abundant and filled with soft, clean sand. There are few out-of-bounds areas. If hackers can find their ball in the trees, they're welcome to play it as it lies. St. Croix National is not an easy course, but it is a very enjoyable course. Trouble can be avoided by playing conservatively, rather than aggressively. Golfers of all levels will truly enjoy the beauty and challenge presented here. If the course gets the best of you on your first round, you can commiserate with the gracious clubhouse staff.

ID: 5402509WI

TEAL WING

12425 North Ross Road
Hayward, WI 54843
Clubhouse: 715-462-3631
Golf Shop: 715-462-3631
Type: Public   Par: 72
www.teallake.com

Region: Wisconsin

Course Rating

HOSPITALITY	8.75
PLAYABILITY	8.22
USABILITY	8.66
FACILITY	8.52
VALUE	7.46

OVERALL SCORE
841

Tees	Men's	Women's	Yards
Blue	69.1/132	74.0/138	5723
Green	71.0/136		6142
Gold	72.1/139		6379

Green Fee: $49 (weekend)
1/2 Cart Fee: $15 (weekend)

Located 20 miles east of Hayward, Wisconsin, Ross' Teal Wing Golf Club lives up to its own description as a "joyful mix of natural northern beauty and good golf." Surrounded by a national forest and designed with respect for the environment, the course is rated by Golf Digest as #48 on its list of "America's Top 50 Toughest." At first glance, it appears to be too intimidating for hackers, however, with tees ranging from 5723 to 6379 yards, players of all levels can enjoy this beautiful course.

A small stand designates the driving range. A sign on the range stand indicates if no one is there to greet you, just grab a cart and make your way to the gazebo where someone will help you. The gazebo is a rustic screened structure the serves lunch and doubles as the clubhouse and pro shop. The practice green is located just outside the gazebo. Restroom facilities are modest (i.e., portable bathroom located by the gazebo and at strategic locations on the course). While the facilities at Teal Wing may be modest, the real attraction of the course is the stunning scenery as the course winds through the woods. The fairways are narrow and tree-lined with thick undergrowth and require accurate tee shots. Most of the holes are doglegs, so it's rare to be able to see the green from the tee. Each tee sign shows a diagram of the hole with yardages and a paragraph with the pro's advice on how to play the hole. There's also a paragraph about the nature aspects of the hole.

Additionally, the course is friendly for the whole family, frequently offering special discounts. Interestingly, Teal Wing has 4-seater carts that allow the whole family to ride together. It's also worth noting they encourage riders and walkers on the course and don't charge for them. For an excellent experience that combines an inspiring trip through the northern Wisconsin woods and a round of golf that will test you whatever your level, we highly recommend Teal Wing Golf Club.

ID: 5484309WI

TREMPELEAU MOUNTAIN

W24411 Fairway Drive
Trempealeau, WI 54661
Clubhouse: 608-534-7417
Golf Shop: 608-534-7417
Type: Public   Par: 71

www.golfthemountain.com

Tees	Men's	Women's	Yards
Red		71.3/117	5360
Gold	68.5/116	74.4/123	5884
White	69.8/119		6178
Blue	71.3/122		6481

Course Rating

HOSPITALITY	8.60
PLAYABILITY	8.67
USABILITY	8.85
FACILITY	8.78
VALUE	7.75

OVERALL SCORE
861

Green Fee: $30 (weekend)
1/2 Cart Fee: $15 (weekend)

We have a love-hate relationship with this course. We love it. It hates us. Many of the locals share our view. They come out here weekly to be physically abused by it and can't wait to come back the next week for more.

This course is a good journey by car from anywhere…between La Crosse and Winona as the cow flies (we're in Dairyland dontcha know)…and yet worth every nickel per drop of gas. When you figure in the sheer beauty and condition of the course, you'd gladly pay MORE than what you have to, in order to play here. And they have GPS on their carts! Dollar for dollar, this is hands-down the best-valued golf experience in the La Crosse area.

There's no trick to the course. You see it all right in front of you. No blind shots, limited trees, few hazards (other than fescue) and very few places you could lose a ball if anyone's watching. The greens are undulated and tiered… perfectly paced… the fairways like carpet, and for a flat course the elevation changes are quite impressive. The only arguable flaw is the tee shot on #13. And that's being nitpicky. It is a paradise of many sorts to a golfer of any level, fervently maintained like a country club. We'd venture that Thoreau might have authored "On Trempealeau Pond" had he ever played here. And speaking of water. It does come into play on four holes here. You get the "island green" experience on the peninsula at 14, and the threat off the tee on 12 and 13. Otherwise you'd have to be a camel in the desert to find other water holes.

We mentioned this course has GPS on the carts. Even without a cart there is little uncertainty in your distance calculations to the green because the course is so well marked. Big name courses like Troy Burne and Big Fish could learn a lot from this one. Without a doubt, if it weren't for the 20-minute drive from La Crosse, this course would be the busiest area course every day of the summer. As it is, enough golfers know a great thing when they find Trempealeau Mountain. Come play "The Mountain."

330

TROY BURNE

295 Lindsay Road
Hudson, WI 54016
Clubhouse: 715-381-9800
Golf Shop: 715-381-9800
Type: Public   Par: 71
www.troyburne.com

Tees	Men's	Women's	Yards
Front	65.2/117	68.7/123	4932
Resort	68.3/126	74.1/133	5837
Champion	71.8/131		6505
Lehman	74.3/136		7034

Region: Wisconsin

Course Rating

HOSPITALITY	7.49
PLAYABILITY	8.65
USABILITY	7.99
FACILITY	8.33
VALUE	5.23

OVERALL SCORE
784

Green Fee: $79 (weekend)
1/2 Cart Fee: $17 (weekend)

Cut through the St. Croix Valley, Troy Burn Golf Club is a stunning and beautiful championship course. This Tom Lehman signature course located just across the border in Hudson, Wisconsin, is perfect for golfers with a handicap of 20 or less. However, this is not a course for beginners.

Driving past hole #6 on the way to the course, you might notice the nine bunkers that line the fairways of this par 4. This hole is not an anomaly; in fact, there are over 120 bunkers at Troy Burne. The front nine features sprawling mounds and native fescue grasses, while the back incorporated more of the native pine, birch, oak and maple trees. Calculating approach shots will keep golfers on their toes here. Sand traps and lakes menacingly guard each green. The bentgrass greens are lightening fast. Those who are able to one-putt at Troy Burne deserve a medal. With this in mind, we strongly recommend using the practice green before your round; it's an exact template of what you'll encounter out on the course.

Missing short or long on the par 3s can spell trouble. The wooded back nine is also more challenging than the front and the 10th hole is no exception. This narrow par 4 that's a dogleg left has not only a lake, but also a waste bunker guarding the entire left side of the fairway. Only golfers who are truly confident (or truly foolish) will attempt to reach the par-5 12th hole in two. The hole isn't long (just 446 yards from the black tees) but the fairway is extremely narrow and nearly three quarters of the green is surrounded by water. The 15th hole is the shortest on the course and features a greenside bunker with an 8–10 foot lip. It's quite literally one unforgettable hole after another here.

But with all the good there is some bad. The hole-to-hole signage is poor and a total absence of any basic and consistent yardage markers is unforgivable. At $96 per round, Troy Burne is also not cheap, but it is a memorable experience and one you're not likely to soon forget.

ID: 5401609WI

TURTLEBACK

1985 18½ Street
Rice Lake, WI 54868
Clubhouse: 715-234-7641
Golf Shop: 715-234-7641
Type: Public   Par: 71

www.turtlebackgolf.com

Tees	Men's	Women's	Yards
Red	68.2/121	69.8/117	5163
White	68.2/121	74.2/124	5818
Blue	70.0/125		6222
Black	71.5/129		6604

Region: Wisconsin

Course Rating

HOSPITALITY	8.29
PLAYABILITY	9.07
USABILITY	7.96
FACILITY	8.51
VALUE	5.68

OVERALL SCORE
823

Green Fee: $53 (weekend)
1/2 Cart Fee: included in fee

Turtleback, in Rice Lake, Wisconsin, sounds like a fun place to play golf. And it is. It's also challenging; the designers of this course made exceptional use of the land and created a masterpiece that should certainly be lauded much higher than it already is.

This course lacks very little. The practice areas offer the same turf conditions you'll find on the course. The clubhouse is enormous and majestic, with locker rooms, a bar, a full-service restaurant, and space galore for any conceivable event. Although the green fee has increased over time, the rate for 18 holes with a cart after 3:30 pm is just $30. That's a good deal at any course and it's a great deal at Turtleback.

The course caters to all playing abilities, equally tough yet fair for everyone. Those new to the course should check out the tour available on Turtleback's website; it offers hints and tips on how to play each hole. While it may prove too challenging for the first round of the season, golfers should be fine here the rest of the year, assuming they play the appropriate tees. You'll feel great if you shoot your handicap, but still love the course even if you don't. It is very well manicured and efficiently run. The service is professional, like a private country club, yet anyone is welcome.

We would argue the par-3 13th is the signature hole. Players are welcomed to the tee by a carved turtle. This hole's green is also turtle-like. Its surface is every bit as concave and slippery as a turtle's shell with bunkers as its feet. To be perfectly honest, this hole is a little unfair. But we loved it and would play it again in a heartbeat!

Nine, fifteen and eighteen are some of the most serene holes on the course. As you climb the hill back to the clubhouse after either nine, you'll feel lucky to have played here and you'll want to come back to Turtleback.

ID: 5486809WI

VIROQUA HILLS

Region: Wisconsin

1110 Highway 14 South
Viroqua, WI 54665
Clubhouse: 608-637-7615
Golf Shop: 608-637-7615
Type: Public   Par: 71/72
www.viroquahillsgolf.com

Course Rating

HOSPITALITY	9.05
PLAYABILITY	8.27
USABILITY	8.44
FACILITY	7.94
VALUE	6.33

Tees	Men's	Women's	Yards
Red		69.7/124	5118
Gold	65.8/111		5263
White	68.6/119		5904
Blue	70.8/123		6376

NOTE: website was not working at presstime (Jan-2010).

OVERALL SCORE
825

Green Fee: $31 (weekend)
1/2 Cart Fee: $16 (weekend)

Viroqua Hills Golf Course is nestled in the hills of Vernon County, Wisconsin. We visited on a weekday when the play was light and we were able to finish our round in four hours, while still enjoying the scenery. There was no beverage cart on the day we played, but there are vending machines and restrooms on the course. For those looking to warm up before playing, there are two practice greens and a driving range near the entrance.

The clubhouse serves sandwiches, wraps, appetizers, drinks and some entrees at reasonable prices. There's a different special available every weekday, as well; some are as cheap as $2. Golfers can enjoy their on their food on the deck overlooking the first tee. While the pro shop display is limited, signage indicated additional apparel and goods are available. The staff and other golfers were friendly, courteous and welcoming.

Viroqua Hills's wide fairways are edged with mature pine, oak and birch trees, providing a boundary from tee to green. Sand traps border the greens on 14 holes, while 6 holes have fairway traps. Water hazards come into play on five holes golfers will have to avoid the out-of-bounds markers on the nine holes around the course's perimeter. Holes 1–3 and 13–18 have a compact, traditional and fairly straight layout. These were the original nine holes when the course was established in 1930. After hole #3, there's a lengthy ride under the highway and up a hill to holes 4–12, which feature a more open arrangement and were built in 1996, and along the way, be sure to enjoy the pleasant views from several elevated greens. The 11th hole is especially pretty; it's a 503-yard par 5, with a tee box 100 feet above the fairway.

On the course, etched granite hole markers show tee placement, distance and an aerial view. The course's website has a map, event calendar, rate and membership information, scorecard and a course tour with links to photos and descriptions for each hole. Those new to Viroqua Hills will likely find this information useful.

ID: 5466509WI

WHITE EAGLE

316 White Eagle Trail
Hudson, WI 54016
Clubhouse: 715-549-4653
Golf Shop: 715-549-4653
Type: Public   Par: 72

www.whiteeaglegolf.com

Region: Wisconsin

Course Rating

HOSPITALITY	8.55
PLAYABILITY	8.32
USABILITY	7.62
FACILITY	8.53
VALUE	7.19

OVERALL SCORE
816

Green Fee: $69 (weekend)
1/2 Cart Fee: included in fee

Tees	Men's	Women's	Yards
Red		69.8/121	4995
Gold		73.7/129	5731
White	70.6/134		6190
Blue	72.8/140		6646
Black	75.2/142		7178

While it requires a drive across the border into Hudson, Wisconsin, White Eagle Golf Club is worth every minute of the drive. The staff is friendly and the medium-sized pro shop has plenty of equipment. Service on the course was fantastic as well, from the beverage cart service to a post-round drink at the clubhouse bar—we felt welcomed throughout the entire day. The carts with GPS are a nice amenity, also allowing golfers to order food and beverages straight from the screen.

The course is a beautiful mix of straight and doglegged holes. The elevation changes and inclines on several holes make for an interesting, but challenging round. Golfers who are able to hit the ball a long way can test themselves with the black tees, which are 7178 yards. Fortunately, for those less confident in their golfing abilities, there are four other sets of tee boxes. There are many trees on the course, so it's more important than ever to hit the fairway. At least you won't find crazy rough or different types of grasses to battle. Water does comes into play on a few holes, but the hazards are well placed, for the most part.

We enjoyed the par-3 5th hole, which the course has named "Soaring Eagle." A huge elevation drop makes this hole not as long as it appears and the tree-lined backdrop is so pretty, it might cause players to lose focus on their game. Also, the par-4 18th is an inspiring uphill finish to a green with a waterfall behind it.

While it seems like some courses' websites list their rates and little else, White Eagle's is packed with information. Those new to the course should definitely check out the hole-by-hole tour with hints and tips (like when to cut the corner on those dogleg holes). The $69 green fee can seem a bit steep, but it's absolutely worth it.

ID: 5401609WI

WHITETAIL

E8414 760th Avenue
Colfax, WI 54730
Clubhouse: 715-962-3888
Golf Shop: 715-962-3888
Type: Public   Par: 72
www.whitetailgolf.com

Region: Wisconsin

Course Rating

HOSPITALITY	8.74
PLAYABILITY	8.03
USABILITY	8.99
FACILITY	8.46
VALUE	7.53

OVERALL SCORE
841

Green Fee: $22.50 (weekend)
1/2 Cart Fee: $12.50 (weekend)

Tees	Men's	Women's	Yards
Red		67.0/106	5152
Gold	73.5/123		5602
White	67.6/114		6072
Blue	69.6/118		6432

Whitetail Golf Course was a pleasant surprise. Located roughly 6 miles off Interstate 94 south of Colfax, Wisconsin, it is very easy to get to.

This extremely well-groomed course is also very conveniently laid out. Golfers come by the clubhouse three times during their round. The banquet facilities inside the clubhouse seat up to 200 people. The lunch menu was limited to sandwiches and grill items that were inexpensive. Bar prices were more reasonable than most places. A 6-pack of beer was just $12.

Oddly, the pro shop is on the opposite side of the building from where you check in, so it's easily missed. They have little inventory, but the staff was very friendly and helpful. Other golfers we encountered were considerate.

The front nine is much more open, with wider fairways and ample landing areas. The back nine features many more trees and requires precision. There are some pars to be had, but there are some challenging holes that, for the average golfer, will result in a few 7s and 8s. Heavily undulated greens mean very few straight putts. This is a fun course to play, but don't expect to shoot par.

Whitetail has a reputation for being well manicured. For example, most of the tree areas are mowed underneath. Hackers who hit into trouble can normally find their ball and play it. The course is walkable, but we would suggest a cart because it's fairly hilly and there are some longer walks between tees.

Whitetail is very affordable; the weekday green fee is only $20.50 and the weekend fee is just $2 more. Even better deals can be found on their website. Hackers will likely be impressed with the quality of play for the rates this course charges.

ID: 5473009WI